Lynda Weinman's | Hands-On Training

Includes CD-ROM with Exercise Files and Demo Movies

MACROMEDIA®

Flash™ MX

H·O·T™

Hands-On Training

lynda.com/books

By **Kymberlee Weil**
developed with **Lynda Weinman**

Macromedia Flash MX | H·O·T
Hands-On Training

By Kymberlee Weil
Developed with Lynda Weinman

lynda.com/books | Peachpit Press
1249 Eighth Street • Berkeley, CA • 94710
800.283.9444 • 510.524.2178 •
510.524.2221 (fax)
http://www.lynda.com/books
http://www.peachpit.com

lynda.com/books is published
in association with Peachpit Press,
a division of Pearson Education
Copyright ©2003 by lynda.com

ISBN: 0-321-11272-5

0 9 8 7 6

Printed and bound in the
United States of America

H•O•T | Credits

Original Design: Ali Karp, Alink Newmedia *(alink@earthlink.net)*

lynda.com Director, Publications: Garo Green *(garo@lynda.com)*

Peachpit Project Manager: Suzie Lowey

Peachpit Copyeditor: Rebecca Pepper

Peachpit Proofreaders: Leslie Ayers and Darren Meiss

Peachpit Production: Myrna Vladic

Peachpit Compositors: Rick Gordon, Emerald Valley Graphics; Deborah Roberti, Espresso Graphics

Beta Testers: Garo Green, Mark Siler, Ellen Noorgard

Cover Illustration: Bruce Heavin *(bruce@stink.com)*

Exercise Graphics: Domenique Sillett (*www.littleigloo.com*)

Indexer: Steve Rath

H•O•T | Colophon

The preliminary design for the H•O•T series was sketched on paper by Ali Karp | Alink Newmedia. The layout was heavily influenced by online communication—merging a traditional book format with a modern Web aesthetic.

The text in Macromedia Flash MX H•O•T was set in Akzidenz Grotesk from Adobe, and Triplex from Emigré. The cover illustration was painted in Adobe Photoshop and Adobe Illustrator.

This book was created using QuarkXPress 4.1, Adobe Photoshop 6, Macromedia Fireworks MX, Microsoft Office 2001, and Flash MX using Windows XP. It was printed on 60# Sonoma Matte at Von Hoffman Printing.

Dedication

To Marie Burger and Holly Weil.

Your strength, positive attitudes and will power are incredible inspiration to me each and every day.

Love, Kymberlee

Macromedia Flash MX | H•O•T _____ **Table of Contents**

Introduction

H•O•T

Macromedia Flash MX

A Note from Lynda Weinman

In my opinion, most people buy computer books in order to learn, yet it is amazing how few of these books are actually written by teachers. I take pride in the fact that this book was written by an experienced teacher who is familiar with training students in this subject matter. In this book, you will find carefully developed lessons to help you learn Macromedia Flash MX— one of the most powerful animation and interactivity tools for the Web.

This book is targeted towards beginning-level Web developers who need a tool to create creative, powerful, and interactive Web sites. The premise of the hands-on exercise approach is to get you up to speed quickly in Macromedia Flash MX, while actively working through the book's lessons. It's one thing to read about a product, and an entirely other experience to try the product and get measurable results. Our motto is, "read the book, follow the exercises, and you will know the product." We've received countless testimonials to this fact, and it is our goal to make sure it remains true for all of our hands-on training books.

Many exercise-based books take a paint-by-numbers approach to teaching. While this approach works, it's often difficult to figure out how to apply those lessons to a real-world situation, or understand why or when you would use the technique again. What sets this book apart is that the lessons contain lots of background information and insights into each given subject, and they are designed to help you understand the process as well as the exercise.

At times, pictures are worth a lot more than words. When necessary, we have also included short QuickTime movies to show any process that's difficult to explain in text. These files are located on the H•O•T CD-ROM inside a folder called movies. It's our style to approach teaching from many different angles, because we know that some people are visual learners while others like to read, and still others like to get out there and try things. This book combines a lot of teaching approaches so you can learn Flash MX as thoroughly as you want to.

This book didn't set out to cover every single aspect of Macromedia Flash MX. The manual and many other reference books are great for that! What we saw missing from the bookshelves was a process-oriented tutorial that taught readers core principles, techniques, and tips in a hands-on training format.

We welcome your comments at flmxhot@lynda.com. Please visit our Web site as well, at **http://www.lynda.com**.

The support URL for this book is **http://www.lynda.com/products/books/flmxhot/**

It's my hope that this book will give you a strong foundation in Macromedia Flash MX and give you the necessary skills to begin developing animations and interactive Web sites. If it does, then we've accomplished the job we set out to do!

–Lynda Weinman

NOTE | About lynda.com/books and lynda.com

lynda.com/books is dedicated to helping Web designers and developers understand tools and design principles. lynda.com offers hands-on workshops, training seminars, conferences, on-site training, training videos and CDs, and "expert tips" for Web design and development. To learn more about our training programs, books, and products, be sure to give our site a visit at **http://www.lynda.com**.

About the Author

Kymberlee Weil

It all started with a Web-development class at UCLA. After attending just a few sessions, Kymberlee fell in love with the technology and decided to pursue a career where she was excited to go to work each and every day. When she was introduced to Flash for the very first time, Kymberlee knew she had found her passion. She states, "Flash is like playing with Play Doh—you can use your imagination to create anything you want and you can have so much fun doing it!"

Kymberlee is an accomplished author with one book already under her belt: *Flash 5 Hands-On Training*. Kymberlee has also worked as a conference speaker and as an instructor for lynda.com, as well as UCLA Extension. She has written courseware for lynda.com and been involved in the beta testing of several lynda.com books. Kymberlee has additionally worked on creating the conference manuals for the first four Flashforward conferences. After completing her MBA at Pepperdine in December of 2000, Kymberlee added consulting to her bag of tricks. She has even been selected to work with a team of individuals on several government projects.

Kymberlee was a featured speaker at Flashforward 2001 and 2002 in New York. She presented a session on Business Strategy for Flash developers and another half day session on the Fundamentals of Flash MX.

After speaking at Flashforward 2002, Kymberlee has just accepted the new position of Conference Coordinator for Flashforward conferences and the Flash™ Film Festival. In this role, she will be able to utilize all her hard earned skills including organization, planning, project management, strategy, writing, and most of all, schmoozing!

Currently, Kymberlee also runs a small multimedia development firm, VolcanicLab.com, in California, which specializes in Flash-based projects. VolcanicLab.com is a full-service business, offering services from consulting to Web project development to CD-ROM development.

When she isn't working on something computer-related, Kymberlee can be seen addressing her stress relief in either Tae Bo or martial arts training.

Snapshots

Kymberlee has found the perfect contrast to spending hours behind one of her computers: martial arts. She is seen here during one of her martial arts training sessions.

Lynda and Kymberlee take a moment to rest and smile for the camera.

Fool-proof recipe for book writing: 1 part experience with the subject matter, 1 part creativity, 1 part drive and determination and a whole lot of Red Bull daily!

Do these hands look familiar? After all this writing, Kymberlee's hands were in top condition and this resulted in her becoming a hand model for an orthopedics company.

Acknowledgments from Kymberlee

This book could not have been possible without the assistance and support of many important individuals.

My warmest aloha and mahalo to:

Lynda Weinman, my role model. Thank you for giving me this wonderful opportunity to utilize my passion for Flash and create another book with you. You have continued to inspire and motivate me to reach goals that seemed impossible during the writing of this book. Your positive feedback and encouragement all along the way have meant the world to me.

Garo Green. Thank you for all your tireless effort and support during the writing of this book. Your suggestions and ideas were essential in making this book the best that it can be!

Domenique Sillett. Thank you for all the time you spent creating the artwork for this book. Your design skills have helped enhance this book many times over!

Robert Reinhardt. Your Flash knowledge and guidance continues to inspire me in all my work.

Shane Rebenschied and **Tony Winecoff.** Thank you Shane for helping me with your knowledge along the way and for donating your voice for the sound chapter! Tony, thank you for your continued moral support and encouragement throughout the book writing process!

The beta testers. Thanks for all your hard work, dedication, and attention to detail.

The Macromedia Flash Folks. Thank you for creating another outstanding product that I can work with every day in some capacity, so that I can truly say I love what I do for a living!

The Entire Peachpit Gang. It has been a pleasure to work on another publication with such talented individuals.

Charles Hollins. Thank you for believing in me and for introducing me to this industry. I look forward to making you proud that one of your students has started with your class as a foundation and continued on a rampage to achieve everything possible in this business and more.

John Barron. Thank you for your guidance and encouragement, not to mention your humor here and there, through the writing of book #2. Your advice and support continues to mean the world to me. I can't tell you enough how much I appreciate you being there for me all along the way!

My Family and Close Friends. Mom and Phil, Dad and Sandy, Beverly and Joe, Grandpa, Jack and Marie, William, Roy, Chris, Guy, Lisa, Dayna, Jackie, Dave, Rob, Meg, and all my Volcanic Lab clientele. I can't believe you all still talk to me after the writing of my second book! I can't thank you all enough for standing by me and offering encouragement and continuous support, all along the way during the writing of this book, not to mention the Red Bull and Rock Star donations to the "cause." You are all wonderful and mahalo to everyone for your patience with me over the last six months.

How To Use This Book

Please read this section—it contains important information that's going to help you as you use this book. The list below outlines the information that is covered:

• The Formatting in This Book

• Interface Screen Captures

• Mac and Windows System Differences

• Opening Windows Files on a Mac

• A Note to Windows Users

• Making Exercise Files Editable on Windows Systems

• Making File Extensions Visible on Windows Systems

• Flash System Requirements—Authoring and Playback

• H•O•T CD-ROM Contents

The Formatting in This Book

This book has several components, including step-by-step exercises, commentary, notes, tips, warnings, and movies. Step-by-step exercises are numbered, and file names and command keys are bolded so they pop out more easily.

Captions and commentary are in italicized text: *This is a commentary*. File names/folders, Command keys, and Menu commands are bolded: **images** folder, **Ctrl+Click**, and **File > Open**... And URLs are in light serif font: http://www.ultrashock.com

Interface Screen Captures

Most of the screen captures in the book were taken on a Windows machine using the XP operating system. The only time Macintosh shots were taken was when the interface differed from the Windows interface. I also own and use a Macintosh system, so I noted important differences when they occurred, and took screen captures accordingly.

Mac and Windows System Differences

Macromedia did a great job of ensuring that Macromedia Flash MX looks and works the same between the Macintosh and Windows operating systems. However, some differences do exist. If you are using this book with one of the Windows operating systems, please be sure to read the section titled "A Note to Windows Users," carefully.

Opening Windows Files on a Mac

As you work with Macromedia Flash MX, you might need to open a PC-created file on a Macintosh. Because of this, I wanted to make sure you were aware of a little glitch that could cause you some confusion. The Macintosh has difficulty recognizing .fla files that were created on a PC. This means when using a Mac, you may not be able to simply double-click on the .fla file that was created on a PC to open it. Instead, you will need to open Flash and then choose **File > Open**. At this point, you still may not see some of the .fla files when you use the browse dialog box. You can get around this by changing the **List Files of Type** option to **All Files**. This will display all files in the folder. You can then save the file on your Mac and it should then open normally when double-clicked.

A Note to Windows Users

This section contains essential information about making your exercise folders editable and making file extensions visible.

Making Exercise Files Editable on Windows Systems

By default, when you copy files from a CD-ROM to your Windows 95/98/2000/XP hard drive, they are set to read-only (write protected). This causes a problem with the exercise files, because you need to write over some of them. To remove this setting and make the files editable, follow the short procedure below:

1. Copy the **chapter** folder from the **H•O•T CD-ROM** to your hard drive.

2. Right-click on the **chapter** folder and choose **Explore**.

3. Press **Ctrl+A** to select all of the files inside the **chapter** folder.

4. Right-click on any of the folder icons and choose **Properties**.

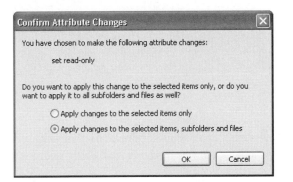

5. Uncheck the **Read-only** checkbox. This will change the setting for all of the files that were selected. If Archive is selected, you can remove that check as well.

6. Click **OK**.

Note: If there are other folders inside the chapter folder, change the attributes of those folders as well by selecting **Apply changes to the selected items, subfolders and files** when the above dialog box appears.

Making File Extensions Visible on Windows Systems

In this section, you'll see three different examples of how to turn on file extensions for Windows 95, Windows 98, Windows 2000, and Windows XP. By default, Windows 95/98/2000 users will not be able to see file extension names such as .fla or .swf. Fortunately, you can change this setting!

Windows 95 Users:

1. Double-click on the **My Computer** icon on your desktop. Note: If you (or someone else) changed the name, it will not say My Computer.

2. Select **View > Options**. This will open the Options dialog box.

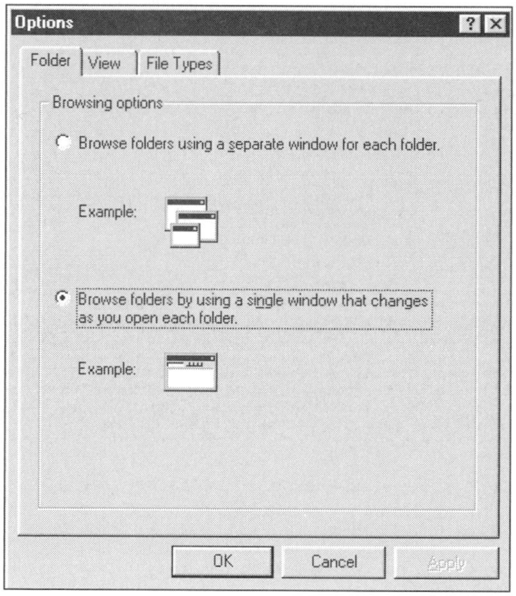

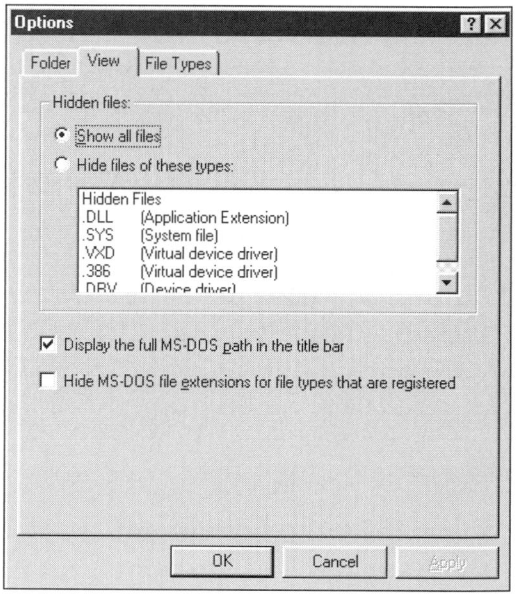

3. Click on the **View** tab at the top. This will open the View options screen so you can change the view settings of Windows 95.

4. Make sure there is no checkmark in the **Hide MS-DOS file extensions for file types that are registered box**. This will ensure that the file extensions are visible, which will help you better understand the exercises in this book!

Windows 98 Users:

1. Double-click on the **My Computer** icon on your desktop. Note: If you (or someone else) changed the name, it will not say My Computer.

2. Select **View > Folder Options**. This will open the Folder Options dialog box.

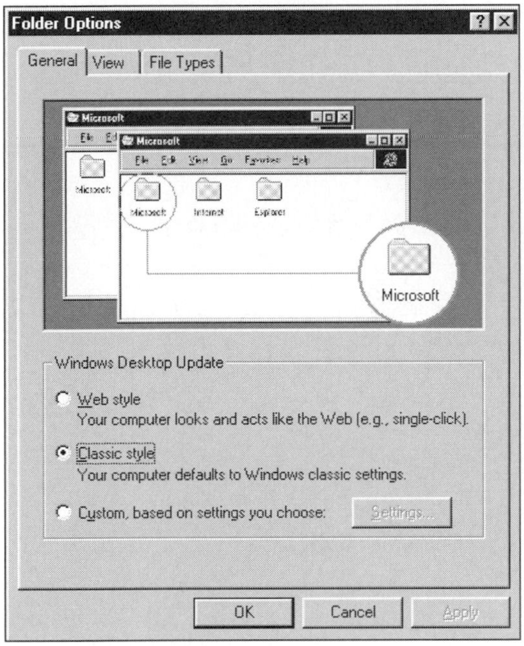

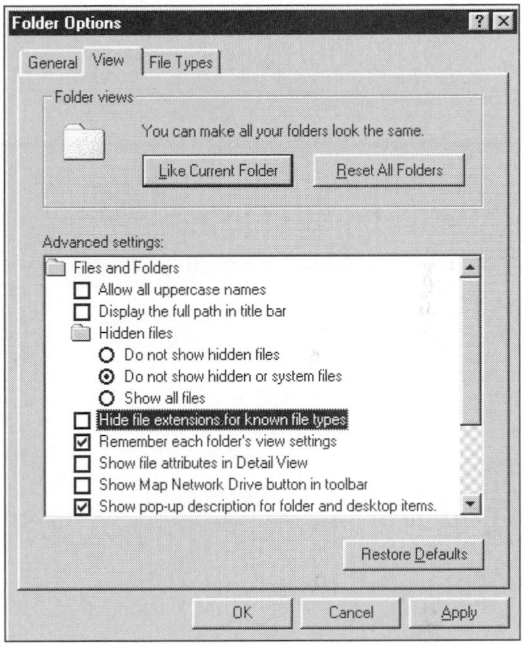

3. Click on the **View** tab at the top. This will open the View options screen so you can change the view settings of Windows 98.

4. Uncheck the **Hide file extensions for known file types** checkbox. This will make all of the file extensions visible.

Windows 2000 Users:

1. Double-click on the **My Computer** icon on your desktop. Note: If you (or someone else) changed the name, it will not say My Computer.

2. Select **Tools > Folder Options**. This will open the Folder Options dialog box.

3. Click on the **View** tab at the top. This will open the View options screen so you can change the view settings of Windows 2000.

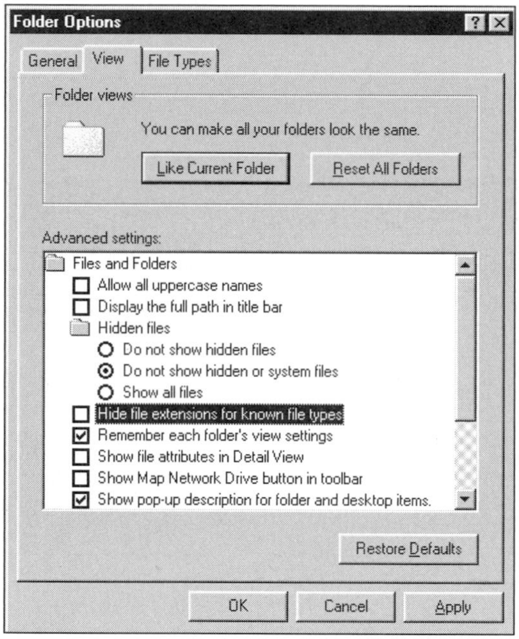

```
┌─────────────────────────────────────────────┐
│ Folder Options                        ? X    │
├─────────────────────────────────────────────┤
│  General  View  File Types                   │
│  ┌ Folder views ──────────────────────────┐  │
│  │      You can make all your folders      │  │
│  │      look the same.                     │  │
│  │      [ Like Current Folder ] [ Reset All Folders ] │  │
│  └─────────────────────────────────────────┘  │
│  Advanced settings:                           │
│  📁 Files and Folders                          │
│    ☐ Allow all uppercase names                │
│    ☐ Display the full path in title bar       │
│    📁 Hidden files                             │
│      ○ Do not show hidden files               │
│      ⦿ Do not show hidden or system files     │
│      ○ Show all files                         │
│    ☐ Hide file extensions for known file types│
│    ☑ Remember each folder's view settings     │
│    ☐ Show file attributes in Detail View      │
│    ☐ Show Map Network Drive button in toolbar │
│    ☑ Show pop-up description for folder and desktop items. │
│                      [ Restore Defaults ]     │
│         [ OK ]   [ Cancel ]   [ Apply ]       │
└─────────────────────────────────────────────┘
```

4. Make sure there is no checkmark next to the **Hide file extensions for known file types option**. This will make all of the file extensions visible.

Windows XP Users:

1. From the Start menu, select **Control Panel**.

2. Choose the **Appearance and Themes** link.

3. Select the **Folder Options** button. This will open the Folder Options dialog box.

4. Click on the **View** tab at the top. This will open the View options screen so you can change the view settings of Windows XP.

5. Make sure there is no checkmark next to the **Hide extensions for known file types option**. This will make all of the file extensions visible.

Macromedia Flash MX System Requirements

This book requires that you use either a Macintosh operating system (Power Macintosh running System 8.5 or later) or Windows 95/98/2000/Me/XP or Windows NT 4.0/2000. You also will need a color monitor capable of 800 x 600 resolution and a CD-ROM drive. We suggest that you have at least 64 MB of RAM in your system, because it's optimal if you can open Macromedia Flash MX and a Web browser at the same time. More RAM than that is even better, especially on Macintosh computers, which do not dynamically allocate RAM like Windows. Here's a little chart that cites Macromedia's system requirements:

Macromedia Flash MX System Requirements	
AUTHORING	
Windows	**Macintosh**
200 MHz Intel Pentium processor Windows 98 SE, Windows Me, Windows NT4, Windows 2000, or Windows XP	Macintosh OS 9.1 and higher, or OS X version 10.1 and higher
64 MB of free available system RAM (128 MB recommended)	64 MB of free available system RAM (128 MB recommended)
85 MB of available disk space	85 MB of available disk space
1024 x 768, 16-bit (thousands of colors) color display or better	1024 x 768, 16-bit (thousands of colors) color display or better
CD-ROM drive	CD-ROM drive
PLAYBACK	
Microsoft Windows 95, 98, Me	Internet Explorer 4.0 or later; Netscape Navigator 4 or later; Netscape 6.2 or later, with standard install defaults; AOL 7; Opera 6
Microsoft Windows NT, 2000, XP, or later	Internet Explorer 4.0 or later; Netscape Navigator 4 or later; Netscape 6.2 or later, with standard install defaults; CompuServe 7 (Microsoft Windows 2000 XP only); AOL 7; Opera 6
Macintosh OS 8.6, 9.0, 9.1, 9.2	Netscape 4.5 or later; Netscape 6.2 or later; Microsoft Internet Explorer 5.0 or later; Opera 5
Macintosh OS X version 10.1 or later	Netscape 6.2 or later; Microsoft Internet Explorer 5.1 or later; Opera 5

What's on the CD-ROM?

Exercise Files and the H•O•T CD-ROM

Your exercise files are located inside a folder called exercise_files on the H•O•T CD-ROM. These files are divided into chapter folders, and you will be instructed to copy the chapter folders to your hard drive during many of the exercises. Unfortunately, when files originate from a CD-ROM, the Windows operating system defaults to making them write-protected, meaning that you cannot alter them. You will need to alter them to follow the exercises, so please read the Note to Windows Users on pages xx–xxi for instructions on how to convert them to read-and-write formatting.

Demo Files on the CD-ROM

In addition to the exercise files, the H•O•T CD-ROM also contains a free 30-day trial version of Macromedia Flash MX for Mac or Windows. All software is located inside the software folder on the H•O•T CD-ROM. I have included trial versions of:

• Macromedia Flash MX
• Macromedia Dreamweaver MX
• Macromedia Fireworks MX
• QuickTime 5
• Sorenson Squeeze

I also have included several players on the H•O•T CD-ROM. If you don't have these players installed already, you should do that before working with any exercise in this book that calls for one of them. All of the players are located inside the software folder. I have included the following:

• Flash MX Player
• Flash_Shockwave MX Player
• QuickTime 5.0 Player

In addition, Patrick Miko and Michel Orthier were generous enough to donate a collection of audio files for you to use with the exercises in this book and your own projects. These files are located inside the chap_13 folder. There is a folder for Macintosh users, which contains audio files in the .aiff format and another folder for Windows users, which contains audio files in the .wav format. Be sure to visit **http://www.ultrashock.com** and **http://www.breakout4u.com** for access to even more sounds to use in your Macromedia Flash MX projects. Thanks again to Patrick and Michel!

Also, the media files for this book including the bitmap graphics (found thoughout the exercise folders) and all the video footage (located in the chap_15 folder) were graciously donated for you to use with the exercises in this book and with your own projects. I would like to give a very special mahalo to those who contributed these files to make this book come to life, including Charles Hollins, the photographs that were donated from Mountain High Ski Resort (Wrightwood, CA) and the video footage from Tim Sigafoos.

I.

Background Information

| Why Macromedia Flash MX? | What's New in Macromedia Flash MX? |
| Macromedia Flash MX as Project, Player, or Projector? |
| File Types Associated with Macromedia Flash MX |
| Macromedia Flash MX and Shockwave Players |
| Beyond Macromedia Flash MX |

no exercise files

Macromedia Flash MX
H•O•T CD-ROM

Most likely, if you've purchased a copy of Macromedia Flash MX, you already know why you want to use the program. You might have experience building Web pages or using other graphics programs and want to increase your software skills for today's job market. However, some of you might not know the benefits of using Macromedia Flash MX versus HTML for authoring a Web site. This chapter answers the question, "Why use Macromedia Flash MX?" It also contains a quick summary of some of the notable new features and outlines some of the ways you can extend Macromedia Flash MX content using other technologies such as CGI, XML, and JavaScript. I suspect that you are eager to dive into the hands-on exercises, so feel free to skim over this chapter. However, be sure to take a look at the "What's New in Macromedia Flash MX?" section so that you can whet your appetite for what's in store for you!

Why Use Macromedia Flash MX?

Macromedia Flash MX has several key benefits, such as small file size and fast downloading speed, precise visual control, advanced interactivity, and the ability to combine bitmap and vector graphics, include video and/or animation, scale to any dimensions, and offer streaming content.

Download Speed

If you want to design a Web site that contains an abundance of visual content, download speed can be a major problem. As most of you know, nothing can be more frustrating than a slow-loading site. Even liberal use of the compressed bitmap graphic file formats that are used for the Web (GIF and JPEG) can result in slow Web sites that frustrate visitors. Because of this, Web developers are often forced to alter their designs to be less visual.

Macromedia Flash MX content is often smaller than HTML content because it uses its own compression scheme that optimizes vector and bitmap content differently than GIFs or JPEGs. For this reason, Macromedia Flash MX has become the delivery medium of preference for graphic-intensive Web sites.

Visual Control

Another great benefit of Macromedia Flash MX is that it frees Web designers from many of the restraints of traditional HTML (**H**yper**T**ext **M**arkup **L**anguage). Macromedia Flash MX gives you complete and accurate control over position, color, fonts, and other aspects of the screen regardless of the platform (Mac or Windows) or browser (Explorer or Netscape) from which it is displayed. This is a radical and important departure from traditional HTML authoring, which requires precise planning to ensure that graphics appear relatively similar on different computers and with different Web browsers. Macromedia Flash MX allows designers to focus on design instead of HTML workarounds.

Enhanced Interactivity

While Macromedia Flash MX is often known as an animation program, it also provides powerful interactivity tools that allow you to create buttons or free-form interfaces for site navigation that include sound and animation. With the release of Macromedia Flash MX, powerful improved scripting makes it possible to create presentations that are far more complex than standard HTML or JavaScript can provide. This book covers interactivity in a number of later chapters.

Combine Vectors and Bitmaps

Most graphics on the Internet are **bitmap** graphics such as GIFs and JPEGs. The size of a bitmap file depends on the number of pixels it contains. Because of this, as the image dimensions increase, so does the file size and download time. In addition to file-size disadvantages, bitmap images that are enlarged to a size other than the original size of the image often appear distorted, out of focus, and pixilated.

Graphics created within Macromedia Flash MX are composed of **vectors**. Vector graphics use mathematical formulas to describe the images, unlike bitmaps, which record information pixel by pixel and color by color. Vector graphics can offer much smaller file sizes and increased flexibility for certain types of images, such as those with solid color fills and typographic content. Some images will have a smaller file size as bitmaps, and some will be smaller as vectors. The neat thing about Macromedia Flash MX is that you can use either kind of image.

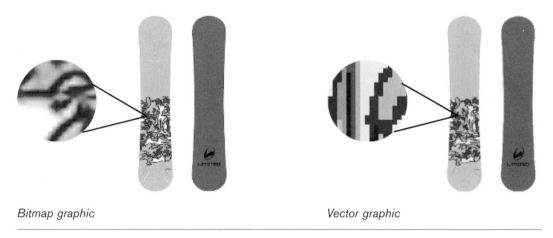

Bitmap graphic   *Vector graphic*

A bitmap graphic is built pixel by pixel and color by color, while a vector graphic is built from mathematical formulas. This means that a vector graphic will be the same file size regardless of its physical dimensions, while a bitmap graphic will grow and shrink in file size depending on how large or small it is. This makes it possible for Macromedia Flash MX to create and display large vector images and animations without increasing file size.

Video

With the release of Macromedia Flash MX, the ability to embed video inside .swf files is a huge accomplishment for the program. This change opens the floodgates even further for the types of projects you can create using Macromedia Flash MX. You will have the chance to learn about about the ins and outs of video in Chapter 15, "*Video*."

Scalability

Because Macromedia Flash MX movies can use vectors, they can be resized in any Web browser window and still retain their original scale and relative position. Most importantly, the file size of vector graphics is independent of their display size. This means it is possible to create full-screen vector animations that display at any resolution and that are only a fraction of the file size of a comparable bitmap graphic.

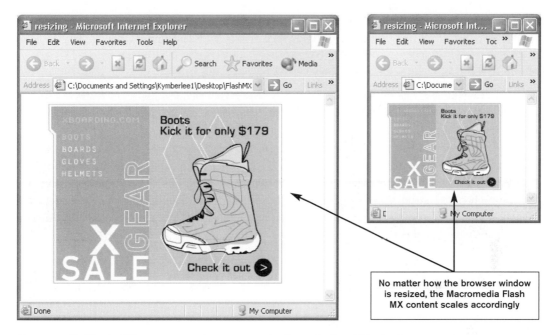

Macromedia Flash MX content can be set to scale dynamically within the browser window, as shown here.

Does all of this mean you should use only vectors in your Macromedia Flash MX movies? Absolutely not. While Macromedia Flash MX is known for its vector capabilities, its support of bitmap images is superb and far exceeds the support offered by HTML. Specifically, if you scale a bitmap image larger than its original size in HTML, the graphic will become distorted and unattractive. Macromedia Flash MX allows bitmaps to scale, animate, and transform (skew, distort, etc.) without much image degradation. This means that you can, and often will, combine bitmap and vector images in your movies. The ability to deliver both bitmap and vector graphics together lets you create movies that look good at different resolutions and that still have a bandwidth-friendly file size. Macromedia Flash MX can even be used to convert bitmap images into vectors, which you will learn to do in Chapter 8, "*Bitmaps.*"

Streaming Content

Vectors are not the only way Macromedia Flash MX makes itself more bandwidth-friendly. Macromedia Flash MX files download to Web browsers in small units. This allows the files to display some content while the rest is still downloading in the background. Ideally, the content will play more slowly than it downloads, so that the viewing experience is not interrupted. This method of playing one part of an entire Web site while the rest is still downloading is called **streaming**. It differs significantly from the way HTML files are downloaded and displayed in a browser, which takes place a page at a time.

Macromedia Flash MX is sometimes difficult to understand because of the way information is organized within it. With HTML, all content is organized into pages (HTML files). When you load a page, all the parts of its content are downloaded to the browser and then displayed. Macromedia Flash MX movies, on the other hand, can be organized in a very different way.

Imagine a Web site with four or five pages. If it were a pure HTML site, every time you traveled from one page to another you would have to wait for the new page to download. With a site based on Macromedia Flash MX, however, all of the "pages" could be contained in a single movie. When you visited the site, the first page would download and be displayed. Unlike the HTML-only site, the other pages would be downloading in the background while you were reading the first page. When you clicked on a link to go to another page, it would be displayed instantly, with no download wait! This is the real beauty of streaming. When used correctly, it can allow you to build a site that eliminates a lot of the waiting that plagues the Web. You'll learn more about how to optimize your Macromedia Flash MX content for streaming in Chapter 16, "*Publishing and Exporting*."

What's New in Macromedia Flash MX?

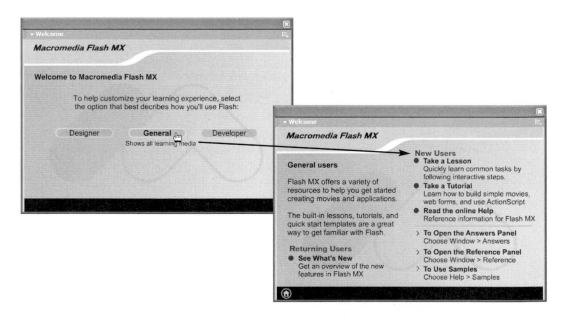

This version of Macromedia Flash offers many upgraded and new features that enhance the program and make it even easier to work with. When you open the program, you will be prompted with a welcome message that allows you to choose the option that best suits the way you plan to work with the program. Depending on which option you select, a window will appear with settings specific to your selection. You can close this window by clicking on the "X" in the upper right corner, and you can always reopen it again by choosing **Help > Welcome**.

A chart follows outlining some of the notable new features in Macromedia Flash MX.

New and Enhanced Features	
Feature	**Description**
Break Apart Text	Creates a separate text block for each character so that you can work with each letter more easily. In Chapter 5, "*Shape Tweening*," you will learn how to do this.
Code Hinting	Speeds up the writing of ActionScript by detecting the command being written and displaying hints, which show the correct syntax of the command. You will learn more about code hinting in Chapter 11, "*ActionScripting Basics.*"
Color Mixer	Simplifies creating and working with colors and gradients.
Components	Offer drag-and-drop interface elements such as check boxes, push buttons, and scroll bars. You will learn how to work with components in Chapter 14, "*Components and Forms.*"
Distribute to Layers	Allows you to select multiple objects on one layer (such as broken-apart text) and instantly distribute each object to its own layer. You will learn to do this in Chapter 5, "*Shape Tweening.*"
Edit in Place	Allows you to modify symbols in place, right inside the context of their movies. You will learn to use this in Chapter 6, "*Symbols and Instances.*"
Free Transform Tool	Allows you to apply various combined object transformations at one time. You will learn more about the Free Transform tool and have a chance to use it in many chapters throughout the book.
Library: **Drag and Drop** **Conflict Resolution**	Simplifies the ability to move symbols between Macromedia Flash MX files by allowing you to drag and drop items from one location to the next. A new feature in the Library allows for conflict resolution when you add a library item to a Macromedia Flash MX file that already has an existing item with the same name. You will learn more about Conflict Resolution in Chapter 17, "*Putting It All Together.*"
	continues on next page

New and Enhanced Features *continued*	
Feature	**Description**
Named Anchors	Allow users who are viewing your Macromedia Flash MX movies to at last be able to use the Forward and Back buttons in their browser. This is now possible thanks to the addition of the named anchors feature in Macromedia Flash MX. Named anchors allow the user to navigate from scene to scene in a video clip or from named anchor point to named anchor point in the Macromedia Flash MX movie. You will learn about anchor points in Chapter 15, "*Video.*"
Property Inspector	Allows easy access to the most common attributes of your movie through a panel with settings that change to reflect what is selected in the project file. You can make modifications quickly right inside the Property Inspector, rather than having to find the correct panel or menu containing the feature you wish to alter.
Save as Flash 5	Allows you to work inside Macromedia Flash MX but save the project file in Macromedia Flash 5 format. You will learn more about saving different Macromedia Flash MX file types in Chapter 16, "*Publishing and Exporting.*"
Sound Controls	Offer more control of sound within your movie by introducing the ability to better synchronize movie events with the beginning or end of a sound clip. You will learn how to use sound controls in Chapter 13, "*Sound.*"
Templates	Allow you to either create your own template or use one of the starter templates to make the development of a new movie easier.
Timeline	Includes more options such as the ability to organize layers using folders and more versatility in working with multiple frames. You will learn all about the Timeline in Chapter 2, "*Interface.*"
Vertical Text	Allows you to create vertical text blocks in addition to the standard horizontal text blocks. You will learn about vertical text in Chapter 12, "*Working with Text.*"
Video	Allows to you import video into Macromedia Flash MX and export from inside your Macromedia Flash MX movie. You will be learning to work with video clips in Chapter 15, "*Video.*"

Macromedia Flash MX as Project, Player, or Projector?

"Flash" as a term can be confusing. Macromedia uses the word interchangeably to include Macromedia Flash as an authoring tool, Macromedia Flash as a player, and Macromedia Flash as a stand-alone projector. The following chart should help set the groundwork for understanding the difference between the authoring tool, the player, and the stand-alone projector.

Macromedia Flash Applications	
Application	**Description**
Macromedia Flash Authoring Tool	Creates the actual Macromedia Flash content. Macromedia Flash MX is the application that allows you to create and edit artwork and animation and add sound and interactivity. The projects that you create using the Macromedia Flash MX authoring tool are stored in the .fla file format. You cannot publish the .fla file to the Web, since it's a file that you use internally to edit and create Macromedia Flash MX content. From the .fla file, you can export the .swf file format, which is inserted into an HTML document and published to the Web.
Macromedia Flash Player	The Macromedia Flash Player must be installed in the Web browser for end users to see Macromedia Flash MX content in the .swf file. This player comes preinstalled in current Web browsers and/or can be downloaded from the Macromedia Web site for free.
Macromedia Flash Projector	Macromedia Flash MX content can also be stored in stand-alone projectors that do not require the Web browser in order to play. These files can be distributed via email, on CD-ROMs, or on disk but are not typically distributed over the Web. The file extension for a Macromedia Flash MX projector is .exe (Windows) or .hqx (Mac).

File Types Associated with Macromedia Flash MX

Macromedia Flash MX media can be saved and output in many formats. The most common types of Macromedia Flash MX files are project files, movie files, and projector files. The file types can become very confusing, because all of these are commonly referred to as "movies." The following list explains the three most prominent Macromedia Flash MX formats. You will learn about all the file types that Macromedia Flash MX can produce in detail in Chapter 16, "*Publishing and Exporting*."

File Types	
File Type	**Description**
Project File (.fla) Untitled.fla	The master project file format, which stores all the settings and resources for your Macromedia Flash MX project. You can reopen and reedit the .fla file at any time using the Macromedia Flash MX Authoring Tool. (.fla stands for **FLA**sh.)
Movie File (.swf) Untitled.swf	The movie format that can be embedded in Web pages for Web-based Macromedia Flash MX presentations. These files are generally not editable. (.swf stands for **S**hock**W**ave **F**lash.)
Windows Projector File (.exe) Untitled.exe **Mac Projector File (.hqx)** Untitled Projector	A stand-alone projector file that can play on any computer without needing the Macromedia Flash player to run. Macromedia Flash MX writes both Windows and Mac format projector files.

Caution: Player Required!

Macromedia Flash MX content is not visible in a Web browser unless either the Macromedia Flash MX Player or the Shockwave Player has been installed in that browser. In the past, this has been seen as a serious limitation of the format, although over the past few years the number of Internet users who have the player has increased exponentially.

Macromedia has hired an independent consulting firm to maintain an estimate of the number of Macromedia Flash Players that are in use. At the time of this writing, over 450 million Web users worldwide had a version of one of these players installed. The Macromedia Flash Player 6 comes preinstalled on all new browsers shipped by AOL, CompuServe, Microsoft, and Netscape. Additionally, all versions of Microsoft Windows 98 and newer and Apple OS 8 and newer include the plug-in.

Players	
Macromedia Flash Player	The Macromedia Flash Player is used for viewing Macromedia Flash content on the Web. You can download the latest version of the Macromedia Flash Player at `http://www.macromedia.com/software/downloads/`. This player installs inside the player folder for your Web browser of choice.
Shockwave Player	The Shockwave Player is used for viewing Macromedia Director content on the Web. You can download the latest version of the Shockwave Player at `http://www.macromedia.com/software/downloads/`.

Beyond Macromedia Flash MX

Macromedia Flash MX is an incredibly powerful tool by itself. However, there are a few functions it can't perform. Here are some of the Web technologies you should know about if you want to extend Macromedia Flash MX beyond its basic capabilities.

What's CGI?

A CGI (**C**ommon **G**ateway **I**nterface) script is a program that defines a standard way of exchanging information between a Web browser and a Web server. CGI scripts can be written in any number of languages (Perl, C, ASP, and others). If you plan on creating a complex Web application that requires the use of something like CGI, I recommend you work with a Web engineer who has experience creating these kinds of scripts. Macromedia Flash MX can communicate with CGI scripts, although that topic is way beyond the scope of this book.

For further information on using CGI, please check out the following links:

`http://www.cgidir.com/`

`http://www.cgi101.com/`

`http://www.icthus.net/CGI-City/`

What's XML?

XML (**EX**tensible **M**arkup **L**anguage) is a standard that has been developed to handle the description and exchange of data. XML enables developers to define markup languages that define the structure and meaning of information. Therefore, an XML document is much like a database presented in a text file. XML content can be transformed into a variety of different formats, including HTML, WML, and VoiceXML.

XML differs from HTML in that it is not predefined—you can create the tags and attributes. You can also use XML to create your own data structure and modify it for the data you want it to carry. In Macromedia Flash MX, you can use the XML object to create, manipulate, and pass that data. Using ActionScripting, a Macromedia Flash MX movie can load and process XML data. As a result, an XML-savvy Macromedia Flash MX developer can develop a movie that dynamically retrieves data from the external XML document instead of creating static text fields within a project file.

Just as HTML provided an open, platform-independent format for distributing Web documents, XML promises to be the open, platform-independent format for exchanging any type of electronic information. Like CGI, XML is also a topic beyond the scope of this book.

For further information on XML, take a look at the following links:

`http://www.ait-usa.com/xmlintro/xmlproject/article.htm`

`http://www.Macromedia Flashkit.com/tutorials/3rd_Party/`
   `Macromedia Flash_5_-Chris_Sm-213/index.shtml`

`http://www.xml.com/`

`http://www.xml101.com/`

JavaScript and Macromedia Flash MX

Macromedia Flash MX's scripting language is referred to as **ActionScripting**. In Macromedia Flash MX, ActionScript is based on another scripting language you may have heard of called **JavaScript**. Although they share a similar syntax and structure, they are two different languages. One way to tell them apart is that ActionScript uses scripts that are processed entirely within the Macromedia Flash Player, independently of the browser that is used to view the file. JavaScript, on the other hand, uses external interpreters that vary according to the browser used.

ActionScript and JavaScript can be used together due to the fact that Macromedia Flash MX gives you the ability to call JavaScript commands to perform tasks or to send and receive data. For many Macromedia Flash MX developers, a basic knowledge of JavaScript makes learning ActionScript easier, because the basic syntax of the scripts and the handling of objects is the same in both languages. However, this is not a requirement for learning ActionScripting.

You will be introduced to ActionScripting in Chapter 11, "*ActionScripting Basics*." That chapter will give you hands-on experience in applying Macromedia Flash MX's powerful scripting language. For further information and tutorials about JavaScript and how to use it in conjunction with Macromedia Flash MX, check out the links below:

`http://www.javascript.com/`

`http://javascript.internet.com/`

`http://www.jsworld.com/`

`http://www.flashkit.com/links/Javascripts/`

That's a wrap for this chapter. Time to move on to the hands-on exercises!

2.

Interface

Document Window	Timeline
Layer Controls	Information Bar
Toolbox	Panels
Custom Keyboard Shortcuts

---

no exercise files

Macromedia Flash MX
H•O•T CD-ROM

Whether you are new to Macromedia Flash or you are a veteran of previous versions, you should not skip this chapter. Although you might be tempted to jump right in and begin with the hands-on exercises, take the time to read through this chapter first so you have a grasp of the new Macromedia Flash MX interface.

This chapter begins with an overview of the main components: the Timeline, Stage, Work Area, and Toolbox, as well as the new panels in Macromedia Flash MX. This will be relatively short so you can get to the actual exercises as quickly as possible. After all, that's the best way to learn how these tools work. The overview in this chapter will make it easier for you to work with the various elements throughout the rest of the book.

The Document Window

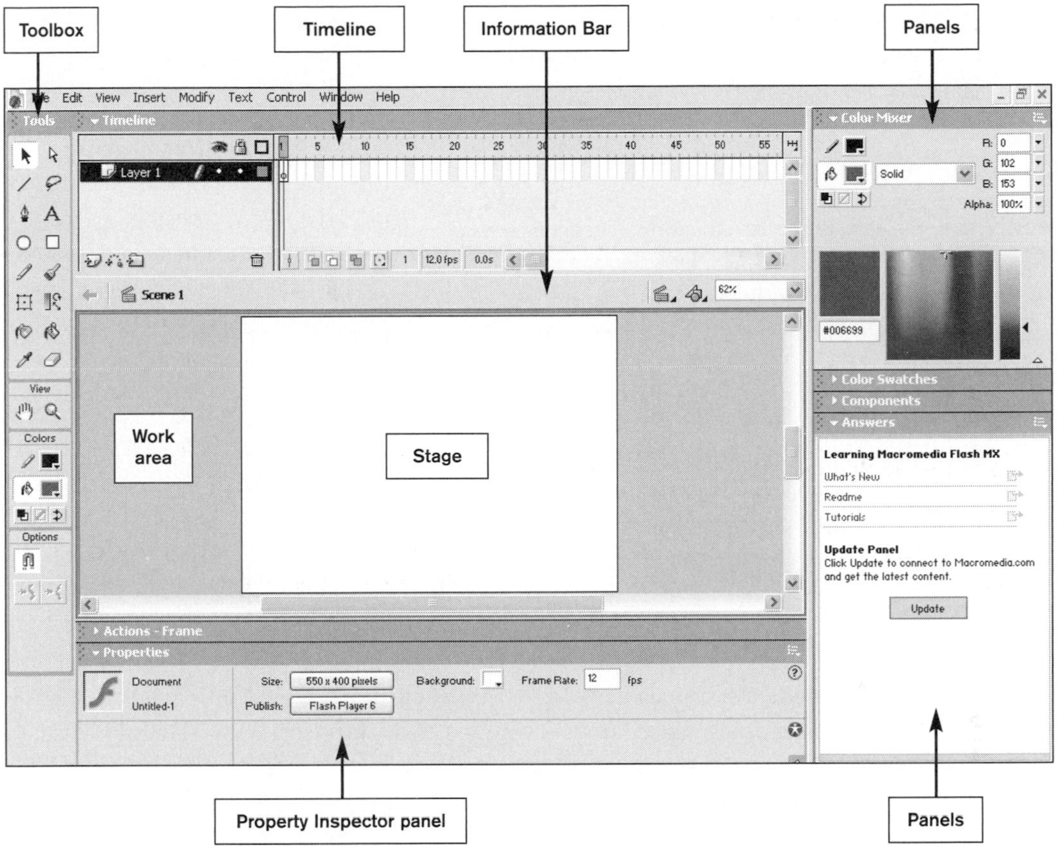

The Document Window contains six main elements: the Timeline, the Stage, the Work Area, the Information Bar, the Toolbox, and, new to Macromedia Flash MX, the panels, including the Property Inspector panel shown here.

Each time you create a new document in Macromedia Flash MX, you are presented with a new blank **Document Window**. This window is divided into six main components:

Timeline The Timeline is where you control the static and moving elements in the project file, using layers, the Playhead, frames, and the Status Bar. All are described in detail in the next few pages.

Stage The Stage is where your animation and images appear. It represents the visible area of your project. You will learn how to modify the properties of the Stage, such as size, color, and frame rate, in Chapter 4, "*Animation Basics.*"

Work Area The light gray area around the Stage is referred to as the Work Area. Nothing in the Work Area will be visible to the end user after you publish your movie. You can place objects here until you want them to appear on the Stage. For example, if you want to animate a bird flying in from offstage, you can place the bird artwork offscreen in the Work Area so it appears to fly in from outside the Stage area.

Information Bar The Information Bar displays your current location inside the project file such as the name of the current scene, a number of buttons that let you edit scenes and symbols, and the Zoom box. This bar may change location based on whether your Timeline is docked or not. Docking and undocking the Timeline is discussed later in this chapter.

Toolbox The Toolbox contains tools that are necessary when creating and editing artwork. This long vertical bar gives you access to just about every tool you will need to create and modify the objects in your Macromedia Flash MX projects.

Panels Panels are windows that contain tools and information to help you work in your project file more efficiently. Each of the panels can be used to view and modify elements within your project file. For example, the Property Inspector panel changes depending on what is selected, and it allows you to make changes to the current selection quickly, right inside the panel. You will learn more about panels later in this chapter.

TIP | The Status Bar

Use the Paint Bucket to fill enclosed areas of the drawing with color

If you're a Windows user, you can choose **Window > Toolbars > Status** to extend the bottom for your screen to display helpful hints. When the Status option is selected, this area will display a description of the tool or menu item that your pointer is over, allowing you to see what it does before you select it.

The Timeline

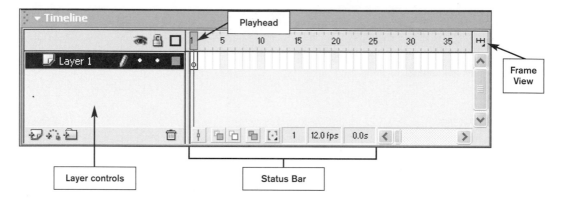

The **Timeline** controls and displays all of the static and moving elements of your project over time, using frames and layers. In this section, you'll learn about the main elements of the Timeline. As I cover each of these elements, don't forget that you will get hands-on experience later as you go though the exercises.

Playhead The Playhead indicates which Timeline frame is currently displayed on the Stage. Once you have artwork on the Stage and have created different frames (which you'll learn to do in Chapter 3, "*Drawing and Color Tools*"), you can click and drag the Playhead to move it to a specific frame. Many people also scan through the Timeline (a process called **scrubbing**) to quickly preview animations. You will get a lot of practice doing this in the animation portions of this book.

Layer controls This region lets you control the features of the layers, including adding, organizing, hiding, and locking layers, as well as displaying the content of layers as outlines. Because there are so many options here, I will wait until later in this chapter to describe them in more detail.

Status Bar The Status Bar gives you feedback about the current frame, the number of frames per second (fps), and the elapsed time of your movie. It also controls some animation tools, such as onion skinning. All of these issues will be addressed fully in Chapter 4, "*Animation Basics*."

Frame View This not-so-obvious drop-down menu lets you control the appearance of your Timeline. You can change the appearance of the individual frames and the entire size of the Timeline itself. As you will see in Chapter 13, "*Sound*," this can be helpful with certain projects.

Docking and Undocking the Timeline

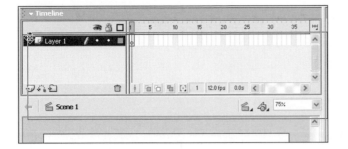

If you have the luxury of working with a large monitor or multiple monitors, you will be pleased to know that you can easily dock and undock the Timeline from the main document window. This feature allows you more flexibility in arranging your work environment. For example, you can place the Stage on one monitor and stash all the Macromedia Flash MX panels on your second monitor, giving you an uncluttered view of your work. By the way, if you find the ability to undock the Timeline annoying, you can disable this feature in the Preferences.

Docking and undocking the Timeline can be done in one or two easy steps: Move your cursor over the upper left corner of the Timeline until you see a series of dots and the cursor turns into either an icon with four arrows (Windows) or a Hand icon (Mac). Click and drag in that area (as shown above) to undock the Timeline. A thin outline will appear when you click, indicating that you have grabbed the Timeline and are moving it.

Release the mouse button and your Timeline will be undocked from the Document Window and will appear as its own window. Once it is undocked, you can click in the Timeline header to drag it around.

If you want to redock the Timeline, you can choose from four locations: its default position above the Stage, the right side of the Document Window, the left side of the Document Window, or the bottom of the document window. To redock it, simply click in the Timeline header, drag it back to one of the four locations, and release the mouse button.

The Layer Controls

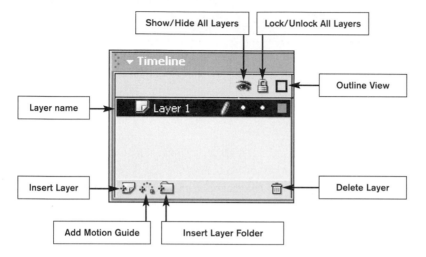

Macromedia Flash MX allows you to use **layers** to organize your artwork, just like other graphics programs you might be familiar with, such as Macromedia Fireworks, Adobe Photoshop, etc. The Timeline's Layer controls play an important role in your workflow. This is where you add, modify, delete, and organize layers and where you can hide, lock, and control the appearance of the layer contents. As you add layers in Macromedia Flash MX, the artwork on the topmost layer in the Timeline will appear closest to you on the Stage. At any time you can change the stacking order of the artwork simply by dragging and dropping the layers higher or lower in the Timeline. The following list explains the Layer controls in detail.

Layer name The default layer names are Layer 1, Layer 2, and so on. Double-click a name to change it.

Insert Layer Adding new layers to your projects is as easy as clicking this button. Each time you click, a new layer is added on top of the one that is currently selected.

Add Motion Guide This button adds a Guide Layer on top of the currently selected layer. You will work with Guide Layers in Chapter 7, "*Motion Tweening.*"

Insert Layer Folder This button is a new feature in Macromedia Flash MX. It adds a special Layer Folder that can hold other layers. This is helpful in organizing your layers into groups that can be easily expanded and collapsed.

Delete Layer There's not much mystery to this trash can button. Clicking this button deletes the layer that is currently selected. Don't worry, though: If you click this button by accident, you can undo it by choosing Edit > Undo. Phew!!

Show/Hide All Layers Clicking the Eye icon will temporarily hide the artwork on the Stage and Work Area on all layers in the Timeline. **Note:** This will not hide your artwork in the published movie.

Lock/Unlock All Layers Clicking the Padlock icon to lock the layer makes it impossible to edit anything on this layer. This control can be useful when you start working with multiple layers, especially ones with overlapping content.

Outline View Clicking this icon displays all of the contents of all of the layers in the Timeline in Outline view, in which solid shapes are represented as outlined shapes with no solid fill. This feature can be very helpful when you are working with multiple layers with overlapping content.

The Information Bar

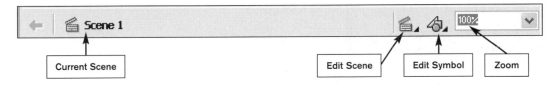

The **Information Bar** is very useful for quick visual feedback as to where you are located in your movie. It contains buttons and a drop-down menu that give you quick access to the scenes and available zoom levels. Here is a brief description of each feature in the Information Bar.

Current Scene The Current Scene readout on the left side of the Information Bar displays the name of the scene that is currently open on the Stage. You will learn about scenes in Chapter 11, "*ActionScripting Basics*."

Edit Scene menu If your movie contains more than one scene, this drop-down menu displays a list of all the scenes in your project file. You will learn how to use multiple scenes in Chapter 11, "*ActionScripting Basics*."

Edit Symbol menu This drop-down menu displays all of the symbols in your project. You'll learn about symbols in Chapter 6, "*Symbols and Instances*."

Zoom box It might seem like a little thing, and maybe it is in size, but the Zoom box is a handy drop-down menu that lets you quickly zoom into and out of the contents of your Stage.

The Toolbox

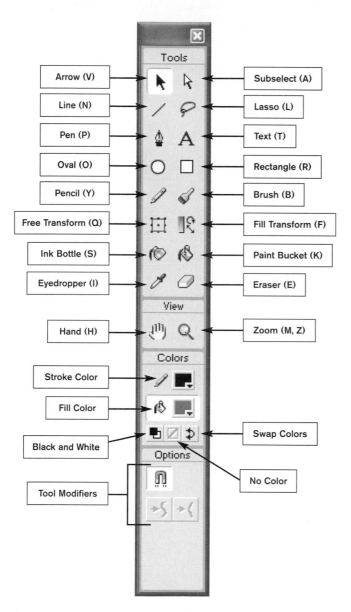

As in most drawing programs, the **Toolbox** contains tools that are necessary when creating and editing artwork. This long vertical bar gives you access to just about every tool you will need to create and modify objects in your Macromedia Flash MX projects. Each of the main tools has an associated keyboard shortcut, which is listed in parentheses next to the tool name above.

Other than docking and undocking the Toolbox and moving it around the desktop, there is only one option for working with the Toolbox. When you hover over a Toolbox icon, a small ToolTip will appear with the name and keyboard shortcut for that option. You can disable this feature in the General Preferences by choosing **Edit > Preferences > General. Tip:** You can temporarily hide the Toolbar by pressing the Tab key on the keyboard. Press the Tab key again to see the Toolbar again.

WARNING | Docking the Toolbox on Windows vs. Macintosh

There is one minor difference between the Mac and Windows operating systems when it comes to docking the Toolbox. On the Macintosh, you can't dock the Toolbox. You can, however, click and drag to reposition the Toolbox freely around the screen. In the Windows operating system, the Toolbox can be docked only along either side of the document window.

The Panels

Macromedia Flash 5 saw the company's first significant movement toward a common user interface among all of their Web applications, including Dreamweaver, Fireworks, Freehand, Flash, and UltraDev. With the release of Macromedia Flash MX, the ability to completely customize the work area has streamlined users' workflow even further. **Panels** are windows that contain tools and information to help you work in your project file more efficiently. Each of the panels can be used to view and modify elements within your project file. The options within the panels allow you to change settings such as color, type, size, rotation, and many others. You have the ability to display, hide, move, resize, group, and organize the panels so that you can customize the work area in any way you wish.

In the next few sections, you will learn the basic ins and outs of working with panels, including how to dock, resize, and work with panel sets. At the end of this section is a list that provides a quick reference to the panels in Macromedia Flash MX.

Undocking and Docking Panels

Don't think for a moment that you are stuck with the default panel layout. Just like the Timeline mentioned earlier in this chapter, the panels can easily be undocked and docked to create new combinations that better fit the way you work.

To undock a panel, move your mouse toward the left of the panel name, over the area where you see a series of dots. You will notice that the pointer becomes either an icon with four arrows (Windows) or a Hand icon (Mac). Click and drag the panel away from its current docked position and let go of the mouse button to undock it.

Once the panel is undocked, you can drag it around the work area by clicking either on the solid bar above the panel name or on the dots to the left of the panel name and dragging.

To redock a panel or add it to another panel group, click on the dots to the left of the panel name (you will see the pointer change to an icon) and drag the panel onto another panel. Once you are hovering over the other panel, you will see a dark outline appear over that panel, indicating that if you release your mouse, you will add the panel you are dragging to the panel group you are hovering over.

Tip: A few of the panels (such as the Property Inspector) will lose their dots once you undock them. In such cases, simply click on the panel's solid bar and drag it over another panel until that panel is outlined and let go of the mouse to dock it again.

Resizing Panels

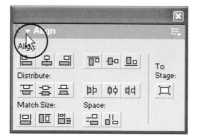

Macromedia Flash MX not only allows you to completely customize the layout and arrangement of the panels, but also lets you change the size of each panel. To resize a panel, either drag the panel's border (Windows) or drag the lower right corner (Mac).

Note: A few of the panels, such as the Property Inspector and the Toolbox, cannot be resized. In panels that can't be resized, the pointer will not turn into the resize arrows when you move it over the border (Windows) or you will not see the lines in the right corner of the panel (Mac).

Expanding, Collapsing, Hiding, and Closing Panels

Panel expanded   *Panel collapsed*

To expand a panel when you see only its title, click the arrow next to the panel name once. Click the arrow again to collapse it. (You can also simply click to the right of the panel name to either expand or collapse the panel.)

Press the **Tab** key on the keyboard to show or hide all of the panels in your document.

Choose **Window > Close All Panels** to close all of the panels.

Using the Panel Options Menu

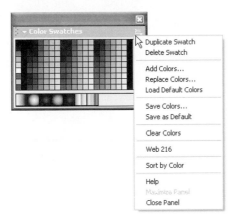

In addition to what you see in each panel, many of the panels have a control that displays a pop-up Options menu when clicked. To display this menu, click the **Options Menu control** in the upper right corner of the panel. You cannot access the pop-up Options menu if the panel has been collapsed.

Creating and Saving Panel Sets

Macromedia Flash MX gives you the flexibility to group panels in any combination you like. In addition, you can save these custom configurations. This means that with the click of the mouse, you can completely modify the arrangement of your panels. The following steps walk you through the process of saving a custom **panel set**.

Organize your panels in any way you want. For example, you can create different panel sets for different tasks, such as drawing, animation, and working with ActionScripts. This feature allows you to quickly organize your workspace for specific tasks.

1. Choose **Window > Save Panel Layout**. This opens the **Save Panel Layout** dialog box, which prompts you to assign a name for this arrangement.

2. Enter any name you want and click **OK**. That's all there is to it!

Switching to Another Panel Set

Changing from one panel set to another is as easy as selecting a menu option. Choose **Window > Panel Sets**, and select the name of the layout you want to display. Your panels will quickly be rearranged into that specific arrangement.

Note: Selecting **Default Layout** will return the panels to their default positions.

> **TIP | Deleting Panel Sets**
>
> What do you do if you create a panel set that you just aren't happy with? While there is no mechanism for deleting them, it is still a relatively simple process. All of the panel sets are stored in a folder on your hard drive: the **Macromedia Flash MX > Panel Sets** folder. If you want to remove one, just delete the appropriate file from this directory, and it will be gone forever.

The Panels Defined

This section briefly describes each of the panels in Macromedia Flash MX. It may seem like a lot of new information. If so, just skim over it for now and then come back to it later as you read through the book. You will have the chance to work with each of the panels described here in depth as you navigate through the exercises in this book.

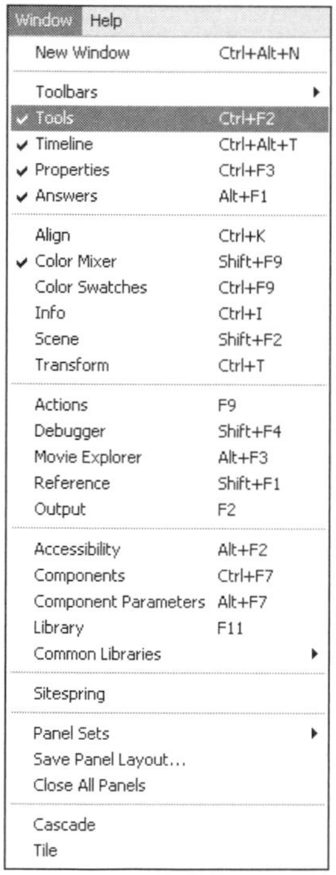

Window	Help	
New Window	Ctrl+Alt+N	
Toolbars	▶	
✔ Tools	Ctrl+F2	
✔ Timeline	Ctrl+Alt+T	
✔ Properties	Ctrl+F3	
✔ Answers	Alt+F1	
Align	Ctrl+K	
✔ Color Mixer	Shift+F9	
Color Swatches	Ctrl+F9	
Info	Ctrl+I	
Scene	Shift+F2	
Transform	Ctrl+T	
Actions	F9	
Debugger	Shift+F4	
Movie Explorer	Alt+F3	
Reference	Shift+F1	
Output	F2	
Accessibility	Alt+F2	
Components	Ctrl+F7	
Component Parameters	Alt+F7	
Library	F11	
Common Libraries	▶	
Sitespring		
Panel Sets	▶	
Save Panel Layout...		
Close All Panels		
Cascade		
Tile		

It is important to know before beginning that panels are accessed in one of two ways. First, you can display the **Window menu** (shown above) and then choose the panel you want. Second, you can use the panel's associated keyboard shortcut. The method you use is a matter of personal preference, but it's a good idea to find one consistent way to work; it makes using Macromedia Flash MX easier.

Here is a description of each of the panels in Macromedia Flash MX.

Toolbox Contains all the tools that are necessary to create and edit artwork, including drawing, painting, section, and modification tools. The Toolbox is one of the most frequently used panels in the program.

Timeline Controls and displays all of the static and moving elements of your Macromedia Flash MX projects over time.

Controller Provides one way to preview your movie right inside the authoring environment. Although there are several ways to test your movie, the Controller panel contains features similar to those on a remote control, allowing you to stop, rewind, fast-forward, and play your movie using one panel.

Property Inspector Acts as a one-stop shop for displaying and changing all of your most commonly used attributes of the current selection in one panel. This context-sensitive panel allows you to modify the current selection using only one panel, rather than having to open several panels.

Answers Provides assistance for learning Macromedia Flash MX. This panel contains links to sections of the Macromedia Web site (**http://www.macromedia.com**) that contain updated information and tutorials that can help you learn Macromedia Flash MX.

Align Gives you access to several different alignment and distribution options.

Color Mixer Allows you to create new colors in one of three different modes—RGB (red, green, blue), HSB (hue, saturation, brightness), or HEX (hexadecimal). The Color Mixer panel also lets you add alpha and work with different types of gradients.

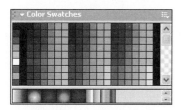

Color Swatches Displays the default 216 Web-safe colors and lets you select, add, sort, replace, save, and clear colors.

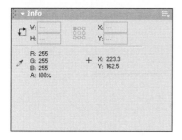

Info Contains numerical information about the size, position, and color of the selected object. This panel is very helpful when you need pixel-specific positions and measurements.

Scene Displays a list of all the scenes within your movie. This panel lets you quickly add, duplicate, delete, name, or rename scenes. The Scene panel also provides a way to jump to different scenes in your document.

Transform Allows you to numerically transform (rotate, scale, and skew) an object. This panel also lets you create a transformed copy of an object.

Actions Allows you to add and modify actions for a frame, button, or Movie Clip. You will learn all about the Actions panel in Chapter 11, "*ActionScripting Basics*."

Debugger Provides a way to check your movie for errors while it is playing in the Macromedia Flash Player.

Movie Explorer Displays the contents of your movie, organized in a hierarchical tree. You can use the Movie Explorer panel to search for specific elements within your project file so that you can quickly select and edit them with a few clicks of your mouse. You will learn about the Movie Explorer panel in Chapter 17, "*Putting It All Together*."

Reference Displays detailed information about ActionScripting usage and syntax. This panel is an essential tool for learning ActionScripting; you will be working with it in Chapter 11, "*ActionScripting Basics*."

Output Provides assistance during troubleshooting by displaying feedback information after you test your movie.

Accessibility Gives you some options that can help make your movies more accessible, so that they can be seen and heard by people with disabilities.

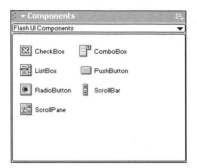

Components Gives you access to the seven default user interface (UI) components. These components are essentially Movie Clips that contain complex ActionScript elements. As you will see in Chapter 14, "*Components and Forms*," the Components panel lets you add powerful functionality to your movie without requiring you to know advanced ActionScripting.

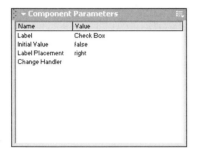

Component Parameters Allows you to set the parameters (attributes) of a component after you have added an instance of that component to your movie.

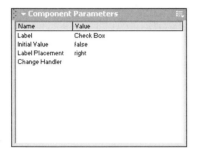

Library Provides a location for you to store and organize specific assets within your project, including symbols, imported artwork, sound files, and video files. You will learn about the Library panel in Chapter 6, "*Symbols and Instances*."

Common Libraries Provides access to sample libraries included with the program. These libraries contain premade buttons, learning interactions, and sounds, which you can use in your movies.

Sitespring Provides a link to Macromedia Sitespring and allows you to access your Sitespring task list. To use this panel, you need a Sitespring user account and access to a Sitespring server.

Custom Keyboard Shortcuts

Keyboard Shortcuts	
Current Set: Flash MX	→ Delete Set
	→ Rename Set
Commands: Drawing Menu Commands	→ Duplicate Set
⊞ File	
⊞ Edit	
⊞ View	
⊞ Insert	
⊞ Modify	← Commands list
⊞ Text	
⊞ Control	
⊞ Window	
⊞ Help	
Description:	
Shortcuts: + −	← Add/Delete Shortcut
	← Shortcuts list
Press Key: Change	
Help OK Cancel	

To further streamline your workflow in Macromedia Flash MX, you can create, modify, and delete sets of custom keyboard shortcuts. Macromedia has even designed an entire interface to make this process easy to do. One of its neatest features is that you can even assign keyboard shortcuts in Macromedia Flash MX that match those used in other programs, like Macromedia Fireworks, Macromedia Freehand, Adobe Photoshop, and even earlier versions of Macromedia Flash. You may think that this feature is only for power users, but you should still be aware of it. Besides, you will be a power user in no time!

The steps that follow outline the process of creating, modifying, and deleting custom keyboard shortcuts. This isn't an exercise that you have to complete; if you like, just make a mental note of it for later use.

Creating a New Shortcut Set

1. Choose **Edit** > **Keyboard Shortcuts** (Windows) or **Flash** > **Keyboard Shortcuts** (Mac) to open the **Keyboard Shortcuts** dialog box.

2. Click the **Duplicate Set** button to create a copy of the current set. This will ensure that you are working from a duplicate so you don't mess up the original set.

3. Enter a name for your custom set. You can name it anything you want, but it's best to stick to a meaningful name that you can recall later. Click **OK**.

4. Click to the left of any of the options in the Commands list to drill down and display the keyboard shortcuts for that menu. Select the option you want to change.

5. Click the **+** button to add a shortcut (click the **–** button to delete the selected shortcut). You can create multiple keyboard shortcuts for one option. (However, that may not be such a good idea.)

6. Click the keyboard shortcut you want to assign to this option or enter it in the **Press Key** text box. Click the **Change** button to confirm your selection and assign it to the menu item. **Note:** If the key combination you selected is already in use, you will get an error message at the bottom of the dialog box.

Well, that's enough of the interface for now. The following chapters are full of hands-on exercises where you will work with these interface elements. So go ahead and turn the page to get started.

3.
Drawing and Color Tools

Drawing Tools Explained	Modifying Strokes and Fills
Working with Multiple Objects	Grouping Objects
Creating Gradients	Color Mixer Panel
Drawing with the Pen Tool	Modifying Paths

chap_03

Macromedia Flash MX
H•O•T CD-ROM

When most people think of Macromedia Flash, they think of one thing: animation. What many people don't know is that the program comes complete with a good set of drawing and color tools that can help you create artwork for making cool and interactive animations.

It's also possible to bring existing artwork into the program from other illustration programs such as Freehand or Illustrator. Chapter 18 "*Integration*," covers how to do this. For some types of artwork, however, you will find it is more convenient to draw right within the program. This chapter introduces you to the distinct characteristics and idiosyncrasies of the native drawing and color tools within Macromedia Flash MX.

Drawing Tools Explained

The drawing tools in Macromedia Flash MX are very powerful, but they can seem somewhat complex as you try to understand their individual behaviors. Here's a handy chart to use for reference. Don't feel compelled to read through everything here if you want to jump into the exercises right away. The keyboard shortcuts for the tools are given in parentheses after the tool name in the chart below and also inside the project file when you move your mouse over a tool in the Toolbox.

Drawing Tools		
Icon	**Name**	**What Does It Do?**
 /	**Line (N)**	The Line tool creates straight lines. Holding down the Shift key with this tool will constrain the lines to 45-degree angles. The lines drawn with the Line tool can be modified with the Ink Bottle tool and/or by using the Property Inspector panel.
 ρ	**Lasso (L)**	The Lasso tool allows you to select artwork or even a specific area of that artwork by drawing a freehand or straight selection around it.
 ♠	**Pen (P)**	The Pen tool creates straight or curved lines. The Pen tool is the only Macromedia Flash MX drawing tool capable of creating Bézier curves.
 A	**Text (T)**	The Text tool allows you to add text or text fields to your movie. The text or text field can be modified using the Property Inspector panel. You will learn all about the Text tool in Chapter 12, "*Working with Text*."
 O	**Oval (O)**	The Oval tool creates circles and ovals composed of fills and strokes, just fills, or just strokes. Holding down the Shift key while using this tool will allow you to create perfect circles.
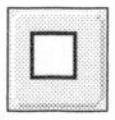 □	**Rectangle (R)**	The Rectangle tool creates rectangles and squares composed of strokes and fills, just strokes, or just fills. Holding down the Shift key while using this tool will allow you to create perfect squares.
 ✐	**Pencil (Y)**	The Pencil tool creates lines in one of three different modes: Straighten, Smooth, and Ink. Holding down the Shift key while using this tool will enable you to create perfect horizontal and vertical lines.

continues on next page

Drawing Tools *continued*		
Icon	**Name**	**What Does It Do?**
	Brush (B)	The Brush tool creates shapes with fills only. You can adjust the size and style of the brush by adjusting the tool options in the Toolbox or by using the Property Inspector. As with the Pencil tool, holding down the Shift key while using this tool enables you to create perfect horizontal and vertical lines.
	Free Transform (Q)	The Free Transform tool allows you to modify objects. You can use this tool to scale, rotate, flip, skew, or even change the center point of an object. Use the Shift key to maintain the aspect ratio while modifying the object.
	Fill Transform (F)	The Fill Transform tool allows you to change the size, direction, or center of a gradient or bitmap fill.
	Ink Bottle (S)	The Ink Bottle tool can be used to change the color or width of a line or to add a stroke to a shape. The Ink Bottle will not change the fill of a shape.
	Paint Bucket (K)	Use the Paint Bucket tool to add a fill inside a shape or to change the color of a fill. The Paint Bucket will never change the stroke of a shape.
	Eyedropper (I)	The Eyedropper tool can be used to copy the fill or stroke attributes of one object and then apply them to another object. This tool is especially useful when you want to copy the exact color of one object to another object.
	Eraser (E)	The Eraser tool can be used to remove any unwanted image areas on the Stage. Holding down the Shift key permits you to erase in perfect horizontal and vertical lines.

Lines, Strokes, and Fills Explained

In addition to learning how each of the drawing tools behave, you need to know the difference between **fills**, **strokes**, **lines**, and **shapes**. These differences can be understandably confusing because the interface refers to both lines and strokes. The chart below gives an example and brief explanation of each.

Lines, Strokes, and Fills		
Lines and Strokes		Lines are created with the Pencil, Pen, and Line tools. Strokes are the outlines that are created using the Rectangle and Oval tools. It is important to note that these terms are used interchangeably in the Macromedia documentation. We will also use both of these terms, since they both can be modified using the same tools. Lines and strokes are independent of any fills, and they are modified using the Ink Bottle, the Color and Tool Modifiers in the Toolbox, the Color Mixer panel, or using the Stroke Color in the Property Inspector.
Fills		Fills are created using the Brush, Paint Bucket, Rectangle and Oval tools. Fills can be created with or without strokes around them. They are modified using the Paint Bucket, the Color and Tool Modifiers in the Toolbox, the Color Mixer panel, or using the Property Inspector.
Strokes, Lines, Fills, and Shapes		Strokes and lines can be attached to fills, as in the pictures on the left, or they can be by themselves, as in the images in the top row. Strokes and lines are added to fills with the Ink Bottle and are modified using the Ink Bottle, the Color and Tool Modifiers in the Toolbox, the Color Mixer panel, or using the Property Inspector. Macromedia Flash MX refers to strokes, lines, fills, or a combination thereof as "shapes" when you select the artwork and view the selection in the Property Inspector.

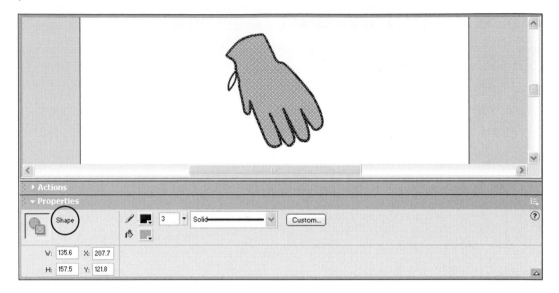

When you select a line, a stroke, a fill, or a combination thereof, the Property Inspector displays the word "Shape." This is how Macromedia Flash MX collectively refers to lines, strokes, and fills.

I. ——————Drawing with the Pencil Tool

The **Pencil tool** is one of the easiest drawing tools to use. It behaves much as you would expect a pencil to behave, drawing a line whenever you click and drag the mouse. By selecting one of the three modes (**Straighten**, **Smooth**, or **Ink**), you can control how the lines are created. In this exercise, you will draw a circle using each of the three modes, so you can better understand how each one works.

1. Copy the **chap_03** folder from the Macromedia Flash MX **H•O•T CD-ROM** to your hard drive. You must copy the files to your hard drive if you want to save changes to them.

2. Open the **pencil.fla** file from the **chap_03** folder. This is just a blank file with the Stage dimensions set to 400 × 200 pixels. This should be enough space for you to draw some shapes.

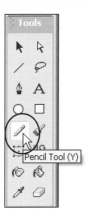

The Pencil tool

The Pencil Mode button appears at the bottom of the Toolbox when the Pencil tool is selected

3. Select the **Pencil** tool from the **Toolbox**. By default, the Pencil tool is in Straighten mode. Tip: If you leave your mouse over the tool long enough, a small ToolTip will appear, with the keyboard shortcut for that tool in parentheses.

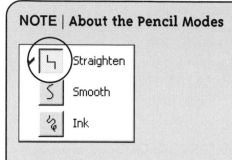

NOTE | About the Pencil Modes

Straighten

Smooth

Ink

In Macromedia Flash MX, the Pencil tool works much the same as the pencil tools in other graphics programs. There are, however, some special drawing modes that can help you control the line's appearance: Straighten, Smooth, and Ink. For example, drawing a perfect circle might be really difficult for some of you (especially after that morning coffee!), but with Straighten mode, it's much easier to create perfect geometric circles.

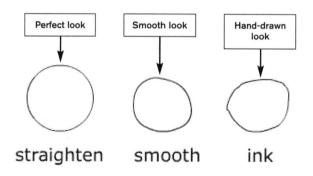

Perfect look   Smooth look   Hand-drawn look

straighten   smooth   ink

This example shows the result of a circle drawn with the Pencil tool, using each of the three modes.

The circle as you draw in Straighten mode

The circle when you release the mouse button

4. On the **Stage**, click and drag with the **Pencil** tool to create a circle. Release the mouse button when you are finished. Notice that the shape snaps to a perfect circle when you release the mouse button. This is the effect of the Straighten mode as it tries to guess what shape you are trying to create.

5. In the **Toolbox**, click the **Pencil Mode** drop-down menu and select **Smooth**. This changes the mode of the Pencil tool to Smooth.

The circle as you draw in Smooth mode

The circle when you release the mouse button

6. Using the **Pencil** tool, draw another circle next to the one you just created. When you release the mouse button, notice that the circle gets smoother, but that the change is less significant than when you used Straighten mode.

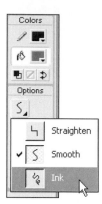

7. Click the **Pencil Mode** drop-down menu and select **Ink**. This changes the mode of the Pencil tool to Ink.

The circle as you draw in Ink mode

The circle when you release the mouse button

8. Using the **Pencil** tool, draw a third circle next to the one you just created. When you release the mouse button, notice that there is very little change in the circle.

9. Enough circles already. Go ahead and try drawing other simple shapes, such as squares, triangles, polygons, etc., with each of the different Pencil modes. This will give you an even better idea of how each of them works and how they can help you create artwork in Macromedia Flash MX.

Tip: If you want to clear the Stage area for more experimenting, press Ctrl+A (Windows) or Cmd+A (Mac) to select everything on the Stage. Then press the Delete key to delete the contents of the Stage.

10. When you are done playing with the Pencil tool, save and close this file—you won't be needing it again.

2. ———————Modifying Lines

Now that you know how to use the Pencil tool, you need to know how to make changes to the lines you create. In this exercise, you will learn how to use the **Property Inspector** as well as the **Ink Bottle** to modify the appearance of lines. Both of these tools let you change an object either by adding a line or by modifying the existing line. In addition, you will learn some of the nuances involved in selecting lines and the reason why you would use the Ink Bottle versus the Property Inspector.

1. Open the **strokes.fla** file from the **chap_03** folder. This file contains some shapes created with lines and fills. You will use these shapes to learn to modify lines and add strokes to shapes.

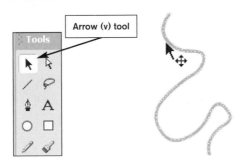

2. Select the **Arrow** tool from the **Toolbox**, and then click on the squiggle drawing to select it. The line gets a bit thicker, and a dotted pattern appears over it, indicating that the line is selected.

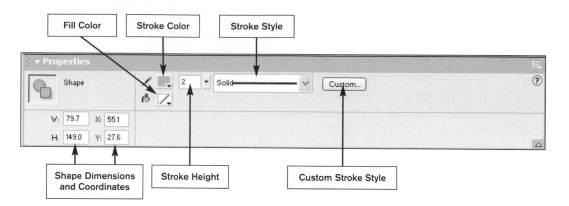

3. Make sure the **Property Inspector** is visible. If it's not, choose **Window > Properties** to make it visible. You must first select a line if you are going to use the Property Inspector to modify the stroke settings.

NOTE | The Property Inspector

One panel that you will become quite familiar with throughout this book is the Property Inspector. It is new to Macromedia Flash MX and is a great addition because it displays and allows you to change features associated with whatever is currently selected, including text, symbols, video, frames, and even tools. The Property Inspector appears in the interface just under the Actions panel below the Stage.

The beauty of the Property Inspector is that this panel allows you to make many different types of changes to the current selection from one easy-to-use panel.

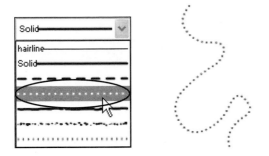

4. With the line still selected, click to see the **Stroke Style** drop-down menu. Select the fourth style from the top, the dotted line style, to change the style of the line from a solid line to a dotted line. Deselect the line by clicking on a blank area of the Stage to clearly see the changes.

You can use the Property Inspector as an easy way to modify artwork you select on the Stage. When you have a line selected, the Property Inspector displays the current settings for that line. This is help-ful when you need to know what the line settings are for a particular object. The default stroke settings are for a 1-point, solid black line.

TIP | Hiding Selections

When lines are selected, it can be very difficult to see the changes you've made. Press **Ctrl+H** (Windows) or choose **View > Hide Edges** (Mac) to temporarily hide the selection mesh so you can see the changes better. Press the keyboard shortcut again to see the selection mesh.

Line deselected to show the changes

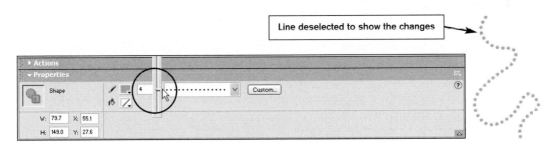

5. Make sure the line is selected on the **Stage** and, in the **Property Inspector**, click on the arrow next to the **Stroke Height** to reveal the slider. Click and drag up on the slider until you reach a setting of **4**. This increases the thickness of the line. The total range of choices is from 0.25 to 10. Deselect the line by clicking on a blank area of the Stage to clearly see the changes.

6. Select the line on the **Stage** again, and from the **Stroke Color** box in the **Property Inspector**, click and select another color. As you can probably guess, this will change the color of the line. Deselect the line by clicking on a blank area of the Stage to clearly see the changes.

TIP | Creating Custom Line Styles

You might be wondering at this point if you can create your own custom line styles. Yes, you can. With the line selected on the Stage, click the box named **Custom** in the **Property Inspector** panel. This opens the Stroke Style dialog box, where you can create your own line style using a number of different options. The changes you make to the settings here are temporary, and they will return to their default settings once you quit the program.

7. Using the **Arrow** tool, move the cursor over the bottom line of the arrow shape in the middle of the Stage. (Don't click just yet.) Notice that as you move the cursor over the line, a small, curved line appears next to the Arrow tool. This indicates that you are over a line, not a fill.

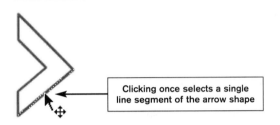

Clicking once selects a single line segment of the arrow shape

8. Using the **Arrow** tool, click on the right lower line segment. Notice that a white selection mesh appears over that line segment only.

9. In the **Property Inspector**, use the **Stroke Height** slider to change the line width to **5**. Notice that only the one selected line segment is changed. In order for a line to be modified, it must be selected before you change the settings in the Stroke panel, and in this case, only one of the six lines of this arrow shape was selected.

10. With the line still selected, change the line width back to **2.75**, the line's original width.

If you know the exact value you want to use, you can change the width of a line by entering a specific numeric value in the small box to the left of the slider.

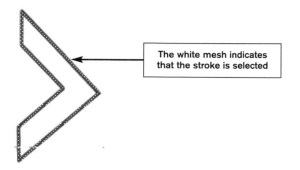

The white mesh indicates that the stroke is selected

11. Click away from the line to deselect it. Double-click on any part of the object and the entire shape will become selected. This shortcut is essential when you need to select entire shapes that are composed of multisegmented lines.

TIP | Selecting Lines in Macromedia Flash MX

Unlike other drawing programs, Macromedia Flash MX breaks lines with hard angles into separate line objects. For example, clicking on the bottom line of the arrow shape selects only the bottom portion of the shape. That's because the shape has six hard angles, which have created six separate lines for this object. Double-clicking on one of the lines will select the entire arrow shape.

12. In the **Property Inspector**, change the style, width, and color of the selected lines. You can choose any settings you like—the point here is to become more comfortable with selecting line styles and changing line preferences using the Property Inspector.

Now you know how to modify an existing line using the Property Inspector, but what do you do when your object doesn't have a line? You add one using the Ink Bottle tool. You will learn how to do this in the following steps.

13. In the **Toolbox**, click to select the **Ink Bottle** tool. The Ink Bottle lets you either add a stroke around a fill object that has no stroke or make changes to the color, width, and texture of existing lines.

Once you select the Ink Bottle tool, you can set the stroke color using the Property Inspector or the Stroke Color options in the Toolbox. Since you have used the Property Inspector quite a bit in this exercise, you will have a chance to use the Toolbox color settings next.

NOTE | Property Inspector or Toolbox?

In Macromedia Flash MX there are often several ways to access and work with the same tools. There is not one *right* way. However, you may find that using the Property Inspector will stream-line your workflow, since it gives you quick access to the attributes of the object or tool selected, all in one panel.

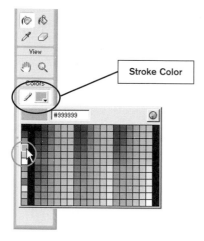

14. In the **Toolbox**, click the **Stroke Color** icon, and in the **color palette** that pops up, choose a light gray color.

15. Using the **Ink Bottle**, click on the outer edge of the snowboard shape. This adds a stroke to the outside of the shape.

NOTE | The Ink Bottle

The Ink Bottle serves several very important purposes. First, it lets you add a stroke to an object, as you just did in step 15. Second, by Shift+clicking on multiple objects, you can use it to modify the line settings for those objects all at once, rather than having to select each object and change its settings individually. This can save you a lot of time when you have several lines to add or modify.

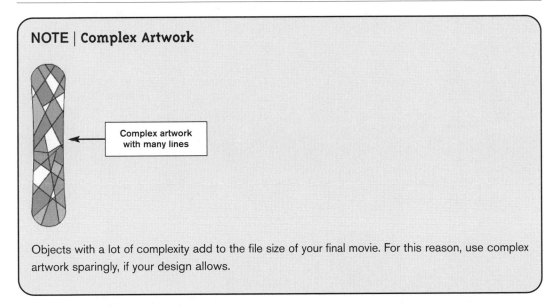

16. Using the **Arrow** tool, double-click to select the stroke around the snowboard shape. The gray selection mesh will appear to confirm that you have selected the stroke. Press the **Delete** key. This will remove the selected stroke. Now you know how to add strokes to objects and remove them in Macromedia Flash MX.

NOTE | Complex Artwork

Complex artwork
with many lines

Objects with a lot of complexity add to the file size of your final movie. For this reason, use complex artwork sparingly, if your design allows.

---

17. Save and close this file—you won't be needing it again.

3. ─────────Using the Oval and Rectangle Tools

The Pencil and Pen tools can be really useful for creating irregular shapes. Sometimes, however, those tools can become somewhat tedious or inefficient for creating simple geometric shapes, such as circles and squares. The **Oval tool** and **Rectangle tool** are good for creating simple shapes, with lines and/or fills that are independent of each other, quickly and effortlessly. In this exercise, you will learn how to use these tools.

1. Open the **shapes.fla** file located inside the **chap_03** folder. This is nothing more than a blank file that has been created for you.

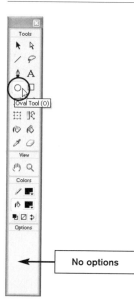

No options

2. In the **Toolbox**, select the **Oval** tool. At the bottom of the Toolbox, notice that there are no options for this tool.

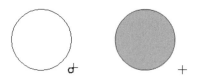

3. Press and hold down the **Shift** key. On the **Stage**, click and then drag the crosshair cursor to the lower right corner with the **Shift** key held down. As you do this, a large, thick circle will appear next to the crosshair. This indicates that you are drawing a perfect circle. Release the mouse button to draw the circle. Notice that Macromedia Flash MX uses the current fill and stroke colors to create the circle.

TIP | Easy Perfect Shapes

When you are using the Oval or Rectangle tools, holding the Shift key down while you draw the shapes will force the tool to draw only perfect circles or squares.

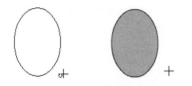

4. Draw another circle, this time in the shape of an oval, but do not use the Shift key. Notice that the small circle around the crosshair is smaller and thinner. This indicates that you are drawing an oval, not a perfect circle.

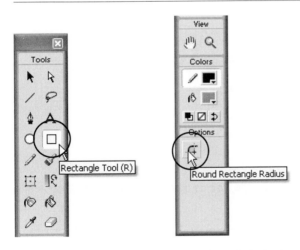

5. In the **Toolbox**, select the **Rectangle** tool. At the bottom of the Toolbox, notice that there is one option for this tool. You'll learn about this option in a bit.

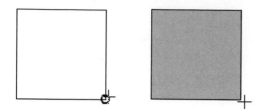

6. Hold down the **Shift** key and click and drag toward the lower right corner of the **Stage**. As you do this, a rectangle preview will appear. Notice the "perfect shape" indicator. It's the same as the one you saw on the Oval tool. In this instance, it indicates that you are drawing a perfect square. Release the mouse button to create the shape. Again, Macromedia Flash MX uses the selected fill and line colors.

7. At the bottom of the **Toolbox**, click the **Round Rectangle Radius** button. This opens the **Rectangle Settings** dialog box.

Rectangle Settings

Corner Radius: 25 points

OK
Cancel
Help

8. Enter **25** for the **Corner Radius** setting. Click **OK**. This will add rounded corners with a 25-point radius to the next rectangle you draw.

Tip: You can enter any value between 0 and 999.

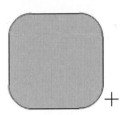

9. Using the **Rectangle** tool, draw another rectangle on the Stage. Notice that the corners of the rectangle are rounded now. Sweet.

TIP | Round Before You Draw

You can't use the Round Rectangle Radius option to round the corners of a rectangle you have already drawn. So creating rounded rectangles does require some forethought. However, you can adjust the points *as you draw* the rectangle. Pressing the Up Arrow key as you draw will decrease the corner radius points, while pressing the Down Arrow key will increase the corner radius points. This is a very cool little shortcut.

10. Save and close this file; you won't be using it anymore.

4. ——————Using the Brush Tool

The **Brush tool** is used to paint shapes. You can create shapes with solid colors, gradients, and even bitmaps as fills. The Brush tool has several painting modes that are unique to Macromedia Flash MX, such as **Paint Fills**, **Paint Selections**, **Paint Behind**, and **Paint Inside**. These modes are covered in detail in the **brushmodes.mov** movie mentioned at the end of this exercise. For now, you will learn to use the Brush tool to create and modify shapes.

1. Open the **paint.fla** file located inside the **chap_03** folder. Once again, this is just a blank file that has been saved for you.

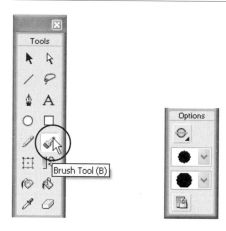

2. In the **Toolbox**, click to select the **Brush** tool. Notice that there are several options for this tool. You will learn about these options as you complete this exercise.

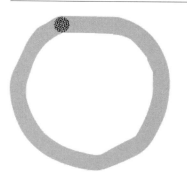

3. On the **Stage**, draw a circle with the **Brush**. Notice that it uses the fill color for this shape, rather than the stroke color. The Brush tool always uses the fill color, as the kind of shape it creates is considered a fill, not a stroke.

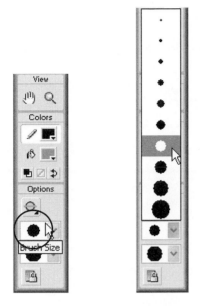

4. At the bottom of the **Toolbox**, click on the **Brush Size** pop-up menu. Select the fourth size from the bottom. This will decrease the size of the next fill that you draw.

5. Draw a smaller circle inside the large one. Notice that the smaller brush size creates a fill shape that is narrower than the first one.

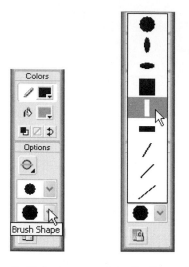

6. At the bottom of the **Toolbox**, click on the **Brush Shape** pop-up menu. Select the fifth shape from the bottom. This will change the shape of the next fill that you draw.

7. Draw another circle on the **Stage**. Notice that it uses the new shape to create the circle. You can produce some pretty cool calligraphy effects using these shapes.

TIP | Using Tablets

Macromedia Flash MX offers support for most pressure-sensitive graphics tablets. Using a tablet can help you create natural-looking shapes that have a hand-drawn look. As you increase pressure on the tablet, the width of the shape will increase, whereas less pressure will create a thinner shape.

8. Go ahead and experiment with the other brush shapes and sizes. If you have a graphics tablet, you might want to use it.

TIP | Adding Lines to Brush Shapes

Because the Brush tool creates shapes that are fills, you can use the Ink Bottle to easily add a stroke to the shapes you create with the Brush.

9. When you are done experimenting with the Brush, save and close this file—you won't need it again.

MOVIE | Brush Modes

If you want to learn about the different Brush modes in Macromedia Flash MX, be sure to check out the **brushmodes.mov** movie, located inside the **movies** folder on the **H•O•T CD-ROM**.

5. ——————Modifying Strokes and Fills

There are several ways to change the fill of a shape. You can specify the fill color before you create the shape, or you can use the **Paint Bucket** to fill uncolored areas of a shape or to change an existing fill color. The Paint Bucket can also be used to modify bitmap and gradient fills. In addition, the Color Mixer panel lets you create solid, gradient, and bitmap fills, which you can then apply to the shapes you create. In this exercise, you will learn how to use the Paint Bucket tool and the Fill color palette to modify the fill of a shape.

1. Open the **modifyFills.fla** file located inside the **chap_03** folder. This file contains a vector graphic of a snowboard.

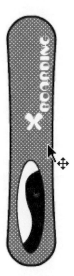

2. Using the **Arrow** tool, select the blue background of the snowboard. When an object is selected, a white dotted selection mesh will appear over it. In this case, it's the background color of the snowboard.

3. Make sure the **Property Inspector** panel is visible. If it's not, choose **Window > Properties**, or use the shortcut **Ctrl+F3** (Windows) or **Cmd+F3** (Mac) to make it visible.

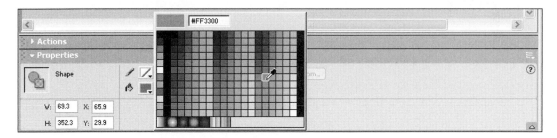

4. In the **Property Inspector**, click on the **Fill Color** box and select a shade of red you like from the Fill color palette. This changes the background color of the snowboard to red.

Notice that some areas of the snowboard are still blue, like the insides of the letters. You will fix this next.

> ### NOTE | Why Didn't Everything Turn to the Color I Selected?
>
> Macromedia Flash MX treats shapes that are one continuous color as one shape. Each time a new color appears, that is a new shape, which means it must be modified individually. In step 4 of this exercise, the middle parts of the letters were treated as separate shapes because they were surrounded by white. You will learn how to quickly fill these remaining blue shapes next.

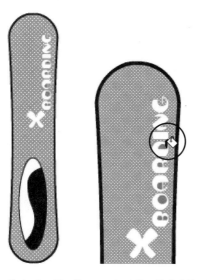

5. In the **Toolbox**, select the **Paint Bucket** tool and click on each of the blue shapes inside the letters to change the color to match the red background color you selected.

Unlike the Property Inspector method, you do not need to select the artwork before you color it with the Paint Bucket tool. If you are having trouble clicking on the small blue regions inside the type, you may want to use the zoom feature. You can use the shortcut keys to zoom in and out by pressing Ctrl+plus or Ctrl+hyphen (Windows) or Cmd+plus or Cmd+hyphen (Mac) on the keyboard.

Tip: *As a safeguard, you can always press Ctrl+Z (Windows) or Cmd+Z (Mac) to undo any mistakes you make.*

TIP | Applying Fills

Using the Fill Color box in the Property Inspector and using the Paint Bucket in the Toolbox are two ways to change the solid fill of an object. Either method will yield the same results; although using the Property Inspector can help speed up your workflow, since you can change and access many features of the selected object using only one panel. It is important to note that you must have the object selected first if you want to change the fill using Property Inspector. However, you can Shift+click to select multiple objects and change them all at once; this is a great way to make several changes quickly.

6. In the **Toolbox**, select the **Arrow** tool and click on the letter **B** on the snowboard. A black dotted mesh will appear indicating the area you have selected.

Rather than fill one letter at a time, you will fill all the letters at once next.

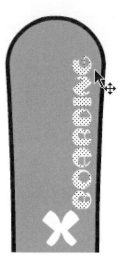

7. Shift+click on each of the remaining letters in the word **boarding** so that all the letters are selected at one time. If you make a mistake and want to start over, you can press the **Esc** key, which will clear all selections.

8. In the **Property Inspector**, choose a new color for the letters by selecting the **Fill Color** box and selecting a new color from the Fill color palette. All the letters will change to the new color you selected!

Up to this point, you have been modifying the fills on the snowboard shape. You will modify the strokes on the snowboard shape next.

9. Using the **Arrow** tool, double-click to select the entire outline of the **snowboard**.

10. Using the **Property Inspector**, choose a new **stroke color** and **stroke style** for the outline of the snowboard. Pretty quick and easy, huh?

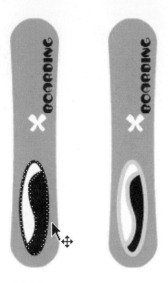

11. Using the **Arrow** tool, double-click on the outline of the yin and yang design on the snowboard to select the entire outline of the design. Back in the **Property Inspector**, choose a new **stroke color** and **stroke height** for the outline of the design. This snowboard has come a long way since you started this exercise!

12. Save and close this file—you won't need it again.

6. —————————Working with Multiple Objects

By now you should have a pretty good idea of how to draw in Macromedia Flash MX. In this exercise, I want to point out some of the nuances involved in drawing, because Macromedia Flash MX behaves differently than most other drawing programs. You will learn how it handles multiple and overlapping objects and you will learn how to protect artwork from being unintentionally modified.

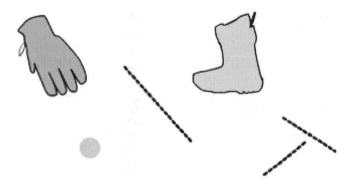

1. Open the **multiple.fla** file located inside the **chap_03** folder. This file contains some simple shapes that you will use to understand the unique drawing behaviors of Macromedia Flash MX.

2. Select the **Arrow** tool, and then move the cursor over the line of the glove. Notice that a small curved line appears at the end of the cursor. This line indicates that you will select the line (rather than the fill) if you click.

3. Double-click to select the entire line around the glove. A gray mesh will appear over the line once it has been selected. Shift+double-click on the black strap to select that also.

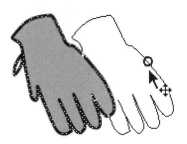

4. Click again on the line and drag to the right. This will pull the line off the glove. As I mentioned earlier, Macromedia Flash MX treats the line and fill as separate objects. Because of this, you can easily separate the two.

5. Press **Delete** to permanently remove the line.

6. Move the cursor over the long line between the glove and the boot. Again, that little curve will appear at the bottom of the cursor. Click once to select the line.

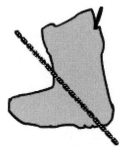

7. Click again on the line and drag it over the boot.

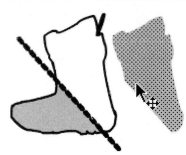

8. Click in the right section of the boot and drag to the right. Notice how the line you dragged on top of the boot has cut the fill into different objects?

Since the fill color of the boot is gray and the line is a different color (black), the line will cut the color beneath it into separate sections.

9. Click on one of the lines to the right of the boot to select it.

10. Click and drag that same line over so that it lies across the other line, then click in a blank area of the Stage to deselect the line.

11. Click to select the top right line segment.

12. Click and drag to the right. Notice that the line was split into four segments simply by having two lines intersect. While this might seem somewhat counterintuitive, it's a great way to create interesting shapes in Macromedia Flash MX.

13. Click and drag the small light blue circle into the middle of the glove.

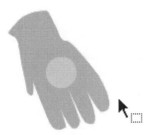

14. Click on any blank area of the Stage to deselect the circle.

15. Click and drag the small circle back to its original location. Notice that it has left a hole in the fill of the glove. **Note:** If this circle were exactly the same turquoise color as the glove, it would not have cut through the circle and made a hole. Instead, it would have combined with the glove into one shape.

16. Save your file, but leave it open; you'll need it for the next exercise.

7. Grouping Objects

Now that you have a good idea of how the drawing features behave in Macromedia Flash MX, this exercise will show you how to create shapes that overlap without cutting into or combining with one another. The following steps will also show you how to create a **grouped object**.

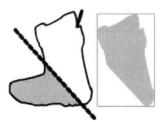

1. Using the **Arrow** tool, click to select the half of the boot you separated.

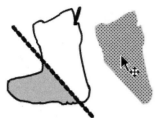

2. Choose **Modify > Group**. When you do this, a thin blue rectangle appears around the object, indicating that this is a grouped object, which protects it from intersecting with other objects on the Stage.

3. Click and drag the gray half of the boot on top of the blue glove.

4. Deselect the gray half of the boot by clicking on any blank area of the Stage.

5. Click and drag the gray half of the boot off of the blue glove. Nothing happens. Phew! As you can see, grouping objects, even single objects, is a quick way of protecting them from being affected by or affecting other objects.

6. With the gray half of the boot still selected, choose **Modify > Ungroup**. This will ungroup the selected object. You can tell that this has been done because the thin blue line goes away and the gray selection mesh returns, both telltale signs that this is a shape in its most primitive form.

7. Now drag that ungrouped gray shape onto the blue glove, deselect it, and then drag it off again. Yikes! Look ma, no fingers! Grouping objects can be a quick and easy way to protect them from unwanted editing.

8. Save and close this file—you won't be needing it again.

What Is the Color Mixer Panel?

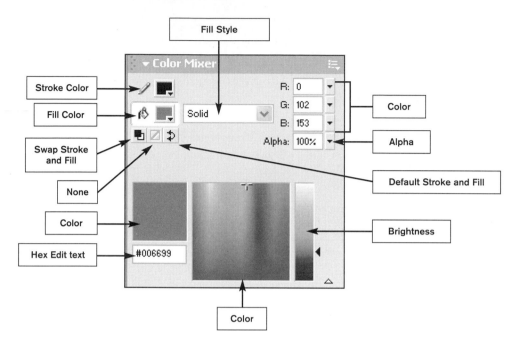

The **Color Mixer panel** gives you precise control over color, all in one panel. This panel is open by default; if you've closed it, you can access it again by choosing **Window > Color Mixer**. The following exercise will show you how to use the Color Mixer panel to create gradient fills.

8. ———————Creating Gradients

Gradients can help you create lots of cool and interesting effects, such as glows and photorealistic spheres, which you will learn more about in Chapter 5, "*Shape Tweening*." Macromedia Flash MX lets you create two types of gradient fills: **linear** and **radial**. In this exercise, you will learn how to use the Color Mixer and Color Swatches panels to create, apply, and change the color of a linear and radial gradient with some shapes in Macromedia Flash MX.

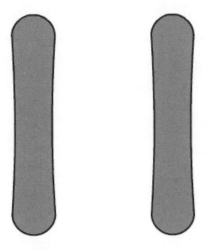

1. Open the **newGradient.fla** file in the **chap_03** folder. This file contains two snowboards. You will be applying gradients to both of these shapes in this exercise.

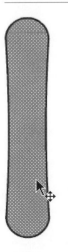

2. Using the **Arrow** tool, click the blue fill on the snowboard on the left to select it.

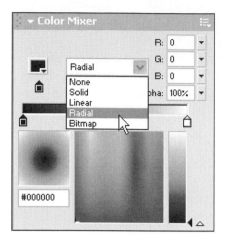

3. Make sure the **Color Mixer** panel is open; if it is not, choose **Window > Color Mixer** to open it. Click the small down arrow to see the **Fill Style** drop-down menu. This menu displays the different types of available fills. Choose **Radial**. This fills the selected shape with a radial gradient, using black and white.

Tip: A radial gradient radiates outward from the center.

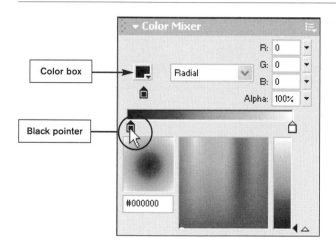

4. Click the **black pointer** in the **Color Mixer** panel. This selects the black color point of the gradient and causes the Fill Color box to display the color of the pointer. This box defines the fill color for the selected pointer.

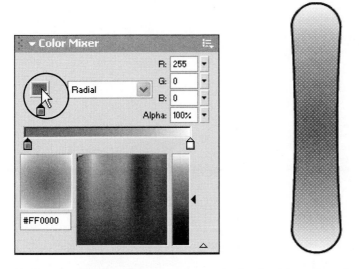

5. Click the **Fill Color** box and select a shade of **red** from the palette. This changes the appearance of the radial gradient—instead of ranging from black to white, it ranges from to red to white.

You have just created your first custom gradient! Next you will make a linear gradient, in which the colors change horizontally or vertically.

6. Using the **Arrow** tool, select the snowboard on the right side of the Stage.

7. In the **Color Mixer** panel, choose **Linear** from the **Fill Style** menu. This creates a linear gradient, using the same color you used for the previous gradient.

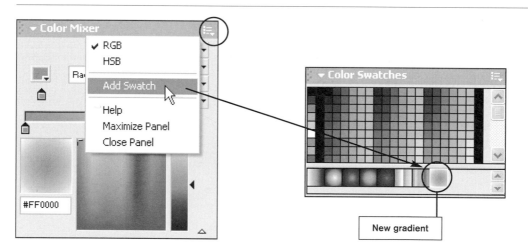

New gradient

8. Click in the top right corner of the **Color Mixer** panel to reveal the Color Mixer pop-up menu, and choose **Add Swatch**. This saves the selected gradient in the Color Swatches panel so that you can access it easily. **Note:** Your Color Swatches panel should be open by default and located under the Color Mixer panel. If it is not, choose **Window > Color Swatches** to open that panel.

9. Save and close this file—you won't need it again.

9. ———————Drawing with the Pen Tool

The **Pen tool** is found in many other vector graphics applications, including Macromedia Freehand and Adobe Illustrator. If you are familiar with how the tool works in those programs, you'll know how to use it in Macromedia Flash MX.

However, if you haven't used it before, the Pen tool can take a little getting used to and will require a good amount of practice before you become really comfortable with it. In this exercise, you will learn to use the Pen tool to draw a few basic geometric shapes. When you are finished with this exercise, you should be a bit more comfortable working with the Pen tool—not only in this program, but in other programs as well.

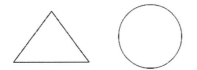

1. Open the **pen.fla** file located inside the **chap_03** folder. This file contains an outline of two separate geometric shapes.

Note: Since you will be using the Pen tool in this exercise, it will be easier to see the results if you use the default settings for this tool. If you just completed the previous exercise, set the stroke settings back to their default values (black, solid, 1 point) using the Property Inspector.

This document has two layers: one for the shape outlines, titled "patterns," and another titled "draw here," which is where you will draw these shapes using the Pen tool. The "patterns" layer is locked so you can't do any damage to the outlines. But have fun drawing on the "draw here" layer.

2. Make sure the **draw here** layer is selected in the **Timeline**. If the **patterns** layer is selected and you try to draw on that layer, you will get an error message asking you to unlock and show that layer. To select the **draw here** layer, click in the first frame, or click where it says "draw here." A pencil appears next to the name of the layer, indicating that it is selected.

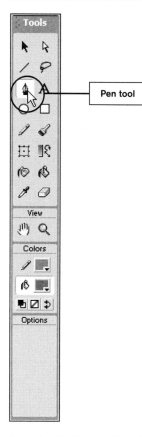

Pen tool

3. In the **Toolbox**, select the **Pen** tool.

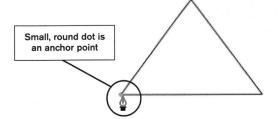

Small, round dot is an anchor point

4. Move your mouse to the bottom left corner of the triangle outline and click. A small circle appears. This is the first **anchor point**, indicating the beginning of your line. Line segments are created between pairs of anchor points to create shapes.

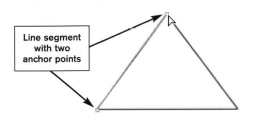

Line segment with two anchor points

5. Click the top corner of the triangle to add the second anchor point, thus creating a line segment, which appears only after you click. The line segment will appear as a red line with two square anchor points. The line segment is the color currently set as the stroke color in the Property Inspector and in the Toolbox.

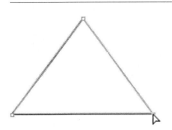

6. Click the lower right corner of the triangle. This will create a second line segment between the upper and lower right anchor points.

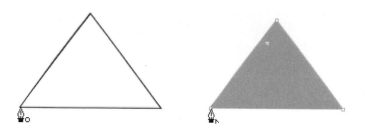

7. Move the cursor to the lower left corner. A small circle appears at the end of the cursor. This indicates that you will close the path if you click. Click to close the path and complete the shape. When you close a path, the shape automatically fills with whatever color you currently have selected for the fill color in the Property Inspector or the Toolbox.

TIP | Pen Preferences

As you learn to work with the Pen tool, there are some preferences you should be aware of that might make your life a bit easier. If you choose **Edit > Preferences**, you can access the Preferences dialog box. Click the **Editing** tab to see the Pen preferences, in the top left corner. There are three preferences you should consider here:

Show Pen Preview (off by default) lets you preview the line segments as you draw with the Pen tool. A stretchy line will appear as a preview of the line segment you will create when you click.

Show Solid Points (off by default) displays unselected anchor points as solid points and selected anchor points as hollow points when you use the **Subselection** tool.

Show Precise Cursors (off by default) causes the Pen cursor to appear as a crosshair. This can be helpful for precise drawing and works great with the grid feature.

Next you'll learn to draw a circle with the Pen tool. This is a bit more complicated than drawing a triangle and will probably take some time to master. Don't worry if you have to do this exercise a few times before you get the hang of things.

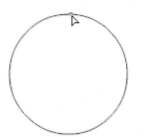

8. Using the **Pen** tool, click at the top center of the circle outline. This will place the first anchor point.

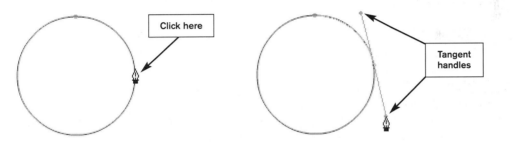

Click here

Tangent handles

9. Click on the middle right edge of the circle and **drag down** to add another control point. As you drag, you will see two **tangent handles** appear. Move the mouse around and watch how the angle of the line changes as you do this. Don't release the mouse button just yet.

10. Drag down toward the bottom right until the line segment seems to match the outline of the circle. Now release the mouse button. **Note:** The circle you draw doesn't have to be perfect here; just try to get comfortable working with the Pen tool.

11. Click on the middle bottom edge of the circle to add another control point. The line will curve automatically when you add the third control point and this will complete half of the circle shape.

12. Click and **drag up** on the middle left edge of the circle to add another control point. As you drag, you will see two tangent handles appear. Don't release the mouse just yet.

13. Drag up toward the top left until the line segment seems to match the outline of the circle. Release the mouse button.

14. Move the cursor to the top of the circle. Click on the first anchor point you created. This will complete the circle and fill it with whatever color you have selected for the fill color.

15. Save the changes you made to this file. After all that hard work, who wants to lose it? Go ahead and leave this file open for the next exercise. Don't worry if it isn't perfect because next you will learn how to modify lines using the shapes you just made.

MOVIE | morepen.mov

If you want to see the Pen tool in action and learn how to create more complicated shapes, make sure you check out the **morepen.mov** movie inside the **movies** folder on the **H•O•T CD-ROM**.

10._____Modifying Paths

Now that you know how to create shapes using the Pencil and Pen tools, it's a good time to learn how to reshape them. In this exercise, you'll use the **Subselection tool** to modify paths using their anchor points or tangent handles. The following steps will expose you to using both the Arrow tool and the Subselection tool to give you a better understanding of how each of these tools works.

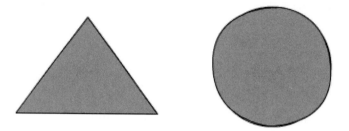

1. The file from the previous exercise should still be open. If it's not, open the **pen.fla** file.

2. In the **Toolbox**, select the **Arrow** tool.

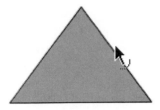

3. Move your cursor over the right side of the triangle. Notice that a small curved line appears at the end of the cursor. This line indicates that you are over a line segment.

4. Click and drag the mouse to the right. The shape will start to distort and stretch as you continue to drag the mouse. (Hey, remember Silly Putty?) Release the mouse button. Notice that both the line and the fill have changed their shape.

The Arrow tool offers a free-form way of transforming shapes, and while it can be fun, it can also lack the precision you sometimes need when creating complex shapes. When you do want pinpoint precision, you can use the Subselection tool, which lets you manipulate the anchor points and tangent handles of paths after you have added them.

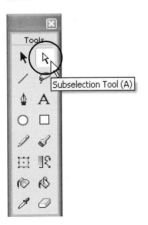

5. In the **Toolbox**, select the **Subselection** tool.

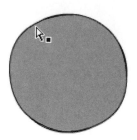

6. Move the cursor over the edge of the circle shape. A small black square will appear indicating that you are over a line.

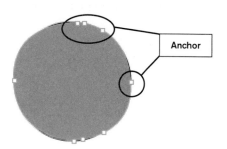

Anchor

7. Click on the edge of the circle to select it. Notice that once the shape is selected, the anchor points become visible. The anchor points are represented by small red squares along the line of the circle. **Note:** Macromedia Flash MX adds anchor points, if necessary, to create the curve. That is why you might see more than the four anchor points you added when drawing the circle.

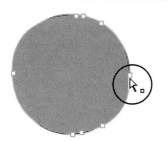

8. Using the **Subselection** tool, move the cursor over the middle right anchor point. A small white square will appear next to the cursor when you are over the anchor point.

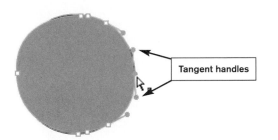

9. Click to select the middle right anchor point. When you do, the tangent handles for that anchor point and the ones above and below it appear. Why? Because all three anchor points work together to create this part of the circle's curve. **Note:** If you don't have as many anchor points as I do in this example, you may not see the three anchor points working together.

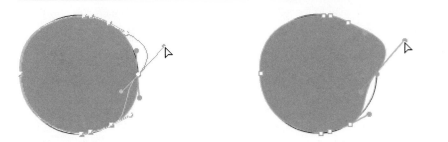

10. Click and drag the top tangent handle of the middle right anchor point over to the right. Release the mouse button. Notice that the top and bottom portions of the curve change together. This is the normal behavior of tangent handles.

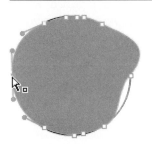

11. Click to select the middle left anchor point.

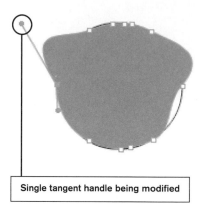

Single tangent handle being modified

12. Press and hold the **Alt** key (Windows) or **Option** key (Mac) as you click and drag the top tangent handle of the middle left anchor point over to the left. Release the mouse button. Notice that only the top portion changes. This is how you modify one part of a curve without changing the other.

13. Using the **Subselection** tool, click on the anchor point on the middle right of the circle and drag down to try to match the circle image in the background. You can click and drag an anchor point to make the circle more perfect in shape.

Now you know how to use the Arrow and Subselection tools to modify the lines you create in Macromedia Flash MX. With the Arrow tool, you can reshape straight or curved lines by dragging the lines themselves. The Subselection tool lets you reshape objects by clicking on and moving the tangent handles and anchor points in an object. Next you will learn how to add, remove, and convert anchor points. Knowing how to do this will give you more control when you are creating shapes in Macromedia Flash MX.

14. In the **Toolbox**, select the **Pen** tool. In addition to drawing shapes, the Pen tool lets you add anchor points to a line.

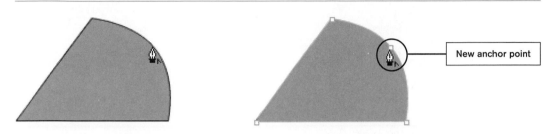

New anchor point

15. Move the cursor over the rounded side of the triangle shape. Notice that when you move over the edge, a small ^ symbol appears next to the cursor. This symbol indicates that a new anchor point will be created if you click. Click to add a new anchor point here.

Converting curves to straight lines is a rather simple process and one you should know how to do. That's exactly what you will do in the following steps.

16. With the Pen tool still selected, move the cursor over the newly added anchor point and notice that the small ^ symbol appears again. This indicates that you will convert the curve point to a corner point if you click.

17. Click the anchor point. The curve point is converted to a corner point. This transforms the curve into a straight-edged shape, and it will look less like a curve. You will no longer have access to any tangent handles for this anchor point.

Converting a corner point to a curve point is even easier to do.

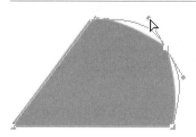

18. Using the **Subselection** tool, click on the anchor point to select it. Now **Alt+click** (Windows) or **Option+click** (Mac) and drag the anchor point you just modified up a bit. When you do this, you will convert that corner point back to an anchor point.

Note: Make sure the anchor point is still selected before you drag it. Selected anchor points are red.

Tip: You can delete anchor points in a number of different ways. One of the easiest ways is to select the anchor point with the Subselection tool and press the Delete key.

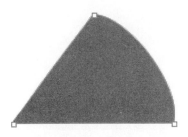

19. With the anchor point still selected, press **Delete**. This removes the anchor point.

20. Save and close this file—you won't be needing it again.

By now, you should feel pretty comfortable working with the drawing and color tools inside Macromedia Flash MX. If you aren't quite there yet, please feel free to take some time to play with the different tools and color settings. You might try drawing some artwork for a project you want to create in Macromedia Flash MX. Nothing will ever replace good old-fashioned practice. It might not make you perfect, but it can make you one heck of an efficient Macromedia Flash designer.

4.

Animation Basics

Timeline	Projects and Movies	Document Properties
Frame Types	Frame-by-Frame Animation	Onion Skinning
Free Transform Tool	Frame Rate	Inserting and Deleting Frames
Copying and Reversing Frames	Testing Movies

chap_04

Macromedia Flash MX
H•O•T CD-ROM

Macromedia Flash MX has a reputation as a powerful and robust animation tool. If you know other animation tools, such as Macromedia Director or Adobe After Effects, you might find yourself looking for similarities. It might surprise you that it's actually easier to learn the animation capabilities of Macromedia Flash MX if you don't know other animation programs, because you have no preconceived notions of how you think it might work. If you've never used an animation tool before, you have an advantage over more experienced animators for this reason! This chapter introduces you to the Timeline, which plays a significant role in producing animation. This is the part of the interface where you will work with keyframes, blank keyframes, frame-by-frame animation, and Onion Skinning. If these are new terms to you, they won't be for long! This chapter also covers setting the frame rate and how the frame rate affects playback speeds. By the end of this chapter, things should really get moving for you, all puns intended!

The Timeline

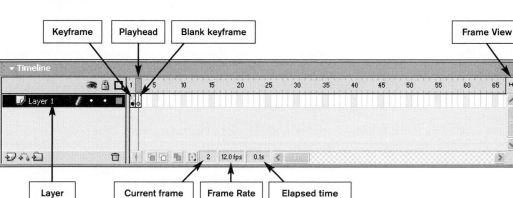

Understanding and working with the **Timeline** is essential to creating animation in Macromedia Flash MX. The illustration above identifies the elements of the Timeline that you will be working with in this chapter. In Chapter 5, "*Shape Tweening*," you will learn all about the options in the Layers section of the Timeline. The following chart gives a detailed description of the features identified above.

Timeline Features	
Feature	**Description**
Layers	Layers are a way of organizing the elements of your animation from front to back on the Stage, so that one object can move in front of or behind another or can make transitions that are independent of other objects. The Layer controls for your movie appear on the left side of the Timeline. Each layer has options for hiding or showing the layer, locking it, and displaying its contents as outlines. You will learn more about layers in Chapter 5, "*Shape Tweening.*"
Current frame	Displays the current position of the Playhead and the frame number of the frame that is currently visible.
Frame Rate	Displays the number of frames per second (or fps) at which the movie attempts to play on your end user's browser or computer. Double-clicking here is a quick way to access the Document Properties dialog box.
Elapsed time	Displays time elapsed from Frame 1 to the current Playhead location at the currently selected frame rate.
	continues on next page

Timeline Features *continued*	
Feature	**Description**
Frame View	This pop-up menu gives you several different options for specifying how the Timeline is displayed. Use it if you want to see fewer or more frames on the Timeline. The default view is usually just fine until you start creating a longer animation. At that point, it's great to be able to see more frames as you work.
Blank keyframe	Blank keyframes are empty locations on the Timeline that are ready to have content placed into them. They can also be used to break up or make changes in your animation.
Keyframe	Keyframes define the moment in the Timeline when actions or animation changes occur. Keyframe content display remains unchanged until another keyframe or a blank keyframe occurs in the Timeline.
Playhead	The Playhead—a red rectangle with a long red line—indicates the current frame that you are viewing in the Timeline. You can click and drag (scrub) the Playhead back and forth in the Timeline to quickly preview your animation.

Projects and Movies

In Macromedia Flash MX, the term "movie" can be used to refer to three separate files—the authoring project file (with the extension .fla), the Macromedia Flash MX content file that is published for the Internet (with the extension .swf), and the content published as a stand-alone file (projector). All of these different types of movies can become rather confusing when you are learning Macromedia Flash MX. To help avoid this confusion, I will be using the terms **project** to identify the .fla file, **movie** to identify the .swf file, and **projector** to identify the projector files. A more comprehensive explanation of these different file types is available in Chapter 1, "*Background Information.*" Here's a handy chart that illustrates the differences between these different types of files:

File Types		
Icon	**File Type**	**Description**
Untitled.fla	**Project**	This file always has an extension of .fla and is the master authoring file used to create Macromedia Flash content.
Untitled.swf	**Movie**	This file always has an extension of .swf and is the only file you will upload to be viewed on the Internet. It is a compiled version of the project file.
Untitled.exe Untitled Projector	**Windows Projector** **Macintosh Projector**	Macromedia Flash MX can produce stand-alone projector files for the Windows and Macintosh operating systems. Windows projector files have an extension of .exe. Macintosh projector files have the word "Projector" appended to the end of the file name.

I. —————————Document Properties

The **Document Properties** are general specifications that affect your entire project. The first thing you should do when you start a new project in Macromedia Flash MX is to set these properties, which include things such as Stage dimensions, frame rate, and background color. This exercise will show you how to set them.

1. Copy the **chap_04** folder, located on the **H•O•T CD-ROM**, to your hard drive. You need to have this folder on your hard drive in order to save files inside it.

2. Create a new file and save it as **movie.fla** in the **chap_04** folder.

3. The **Property Inspector** should be visible near the bottom of the document window. If it is not visible, choose **Window > Properties** to open it.

By default, the Stage dimensions will be 550 × 400 pixels, the movie will have a white background, and the frame rate will be 12 frames per second. You'll learn how to change each of these settings in the steps that follow.

4. In the **Property Inspector**, set the **Frame Rate** to **22**. This sets the frame rate of your movie to 22 frames per second (fps). In other words, for every 22 frames in your animation, 1 second of time will elapse. You will learn more about the frame rate later in this chapter.

5. In the **Property Inspector**, click the **Background Color** box. This will display the default color palette. Select a **light blue** color. This will change the background color of your movie to light blue.

6. With the Property Inspector still open, click on the **Size** button. This will open the **Document Properties** dialog box, which contains all the frame rate preferences, movie dimensions, background color, and rule measurements that you can set for your entire movie.

7. In the **Document Properties** dialog box, for the **Dimensions** settings, enter a **width** of **700** and a **height** of **350**. These options control the absolute pixel dimensions of your Stage. You will learn other ways to control the size of your movie when you get to Chapter 16, "*Publishing*."

8. Click the **Ruler Units** arrow to see the drop-down menu. This menu contains several different methods for displaying the ruler units on your Stage. Make sure you leave this option set to the default of **Pixels**.

9. Click **OK**. Notice that the values in the **Property Inspector**—the dimensions, background color, and frame rate—are changed to your new specifications.

You can quickly use the Property Inspector at any point to change the movie's background color or frame rate. In addition, you can use the Size button in the Property Inspector to access the Document Properties dialog box, where you can change the options not available in the Property Inspector. However, you should avoid changing the dimensions of your movie once you have added content to your Stage. The reason for this is that changing the dimensions once you've started creating artwork and animation causes the position of all your hard work to be offset, which can be difficult to fix.

10. When you are finished, save the changes you made to this file. However, don't close it just yet; you will need it for the next exercise.

TIP | Saving New Default Settings

Document Properties

Dimensions: `700 px` (width) x `350 px` (height)

Match: [Printer] [Contents] [Default]

Background Color:

Frame Rate: `22` fps

Ruler Units: `Pixels`

[Help] (Make Default) [OK] [Cancel]

When you create a new movie, by default you will get a Stage that is 550 × 400 pixels with a white background. This size might not be all that convenient when you are working on projects that should have different settings. But there's good news—you can redefine the default settings so they better fit your needs. Simply change the Document Properties to match the settings you need and click the **Make Default** button. Next time you create a new movie, it will already have all the properties you want. Pretty cool!

What Is a Keyframe?

The term **keyframe** has been used in animation since the early 1900s. It signifies a change in motion, and in Macromedia Flash MX, keyframes are displayed on the Timeline. The Timeline represents the passing of time, with each slot representing an individual frame. If you have artwork in Frame 1 and you don't change it until Frame 20, the image in Frame 1 will persist until Frame 20. You would need to add a new keyframe in Frame 20 in order to make a change to the artwork. If you have artwork in Frame 1 and you want to change it in Frame 2, you would need to add a new keyframe in Frame 2; therefore, you would end up with two keyframes, one in Frame 1 and the other in Frame 2.

This concept might seem abstract to you if you've never worked with keyframes before, but you will have lots of opportunities to work with keyframes in this chapter, so they won't be alien to you for long.

Keyframes in Macromedia Flash MX

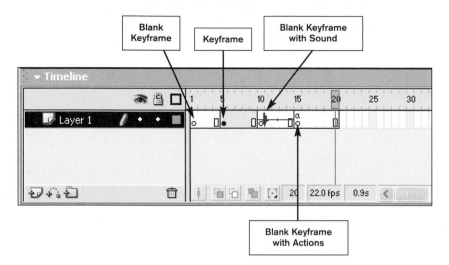

Keyframes are located in the Timeline. A keyframe that contains content displays a solid circle in the Timeline, and a blank keyframe that contains no content on the Stage is represented by a hollow circle in the Timeline. Subsequent frames that you add to the same layer will have the same content as the keyframe.

To complicate things a little more, Macromedia Flash MX has different kinds of frames and keyframes. The following chart describes the different types and gives the keyboard shortcut for each in parentheses.

Frame Types	
Term	**Definition**
Blank keyframe (F7)	A blank or empty keyframe is represented by a hollow circle. It means that there is no artwork on the Stage on that frame. The Timeline, by default, opens with a blank keyframe. As soon as you put content on the Stage, the blank keyframe changes to a keyframe. From that point on, this artwork will be copied to all frames until you define another keyframe or blank keyframe and change the content on the Stage at that frame. To confuse matters a little more, although a blank keyframe contains no artwork, it can contain sound and actions. You will learn more about sound in Chapter 13, "*Sound*," and more about actions in Chapter 11, "*ActionScripting Basics*."
	continues on next page

Frame Types *continued*	
Term	**Definition**
Keyframe (F6)	A keyframe that contains content (meaning that artwork is on the Stage at that frame in the Timeline) is represented by a solid circle. By default, when you add a keyframe in Macromedia Flash MX, the content (except for actions and sounds) is copied from the previous keyframe. To make a change, you must alter the artwork on the Stage at the point on the Timeline where you have defined the new keyframe. Otherwise, Macromedia Flash MX will simply copy the content from the previous change. In other words, simply adding a keyframe will not cause the artwork to change.
Frame (F5)	The Timeline in Macromedia Flash MX looks as though it has lots of frames in each layer, which can be a bit deceiving! While it has slots for frames, you have to specifically define them as frames (or keyframes, etc.). You can do this by clicking in any of the slots and pressing F5 or by choosing Insert > Frame. It's possible to have a different number of frames on different layers. For example, Layer 1 could have 10 frames while Layer 2 has one frame. It is up to you to set the frames for each layer.
Clear Keyframe (Shift+F6)	To clear the content from a keyframe, you use the Clear Keyframe command. You do this when you want to erase the keyframe from the Timeline. Clearing a keyframe removes the content from the keyframe but leaves the frame. This will not reduce the number of frames on a layer but will simply remove the keyframe and change it to a regular frame. This command is usually used to fix (or clear) a mistake.
Remove Frames (Shift+F5)	If you ever want to delete frames that you have set, select those frames and press Shift+F5 or choose Insert > Remove Frames.

2. ————————Frame-by-Frame Animation with Keyframes

This exercise will teach you how to work with keyframes. A common animation technique is to make a word appear as though it is being written before your eyes. This is very simple to do using keyframes, because when you insert a keyframe, the program searches backward in the Timeline until it finds another keyframe and then copies that content to the newly inserted keyframe. You will learn how to make a word appear in the following steps.

1. Open the **movieFinal.fla** file from the **chap_04** folder. This file has been created for you so that you can see the finished version of the exercise.

> **WARNING | Windows Users**
>
> If you don't see a file named **movieFinal.fla** but you do see a file named **movieFinal**, your file extension display may be turned off on your computer. To learn how to make the file extension visible, see the *Introduction*.

2. Press **Enter/Return** on the keyboard to preview the animation on the Stage. You will notice the word "Xboarding" being written right on the screen as it animates. You will be creating this same frame-by-frame animation next.

3. Close the **movieFinal.fla** file.

4. You should still have the **movie.fla** file open from the last exercise, but in case you accidentally closed it, go ahead and open the **movie.fla** file you saved inside the **chap_04** folder in the last exercise.

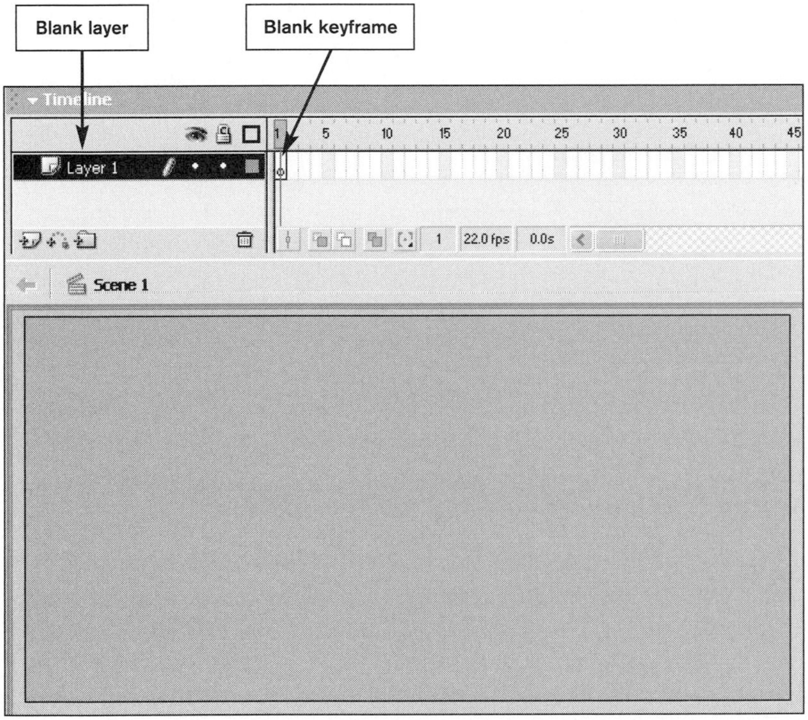

Blank layer

Blank keyframe

Notice that this document has a single layer containing a single blank keyframe. This is the way all new documents appear by default. Every project has to have a starting point, and this is the minimum you need to start drawing. The blank keyframe has a hollow circle and a line around the frame.

5. Select the **Brush** tool from the **Toolbox**. You can use any size, shape, and color (other than white— you will see why in step 11) you want. You are going to be writing the word "Xboarding," one letter at a time, in a series of keyframes.

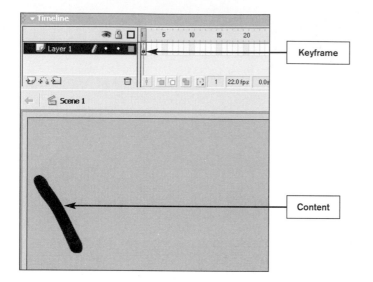

6. Using the **Brush** tool, draw the first part of the capital letter **X** on the left side of the Stage, as shown in the picture above. Notice that the blank keyframe in Frame 1 now contains a small black dot, which signifies that it contains content. Frame 1 is now referred to as a keyframe because it is no longer empty.

To make a change on the Timeline, you must have a keyframe where you want the change to occur. Now that you have filled in the first keyframe of Layer 1, you are going to add another keyframe after it so you can draw the second frame of your animation. Adding a new keyframe after the last one will copy all the content from the last keyframe to this new keyframe. You will draw another stroke in this new keyframe in order to create a change in your animation.

7. Select **Frame 2** and choose **Insert > Keyframe** or press **F6** (the shortcut key). This adds a new keyframe to the Timeline in Frame 2, copying all the artwork in Frame 1 and allowing you to continue drawing.

Tip: F6 is a keyboard shortcut you should learn right away, because you will be using it often to insert keyframes.

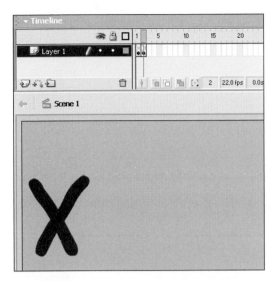

8. Using the **Brush** tool again, draw the second part of a capital **X** in the new keyframe, just like the picture above.

9. Press **F6**. This adds a new keyframe to the Timeline in Frame 3, copying all the artwork from the previous keyframe, Frame 2.

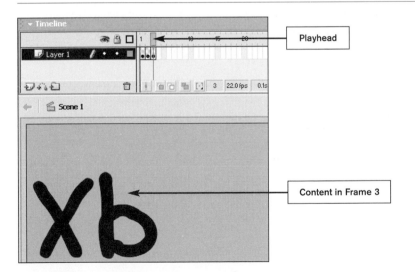

Playhead

Content in Frame 3

10. Now draw a **b** just like the picture above. Believe it or not, you have already created the beginning of your animation! You can click and drag (**scrub**) the **Playhead** back and forth in the **Timeline** to quickly preview the animation. You will see the "X" and the "b" being drawn directly on the Stage.

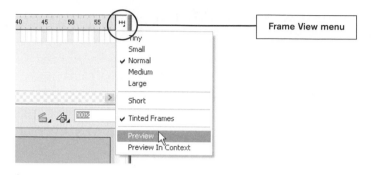

Frame View menu

Looking at a Timeline with a bunch of black dots might seem somewhat abstract to you. The Frame View menu has several options that allow you to display the contents of your individual frames right in the Timeline.

Timeline in Preview mode

11. From the **Frame View** drop-down menu, select **Preview**. This will change your Timeline so that you see a preview of what is on each frame instead of a bunch of black dots. I find this view of the Timeline very helpful when creating frame-by-frame animations.

Note: If you had chosen white for the Brush color, you would not see the artwork in Preview mode since the Timeline frames are white also.

12. Press **F6** to insert another keyframe so you can continue to draw the pieces to spell out the word "Xboarding."

13. Using the **Brush** tool, draw an **o** on the **Stage**. You should be able to see the contents of your fourth frame appear in the Timeline preview.

As you continue to spell out the word "Xboarding," you don't have to draw the whole letter in each keyframe. Instead, you can draw a part of the letter (just as you did with the "X") in one keyframe, press F6 to insert the next keyframe, and draw the remaining parts of the letter in that keyframe for a more realistic drawing animation.

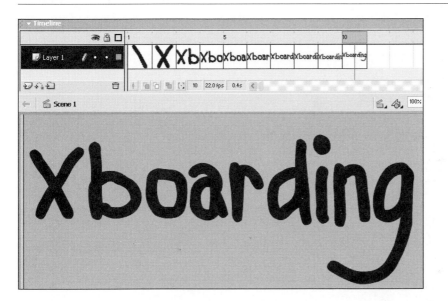

14. Go ahead and continue to spell out the word "Xboarding" by pressing **F6** to add a new keyframe after the previous one and then adding more letters or parts of the letters in each one, using the **Brush** tool. When you are done, your Timeline should look like the one shown above.

You can get a quick preview of your animation right away using one of two methods. You can scrub the Playhead across the Timeline as mentioned in step 10, or you can press Enter/Return and watch the animation play directly on the Stage. So get out the popcorn and watch your first animation!

15. Press **Enter/Return**. Your animation will play once on the Stage and stop at the last keyframe. Unlike scrubbing the Playhead, this time you are seeing an accurate preview of the frame rate for this movie, which you set in the previous exercise: 22 fps. (Frame rate is covered in more detail later in this chapter.) Press **Enter/Return** to preview the animation again as many times as you like.

There are other ways to preview your animations that will be covered later. For now, this exercise is focused on the basics.

16. Save and close this file.

3. ————————Onion Skinning

In the last exercise, you learned to work with keyframes and to add content to each new keyframe you inserted in the Timeline. This exercise will teach you a few new techniques. First, you'll learn to use the **Onion Skinning** feature. This feature allows you to see a ghost image of the previous frame so you can see where you want to place the artwork on each frame in relation to the frames before it. Next you will learn to use the new **Free Transform tool** to modify the artwork. This exercise will also teach you how to use a feature called **Loop Playback**, so you can preview your animation over and over until you get sick of it. Just kidding!

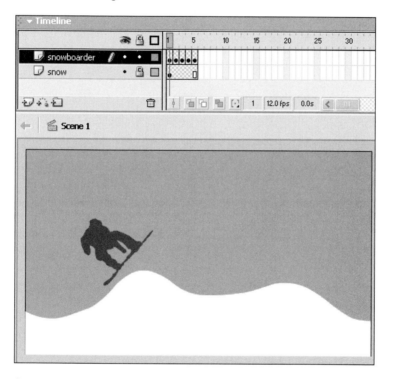

1. Open **onionFinal.fla** file from the **chap_04** folder. This file has been created for you so that you can see the finished version of the exercise.

2. Before you preview the animation, choose **Control > Loop Playback**. This will allow you to see the animation repeat over and over when you preview it.

3. Press **Enter/Return** on the keyboard to preview the animation on the Stage. You will see the snowboarder catching some air! In the following steps, you will be creating this same animation technique. To stop the looping, choose **Control > Loop Playback** again.

4. Close the **onionFinal.fla** file.

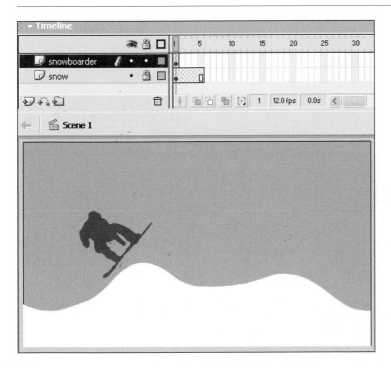

5. Open the **onion.fla** file from the **chap_04** folder. This file contains one keyframe with the snowboarder beginning his jump on the top layer and one keyframe with the snow on another layer. The layer named **snow** has been locked so that you don't accidentally select something on that layer. You will be altering only the artwork on the **snowboarder** layer in the next few steps.

6. Select **Frame 2** and press **F6** to add a keyframe to the frame. Notice that Frame 2 is now a keyframe because it contains a small black dot, which signifies that it contains content.

If you press F6 without first selecting the frame where you want to add a keyframe, nothing happens. Why? When you have more than one layer in your document, you have to select the frame first in order for Macromedia Flash MX to know where you want to place the keyframe.

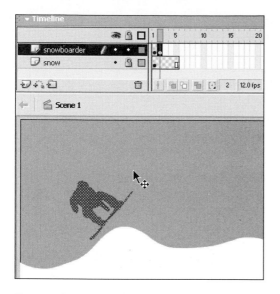

7. In **Frame 2**, click on the snowboarder artwork to select it, and move it up and to the right, as though he is advancing in his jump.

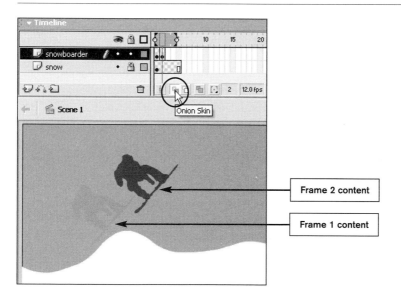

8. At the bottom of the **Timeline** is a row of five buttons. Click the second button from the left. This is the **Onion Skin** button. You will be able to see a faint ghost image of the content in Frame 1 on the Stage. This convenient feature allows you to see the artwork in the previous keyframes and change the artwork relative to the ghost images.

NOTE | Onion Skin Markers

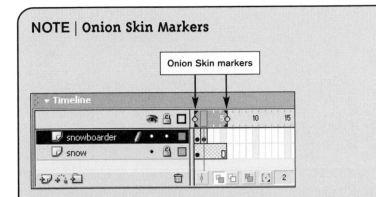

After you click the Onion Skin button, a gray bar with a draggable bracket on each end appears at the top of the Timeline. These are called **Onion Skin markers**. The **Start Onion Skin** marker (the one on the left) is on Frame 1 (the start of your animation), and the **End Onion Skin** marker (the one on the right) is on Frame 5 (the last frame of your animation). If you click and drag your Playhead to the right or left and let go, the Start Onion Skin marker will move. Basically, Onion Skinning will move along with your Playhead. You can always drag one of the Onion Skin markers to include more frames if it is spanning fewer keyframes than you have in the Timeline.

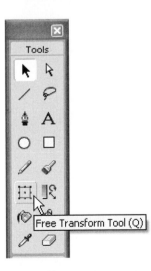

9. With **Onion Skinning** turned on, select the new **Free Transform** tool in the **Toolbox**. This tool allows you to modify your artwork by changing the size, rotation, skew, and distortion of the selected artwork. The chart at the end of this exercise illustrates the functions of the Free Transform tool.

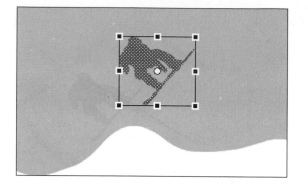

10. With the **Free Transform** tool selected, click on the snowboarder in Frame 2 to select the shape, if it is not already selected. Notice the bounding box that appears around the artwork. This box indicates that you can transform the artwork.

If you move the cursor over different parts of the selected artwork, the cursor will change to indicate what transformation function is available.

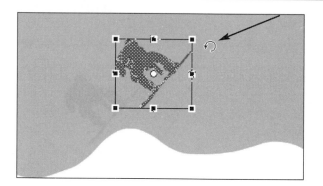

11. Move your cursor just outside the upper right corner of the bounding box until it changes to a round arrow, as shown in the picture above. This icon indicates that you can rotate the artwork. Click and drag to the right to rotate the snowboarder a bit and make the jump look more realistic.

12. Select **Frame 3** and press **F6** to insert another keyframe so you can create the third frame of your animation.

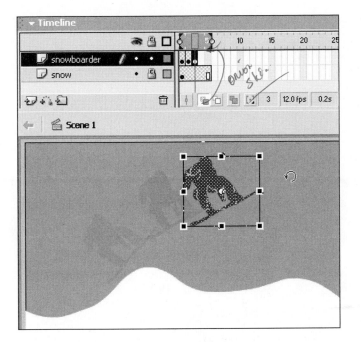

13. With Onion Skinning still turned on, select the snowboarder artwork in **Frame 3** and move it to the right. Select the **Free Transform** tool and rotate the snowboarder again, just as you did in step 11.

14. Finish off the snowboarder jump by repeating steps 12 and 13 twice more, adding two more keyframes to Frames 4 and 5 and modifying the artwork in each keyframe.

15. Choose **Control > Loop Playback** so that you can see the animation repeat over and over.

16. Press **Enter/Return** to test the movie. You will see the snowboarder catching some air!

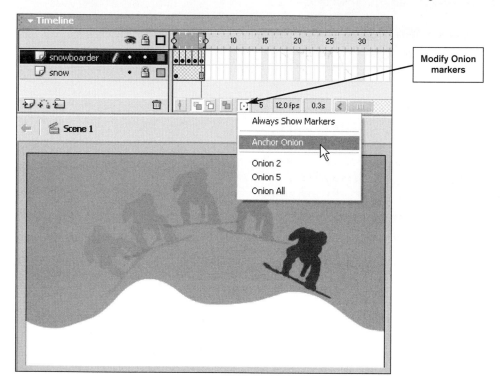

If you do not want the Onion Skin markers to move when you move the Playhead or click on a frame in the Timeline, you can choose Anchor Onion from the menu that appears when you click the Modify Onion Markers button at the bottom of the Timeline. This will lock the Onion Skinning span where it is until you unlock it again or manually drag the Start or End Onion Skin markers.

17. You will have the chance to work with the other features of the Free Transform tool in Chapter 6, "*Symbols and Instances.*" For now, save and close this file.

NOTE | The Free Transform Tool

You can use the Free Transform tool to modify objects in several ways. As you move the cursor over the bounding box around a selected object, it will change to indicate what type of transformation is available to you. As you drag, you will see a preview of the transformation you are about to make. The chart below lists the features of the Free Transform tool.

Free Transform Tool Functions	
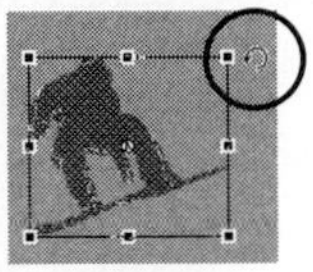	Clicking and dragging up or down on a corner transform handle will rotate the object. The cursor icon will change to a round arrow, as shown in the image at left. This arrow indicates that you can rotate the object.
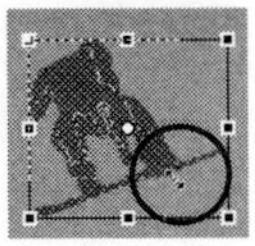	Clicking and dragging diagonally on one of the corner transform handles will modify the scale of the object. The cursor icon will change to a diagonal double-pointed arrow when you can perform this transformation.
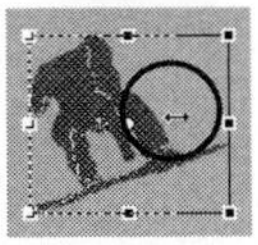	Clicking and dragging on one of the middle side transform handles will modify the width or height of the object. The cursor icon will change to a horizontal (or vertical depending on which side you are on) double-pointed arrow when you can perform this transformation.
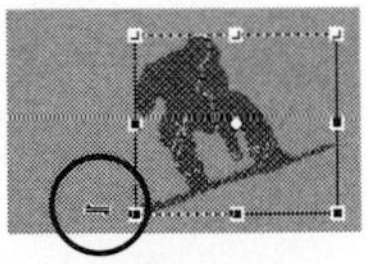	Clicking and dragging between any two transform handles will skew the object. The cursor icon will change as shown at left. This icon indicates that you can skew the object.
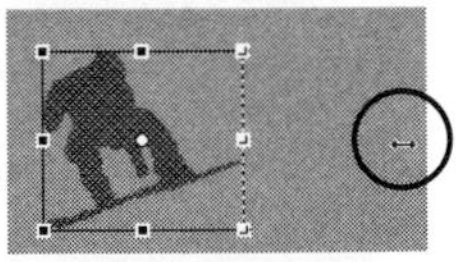	Clicking and dragging one of the middle side transform handles to the other side of the object will flip the object. The cursor will change to a horizontal or vertical double-pointed arrow depending on which side you are on.
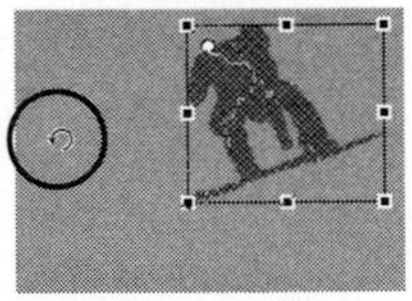	Clicking and dragging the center registration point will modify the center point of the object. After you alter the center point, all transformations will rotate or move in relation to the new center point location.

4. ——————————Understanding Frame Rate

Now that you have created a couple of frame-by-frame animations, it's time to investigate the Frame Rate setting of your movie. The **frame rate** defines how many frames your animation will try to play in one second. I use the word "try" because there is no guarantee that your movie will play back at the specified frame rate, due to the varying processor speeds of the computers that your end users might use. In the following steps, you will start by opening a file that contains a simple frame-by-frame animation of a snowboarder moving down a mountain. You will test the animation to preview the current frame rate and then lower the frame rate to see the impact it has on playback speed.

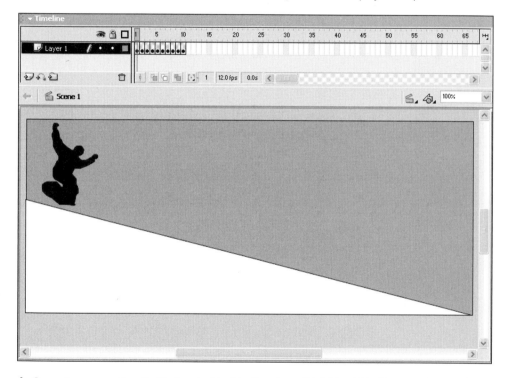

1. Open the **properties.fla** file located inside the **chap_04** folder. This file contains one layer with a frame-by-frame animation of a snowboarder cruising down a mountain.

2. Press **Enter/Return** to watch the animation play on the Stage. The animation will play at the default frame rate of 12 fps.

3. Make sure the **Property Inspector** panel is open. If it is not, choose **Window > Properties** or press **Ctrl+F3** (Windows) or **Cmd+F3** (Mac) to open it.

4. In the **Frame Rate** field, enter **6**. This will lower the frame rate to 6 frames per second, reducing the speed of the animation by half.

5. Press **Enter/Return**. Notice that the animation plays much more slowly and kind of stutters. You are taking twice the time to play the same number of frames. The lower the frame rate, the slower the animation will play.

6. Save and close this file; you won't need it for the next exercise.

What Is the Frame Rate?

The frame rate determines the number of frame your movie plays per second. This rate corresponds directly to the length of time your animation takes to play.

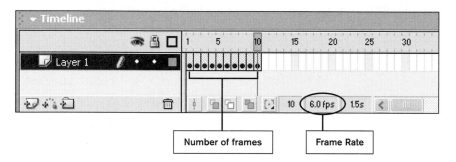

Number of frames · Frame Rate

Here's how to use the frame rate to calculate the playback time of your animation. Take the total number of frames in your Timeline and divide that by the frame rate; the result is the number of seconds it will take to view your movie.

For example, if your Timeline has 10 frames and your frame rate is set to 6 FPS (frames per second), your animation will display in 1.67 seconds. The chart below gives several examples of how the frame rate affects the length of time an animation takes to play.

Number of Frames	/	Frame Rate	=	Time
24 frames	/	12 fps	=	2 seconds
36 frames	/	12 fps	=	3 seconds
48 frames	/	24 fps	=	2 seconds
72 frames	/	24 fps	=	3 seconds

It is important to note that the frame rate affects all of the animations in your movie. In the next exercise you will learn how to make animations play at different speeds in the same Timeline.

Recommended Frame Rates

When you set a frame rate in Macromedia Flash MX, you've set the *maximum* frame rate for your movie, or how quickly the movie "tries" to play. The actual playback frame rate depends upon several factors, including download speed and the processor speed of the computer viewing the movie. If the frame rate is set higher than the computer can display, the movie will play as fast as its processor will allow. So if you set your frame rate to 200 (which is really high), the average computer will not display the movie at that rate. Here's another wrinkle: Frames that have more objects, colors, or transparency than others take more time for the computer to render. Thus, the actual frame rate can vary during playback due to the rendering requirements from one frame to another.

Based on all this information, I would recommend that you use a frame rate of at least 12 fps and not more than 25 fps, so that the average computer can display your movie as you intended. A frame rate of 20 to 22 fps seems to work well most of the time. This rate is very similar to that used in motion pictures, which typically play at a frame rate of 24 frames per second.

5. ——————Inserting and Deleting Frames

As you learn to create frame-by-frame animation and other types of animation, you will at some point want to adjust their speed. In the previous exercise, you learned that adjusting the frame rate will do just that, but it affects the entire movie. That might not be what you want to do, so in this exercise, you will learn how adding and removing frames in your Timeline can help control the timing of your animation. This means that you can have multiple animations playing at different tempos, even though they all share the same frame rate.

1. Open the **frames.fla** file from the **chap_04** folder. This file contains a simple frame-by-frame animation with some text. You'll be learning more about how to use text in Chapter 12, "*Working with Text.*"

2. Press **Enter/Return** to preview the animation on the Stage. The animation will play pretty quickly. In fact, it's playing so fast that you almost lose the effect of the text appearing one letter at a time.

If you adjust the frame rate to slow down this animation, it will also affect every other animation in this project. This could cause some serious problems if you wanted other sections of your movie to play at a different speed. So you must find another way to slow down the animation. One way to do this is by inserting frames at strategic points to lengthen parts of the animation. That's exactly what the following steps will show you how to do.

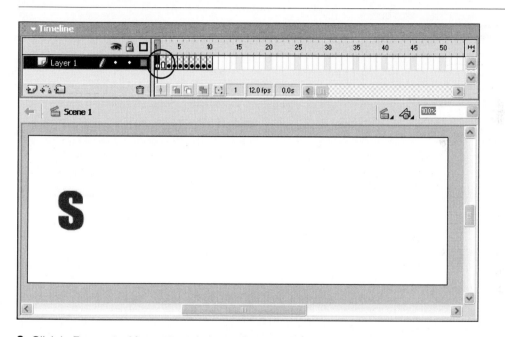

3. Click in **Frame 1** of **Layer 1**, and choose **Insert > Frame** or use the shortcut key **F5**. This will insert a frame between Frames 1 and 2, extending the Timeline by one frame.

4. Press **F5** to insert another frame. Each time you choose **Insert > Frame** or press **F5**, you will insert one frame and extend the Timeline.

TIP | What Do Those Dots Mean?

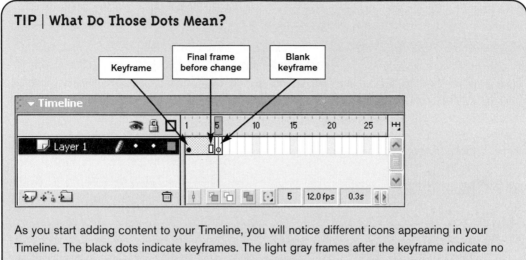

As you start adding content to your Timeline, you will notice different icons appearing in your Timeline. The black dots indicate keyframes. The light gray frames after the keyframe indicate no change in content. The small white square inside a light gray frame indicates the ending point of a frame range, which also means that the next frame will be a blank keyframe or a keyframe. The white frame with a hollow circle, directly after the frame with a hollow square, is a blank keyframe.

5. Press **F5** again so that you have a total of three additional frames between your first two keyframes. By extending the space between the first two keyframes in the Timeline, you are able to control the timing of the animation, as your image will display for a longer period of time.

6. Press **Enter/Return** to preview the animation on the Stage. Now there is a noticeable delay between the letters "s" and "n."

7. Click in **Frame 5** of the **Timeline**. This is where the second keyframe should be located.

8. Press **F5** three times to insert three frames in the Timeline. This will create a short pause between the letters "n" and "o."

9. Repeat this process for the other letters in the animation. When you are finished, your Timeline should look like the one shown above.

---

10. Press **Enter/Return** to preview your animation on the Stage. See how much slower the entire animation plays—and you didn't have to touch the frame rate for the movie. Nice.

Great—you now know that you can control the timing of individual animations without having to adjust the frame rate of your entire movie. You have just seen that by inserting frames you can slow down an animation, so it should be no surprise that you can increase the timing of the animation by deleting frames. You will learn how to do this next.

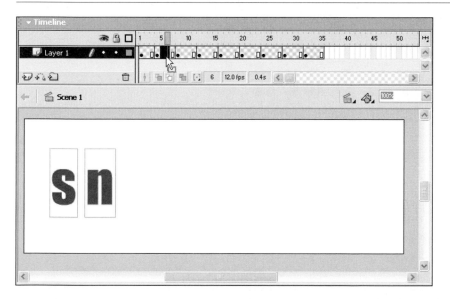

11. Click on **Frame 2** of the Timeline and choose **Insert > Remove Frames**. This will remove the selected frame, shortening your Timeline by one frame and decreasing the amount of time between the "s" and "n" letters in your animation.

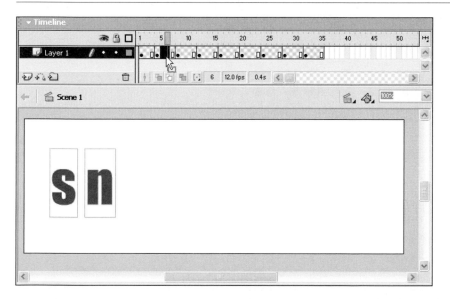

12. Ctrl+click and drag (Windows) or **Cmd+click and drag** (Mac) and select **Frames 5** and **6**. This lets you select a specific range of frames. Make sure you hold the appropriate key down as you click and drag; otherwise you might accidentally move keyframes around.

13. With Frames 5 and 6 still selected, choose **Insert > Remove Frames**. This will remove the selected frames and shorten your Timeline by two frames.

14. Go ahead and use **Shift+F5** (the keyboard shortcut for removing frames) to remove the frames between each of the keyframes in the Timeline (including the ones between Frames 1 and 4) so that there is only one frame between every two keyframes. When you're finished, your Timeline should look like the one shown above.

15. Press **Enter/Return** to preview your animation on the Stage. The animation will play much faster than it did before, because there are fewer frames between the keyframes. Now you know at least two ways to speed up or slow down the timing of your animation.

16. Save and close this file.

6. ———————Copying and Reversing Frames

Creating a looping animation (one that repeats indefinitely) can be a lot of work if you have to draw all the frames over and over. In Macromedia Flash MX, you can quickly and easily copy, paste, and reverse a sequence of frames to create a looping animation. You will learn to do this in this exercise.

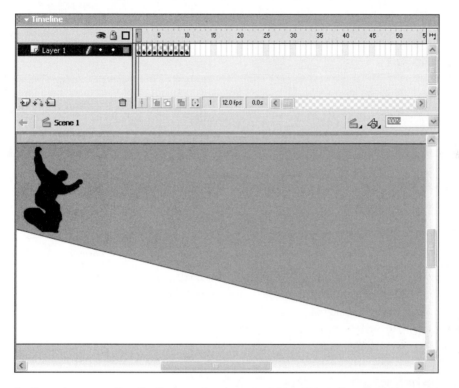

1. Open the **properties.fla** file from the **chap_04** folder. This is the same file you worked on earlier.

2. Using the **Property Inspector**, make sure the **Frame Rate** is set back to **12**.

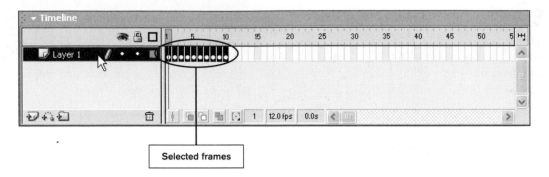

Selected frames

3. Click to the right of the layer name. This is an easy way to select all of the frames on a layer. Before you can copy a range of frames, you want to make sure you have selected them first.

4. Move your cursor over the selected frames. Click and drag to the right. But don't release the mouse button just yet! **Note:** The light gray outline surrounding the frames indicates where they'll be moved when you release the mouse button.

5. While still holding the mouse button down, press the **Alt** (Windows) or **Option** (Mac) key. Notice that a small plus sign appears to the right of the cursor. This indicates that you will duplicate, not move, the frames when you release the mouse button.

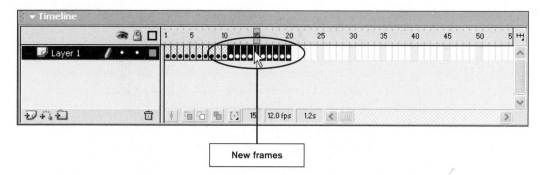

New frames

6. Release the mouse button. This will place a copy of the selected frames in Frames 11 through 20.

7. With **Frames 11** through **20** still selected, choose **Modify > Frames > Reverse**. You won't see any noticeable reversal in your Timeline, but you will when you test the movie.

8. Press **Enter/Return** to preview your animation on the Stage. The snowboarder will race down the hill and then go backward up the hill, as if you were rewinding the film to view an instant replay! Neat! If you choose **Control > Loop Playback**, you can watch the animation preview loop endlessly.

9. Save and close this file.

7.————————————**Testing Movies**

So far, you've been testing your movies by pressing Enter/Return and watching them play on the Stage. This is a great way to test the frame rate, but there are other ways to test your work. In this exercise, you will learn how to preview the movie file (.swf) with the **Test Movie** feature and how to preview your movie in a browser with the **Preview in Browser** feature. You will also learn a really easy way to produce the HTML file needed to hold your .swf file. More in-depth instruction on publishing Macromedia Flash MX content is provided in Chapter 16, "*Publishing and Exporting*."

1. Open the **frames.fla** file from the **chap_04** folder.

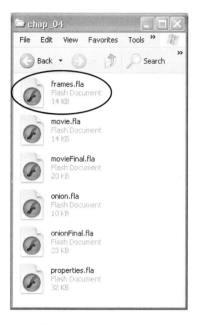

This file should have been saved inside the chap_04 folder. It is important to know where your project file (.fla) has been saved before you use the Test Movie and Preview in Browser features, because as you'll see, Macromedia Flash MX automatically generates new files and saves them with your project files when you use these features. If you saved your file in a different location, make sure you know where it is.

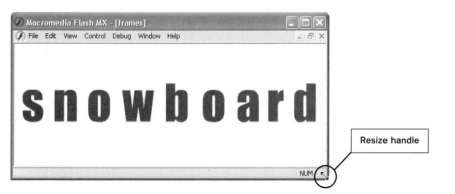

Resize handle

2. Choose **Control > Test Movie**. This will open a new window with a preview of the movie file(.swf) that would be exported if you chose to publish your movie right now.

Tip: You can click on the resize handle of the Preview window and drag to make your window larger. Although the size of the window will change, the snowboard letters will stay the same size. You will learn how to make the content scalable, also using the publish settings, in Chapter 16.

TIP | Loop-de-loop

At this point, you're probably wondering why your animation is looping (playing over and over). This is the default behavior of all movies in Macromedia Flash MX, although you don't see it when you simply press Enter/Return to preview your work (unless you've set the file to Loop Playback). If you uploaded your published file to the Web, however, it would loop. You will learn to control the looping in your final movie (.swf) file in Chapter 11, *"ActionScripting Basics,"* when you learn how to add actions to frames. If all this looping is making you dizzy, you can select **Control > Loop** to deselect this feature and turn it off temporarily.

3. With the .swf file still open, choose **Window > Toolbars > Controller** (Windows) or **Window > Controller** (Mac). You'll see a small toolbar on your screen that looks like the front of your VCR or other media player. This handy little gadget helps you control the playing of your animation.

Stop button

4. Click the **Stop** button. As you probably guessed, this stops your animation.

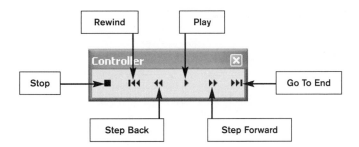

5. Click the **Play** button. Yes, you guessed it; this plays your animation. Go ahead and take a few minutes to try the other buttons on the Controller.

Something else happened, behind the scenes, when you chose Control > Test Movie. Macromedia Flash MX automatically created the .swf file for this movie and saved it in the same location as your project (.fla) file. You'll locate this file next.

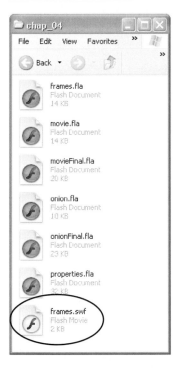

6. Open the **chap_04** folder from your desktop. Notice that there is a **frames.swf** file inside this folder. This file was automatically generated by Macromedia Flash MX. Also notice that the .swf file has a different icon than the .fla files. This can be helpful visual feedback, especially if your file extensions are turned off. The .swf file is the file that you would add to an HTML page, much as you would a .gif or .jpg file.

7. Return to Macromedia Flash MX and close the Preview window.

8. Choose **File > Publish Preview > Default – (HTML)** or use the **shortcut keys Ctrl+F12** (Windows) or **Cmd+F12** (Mac). This will launch your default browser with a preview of your movie file (.swf) inside the browser window. This command provides a quick and easy way to see what your movie files will look like in a browser. You will learn a more appropriate and formal way of publishing your Macromedia Flash movies later in Chapter 16, "*Publishing and Exporting.*"

Again, something extra is happening behind the scenes. When you preview your movie in a browser, Macromedia Flash MX will automatically create an HTML file, as well as the .swf file if there isn't one already, in the same location as the project file (.fla). So make sure you always know where you're saving your project files.

NOTE | How Does Macromedia Flash MX Know Which Browser to Use?

If you have several browsers installed on your system, you can specify which one Macromedia Flash MX uses as the default browser. You can change the default browser to your preferred browser in a few steps. There's a great explanation of how to do this for either a Windows machine or a Macintosh on Macromedia's Web site: **http://www.macromedia.com/support/ flash/ts/documents/browser_pref.htm**.

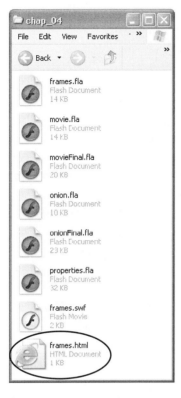

9. Hide Macromedia Flash MX for a moment and look inside the **chap_04** folder on your desktop. Notice that there is a **frames.html** file inside this folder. Macromedia Flash MX generated this file automatically to hold your **frames.swf** file.

At this point, all the files necessary to publish to the Web have been generated automatically. More thorough instructions and details are provided in Chapter 16, "Publishing and Exporting." This exercise simply demonstrated a quick and easy way to generate files.

---

10. Return to Macromedia Flash MX and save the changes you made to this file. You can close this file—you are finished with this chapter! It was a long but essential part of your animation training.

Well, that's about it for the basic stuff. The next three chapters deal with more complex and specific issues, such as symbols and instances, motion tweening, and shape tweening. Now would be a great time for a break—you've worked through a lot of material, and you deserve one!

5.

Shape Tweening

| What Is Shape Tweening? |
Shape Tweening Text	Shape Hinting
Multiple Shape Tweening	Layer Folders
Layer Properties	Animating Gradients

chap_05

Macromedia Flash MX
H•O•T CD-ROM

Most of you have seen animations on the Web or on television that show an object transforming (or morphing) from one shape into another. You can create this same effect in your Macromedia Flash MX movies through a technique called shape tweening.

The exercises in this chapter offer a thorough introduction to shape tweening. By working through them, you will expand your Macromedia Flash MX skill set to include shape tweening, hinting, animating gradients, and multiple shape tweening.

What Is Shape Tweening?

Shape tweening works like this. If you wanted to create an animation that showed a square transforming into a circle, you could create the starting point of the animation—the square—and the ending point—the circle—by placing them on separate keyframes, leaving empty frames between them. You could then set up a shape tween and have Macromedia Flash MX automatically generate the art for the empty frames between the two images.

Before I describe shape tweening in more detail, I first need to define a few terms—**shape**, **keyframes**, and **tweening**. Here's a handy chart to refer to if these terms are new to you:

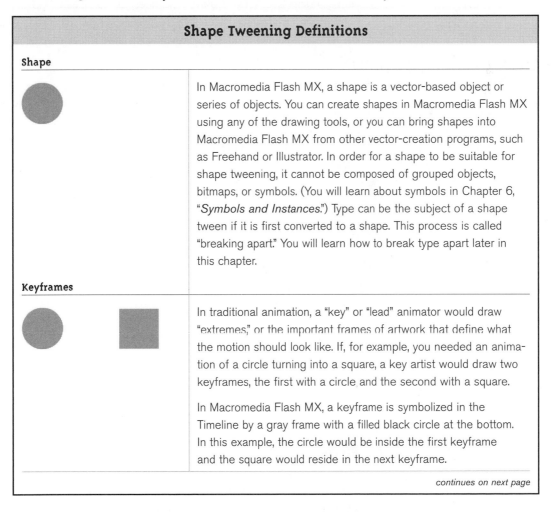

Shape Tweening Definitions	
Shape	
	In Macromedia Flash MX, a shape is a vector-based object or series of objects. You can create shapes in Macromedia Flash MX using any of the drawing tools, or you can bring shapes into Macromedia Flash MX from other vector-creation programs, such as Freehand or Illustrator. In order for a shape to be suitable for shape tweening, it cannot be composed of grouped objects, bitmaps, or symbols. (You will learn about symbols in Chapter 6, "*Symbols and Instances*.") Type can be the subject of a shape tween if it is first converted to a shape. This process is called "breaking apart." You will learn how to break type apart later in this chapter.
Keyframes	
	In traditional animation, a "key" or "lead" animator would draw "extremes," or the important frames of artwork that define what the motion should look like. If, for example, you needed an animation of a circle turning into a square, a key artist would draw two keyframes, the first with a circle and the second with a square.
	In Macromedia Flash MX, a keyframe is symbolized in the Timeline by a gray frame with a filled black circle at the bottom. In this example, the circle would be inside the first keyframe and the square would reside in the next keyframe.

continues on next page

Shape Tweening Definitions *continued*	
Tweening	
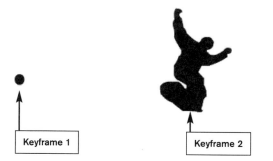	The term "tweening" is borrowed from traditional cel animation terminology, and is slang for "in-betweening." In cel animation, a person called an "in-betweener" would take the keyframes that a lead animator creates and draw all the frames that go between them that describe the motion. For example, the in-betweener would take the two keyframes just described and would use them to draw a series of images of the shapes in various stages of morphing from one object, the circle, into the other object, the square.

Macromedia Flash MX lets you use shape tweening to animate between lines and shapes and to animate the colors and gradients that are applied to them. This process is often referred to as **morphing**. The illustrations that follow are a good example of a shape tween:

Keyframe 1	Keyframe 2

The first step in creating a shape tween is to create two unique keyframes.

The next step is to apply a shape tween to the frames with a few clicks of the mouse. Macromedia Flash MX will then interpolate the difference between the keyframes and automatically generate all of the frames in between.

Shape tweening is the only process in Macromedia Flash MX that lets you quickly animate from one distinct shape to another. It can also be used to animate from one gradient to another, from one color to another, and/or from one position to another. As you might imagine, creating this kind of animation by drawing each frame of the artwork would be rather tedious. The shape tweening feature in Macromedia Flash MX automates this process.

The lists that follow outline some of the things that you can and can't do with shape tweens in Macromedia Flash MX.

What Shape Tweening Can Do

• Tween the shape of an object

• Tween the color of an object (including a color with transparency)

• Tween the position of an object on the Stage

• Tween the transformation (scale, rotation, skew) of an object

• Tween text that has been broken apart

• Tween gradients

What Shape Tweening Can't Do

• Tween grouped objects

• Tween symbols

• Tween text that has not been broken apart

I. Shape Tweening Text

In the steps that follow, you will create an animation of a snowboard changing into the letter "X." This will introduce you to the basics of shape tweening.

1. Copy the **chap_05** folder, located on the **H•O•T CD-ROM**, to your hard drive. You will need to have this folder on your hard drive in order to save changes to the files inside it.

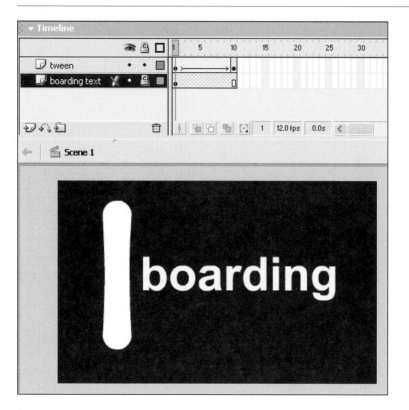

2. Open the **textTweenFinal.fla** file from the **chap_05** folder. This is a finished version of the animation you will create in the following steps.

3. Press **Enter/Return** on the keyboard to preview the shape tweening animation. You will see the snowboard artwork turn into the letter "X." You will create this shape tween next.

4. Close the **textTweenFinal.fla** file.

5. Open the **textTween.fla** file from the **chap_05** folder. This file contains two layers: one named **boarding text** with the word "boarding" on it and one named **tween** with the snowboard shape on it. You will be working on the layer named **tween**.

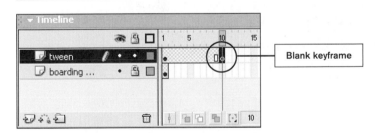

6. On the **tween** layer, press **F7** on **Frame 10**. This adds a blank keyframe to Frame 10. You are adding a blank keyframe rather than a keyframe because you want to add new artwork on Frame 10, not copy the artwork from Frame 1.

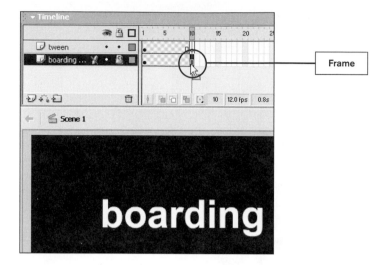

Frame

7. Notice that after the first frame, the word "boarding" disappears. This happens because the **boarding** layer has only one frame, while the **tween** layer now has 10 frames. In order for the word "boarding" to appear throughout the entire animation, the **boarding** layer must also contain 10 frames. Click on **Frame 10** and press **F5** on Frame 10 in the **boarding** layer to add frames up to Frame 10 on that layer.

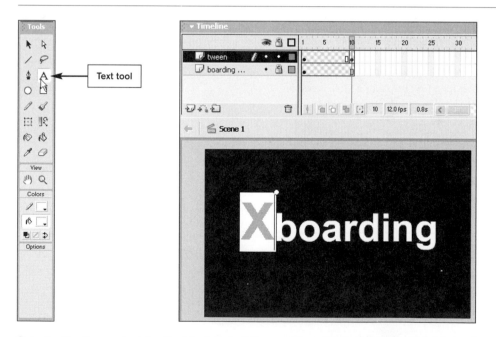

Text tool

8. In the **Toolbox**, select the **Text** tool. Select **Frame 10** on the **tween** layer, click on the **Stage**, and type the capital letter **X** in **Frame 10** just before the letter "b" in the word "boarding," as shown above.

Note: *I used the Arial font, size 78, white, and bold to type the "X," but you can use whatever font and size you like. You will learn more about the text options in Macromedia Flash MX in Chapter 12, "Working with Text."*

9. Using the **Arrow** tool, click to select the large **X** on the **Stage**. Drag the **X** to position it before the letter "b," with a little space between the "X" and the "b," as shown above.

When you type text using the Text tool, the "X" is still in an editable format, which means you can double-click on it at any time and change the letter to something else. If you deselect the text and use the Arrow tool to select it again, you will see a blue bounding box and no selection mesh, indicating that it is not a shape.

To use text in a shape tween, you have to make it a shape by breaking it apart. The act of breaking text apart converts it from editable text into an editable shape. You must do this because editable type cannot be the source of a shape tween. It's one of the rules of shape tweening–you can't use grouped objects or symbols either. While you might not think of type as a grouped object, by Macromedia Flash MX's definition it must be broken apart to become a shape. You will learn more about working with text tools in Chapter 12.

Broken-apart text with selection mesh

10. With the **X** still selected, choose **Modify > Break Apart**. The text is broken apart and converted into a shape, ready to be shape tweened. The selection mesh over the "X" indicates that you are now working with a shape. This will be the last keyframe of your animation.

11. Click anywhere between the two keyframes to select a frame in the middle of that range of frames.

12. Make sure the **Property Inspector** is open. If it is not, choose **Window > Properties**.

13. In the Property Inspector, click to see the **Tween** drop-down menu and select **Shape** to apply a shape tween between the two keyframes.

Once you have applied a shape tween between two keyframes, the Timeline will be shaded green and a long arrow will appear between the keyframes. This is a visual indication that a shape tween is active.

14. Press **Enter/Return** to test your tween. You will see the snowboard turning into the letter "X".

15. When you are finished testing, save this file and keep it open for the next exercise.

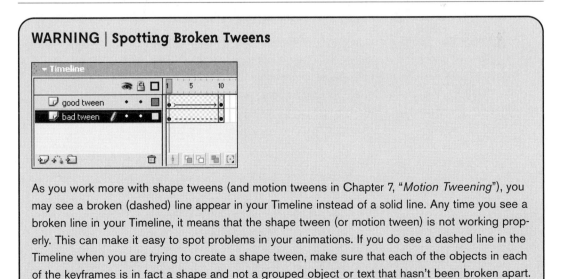

WARNING | Spotting Broken Tweens

As you work more with shape tweens (and motion tweens in Chapter 7, "*Motion Tweening*"), you may see a broken (dashed) line appear in your Timeline instead of a solid line. Any time you see a broken line in your Timeline, it means that the shape tween (or motion tween) is not working properly. This can make it easy to spot problems in your animations. If you do see a dashed line in the Timeline when you are trying to create a shape tween, make sure that each of the objects in each of the keyframes is in fact a shape and not a grouped object or text that hasn't been broken apart. You'll learn more about the causes of broken shape tweens when you learn about symbols in future chapters.

2. ————————Shape Hinting

When working with shape tweening, Macromedia Flash MX will automatically determine how to change from one shape to the next. Because this is an automatic process, you don't have complete control over how the tween occurs. **Shape hinting** is a feature that helps you regain some control over a tween. It is used primarily to fix a shape tween that does something you don't want it to do. In this exercise, you will take the shape tween that you created in the previous exercise and add shape hints to better control how the snowboard morphs into the "X".

1. You should still have the file from the previous exercise (**textTween.fla**) open. If you don't, go ahead and open it now.

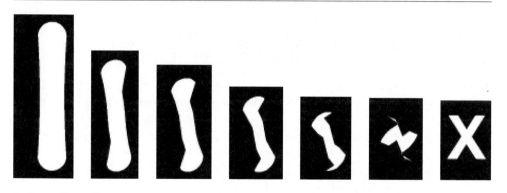

2. Press **Enter/Return** to preview this shape tween.

Notice that, as the shape tween progresses, the snowboard appears to crumple up like a piece of paper and then all of a sudden pop into the letter "X." That is how Macromedia Flash MX decided to create this shape tween. What if you want the tween to appear more fluid? You'll learn how to do this using shape hinting in the steps that follow.

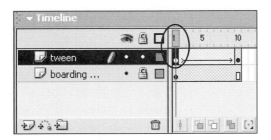

3. Make sure the **Playhead** is over **Frame 1**. When you add shape hints, you must start on the first frame of your animation.

4. Choose **Modify** > **Shape** > **Add Shape Hint**.

5. A red circle with an "a" in it will appear in the middle of the snowboard. This is a shape hint. Click and drag the **shape hint** to the upper left corner of the snowboard shape. **Note:** You must use the **Arrow** tool from the **Toolbox** to do this.

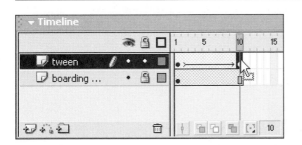

6. Move the **Playhead** to the last frame (**Frame 10**) of your animation.

7. Click and drag the **shape hint** (the small "a") to the upper left inside corner of the **X**, as shown above. This will make sure that the upper left corner of the snowboard ends up as the upper left corner of the letter "X."

When you let go of your mouse, notice that the shape hint changes from red to green. Why? This is how you know that the shape hint has been accepted. When your shape hint doesn't turn green on the ending keyframe, it means that it was not placed in the same (or in a similar) location as the first shape hint. The Macromedia documentation states that shape hints are yellow in the starting keyframe, green in the ending keyframe, and red when they are not on a curve. However, this is not always the case, as shown in this exercise, where the "X" shape has no curves but the hints still turn green. In order for shape hints to work properly, your best bet is to place them in similar locations on each keyframe and to pay more attention to how the tween animates than to the color of the hints. If necessary, try repositioning your shape hint for a better tween effect. Sometimes it takes just a small adjustment for Macromedia Flash MX to get the hint (pun intended)!

8. Press **Enter/Return** to preview the effect of changing the shape tween by using a shape hint. Notice that the shape tween looks better. You will make the transition even smoother by adding more shape hints next.

9. In the **Timeline**, click on **Frame 1** to make sure the Playhead is over the first frame. Choose **Modify > Shape > Add Shape Hint** to add another shape hint.

10. The second shape hint will appear as a small "b" in the middle of the snowboard. Click and drag the second **shape hint** to the upper right corner of the snowboard shape, as in the picture above.

TIP | Multiple Shape Hints

After you add a second shape hint, it appears as a red circle with the letter "b" rather than an "a" in the middle of it. The next shape hint after that will be "c", and so on. I think you see the pattern here. When you get to "z", that's it! You're all out of shape hints. You're given a total of 26 shape hints per shape tween. But don't worry; 26 shape hints should be far too many for most animations. If you find yourself needing more than 26 shape hints, you might want to rethink the complexity of your animation, as by then it is probably going to put a lot of strain on the end user's computer processor.

11. Move the **Playhead** to the last frame (**Frame 10**) of your animation. Click and drag the second **shape hint** ("b") to the upper right outside corner of the **X**, as shown above.

12. Press **Enter/Return** to preview the effect of changing the shape tween by adding another shape hint. Notice that the shape tween transition is getting better.

13. In the **Timeline**, click on **Frame 1** to select the first frame. Repeat steps 9, 10, and 11 two more times to add two more shape hints, moving them to the remaining corners of the "X." When you are finished, Frame 1 and Frame 10 should look like the pictures above.

14. Press **Enter/Return** to test the shape tween with four shape hints.

Try experimenting by moving the shape hints around. Moving them even slightly can give a completely different look to your shape tween. Now that you know how to add shape hints, you should learn how to remove them as well. The following steps show you how to remove a shape hint.

15. Click and drag the **Playhead** back to **Frame 1**.

16. Right-click (Windows) or **Ctrl+click** (Mac) on the **shape hint** with a "d" on it. Choose **Remove Hint** from the pop-up menu. This will remove the selected shape hint and returns the animation back to the point of using just three shape hints.

17. Press **Enter/Return** to test the shape tween animation again. Go ahead and experiment removing another shape hint and notice how it affects the animation.

18. When you are finished, save and close this file—you won't need it to complete the next exercise.

TIP | Quickly Removing Shape Hints

If you add too many shape hints and really mess up your animation, don't worry. You can remove them all with just a few clicks. Right-click (Windows) or Ctrl+click (Mac) on any shape hint and select **Remove All Hints** from the pop-up menu. You can also select **Modify > Shape > Remove All Shape Hints**. Either option will remove every shape hint from your animation. Thank goodness for this feature!

3. ———————Multiple Shape Tweening

So far, you have learned how to create single shape tweens. There will likely come a time, however, when you will want to create more than one shape tween in your project. In this exercise, you will learn how to create **multiple shape tweens** by placing them on separate layers using the **Distribute to Layers** feature (new to Macromedia Flash MX). Working with multiple layers is the only way to choreograph animations with multiple tweens. This exercise will also introduce the **Layer Folder** feature (also new to Macromedia Flash MX), which is a wonderful way to organize and consolidate animations that contain many different layers.

1. Open the **mutplShpTwnFinal.fla** file from the **chap_05** folder. This file contains a finished version of the shape tween animation you are about to create.

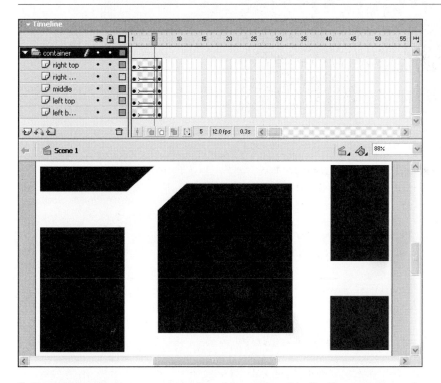

2. Press **Enter/Return** on your keyboard to preview this file. If you can't see the entire Stage, choose **View > Magnification > Show All** so that you can see the whole multiple shape tween animation. Notice the Folder icon in the Layers section of the Timeline, with all the layers in it. This designates a Layer Folder, which you'll learn about near the end of this exercise. When you are finished previewing, close the file. You will learn to create this same animation in the steps that follow.

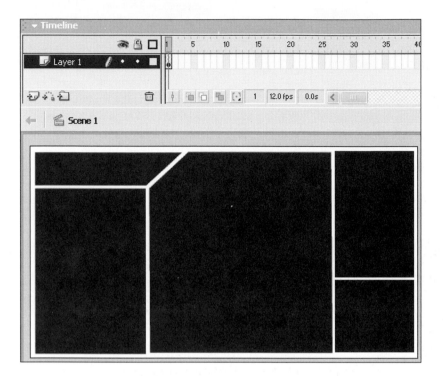

3. Open the file named **mutplShpTwn.fla** located inside the **chap_05** folder. Currently, this file has one layer with six different shapes on it.

Up to this point in the chapter, you have been creating shape tweens in which one shape turns into another on one layer. While it is possible to tween one shape into many shapes using only one layer, some effects require you to place your shapes on separate layers. The following steps show a good example of when it's necessary to put your shapes on separate layers.

4. Click on **Frame 1** to select all the shapes on Frame 1, and choose **Modify > Distribute to Layers**.

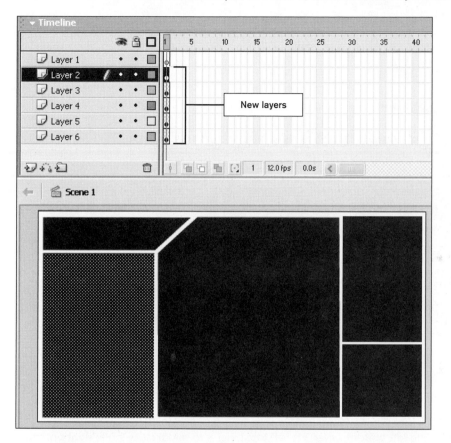

The Distribute to Layers feature will take each selected shape and place it on its own layer. You can click on any of the shapes on the Stage, and you will see the corresponding layer become highlighted in the Timeline, as shown above.

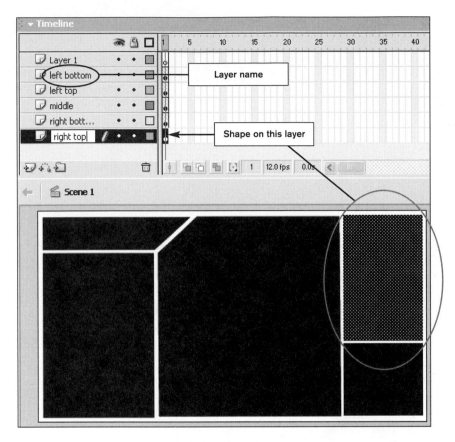

5. Starting with **Layer 2**, double-click on each of the layer names to give them new, more descriptive names. Change Layer 2 to **left bottom**, Layer 3 to **left top**, Layer 4 to **middle**, Layer 5 to **right bottom**, and Layer 6 to **right top**, just as you see in the picture above. Make sure that the name you give to each layer matches the shape's location on the Stage. This makes it easier to know what shapes are on each of the layers.

TIP | Revealing More of the Timeline

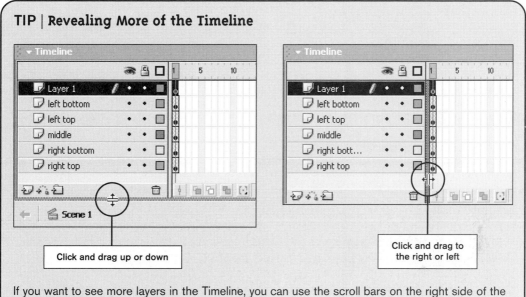

Click and drag up or down

Click and drag to the right or left

If you want to see more layers in the Timeline, you can use the scroll bars on the right side of the Timeline, or you can click and drag to reveal more layers or even to see more of the layer names, as shown above.

6. Starting with **Frame 6** on the layer named **left bottom**, click and drag down to select **Frame 6** on all the layers below the **left bottom** layer, as shown above.

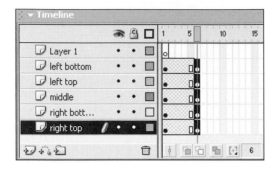

7. Press **F6** to add a keyframe on **Frame 6** of each layer you selected. Inserting a keyframe will copy the artwork from Frame 1 of each layer in the Timeline. This will serve as the ending keyframe of your shape tween animation.

8. Move the **Playhead** back to **Frame 1**. In the following steps, you will be altering the size of each shape in Frame 1, to serve as the beginning point of the shape tween animation.

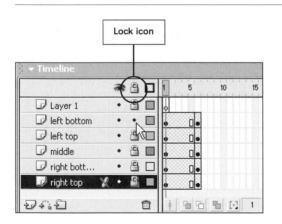

9. In the Timeline, click the **Lock** icon, next to the small Eye icon, to lock all the layers at once. Click the **Lock** icon for the **left bottom** layer to unlock just that layer. This makes it much easier to work on just the shapes on the **left bottom** layer without affecting any of the other shapes.

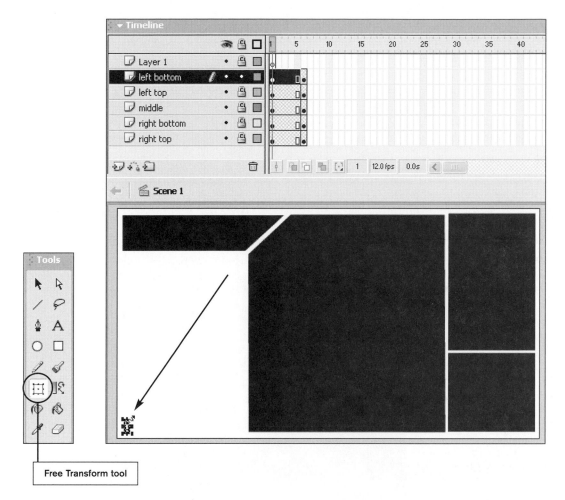

Free Transform tool

10. Click on **Frame 1** on the **left bottom** layer to select it. In the **Toolbox**, select the **Free Transform** tool, and then click and drag the upper right resize handle toward the lower left portion of the Stage. This will scale the shape down to create the starting point of the animation for the **left bottom** layer.

11. Click on the **dot** in the **Lock** column on the **left bottom** layer to lock that layer. Then click on the **Lock** icon for the **left top** layer to unlock that layer. You will be altering the size of the shape on this layer next.

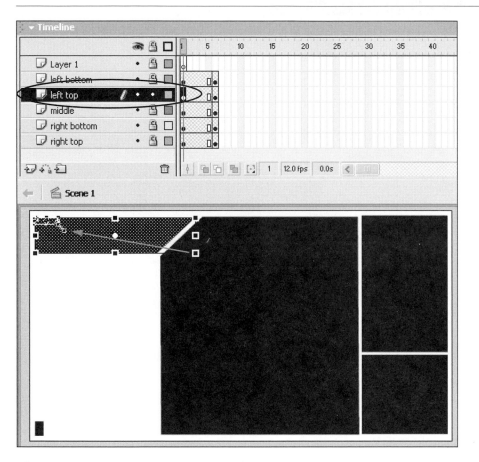

12. Click on **Frame 1** on the **left top** layer to select it. In the **Toolbox**, select the **Free Transform** tool, and then click and drag the lower right resize handle toward the upper left of the Stage, just as you see in the picture above. This will scale the shape down to create the starting point for the animation in the **left top** layer.

13. Repeat steps 11 and 12 for the **middle**, **right top**, and **right bottom** layers. When you are finished, the shapes on all the layers on Frame 1 should look like the image above. You may need to use the Arrow tool to reposition the middle shape near the center of the Stage.

To animate the shapes, all you have left to do is to add a shape tween to each layer. You can add shape tweens to multiple layers at one time, as you will see next.

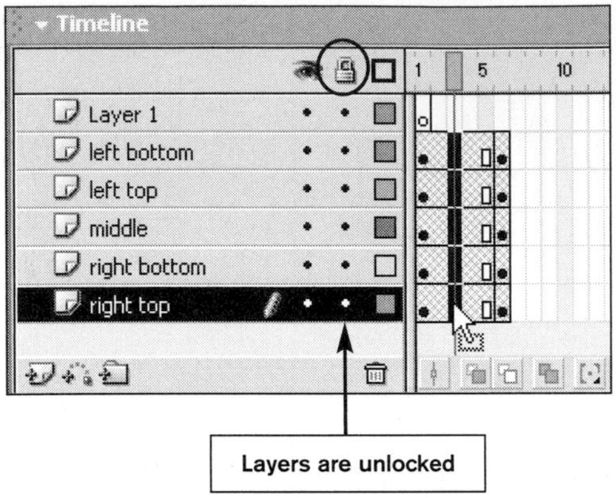

Layers are unlocked

14. Unlock all the layers in the **Timeline**. Starting with the layer named **left bottom**, click and drag down between the two keyframes to select all the layers below the **left bottom** layer, as shown above.

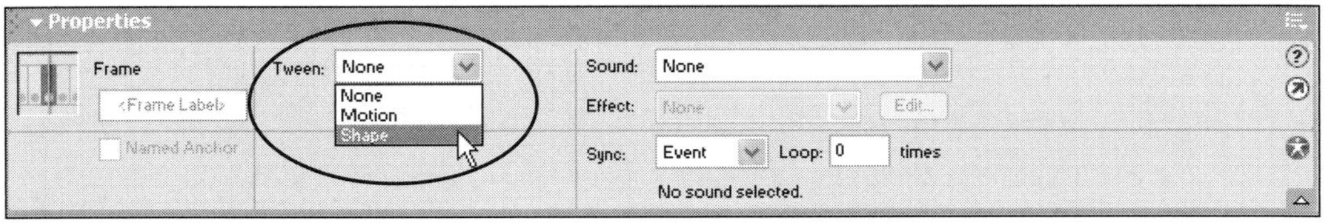

15. Make sure the **Property Inspector** is open. If it is not, choose **Window > Properties**. Select **Shape** from the **Tween** drop-down menu. This will automatically generate a shape tween between each of the two keyframes on all the layers.

16. Press the **Enter/Return** key to see the shape tweens in action! By using a multiple shape tween, you can have different animations on different layers all happening at the same time.

You are almost done! All you have left to do is to put your shape tween layers into a Layer Folder layer and you will learn how to do this next.

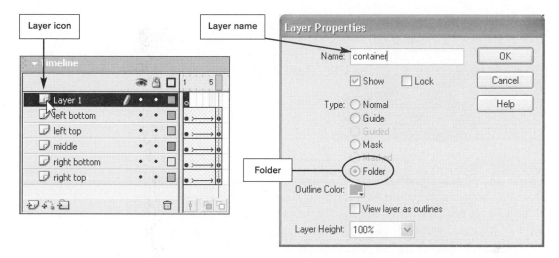

Layer icon

Layer name

17. Double-click on the **Layer 1** icon. This opens the **Layer Properties** dialog box. For the **Name**, type **container** and for the **Type**, select **Folder**. This changes Layer 1 into a Layer Folder and names the folder **container**. Click **OK**. A chart describing all the layer properties found in this dialog box is provided at the end of this exercise.

NOTE | What Is a Layer Folder?

A **Layer Folder** is a special kind of layer that can hold other layers inside of it. It is important to note that you cannot have artwork in a Layer Folder—the Layer Folder's sole purpose is to hold multiple layers so that you can keep your Timeline compact and organized.

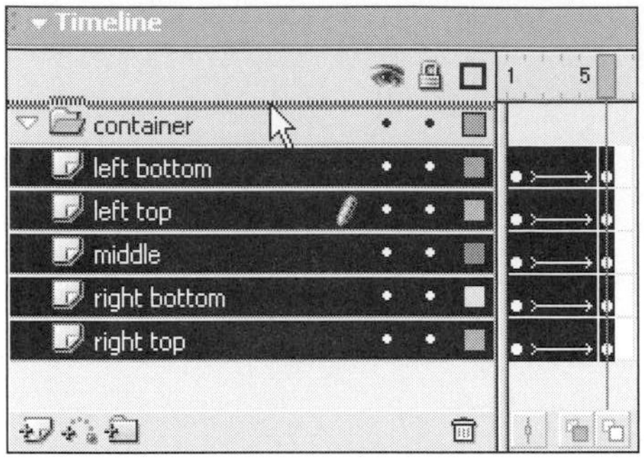

18. In the **Timeline**, click on the **right top** layer name to select that layer, and then Shift+click on the **left bottom** layer name to select that layer and all of the layers in between. With all the layers selected, drag the layers onto the **container** layer. This will place all the layers in the Layer Folder. After you do this, notice that the layers are all indented under the Layer Folder.

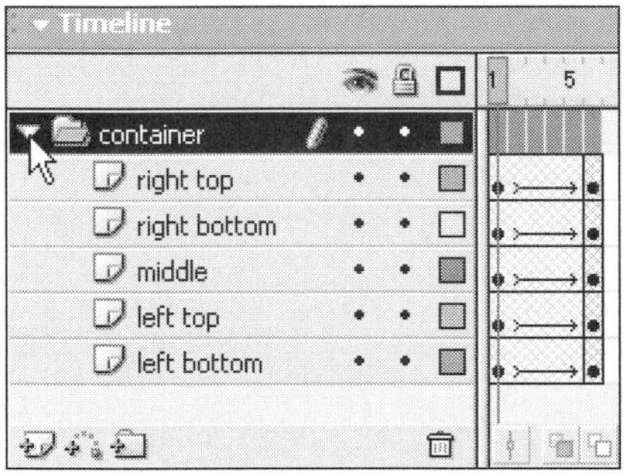

Layer Folder expanded

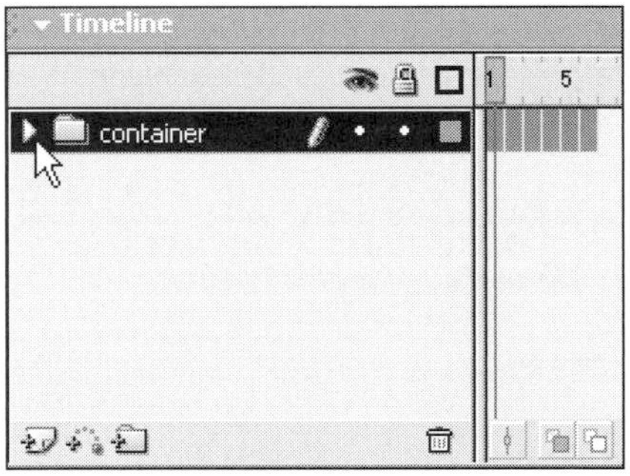

Layer Folder collapsed

19. Click on the **arrow** to the left of the **container** layer name to collapse the folder. Now you see the layers, now you don't! This is organization! You will really come to appreciate this feature when you work on projects that have tons of layers.

20. Press **Enter/Return** to preview your multiple shape tween animation again. Although you've moved the layers into a Layer Folder, the animation is left untouched.

21. When you are finished, save and close this file.

Layer Properties Defined

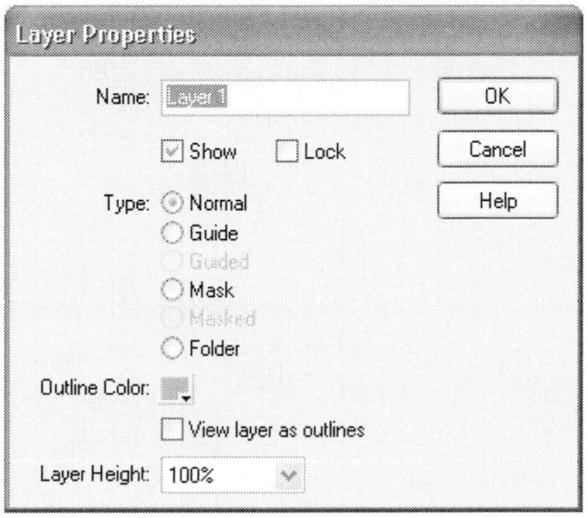

The Timeline offers a number of ways of controlling layers, but other options are available in the Layer Properties dialog box that aren't visible in the Timeline. The following chart covers these additional options.

Layer Properties	
Option	**Description**
Guide	This option enables you to use the contents of a layer as a tracing image (or guide), which helps you create artwork on other layers. Guide layers are the only layers that are not exported with the movie. You will work with a Guide layer in Chapter 7, "*Motion Tweening*."
Guided	A Guided layer is a layer that is linked to a Guide layer. The artwork on this layer can follow the path of the Guide layer it is linked to. Chapter 7, "*Motion Tweening*," will give you hands-on experience working with Guided layers.
Mask	Selecting this option will turn the layer into a Mask layer. You will learn more about this layer type in Chapter 8, "*Bitmaps*."
Masked	Selecting this option will cause the layer to be masked by the Mask layer above it. You will learn how to work with this option as well in Chapter 8, "*Bitmaps*."
	continues on next page

Layer Properties *continued*	
Option	**Description**
Folder	Choosing this option will turn the layer into a Layer Folder so that you can organize your layers.
Outline Color	This option specifies the color that will be used if you select the "View layer as outlines" option. By default, each layer will have a different color. This just gives you an extra bit of organizational control.
Layer Height	This option makes a layer's Timeline display "taller" when you increase the line height of a specific layer. You can choose 100% (the default), 200%, or 300%. This feature is especially useful for working with sounds on the Main Timeline. Allowing the layer containing the sound to be taller makes it easier to work with the waveforms and to synchronize the sound with your animation. You will try this later in Chapter 13, "*Sound*."

4. ————————Animating Gradients

Shape tweening can be used to create additional effects besides morphing one shape into another. You can also use the shape tween process to animate gradients. This can produce dramatic lighting effects, such as glows and strobes. In this exercise, you will learn how to modify and animate a gradient.

1. Open the **animatedGradientFinal.fla** file from the **chap_05** folder.

2. Press **Enter/Return** to preview the animation. Notice that the gradient appears to move from left to right. This is a finished version of the animated gradient effect you will create in the following steps.

3. Close the **animatedGradientFinal.fla** file and open the **animatedGradient.fla** file from the **chap_05** folder. This file contains two layers: one with the dot on it, which is locked, and one named **text**, which is where you will create the gradient tween.

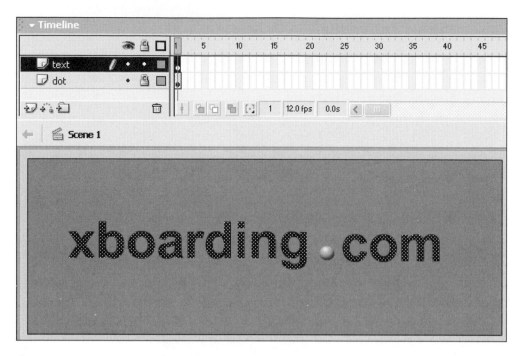

4. Click on **Frame 1** of the **text** layer to select the artwork in that frame. It contains text that has been broken apart so that you can apply a gradient fill to it.

TIP | Why Is the Text Broken Apart?

The text in this exercise file was broken apart because you can't apply a gradient to text, but you can apply a gradient to a shape. In order to re-create the animation of the gradient moving from one side of the word to the other, you have to work with shapes, so the text was broken apart for you ahead of time.

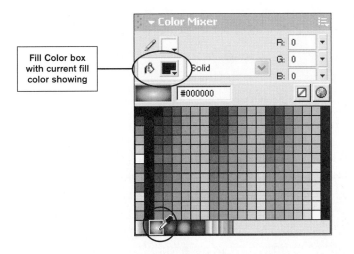

Fill Color box with current fill color showing

5. Make sure the **Color Mixer** panel is open. If it's not, choose **Window > Color Mixer**. With **Frame 1** in the **text** layer still selected, click on the **Fill Color** box to open the **Fill Color** palette. At the very bottom of this palette are some gradients. Choose the black and white radial gradient; it is second from the left.

As soon as you select the black and white radial gradient, the letter shapes on the Stage will change to reflect the new gradient fill color because they were already selected. You can click anywhere away from the Stage to deselect the shapes and see the gradient fill better. To create the effect of the gradient moving from one side of the word to the other, you will change the center of the gradient next.

6. Click on **Frame 1** of the **text** layer to select all the shapes again.

7. In the **Toolbox**, select the **Paint Bucket** tool and click in the top left corner of the letter **X**, as shown above. The spot where you click defines the center of the radial gradient. Because the radial gradient is white in the center and black on the outside, the place where you click is where the white point of the gradient will be.

8. On the **text** layer, press **F6** on **Frame 30** in the **Timeline** to add a new keyframe to the frame. As you might remember from Chapter 4, "*Animation Basics*," pressing F6 copies the content from the previous keyframe and places it on the new keyframe. This can save you from having to re-create entire pieces of artwork, and it's especially useful when you want to make only minor changes.

9. On the **dot** layer, press **F5** on **Frame 30** to add frames up to Frame 30 on this layer. This will allow the dot to be visible through Frame 30.

Tip: Even though the dot layer is locked, you can still add and delete frames in the Timeline—you just can't select the artwork or objects on the Stage in a locked layer.

10. Click on **Frame 30** in the **text** layer to select it. In the **Toolbox**, make sure the **Paint Bucket** tool is still selected, and this time click on the top right of the letter **m**, as shown above. Now it appears as though a light source is coming from the opposite side of the word. This is the ending frame of your animation.

11. On the **text** layer, click anywhere between the two keyframes.

12. In the **Property Inspector**, choose **Shape** from the **Tween** drop-down menu to create a shape tween between the two keyframes.

13. Press **Enter/Return** to test your shape tween. Now it looks as though the word "xboarding.com" is being lit by a moving light source.

Don't be deceived by the word "shape" in "shape tweening." As you've just seen, shape tweens can be used to create animations that don't involve changing one shape into another. In this example, shape tweening was used to animate a gradient.

14. When you are finished, save and close this file—you won't be needing it anymore.

I hope this chapter uncovered the many secrets and nuances of shape tweening. You started with the simple concepts, using simple exercises, and then progressed quickly to a fairly advanced level with the multiple shape tweening and animated gradient exercises. As you gain experience in Macromedia Flash MX, shape tweening will likely become a technique you use often for many different types of effects. If you have the stamina, keep pressing forward to the next chapter. There's no rush though; the book will still be here tomorrow.

6.

Symbols and Instances

| Symbol and Instance Structure | Creating Graphic Symbols
| Library | Registration Point | Creating Symbol Instances |
| Editing Symbols and Instances | Color Styles |
| Animating Graphic Symbols |

chap_o6

Macromedia Flash MX
H•O•T CD-ROM

Effective Macromedia Flash MX movies, even very simple ones, often rely on symbols and instances. Just what can symbols and instances do for you? Symbols enable you to create very complex movies that are faster to download. How? Symbols are downloaded only once, regardless how many copies (called "instances") you have in your movie. For example, if you had a symbol of a tree and you added 50 instances of that tree to the Stage, the file size would be not be that much larger. However, if you were to instead draw 50 separate trees, the user would have to download all 50 trees, and the file size would increase dramatically.

The concept of symbols and instances is often one of the hardest things to teach and learn in Macromedia Flash MX, because this way of working doesn't exist in many other common graphics, animation, or interactive programs. I am confident, however, that if you try these exercises you will better understand how to work more easily with symbols and instances than if you just read about them. Here's where the premise of a hands-on training book is really worth its weight in gold. For many, trying something and gaining first-hand experience is the key to understanding!

The Symbol and Instance Structure

A Macromedia Flash MX **symbol** is a master object of sorts. You create a symbol once—it can be a simple shape or something very complex—and use it multiple times throughout your movie. Each time you reuse a symbol in your project file, it is called an **instance**, which is a copy of a symbol.

The concept of symbols and instances is the key to reducing the download weight of your Macromedia Flash MX documents, because the symbol is downloaded only once, while the instances are simply described in a small text file by their attributes (scale, color, transparency, animation, etc.). That is why instances add very little to the file size of your final movie. To reduce the file size, you should create symbols for any object that you reuse in your projects. Besides reducing the final file size, symbols and instances can also help you make quick updates to objects across your entire project file. Later in the book, as you learn about more advanced animation techniques, you'll see that symbols and instances play another dramatic role. But that's skipping ahead! This chapter focuses on one concept alone—how to create and manipulate symbols and instances.

There are three types of symbols in Macromedia Flash MX: Graphic symbols, Button symbols, and Movie Clip symbols. In this chapter, you will be working with **Graphic symbols**. Hands-on exercises for creating Button and Movie Clip symbols are covered in later chapters.

Here's a handy chart that explains some of the terms found in this chapter:

Symbol Definitions	
Term	**Definition**
Symbol	A reusable object that serves as a master from which you can create copies (instances). Once a symbol is created, it automatically becomes part of the project file's Library. You will learn about the Library later in this chapter.
Instance	A copy of the original symbol. You can alter the color, size, shape, and position of an instance without affecting the original symbol.
Graphic Symbol	One of the three types of symbols. It consists of artwork that can be either static or animated. The Graphic Symbol Timeline is dependent on the Main Timeline—it will play only while the Main Timeline is playing. You'll learn more about this behavior as you work through the exercises in this book.

Symbol Naming Conventions

As you learn to create symbols and instances in this chapter, you'll need to create names for them. In past versions of Macromedia Flash, it didn't matter what name you gave to symbols or instances. With ActionScripting in Macromedia Flash MX (which you will learn about later in this book), naming conventions are more important than they used to be. This is especially true for Movie Clip symbols. For this reason, I recommend that you get used to naming all your symbols in Macromedia Flash MX following the same rules, so you don't develop bad habits that bite you down the road. Here's a handy chart that explains the rules.

Naming Symbols	
Convention	**Explanation**
No spaces	Don't use any spaces. Instead, string the words together or add underscores. For example, instead of *my first symbol*, use the name *myFirstSymbol* or *my_first_symbol*.
No special characters	Special characters—such as Δˊ¨©¢∞£¢¬∂˚Δˇ∑Δ∑ˊ°ø)@#(%$T(%— are forbidden. Some special characters have specific meaning to the Macromedia Flash MX Player and can mess up ActionScripting in the future, so be sure to avoid them.
No forward slashes	Forward slashes are often misinterpreted as path locations on a hard drive, instead of as the name of an object. So, for example, don't use the name *my/first/symbol*.
Begin with a lowercase letter	Symbol names that begin with numbers can cause confusion in ActionScripting. For this reason, always start your symbol names with a lowercase letter. Names can contain numbers, but the first character should be a letter.
No dots	Don't put dots in your file names, such as *snow.boarder*—dots are reserved for ActionScripting syntax.
Use a descriptive name	It is good practice to use descriptive names for symbols. Rather than *symbol6*, you should choose a name that is more easily recognized, like *gfxLogoBkgd*. When you use multiword names for symbols, capitalize the first letter of all words except the first so that you can read it more easily. When you refer to an object in ActionScripting (which you'll get to try in later chapters), you must refer to the symbol with the same capitalization you used in its name.

Important Timeline Vocabulary Terms

This chapter reintroduces you to the Timeline. In the following exercises, you will learn that a symbol has a Timeline too, and therefore you may have one Macromedia Flash MX project that contains several different Timelines. The following chart will help you further understand the distinctions among the various types of Timelines.

Timeline Definitions	
Term	**Definition**
Main Timeline	When you open a Macromedia Flash MX project (.fla), it always defaults to showing the Timeline of Scene 1. This is also called the Main Timeline in the Macromedia Flash MX documentation. The Main Timeline is the Timeline that is visible when you're inside a scene. (You will learn all about scenes in Chapter 11, "*ActionScripting Basics*.")
Graphic Symbol Timeline	Each Graphic symbol has its own Timeline, called a Graphic Symbol Timeline. The Timeline for a symbol and the scene in which the symbol is placed must have the same number of frames, or the symbol's animation will not play properly. This is important because Movie Clip symbols, which you'll learn about in Chapter 10, "*Movie Clips*," do not behave this way.
Scene's Timeline	Every Macromedia Flash MX project (.fla) has a Main Timeline in the form of Scene 1's Timeline. You'll see in later chapters that Macromedia Flash MX projects can have multiple scenes. In those cases, each scene is considered part of the Main Timeline. Learning the difference between a scene's Timeline and a symbol's Timeline is one of the key foundations to working successfully with Macromedia Flash MX.

I. _____Creating Graphic Symbols

Symbols are used for many purposes in Macromedia Flash MX. Before you learn hands-on what they're good for, you'll need to know how to create them. This first exercise shows you how to create a Graphic symbol. Later in the book, you'll learn to work with the two other symbol types—Buttons and Movie Clips—which are more difficult.

1. Copy the **chap_06** folder, located on the **H•O•T CD-ROM**, to your hard drive. You need to have this folder on your hard drive in order to save changes to the files inside it.

2. Open the **graphicSymbol.fla** file from the **chap_06** folder. This file contains one layer with a snowflake shape in Frame 1. You will be converting this shape into a Graphic symbol in the steps that follow.

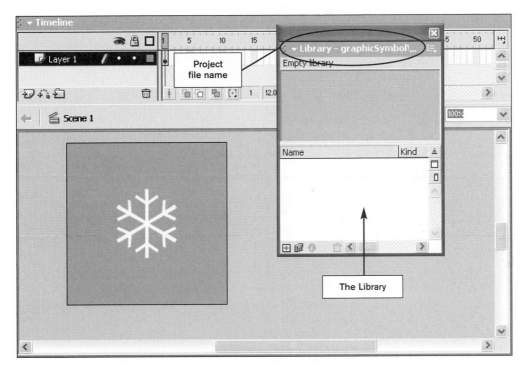

3. Choose **Window > Library** to open the **Library** panel. Notice that the project file name is displayed at the top of the Library panel.

NOTE | What Is the Library?

The **Library** is a container where Macromedia Flash MX stores and organizes symbols, bitmap graphics, sound clips, and video clips. For designers, it can be one of the most useful and frequently used interface elements in the program. The Library is attached to the movie that you're working with. If you give your project file (.fla) to someone else and that person opens it, he or she will see the same Library that you see when you have that file open. Additionally, you can even open just the Library from another project file by choosing **File > Open as Library**.

Inside the Library, you can sort the contents by name, type, usage, and linkage. As your files become more complex, you will find it useful to create folders within your Library to help separate your symbols into different categories. Since you will frequently work with the Library in Macromedia Flash MX, it's useful to learn the two shortcuts to bring the Library to the screen: **F11** or **Ctrl+L** (Windows) or **Cmd+L** (Mac). You will get an in-depth look at the Library and all its functions in later chapters.

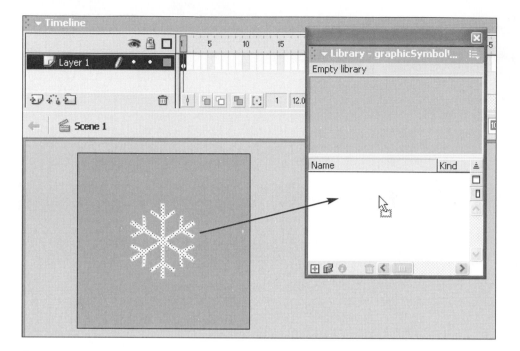

4. Using the **Arrow** tool, select the **snowflake** on the **Stage** and drag it into the lower half of the **Library** panel. This will open the **Symbol Properties** dialog box.

Note: Instead of dragging the shape into the Library, you can also select the shape and choose Insert > Convert to Symbol to open the Symbol Properties dialog box.

NOTE | The Symbol Properties Dialog Box

Convert to Symbol ☒

Name: [Symbol 1]

Behavior: ○ Movie Clip   Registration: ⊞⊞⊞   [OK]
          ○ Button   [Cancel]
          ⊙ Graphic   [Advanced] [Help]

← [**Basic view**]

Convert to Symbol ☒

Name: [Symbol 1]

Behavior: ○ Movie Clip   Registration: ⊞⊞⊞   [OK]
          ○ Button   [Cancel]
          ⊙ Graphic   [Basic]   [Help]

Linkage
    Identifier: [   ]

    Linkage: ☐ Export for ActionScript
             ☐ Export for runtime sharing
             ☐ Import for runtime sharing
             ☐ Export in first frame

    URL: [   ]

Source
    ☐ Always update before publishing
    File: [Browse...]
    Symbol Name: Symbol 1   [Symbol...]

← [**Advanced view**]

The **Symbol Properties dialog box** offers two views: basic and advanced. For now, we will stick to the basic view. Inside the Symbol Properties dialog box are three settings to be determined next: the name, the behavior, and the Registration Point of the symbol.

5. For **Name**, type **snowflake**; for **Behavior**, select **Graphic**; and for **Registration**, make sure the box in the middle of the square is selected. Click **OK**.

Note: I promise that you'll get to learn about Movie Clip and Button symbols in later chapters. For now, you'll focus on Graphic symbols only.

NOTE | What Is a Registration Point?

When you convert a shape into a symbol, Macromedia Flash MX needs to know where you want the center point to be located on that shape. Who cares, you might be thinking. Well, it becomes very important when you create animation using rotation because the symbol will rotate around its **Registration Point**. If this seems a bit abstract to you, it will make more sense once you have completed Exercise 5 later in the chapter. For now, make sure the Registration Point is in the middle.

Registration Point

Selected snowflake shape before it is converted to a symbol

Selected snowflake shape after it is converted to a symbol

Once you click OK, the snowflake on the stage will change slightly. Notice the bounding box and the circle with a crosshair in the middle of the snowflake. This provides visual feedback that your snowflake is now a Graphic symbol. The circle and crosshair in the middle of the snowflake act as a marker, telling you where the center (or Registration Point) of the symbol is. This is an important indicator because it affects how all of the instances (which you will learn about in the next exercise) of this symbol are rotated and scaled. You will also learn how to rotate and scale instances later in this chapter.

6. After you click OK in the Symbol Properties dialog box, notice that you now have two snowflakes in your project file: the snowflake symbol, which is located in the Library, and an instance (a copy of the original symbol) on the Stage. Instances are placed on the Stage, and symbols are stored in the Library.

Congratulations! You have just made your first Graphic symbol. In the next exercise, you will learn to work with symbol instances.

7. Save and close the file.

TIP | Five Ways to Create a Symbol

When you are working with Macromedia Flash MX, there are five different ways to create a symbol. You can create a symbol using artwork that already exists on the Stage or create a new symbol from scratch on a blank Stage. The five ways are explained below:

1. Select premade artwork on the Stage and drag it into the Library, as you did in step 4 of the previous exercise. This will turn the artwork you select into a symbol.

2. Select premade artwork on the Stage and choose **Insert > Convert to Symbol**, or use the shortcut key **F8**. This will also turn the artwork you select into a symbol.

3. Choose **Insert > New Symbol** or use the shortcut key **Ctrl+F8** (Windows) or **Cmd+F8** (Mac). This places you in symbol editing mode with a blank canvas ready for you to add or create artwork.

4. Choose **New Symbol** from the **Library Options** menu in the upper right corner of the Library. This places you in symbol editing mode with a blank canvas ready for you to add or create artwork.

5. Click the **New Symbol** button in the bottom left corner of the Library. This will place you in symbol editing mode with a blank canvas ready for you to add or create artwork.

2. —————————Creating Symbol Instances

In the last exercise, you learned how to create a symbol. In this exercise, you will learn how to create instances of a symbol in the Library. Instances are copies of the original symbol that can be modified individually without affecting the symbol in the Library. You will learn to do this in the following steps.

1. Open the **instances.fla** file from the **chap_06** folder. This file contains two layers: a layer named **background**, which contains a bitmap image, and a layer named **instances** where you will place instances of a symbol just like the one in the last exercise. The background layer has been locked so that you don't accidentally add instances to that layer.

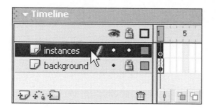

2. Make sure the **instances** layer is selected. If it's not, click to the right of the layer name to select that specific layer.

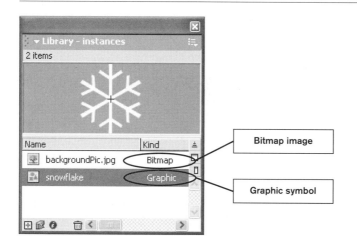

3. Make sure the **Library** is open. If it is not, choose **Window > Library** (or press **F11**) to open the Library for this file. Notice that there are two items in the Library: the snowflake symbol and something called **backgroundPic.jpg**. You might be wondering how those elements got there. The snowflake was saved as a symbol in this project file, and it automatically appears in the Library whenever you open this project file, just like the snowflake symbol you created in Exercise 1. The backgroundPic item is a bitmap that was also saved as a Library element and is located on the **background** layer.

NOTE | Library Assets

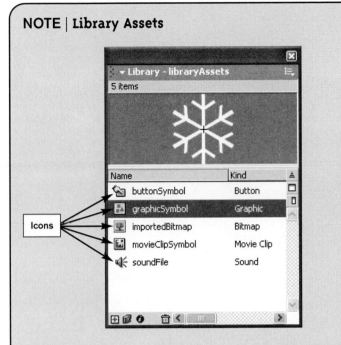

In addition to storing symbols, the Library also stores other assets, such as imported bitmap and vector graphics, sound clips, and video clips. It is easy to identify the different assets inside the Library at a glance, since each type has a different icon associated with it.

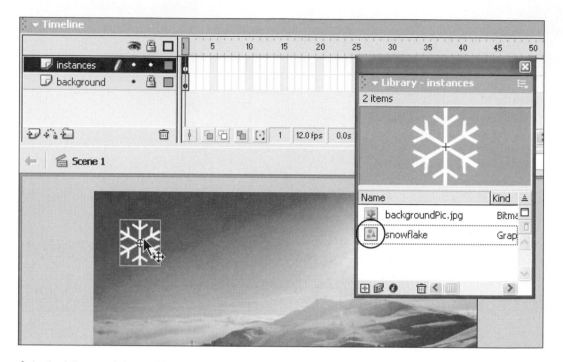

4. In the **Library**, click on the snowflake's **Graphic symbol** icon, and drag it onto the **Stage**. When you release the mouse button, an instance of the snowflake is placed on the Stage.

One key point to remember is that symbols are stored in the Library and instances are located on the Stage. From every symbol, you can create as many instances as you want.

5. Click and drag seven more snowflakes from the Library. This will create a total of eight instances on your Stage. You can also insert instances by clicking in the Library's Preview Window and dragging an instance onto the Stage.

Clicking and dragging from the Library is one way to create instances on your Stage, but you can also Ctrl+drag (Windows) or Option+drag (Mac) an instance on the Stage to create a duplicate of it without opening the Library.

6. Save the changes you made to this file. Keep this file open for the next exercise. You will learn how to edit symbols next.

3. ——————————Editing Symbols

The instances on your Stage have a special relationship with the symbol in the Library. This is often referred to in computer programming circles as a **parent/child relationship**. One of the advantages of this relationship is that if you change a symbol in the Library, all of the instances on your Stage will be updated. As you can imagine, this can save you a lot of time when you need to make large updates across an entire project. This ability to make quick—and sometimes large—updates is one of the powerful advantages of using symbols and instances. In this exercise, you will modify the appearance of the snowflake symbol to change all eight instances on the Stage.

1. The file from the previous exercise should still be open. If you closed it, go ahead and open the **instances.fla** file from the **chap_06** folder.

2. Make sure your **Library** panel is open. If it's not, press **F11** to open it now.

Your Stage should look similar to the one shown above. If for some reason it does not, refer to the previous exercise to learn how to create multiple instances of the snowflake symbol.

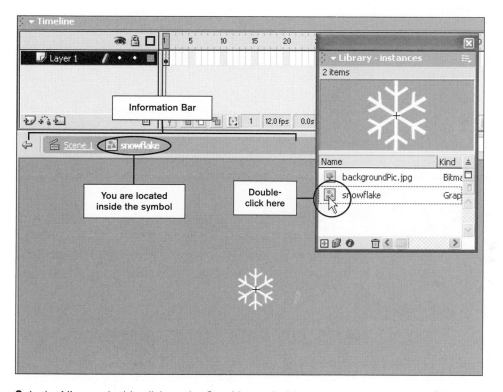

3. In the **Library**, double-click on the **Graphic symbol** icon to the left of the **snowflake** symbol name. Your Stage will change, because you are now editing the Timeline for the symbol, where you can create or modify its contents. At this point, you are no longer working in the Main Timeline. Notice that the gray (work) area around your Stage is gone, as is the bounding box around the symbol. When you're in symbol editing mode (inside a symbol), you will not see the work area, unless you are using the Edit in Place feature, which you will learn about later in this exercise. Notice also that the Information Bar above the Stage shows two names: **Scene 1** and **snowflake**. This is another indicator that you are no longer working on the Main Timeline. Instead, you are inside the editing interface and Timeline for the snowflake Graphic symbol.

TIP | Know Your Location

There are several ways to get into symbol editing mode. It's so easy to get into and out of this mode that you may not even be aware that you have switched views, so be constantly aware of where you are while you work. Keep an eye on the Information Bar and make sure that you are drawing, animating, or creating in the correct location of your project.

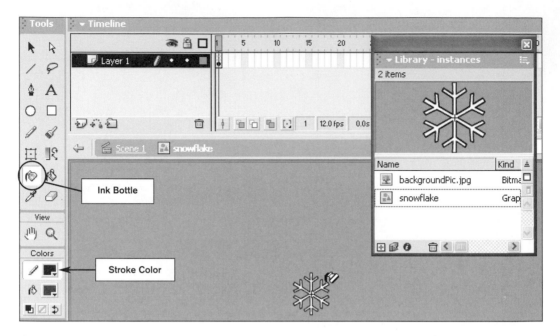

4. In the **Toolbox**, select the **Ink Bottle** tool, and select **black** for the **Stroke Color**. Click on the **snowflake** to add a stroke to the snowflake shape. Notice that as soon as you click on the shape with the Ink Bottle tool, the Preview Window in the Library is updated instantly to reflect the change you made.

Note: In the Macromedia Flash MX documentation, the terms "outline" and "stroke" are at times used interchangeably. As you may recall from Chapter 3, "Drawing and Color Tools," you can add strokes (sometimes called outlines) to objects that don't already have a stroke applied to them with the Ink Bottle, as you did in the previous step. You can also modify an existing stroke by selecting it and then changing its width and appearance using the Property Inspector.

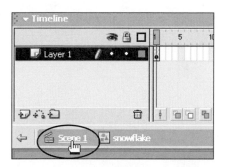

5. In the **Information Bar**, click on the underlined **Scene 1** to return to the **Main Timeline**. You should see the bitmap with the snow and sky again.

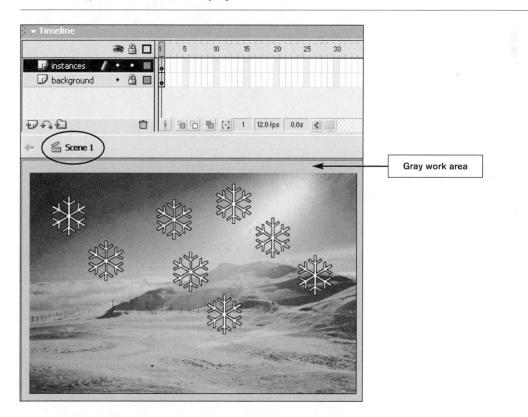

As soon as you click on the Scene 1 name, the gray work area appears again, and you see only the Scene 1 name, without the snowflake name next to it. Notice also that all of the instances of the snowflake now have a black stroke around them. Every time you modify a symbol, it affects all of the instances you have in your project file, just as you saw here. This can be a very powerful way to make changes throughout your project.

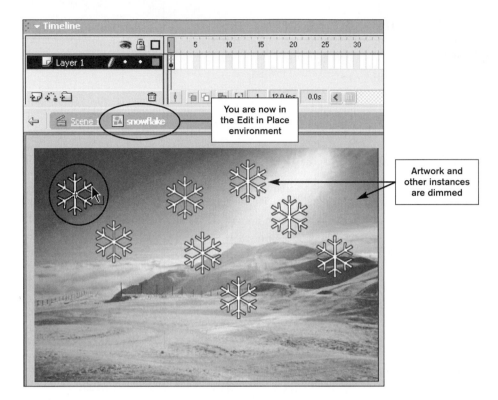

6. Choose a **snowflake** instance on the **Stage**, and double-click on it. This will allow you to edit the symbol in place, which means in the context of the other instances on the Stage. When you edit a symbol in place, all the other objects on the Stage are dimmed to differentiate them from the symbol you are editing. You can also edit the symbol in place by choosing **Edit > Edit in Place**.

TIP | Techniques for Editing Symbols

Editing an instance in place (double-clicking on the instance on the Stage) will produce the same end result as editing the symbol in the Library (double-clicking on the Graphic symbol icon to the left of the symbol name in the Library). Both techniques change the appearance of the master symbol as well as all of its instances. The difference between the two techniques is that when you edit the symbol in the Library, you cannot see the Main Timeline. When you edit an instance in place, you see a dimmed version of the Stage, and you can preview your changes in context with the rest of the Stage on the Main Timeline before returning to the Main Timeline.

7. Using the **Arrow** tool, double-click on the **stroke** around the snowflake to select it. Press the **Delete** key to remove it. Instead of the stroke, you'll make a change to the fill this time. It's easy to change the artwork for the symbol whenever the mood strikes you!

8. Use the **Arrow** tool to select the **snowflake** shape.

9. In the **Property Inspector**, click on the **Fill Color** box and choose a different shade of gray. Because the snowflake was already selected, Macromedia Flash MX automatically updates the color of the snowflake as soon as you select a color. Again, notice that all the other instances of the snowflake change color as well!

10. In the **Information Bar**, click on **Scene 1** to return to the **Main Timeline**. You should see the background bitmap and the snowflake instances in full color.

11. Save the changes you made to this file. Leave this file open because you will use it in the next exercise.

4. Editing Symbol Instances

In the previous exercise, you learned how to modify a symbol to make changes to all of the instances on the Stage. But what do you do if you want to change the color of only one instance or of each instance individually? You can do this by selecting the instance on the Stage in the Main Timeline and modifying the setting in the Property Inspector. The Property Inspector will let you change the tint, brightness, and alpha settings of symbol instances. This is the only way to change the color values of an instance because the Paint Bucket and Brush tools work only on shapes, not on symbol instances. In this exercise, you will use the Property Inspector and the Free Transform tool to change the appearance of individual snowflakes.

1. The file from the previous exercise should still be open. If it's not, open the **instances.fla** file from the **chap_06** folder.

2. Click to select the **snowflake** instance in the upper left corner of the **Stage**.

It's very important that you select the snowflake instance by clicking on it only once. If you double-click it accidentally, you will be editing the symbol, not the instance. If this happens, go back to the Main Timeline by clicking on the Scene 1 link in the Information Bar.

3. Make sure the **Property Inspector** is open and visible. If it's not, choose **Window > Properties** or use the shortcut **Ctrl+F3** (Windows) or **Cmd+F3** (Mac) to open it.

4. From the **Color Styles** box in the **Property Inspector**, choose **Brightness**. Click the **slider** to the right of the menu and drag it up to **100%**. This will increase the brightness level of the selected object as you drag up.

Note: The Brightness option controls the brightness value of the instance and has a range of −100% to 100%, with −100% being completely black and 100% being completely white.

5. Click to select a different **snowflake** on your **Stage**. You can choose any snowflake you want.

6. From the **Color** Styles box in the **Property Inspector**, choose **Tint**. The Tint option applies a tint to the base color of your instance.

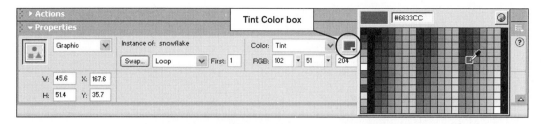

7. Click inside the **Tint Color** box and, from the pop-up color palette select a shade of **purple**.

8. Click and drag the **Tint slider** up to **75%**. As you drag the slider up, notice how the color becomes brighter. The Tint option has a range of 0% (no tint) to 100% (fully saturated). Basically, this is changing the amount of color that is applied to the instance. It also changes the RGB values in the Property Inspector.

Note: You control the color of the instance by modifying the percentage of the tint being applied and the individual RGB (red, green, and blue) values. The Tint option is the only way you can change the color of an instance, other than using the advanced settings, where you can set the RGB values. This option also changes both the Fill and Stroke settings to the value you specify. You cannot change these settings separately when editing the instance; this can be done only by editing the symbol.

9. Click to select another **snowflake** on the **Stage**. Just make sure you select one that has not been modified yet.

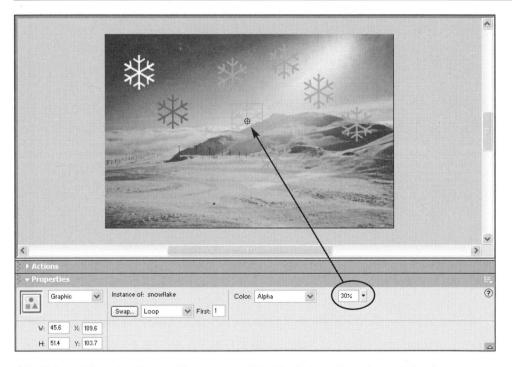

10. From the **Color Styles** box in the **Property Inspector**, choose **Alpha**. This option, which has a range of 100% (opaque) to 0% (transparent), lets you control the transparency value of the selected instance.

11. Click and drag the **Alpha slider** down to **0%**. Watch the selected snowflake disappear as you drag the slider down. Return the Alpha slider to **30%**.

In the next few steps, you will learn about the Advanced option in the Color Styles drop-down menu. This option lets you modify multiple settings for a selected object. For example, you can use this option to adjust the Tint and Alpha settings of the selected instance. The best way to learn about it is by using it, and that's exactly what you are going to do.

12. Click to select another unmodified **snowflake** on the **Stage**.

13. From the **Color Styles** box in the **Property Inspector**, choose **Advanced** from the drop-down menu. Click the **Settings** button.

14. In the **Advanced Effect** dialog box, click the arrow and drag the **Red slider** to **20%**. Click and drag the **Green slider** down to **60%**. Click and drag the **Alpha slider** to **50%**. The end result should be a snowflake that is a nice shade of blue.

The left column of fields in the Advanced Effect dialog box allows you to manipulate the colors using percentages, while the right column of fields allows you to manipulate the colors using numbers that correspond with color values.

Note: *Your snowflake might look a bit different if you didn't select the same gray for your snowflake symbol as I did in the last exercise.*

15. Go ahead and recolor as many snowflakes as you want. It never hurts to practice! For your reference, I have provided a chart at the end of this exercise that outlines all of the options in the Color Styles drop-down menu.

NOTE | Removing Color Styles

Up to this point in this exercise, you have added many different color styles to the instances on your Stage. If you want to remove the styles you have applied to an instance, you can simply select the instance and choose the **None** option from the Color Styles drop-down menu. This will turn off any color styles you have applied and restore the instance to its original condition.

So far, you've gained some experience in changing symbol instances by modifying their brightness, tint, and alpha. You can also rotate, scale, and skew instances. In the following steps, you will use the Free Transform tool to modify the instances on your Stage.

---

16. Click to select another **snowflake** on your **Stage**. It doesn't really matter which one you select because you will eventually select them all.

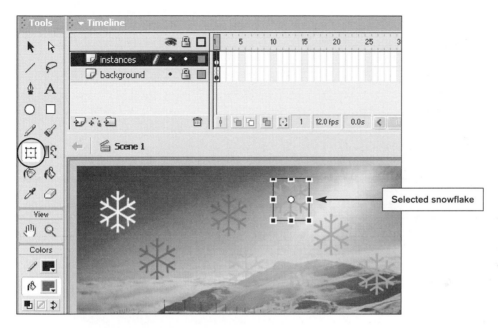

17. In the **Toolbox**, select the **Free Transform** tool.

18. Click on the middle handle on the bottom of the snowflake and drag down. This will increase the height of the snowflake.

19. Move your cursor between the bottom left and middle handles (slightly above the handles) until you see the **skew** cursor icon, as shown in the picture above. Once you see the icon, click and drag to the left. This will skew the selected snowflake.

20. Click to select another **snowflake** instance on the **Stage**.

21. Select the **Free Transform** tool in the **Toolbox** and click and drag diagonally on one of the corner handles. This will scale the snowflake to a bigger size.

Tip: If you hold down the Shift key while you drag one of the handles, the snowflake will scale proportionally on all sides.

22. Click to select a different **snowflake** instance on the Stage.

23. In the **Toolbox**, select the **Free Transform** tool and move your cursor over a corner handle until the **rotate** icon appears, as shown in the picture above. Click and drag down. This will rotate the selected snowflake.

NOTE | Changing the Registration Point

When using the Free Transform tool, you might have noticed that the circle in the center of an instance serves as an anchor from which position, rotation, and scale originate. It is possible to move the center point (Registration Point) if you want to.

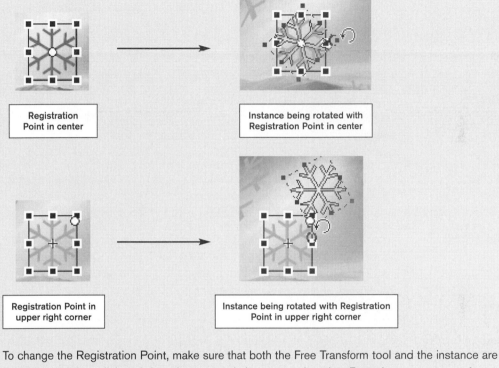

Registration Point in center

Instance being rotated with Registration Point in center

Registration Point in upper right corner

Instance being rotated with Registration Point in upper right corner

To change the Registration Point, make sure that both the Free Transform tool and the instance are selected, and then click and drag the center circle to a new location. From then on, any transformations you make will originate from this new position. Use this technique when you want to rotate from a corner; you can even move the Registration Point off the image to rotate on a distant axis.

24. Go ahead and select the last **snowflake** on the Stage and, using the **Free Transform** tool, apply any transformation you like. Remember, practice makes perfect, so have some fun creating your own transformation of the last unchanged snowflake instance.

25. When you are finished, save the changes you made and close this file. You won't need it anymore.

Color Styles

The chart below explains the different options available in the Color Styles drop-down menu in the Property Inspector. As you learned in this exercise, the Color Styles options can be used to change the color and alpha properties of an instance.

Color Styles Options	
Option	**Description**
Brightness	Controls the brightness (lightness or darkness) of the selected symbol. The percentage slider goes from −100% (black) to 100% (white).
Tint	Allows you to tint a selected symbol a specific RGB color. You can choose a color from the Tint color palette The slider allows you to add a tint to the selected symbol with a percentage of that specific color. You can also choose a color by sliding the R, G, and B color sliders up and down.
Alpha	Allows you to change the transparency of a selected instance. Using the slider, you can have a completely opaque instance (100%) or a completely transparent instance (0%), or any value in between.
Advanced	A complex option that lets you adjust the tint and alpha of an instance. The *Using Macromedia Flash MX* manual has a good explanation of the complex mathematical equations involved with this panel. I find it easier to just play with the different settings to get the right look.

Great job! You've made it this far; now you have only one more exercise to go. Next you will learn how to make an animated Graphic symbol.

5. —————————Animating Graphic Symbols

Up until now, you have been working with static Graphic symbols. Now you will learn how to create a Graphic symbol that contains animation frames. When you use animated Graphic symbols in Macromedia Flash MX, it's important to understand that the number of animation frames inside the symbol have to relate to the number of frames that are set on the Main Timeline. This will make more sense to you after you try it.

In this exercise, you will modify the snowflake Graphic symbol and add a simple shape tween animation to its Timeline to convert it into an animated Graphic symbol. The end result will be a snowflake that turns into a small snowball and fades away.

1. Open the **animSymbolFinal.fla** file from the **chap_06** folder. **Choose Control > Test Movie** to preview the animation. It's snowing! You will play Mother Nature and create the snowing animation next.

2. Close **animSymbolFinal.fla** and open the file named **animSymbol.fla** from the **chap_06** folder. This file is similar to the one you started with in Exercise 2. It contains two layers: one named **background**, which contains a bitmap background image, and one named **animSymbol**, where you will place the animated symbol you are about to create. The **background** layer has been locked so that you don't accidentally modify that layer.

3. Make sure the **Library** panel is open and visible. If it's not, press **F11** to open it. The Library contains two items: **backgroundPic.jpg**, which is the background image, and a snowflake symbol.

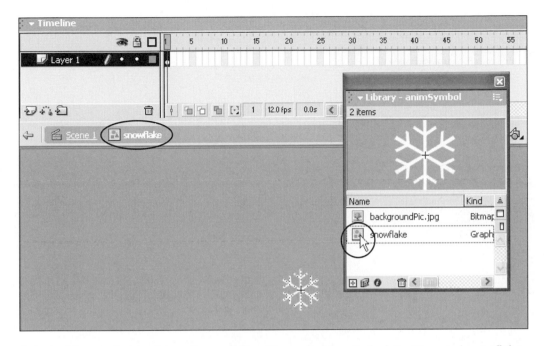

4. In the **Library**, double-click on the small **Graphic symbol** icon to the left of the word **snowflake**. This will take you into editing mode for this symbol. Notice that the contents of your Stage have changed and that the snowflake Graphic symbol icon appears in the Information Bar.

In the following steps, you will create a shape tween animation that will make the snowflake look as though it is falling as it changes into a small snowball and fades away. Keep in mind that you are creating this animation of your snowflake on the Graphic Symbol Timeline, which is different from the Main Timeline in Scene 1. This means that the animation will affect all the instances of this symbol, because you are editing the master symbol.

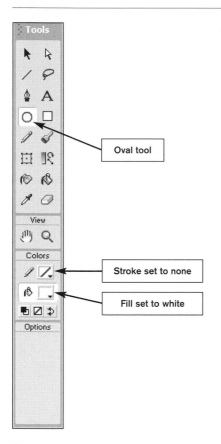

5. In the **Timeline**, press **F7** on **Frame 10** to add a blank keyframe to Frame 10.

Remember, a blank keyframe identifies a change and does not copy any artwork from the previous keyframe.

Oval tool

Stroke set to none

Fill set to white

6. In the **Toolbox**, select the **Oval** tool and set the **Stroke** to **none** and the **Fill** to **white**.

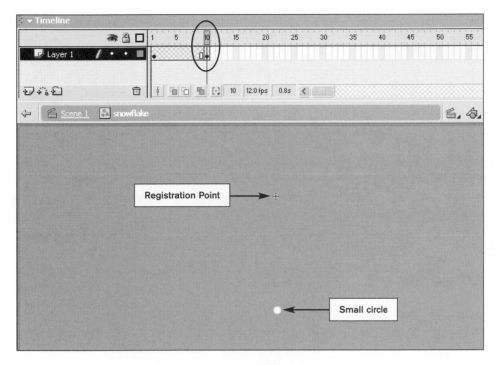

7. Draw a small **circle** directly below the **Registration Point**.

On Frame 1, your snowflake was centered on the Registration Point, and since you want to create an animation of the snowflake falling, you need to draw the circle below the Registration Point.

8. In the **Graphic Symbol Timeline**, click anywhere between **Frame 1** and **Frame 10** to select one of the frames.

9. Make sure the **Property Inspector** is open. If it is not, press **Ctrl+F3** (Windows) or **Cmd+F3** (Mac). Choose **Shape** from the **Tween** drop-down menu.

10. Press **Enter/Return** to get a quick preview of what your animation will look like.

You still have one more tween to add.

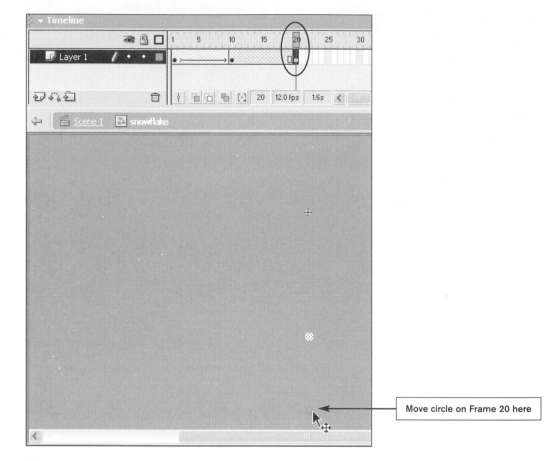

Move circle on Frame 20 here

11. Press **F6** on **Frame 20** to add a keyframe to Frame 20. With the **Arrow** tool, move the **snowball** circle on Frame 20 down, as shown in the picture above.

The snowflake will turn into a snowball from Frame 1 to 10, and then the snowball will disappear from Frame 10 to 20.

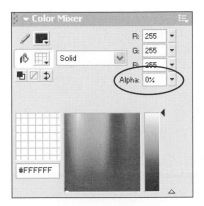

12. With the **snowball** circle still selected, set the **Alpha** to **0%**. This will make the snowball in Frame 20 transparent. Click anywhere off the snowball to deselect it, and you will see it disappear!

13. In the **Graphic Symbol Timeline**, click anywhere between **Frame 10** and **Frame 20** to select one of the frames.

14. Choose **Shape** from the **Tween** drop-down menu. This adds the tween animation of the snowball falling and disappearing.

15. Press **Enter/Return** to preview the entire animation. As it is falling, the snowflake should turn into a snowball, and then the snowball should fade away.

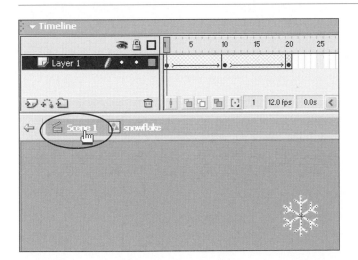

16. When you are happy with your animation, click on **Scene 1** in the **Information Bar** to return to the **Main Timeline**.

17. Drag an instance of the **snowflake** symbol onto the **Stage**. This will add an instance of the ani-mated snowflake symbol to the Main Timeline.

18. Choose **Control > Test Movie**. This will open a new window with a preview of your movie. But wait; the snowflake is not animating. Why not? Close the Preview Window to return to Scene 1's Timeline, and I'll show you how to fix this.

The Timeline of the animated Graphic symbol is directly related to the Main Timeline (the current scene—in this case, Scene 1) of the project. This means that if the Main Timeline is one frame in length, which it is, and the Timeline of the animated Graphic symbol is 20 frames in length, only one frame will be displayed. To fix this situation, you need to extend the Main Timeline to be at least as long as the Timeline of the animated Graphic symbol, which is 20 frames long.

19. Click in **Frame 20** of the **animSymbol** layer and drag down to **Frame 20** of the **background** layer. This will select the range of frames between the layers.

20. Press **F5** to insert frames and extend the Timeline of both layers to 20 frames in length. Now the Main Timeline is at least as long as the Timeline of the animated Graphic symbol, which means that you will see the entire animation play. Your snowflake is about to animate!

Note: You just extended both layers so that the content of these layers is displayed for the same length of time. For example, extending just the animSymbol layer would cause the background layer to disappear when the Playhead reached Frame 2. Extending both layers to Frame 20 ensures that all of the layers are displayed for the same length of time.

21. Choose **Control > Test Movie** once again to preview your movie. There you go: an animating snowflake. However, in order to have the effect of snow falling, you need to add more instances to your Stage. You will do this next.

22. Close the Preview Window.

23. On the **Main Timeline**, drag 11 more instances of the animated **snowflake** symbol onto the **Stage**, to make a total of 12 snowflakes on the Stage.

24. Choose **Control > Test Movie**. This will open a new window with a preview of your movie.

Notice that the snowflakes are all falling in unison, which doesn't look very realistic. The following steps will show you how to change the starting frames of each animated Graphic symbol to create a more natural-looking snowfall.

25. Close the Preview Window.

26. Click to select a **snowflake** on the **Stage**.

27. Enter any number between **1** and **20** in the **First** field, in the middle of the **Property Inspector**. This field sets the frame on which the animation begins. Since this animation has a total of 20 frames, you must select a number between 1 and 20.

28. Repeat this process for all of the snowflakes on your Stage, entering a different **First** value for each one. By changing the starting frame of each animation, you will change the starting point of each animation, and that will produce a more realistic snowfall effect.

29. Choose **Control > Test Movie** to preview your movie. It's snowing! You can go ahead and close the Preview Window.

Could you have achieved this same effect using a different method? The answer is yes. In Macromedia Flash MX, it is often possible to produce the same effect in a number of different ways. However, some ways are more efficient than others. The above example outlines an efficient way of using one symbol to create several instances that look and behave very differently. You could have created and animated each of the snowflakes separately to produce the same effect, but that would have been so much more work.

30. Save the changes you made to this file and close it.

NOTE | Looping

You might have noticed that the 20-frame animation of the falling snowflakes played over and over again when you tested the movie. This type of behavior is called a **loop**, which is an animation sequence that repeats over and over. Macromedia Flash MX defaults to looping whatever is on the Stage, unless you tell it not to through the use of ActionScript. You will learn about ActionScript in Chapter 11, "*ActionScripting Basics.*"

You made it! Congratulations! By now, you should feel a lot more comfortable working with symbols and instances, and you should understand the role they can play in your projects. But you aren't finished yet. Future chapters on Buttons and Movie Clips will continue this learning process. So don't stop now—you are just getting to the good stuff.

7.

Motion Tweening

Basic Motion Tweening	Tweening Effects
Editing Multiple Frames	Using a Motion Guide
Easing In and Easing Out	Exploding Text

chap_07

Macromedia Flash MX
H•O•T CD-ROM

Similar to shape tweening, motion tweening is a method of animation that takes the position and attributes of an object in a start keyframe, and the position and attributes of an object in an end keyframe, and calculates all the animation that will occur between the two. However, unlike shape tweening, motion tweening requires that you use symbols, groups, and text blocks, rather than shapes, to create animation. In addition to position, motion tweens can animate scale, tint, transparency, rotation, and distortion. Throughout the following exercises, you will learn much more than simple motion tweening, including how to edit multiple frames and how to use Motion Guides.

Shape Tweening Versus Motion Tweening

When you start working in Macromedia Flash MX, you might be confused about which type of tween to choose: motion or shape. You may spend unnecessary time trying to figure out why your animation is not working when the solution turns out to be that you simply selected the wrong type of tween. The basic distinction between the two types of tweening is that with shape tweening, you use shapes to create the tweening effect, whereas with **motion tweening**, you use groups, text, or symbols to create the effect. Use the following chart as a reference tool when deciding on the type of tween to use.

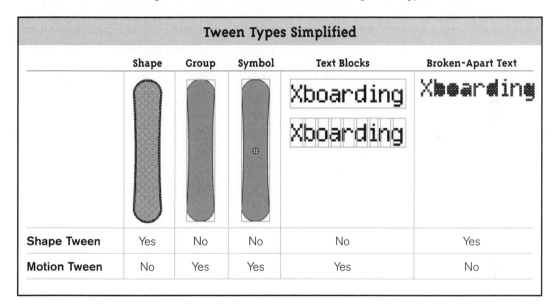

Tween Types Simplified					
	Shape	Group	Symbol	Text Blocks	Broken-Apart Text
Shape Tween	Yes	No	No	No	Yes
Motion Tween	No	Yes	Yes	Yes	No

I. ——————————Basic Motion Tweening

This exercise demonstrates how to create a basic motion tween, using a Graphic symbol. I've created the Graphic symbol for you, but please note that you would need to create a Graphic symbol first if you were creating a motion tween from scratch. Motion tweening itself is very simple, especially once you've learned shape tweening. The big difference is not in the technique but in understanding when to use which type of object: shape, group, symbol, text, or broken-apart text. You may find yourself referring back to the "Tween Types Simplified" chart often, since remembering the rules of objects and tweening is harder than the process itself.

1. Copy the **chap_07** folder, located on the **H•O•T CD-ROM**, to your hard drive. You need to have this folder on your hard drive in order to save changes to the files inside it.

2. In your **chap_07** folder, open the file **motionTween.fla**. This file contains one layer with a background image.

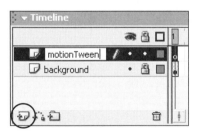

3. Click on the **Insert Layer** button to add a new layer to the Timeline. Double-click on the **Layer 2** name and rename this layer **motionTween**.

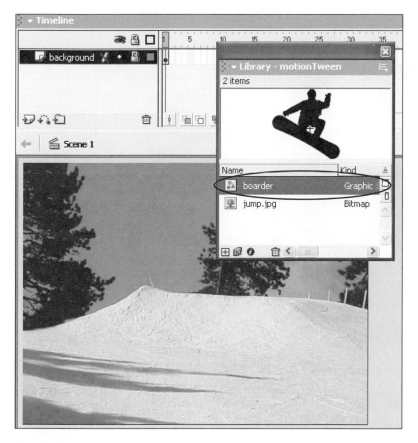

4. Open the **Library** for this movie by pressing **F11**. Click the **boarder** symbol to select it. Once it's selected, you will see a preview of it in the preview portion of the Library window.

Note: In Chapter 5, "Shape Tweening," when you were introduced to shape tweening, you saw that your tween had to be created using a shape. With motion tweening it is the opposite. When working with motion tweening, the graphic that you're tweening cannot be a shape. Instead, it must be a symbol, a text block, or a grouped object.

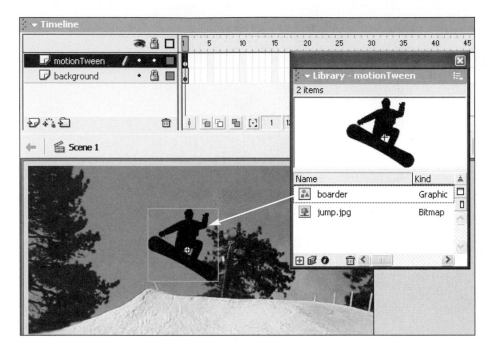

5. Click and drag an instance of the **boarder** Graphic symbol from the **Library** out onto the middle of the **Stage**, just above the jump, as in the picture above. This is where the boarder is going to start its animation.

6. Click inside **Frame 20**, and press **F6** to add a keyframe. This will copy the contents of Frame 1 to Frame 20.

7. Click on **Frame 20** of the **background** layer and press **F5** to add a frame on that layer as well. This way, the background image will be visible throughout the motion tween.

8. Making sure that the **Playhead** is still over **Frame 20**, drag the **boarder** to the bottom right corner of the **Stage**. This will serve as the end point for your animation. Note that Macromedia Flash MX switched you to the motionTween layer when you selected the boarder artwork from the Stage.

Tip: If you can't see the whole background image, choose View > Magnification > Show All to see the whole image.

9. In the **Timeline**, click anywhere between the two keyframes to select one of the frames between Frame 1 and Frame 20.

10. Make sure the **Property Inspector** is open; if it is not, choose **Window > Properties** to open it. From the **Tween** drop-down menu, choose **Motion**. This turns on motion tweening for the range of frames between Frame 1 and Frame 20.

11. Preview your first motion tween by pressing **Enter/Return** on the keyboard. The boarder will move from the middle of the Stage to the lower right-hand side. All you had to do was set up the beginning and ending points and turn on motion tweening, and Macromedia Flash MX did the rest.

12. In the **Timeline**, click anywhere between the two keyframes again to select one of the frames between Frame 1 and Frame 20. You will add a little finesse to the motion tween next.

13. In the **Property Inspector**, choose **CW** for the **Rotate** option. This will make the boarder rotate clockwise (CW) one time during the motion tween.

14. Press **Enter/Return** to preview the motion tween animation again. Now that's a jump!

15. Save this file and leave it open. You will need it for the next exercise.

MOVIE | moTween1.mov

To see a movie of making this motion tween, play **moTween1.mov**, which is located in the **movies** folder on the **H•O•T CD-ROM**.

2. ─────────────**Tweening Effects**

Surprisingly, a motion tween isn't used solely for tweening motion, as its name implies; you can also tween the alpha, tint, brightness, size, position, and skew of a Graphic symbol. The next exercise will show you how. This technique will open the door for you to create a wide range of animated effects— far beyond simply moving an object from one location to another.

1. You should have the file open from the previous exercise. If you closed it, open the **motionTween.fla** file from the **chap_07** folder.

2. Make sure the **Playhead** is over the last frame in the Timeline, **Frame 20**.

3. Select the **boarder** graphic on the **Stage** by clicking on it.

4. In the **Property Inspector (Window > Properties)**, set the **Color Styles** to **Brightness**. Drag the **Brightness** slider up and down and see what effect it has on the instance of the boarder. See how the boarder gets brighter and darker? Set it at **100%**. This will change the brightness of the symbol instance on Frame 20 to 100 percent, or completely white.

Tip: If you already know the percentage you want, you can also simply type it in the window next to the slider rather than using the slider to adjust the brightness of your symbol.

5. Preview the animation by clicking on the **Stage** and then pressing **Enter/Return** on the keyboard. Notice that the boarder animation starts out black and progressively turns to the new color, white.

You just changed the instance of the boarder on the last keyframe but left the first keyframe of your animation unaltered. Since you had motion tweening turned on for this animation, Macromedia Flash MX automatically redrew all of the frames in between the two keyframes to accommodate the changes you made. This technique will carry through not only to brightness but to all of the effects that I mentioned at the beginning of this exercise, such as alpha and tint.

6. Move your **Playhead** to **Frame 1**.

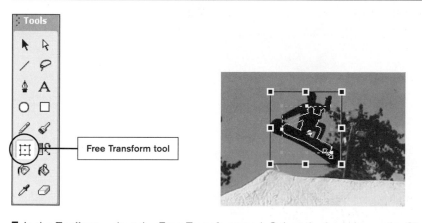

Free Transform tool

7. In the **Toolbox**, select the **Free Transform** tool. Select the **boarder** on the **Stage** by clicking on it. You will see the Free Transform tool's bounding box around the boarder. Click on one of the corner handles, and drag diagonally inward to decrease the size of the boarder. **Note:** Holding down the Shift key while you drag will maintain the original aspect ratio of the image.

8. In the **Timeline**, click on **Frame 20** in the **motionTween** layer.

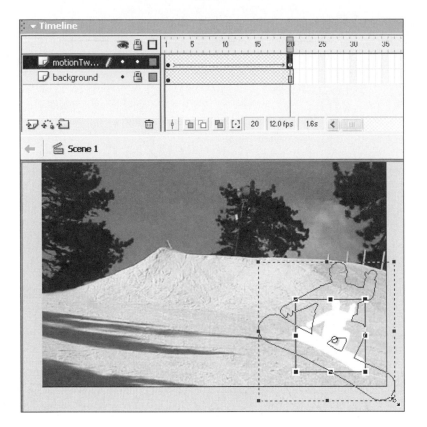

9. Using the **Free Transform** tool, this time click on one of the corner handles and drag diagonally outward to increase the size of the boarder. **Note:** Holding down the Shift key while you drag will maintain the original aspect ratio of the image.

10. Press **Enter/Return** on your keyboard again to see the changes you've made. Now your boarder starts off smaller and gets larger as it moves toward the right-hand side of the Stage. At the same time that the size is tweening, the brightness of your boarder is also changing as it moves! You are now tweening the brightness and scale (not to mention the position) in a motion tween.

11. Go ahead and experiment by making more changes using the **Free Transform** tool to either the first or last keyframe of the motion tween, and see how it changes the animation.

12. When you are finished, save and close this file. You will not be needing it anymore.

3. ——————————Editing Multiple Frames

Suppose you created a motion tween but then decided you would rather have the animation occur across the bottom of the Stage rather than the top. Can you imagine repositioning the items one frame at a time? With the **Edit Multiple Frames** feature, you can bypass that tedious work. The following exercise will show you a method to move the entire animation—including the first and last keyframes—simultaneously.

1. Open the file named **editMultipleFrames.fla** from the **chap_07** folder. This file contains one layer with a background image.

Tip: If you can't see the whole background image, choose View > Magnification > Show All to see the whole image.

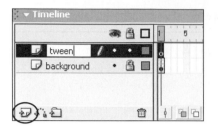

2. In the **Timeline**, click on the **Insert Layer** button to add a new layer to the Timeline. Double-click on the **Layer 2** name, and rename this layer **tween**.

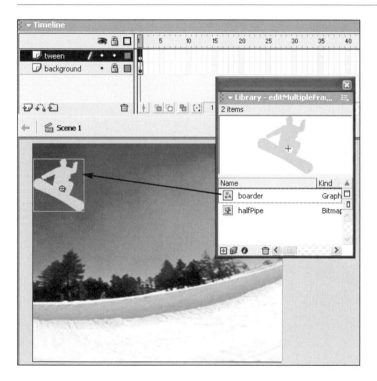

3. Open the **Library** for this movie by pressing **F11**. Click on the **boarder** in the Library and drag it to the upper left corner of the sky in the background image on the **Stage**, as shown in the picture above. This is where the boarder is going to start its animation.

4. Select **Frame 15** and press **F6** to add a keyframe. This will copy the contents of Frame 1 to Frame 15.

5. Select **Frame 15** on the **background** layer and press **F5** to add frames to that layer too. This way, the background image will be visible throughout the motion tween.

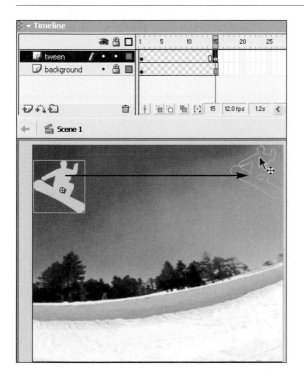

6. Making sure that the **Playhead** is still over **Frame 15**, drag the **boarder** to the right side of the **Stage** in the sky. This will serve as the end point for your animation.

7. In the **Timeline**, click anywhere between the two keyframes to select one of the frames between Frame 1 and Frame 15.

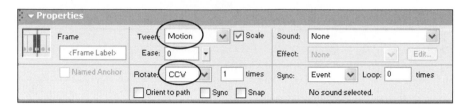

8. In the **Property Inspector**, from the **Tween** drop-down menu, choose **Motion**. Set the **Rotate** option to **CCW**. This will make the boarder rotate counterclockwise (CCW) one time during the motion tween.

9. Press **Enter/Return** on the keyboard to preview the motion tween. Notice that it looks good, but perhaps the animation should occur in the snow rather than in the sky. You will change this next.

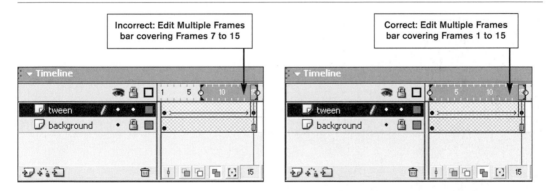

10. Turn on the **Edit Multiple Frames** feature by clicking the **Edit Multiple Frames** button (located in the status bar of the Timeline).

Note: When you click the Edit Multiple Frames button, you'll see a dark bar appear at the top of the Timeline that looks identical to the Onion Skinning bar, which you learned about in Chapter 4, "Animation Basics." Don't be fooled by the similarities, though. Editing multiple frames is quite different from Onion Skinning. When working with Onion Skinning, the Onion Skinning bar represents the range of frames you are seeing at the same time on your Stage. With Edit Multiple Frames, however, the bar represents the range of keyframes you will be editing at the same time.

Incorrect: Edit Multiple Frames bar covering Frames 7 to 15

Correct: Edit Multiple Frames bar covering Frames 1 to 15

11. Position the starting point and ending point of the dark bar (representing your Edit Multiple Frames range) to span from **Frame 1** to **Frame 15**. If either the starting point or ending point is not over the correct frame, click and drag the bar over the correct frame. By doing this, you are defining which keyframes you are going to edit simultaneously.

In the following steps, you will be moving your entire animation to the bottom part of the Stage, so you want to make sure all of the frames are covered by the Edit Multiple Frames bar. Since your animation is composed of two keyframes (Frame 1 and Frame 15), these are the frames that you want the bar to cover.

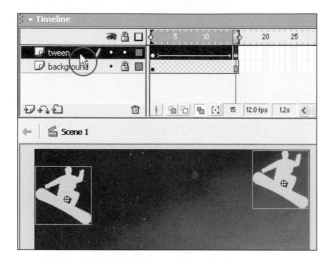

12. Click to the right of the **tween** layer name (in the place shown circled above) to select the entire layer. The layer will turn black in the Timeline when you do. Notice that you can see the boarder on the first keyframe and the boarder on the last keyframe. Unlike Onion Skinning, however, you won't see ghosted representations of all of the frames in between the two keyframes. Also notice that both boarders are selected (they have a turquoise border around them), which means that you can move them together at one time.

13. Click on either one of the boarders on the **Stage** and drag downward. Notice that as you drag, both boarders move.

14. Turn off Edit Multiple Frames by clicking the **Edit Multiple Frames** button again.

It's very important that you turn off Edit Multiple Frames once you have completed your task. If you leave Edit Multiple Frames turned on and continue to work in your movie, Macromedia Flash MX will become confused as to which frame you're working in, and your movie will produce unexpected results. If you do make this mistake, remember, by default you have 100 undo's available to you!

---

15. Preview the animation by pressing **Enter/Return** on your keyboard. Now the whole animation has been moved to the bottom of the Stage and the boarder is moving across the snow rather than in the air!

Note: The Edit Multiple Frames feature is a great technique to use when you need to move the contents of many frames all at once. It is also the only way to move an entire animation together at one time.

---

16. Save this file and close it. You won't need it again.

---

4. ——————Using a Motion Guide

This exercise shows you how to create a motion tween using a **Motion Guide**. A Motion Guide is a type of layer on which you can draw a path. This type of Guide layer allows the symbol used in the motion tween to follow the path, rather than traveling a straight line between two keyframes. This is the only way in Macromedia Flash MX to make a motion tween follow a curved path, so it is an important technique to understand.

1. Open **motionGuideFinal.fla** from your **chap_07** folder. This file is a finished version of the file you are about to create. Choose **Control > Test Movie** to view the movie (.swf) file. Notice how the snowflake moves from side to side in a downward direction before reaching the bottom of the screen. Using a Motion Guide, you will create this same effect next.

2. When you are finished, close the preview window and then close the project file.

3. Now open **motionGuide.fla** from your **chap_07** folder. Notice that this file contains one layer with the background image. You'll be adding the falling snowflake in the following steps.

4. In the **Timeline**, click the **Insert Layer** button to add a new layer to the Timeline. Double-click on the **Layer 2** name and rename this layer **flake**.

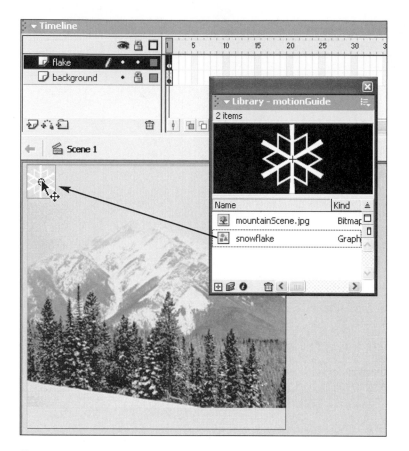

5. If the **Library** is not open, press **F11** to open it, and drag an instance of the **snowflake** symbol onto the **Stage** in the top left corner. This will be the beginning of the animation. You can then close the Library by pressing **F11**.

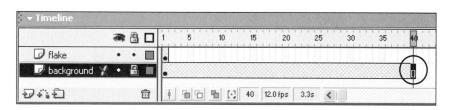

6. In the **Timeline**, click on **Frame 40** of the **background** layer and press **F5** to add frames up to Frame 40. This will make sure the background shows throughout your animation, which you will create next.

7. On the **flake** layer, click on **Frame 40** and press **F6** to add a new keyframe. Make sure the **Playhead** is over **Frame 40**, and then click on the **snowflake** instance and drag it to the lower right corner of the screen. This will serve as the end point of the animation.

8. On the **Timeline**, click anywhere between Frame 1 and Frame 40 to select a frame between the two keyframes. In the **Property Inspector**, select **Motion** from the **Tween** drop-down menu. Press **Enter/Return** to test the motion tween animation.

You just created a simple motion tween like the one you built in Exercise 1 of this chapter. Now you will learn some techniques to enhance a basic motion tween.

Click here to select the layer

Click here to add a Motion Guide

9. Select the **flake** layer by clicking to the right of the layer name. Next, click the **Add Motion Guide** button once—it's at the bottom of the **Timeline**, to the right of the Insert Layer button. This will add a Motion Guide layer to the flake layer. This new layer has automatically been named Guide: flake.

Notice the icon in front of the Guide layer. This icon is visual feedback that this layer is now a Guide layer. Something else has happened that you haven't seen before: The flake layer is indented below the Guide layer. This means that the flake layer is taking instructions from the Guide layer. The flake layer contains your motion tween, and the Guide layer will contain the trail or path that the tween will follow. Before it can follow the path, however, you will have to draw one. That's coming up soon, so keep following along.

10. Lock the **flake** layer so that you don't accidentally put anything on it. You can do this by clicking on the small **dot** below the **Lock** icon on the **flake** layer (the dot turns into a lock).

11. Select the **Guide: flake** layer by clicking once to the right of the layer name. The layer should turn black.

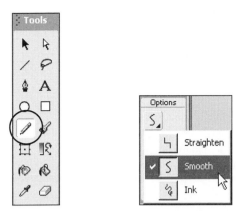

12. In the **Toolbox**, select the **Pencil** tool and, for the **Pencil Mode** option, choose **Smooth**. That way, when you draw the line for the snowflake to follow, Macromedia Flash MX will smooth out any irregularities for you.

13. On the **Stage**, draw a curved line to serve as the trail that the snowflake will follow (as shown above). It doesn't matter what color or stroke width you choose. Macromedia Flash MX is concerned only with the path of the line.

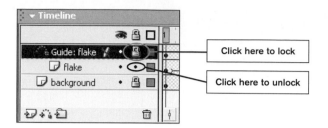

14. Unlock the **flake** layer by clicking on the **Lock** icon (so you can make changes to it), and lock the **Guide: flake** layer by clicking on the **dot** (because you're done with it and you don't want to move or edit it accidentally).

15. Move the **Playhead** so that it is over **Frame 1**. Using the **Arrow** tool, click the little **plus** sign inside the circle in the middle of the **snowflake** instance—this is the Registration Point, as you learned in Chapter 6, "*Symbols and Instances*." Click and drag the **snowflake** to the top point of the line that you drew in the Guide layer. When you get close to the line, the snowflake will "snap" to it and the Registration Point will turn into a small circle. This is where the snowflake will start following the line.

Note: *It is very important that you grab the snowflake symbol instance from the Registration Point in order for the Motion Guide to work properly. You will know if you have done this correctly if the Registration Point turns into a circle, as shown above.*

16. Move the **Playhead** to **Frame 40**, the last keyframe of the animation. Again, click the Registration Point of the **snowflake** symbol instance, and drag the snowflake to the bottom point of the line that you drew on the Guide layer. This is where the snowflake will stop following the line. That's it!

---

17. Preview your animation by pressing **Enter/Return** on your keyboard. Notice that the snowflake now follows the line that you drew on the Guide layer! Now choose **Control > Test Movie**. Notice that now you don't see the line at all! That is because the contents of your Motion Guide layer will not be visually exported to the final movie (.swf) file, but your snowflake will still continue to follow the path. When you choose **Test Movie**, Macromedia Flash MX creates the .swf file for you.

Wouldn't it be nice if the snowflake rotated in the direction of its movement, instead of always facing in the same direction? In other words, if the snowflake is moving down, it should be pointing down, don't you think? You're going to do that next.

---

18. Click on **Frame 1** of the **flake** layer. In the **Property Inspector**, click on the **check box** next to **Orient to path**. This option does what its name implies. When it is selected, Macromedia Flash MX will do its best to orient the snowflake to face in the direction that the path is going.

19. To make the snowflake start off slow and the gradually speed up as it follows the path, move the **Ease** slider to **-50**.

TIP | Easing In and Easing Out

The terms **easing in** and **easing out** have to do with the speed of animation. If you leave the Ease setting at its default of None, animation in Macromedia Flash MX will occur in a **linear motion**, meaning that all the frames will move at the same speed. Easing out means that the animation gradually slows to the last keyframe. Easing in means that the animation gradually speeds up to the last keyframe.

---

20. Preview your animation again by pressing **Enter/Return** on your keyboard.

Just by selecting one check box, you've caused Macromedia Flash MX to point the snowflake symbol instance in the direction that the path is moving, as though the wind was blowing it along. Altering the speed of the snowflake and adjusting the amount of easing have also given a more realistic feel to the snowflake's movement. This is a great (and easy) way to add the visual effect that your graphic is actually following the path.

21. Save and close this file. You won't be using it again.

5. ————————— Exploding Text

In this exercise, you will create the effect of a word exploding on the screen. In the process, you'll get to practice creating a symbol from text, breaking apart the letters, and distributing them to layers.

1. Open the **explodeFinal.fla** file from the **chap_07** folder.

2. Choose **Control > Test Movie** to test the animation. The words explode before your eyes! When you are finished previewing, close the file. You will create this animation next.

3. Open the **explode.fla** file from the **chap_07** folder. This starter file was created for you; it has a red background, and the frame rate has been set to 20 frames per second.

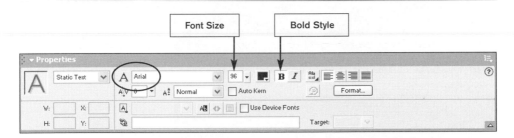

4. Select the **Text** tool from the **Toolbox**. In the **Property Inspector**, set the **Font** to **Arial**, set the **Font Size** to **96**, and select **Bold**.

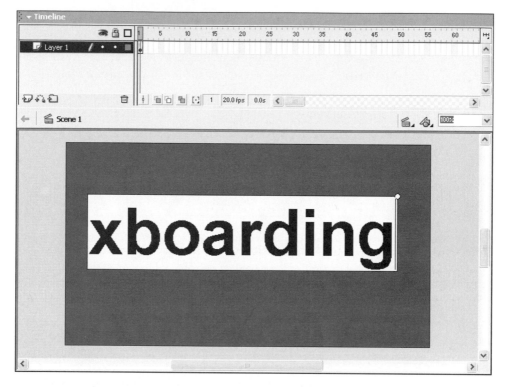

5. Click anywhere on the **Stage** and type the word **xboarding**.

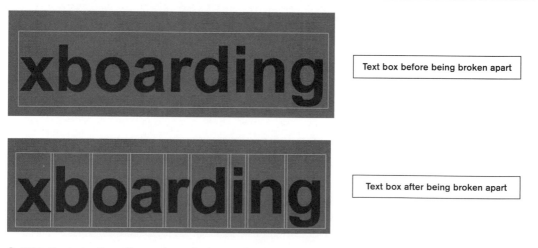

Text box before being broken apart

Text box after being broken apart

6. With the text, **xboarding**, selected, choose **Modify > Break Apart**. This will break the text box into nine individual text boxes, one box for each letter.

7. With all nine text boxes still selected, choose **Modify > Distribute to Layers**. This will place each letter on a separate layer. This step is important because in order to create the effect of many motion tweens occurring at once, each tween must reside on its own layer. Likewise, each symbol (which you will create next) must reside on a separate layer.

---

8. Switch to the **Arrow** tool and click anywhere off the Stage to deselect all nine letters. Using the Arrow tool, select the **x**. Press **F8** to convert the letter **x** into a symbol. In the **Symbol Properties** dialog box, name the symbol **x** and set **Behavior** to **Graphic**. Click **OK**.

NOTE | Motion Tweening Text

You don't have to convert a regular text block to a symbol in order to use it as the artwork for a motion tween. However, you are limited in the effects that you can apply to text boxes. With a text block, you can animate the position and scale, rotation, skew, and flip. However, with a Graphic symbol with text inside, you can animate Color Styles such as color, brightness, alpha, and tint. With a symbol, you have more options for creating effects in your motion tween than you have using a regular text block.

---

9. Using the **Arrow** tool, select the **b**. Press **F8** to convert the letter **b** into a symbol. In the **Symbol Properties** dialog box, name the symbol **b** and set the **Behavior** option to **Graphic**. Click **OK**.

---

10. Repeat step **9** seven more times to make seven more symbols: **o, a, r, d, i, n,** and **g**. You can name the symbols **o, a, r, d, i, n,** and **g**, respectively, in the **Symbol Properties** dialog box.

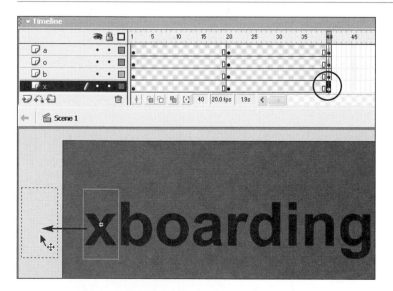

11. On the **Timeline** click on **Frame 20** and drag your cursor down over all nine layers that have a symbol on them. Then press **F6** on the keyboard. This technique will add a keyframe to Frame 20 on all nine layers at once! **Tip:** To view all the layers at the same time, click and drag down on the bottom bar (circled above) of the Timeline.

12. Add a keyframe on **Frame 40** of all nine layers in the same way you did in the previous step. This is where the letters are going to finish their animation.

13. Click anywhere off the Stage to deselect all the symbols. Making sure the **Playhead** is over **Frame 40**, click and drag the **x** symbol off the left side of the **Stage** onto the **work area**. When the **x** explodes, it will end up in this position.

14. In the **Toolbox**, select the **Free Transform** tool. Use this tool to rotate and scale the **x** symbol. The degree of the rotation and scale are completely up to you.

15. Make sure the **Property Inspector** is visible; if it is not, choose **Window > Properties**. In the **Color Styles** box, choose **Alpha** and set the amount to **0%**. I recommend keeping the Alpha setting at 0% on the last keyframe. That way, the **x** will fade out completely as the word "xboarding" explodes into space.

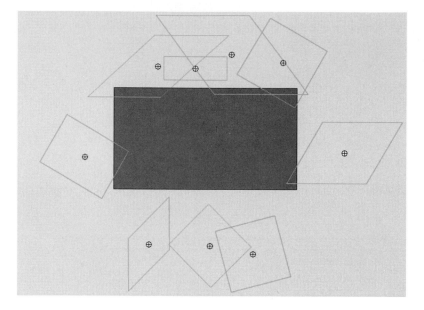

16. Modify the positions of the other Graphic symbols on **Frame 40** as you did in the previous step, scaling, rotating, and adding an alpha effect to each one. Feel free to move the symbols and then use the Free Transform tool to scale, rotate, or even flip and skew each letter in any way you want, but I recommend keeping the Alpha setting at 0%. In the screen shot above, I've selected all of them so that you can see the variety of positions you can choose.

17. Click anywhere between Frames 20 and 40 on the **g** layer and drag down to the **x** layer to select all the layers on that frame. Using the **Property Inspector**, choose **Motion** from the **Tween** drop-down menu. This will add a motion tween to all the layers at once! Nice workflow shortcut, don't you think?

Next you'll use easing to make the explosion look more realistic.

18. Click and drag down to select **Frame 20** on all nine layers.

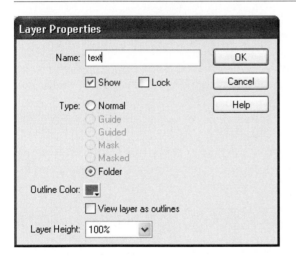

19. In the **Property Inspector**, drag the **Ease** slider up until it reads **80 Out**. Adding easing to the motion tween will cause the animation to start off fast and then slow down as it nears the end of the animation.

---

20. That's it! Choose **Control > Test Movie**, or use the shortcut **Ctrl+Enter** (Windows) or **Cmd+Return** (Mac) to preview the animation.

You are almost done. Just a little housekeeping left to do ....

---

21. In the **Timeline**, double-click to the left of the **Layer 1** name to open the **Layer Properties** dialog box. Name the layer **text** and set the **Type** option to **Folder**. This will turn the layer into a Layer Folder. You learned about Layer Folders in Chapter 5, "*Shape Tweening.*"

---

22. In the **Timeline**, click to the right of the **x** layer name, and then Shift+click to the right of the **g** layer name to select all the layers. Drag the layers on top of the **text** Layer Folder to place the layers inside the folder. **Tip:** If you can't see all the layers, click and drag down on the bottom of the Timeline to reveal them.

23. Click the arrow to the left of the **Layer Folder** icon to collapse the folder. Much better—everything is neat and put away now!

24. You can save and close this file. You will not need it again.

Motion Tweening Options and Limitations

There are many additional options for creating animation using motion tweens. For your reference, here is a list of the things that motion tweening can and can't do.

What Motion Tweening Can Do

Symbol Instances

- Tween position
- Tween brightness
- Tween tint
- Tween alpha
- Tween scaling
- Tween rotation
- Tween skew

Grouped Objects

- Tween position
- Tween scaling
- Tween rotation
- Tween skew
- Tween a text block (editable text)

What Motion Tweening Can't Do

- Tween a shape
- Tween broken-apart text
- Tween multiple items on the same layer

This chapter has taught you how to use symbols to create motion tween animations. You learned that motion tweening can produce many different effects beyond simply moving a symbol from one location to another. The exercises showed you how to use motion tweening to animate scale, rotation, tint, and alpha. You also learned how to create a Motion Guide and make text appear as though it were exploding! That was a lot! Take a break and then get ready for the next chapter, "Bitmaps."

8.

Bitmaps

Benefits of Bitmaps	Compression
Importing and Compressing Bitmaps	Importing Bitmap Sequences
Converting Bitmaps to Vectors	Basic Masking
Animated Masks	Breaking Apart Bitmaps	Stroking a Bitmap
Combining Bitmaps and Vectors

chap_o8

Macromedia Flash MX
H•O•T CD-ROM

So far, although you have used bitmap images as background images in several of the exercise files, you've mostly worked with vector images. Although many people think of Macromedia Flash MX as simply a vector-editing and animation program, you will soon learn that it has some pretty impressive bitmap-editing features as well. This chapter concentrates on bitmap files, examining how Macromedia Flash MX treats them differently from vectors. You will learn how to import bitmaps and how to optimize them. You'll also learn the art of breaking apart bitmaps to edit or crop them, and how to create a static and animated mask of a bitmap. At the end of this chapter, you will learn how to create neat animation effects using bitmaps, including how to convert them to vectors.

Benefits of Bitmaps

Vector graphics are probably best known for their crisp appearance, small file size, and flexibility in scaling. Their efficient file size makes your movie play faster and your site visitors happier. However, vectors do have a few negative aspects. Complex vector artwork made up of many individual vector shapes can actually generate large files. Also, many photographs do not look good as vector artwork. In these cases, you'll want to work with a bitmap file. Bitmap graphics (also known as raster graphics) are stored in the computer as a series of values, with each pixel taking a set amount of memory. Because each pixel is defined individually, this format is great for photographic images with complex details. This also means that bitmap graphics typically have a larger file size than vector graphics.

Conveniently, Macromedia Flash MX has the ability to import graphics of many different formats, including JPEG, GIF, and TIFF. If you have QuickTime 4 or later installed on your machine, the list of files available for import increases even further. A chart listing the bitmap file formats that can be imported into Macromedia Flash MX is given below. For a chart describing the vector file types supported by Macromedia Flash MX, see Chapter 18, "*Integration*."

Bitmap File Types				
File Type	**Extension**	**Windows**	**Mac**	**QuickTime 4 or Later Needed?**
Bitmap	.bmp	x	x	No with Windows, yes with Mac
GIF and animated GIF	.gif	x	x	No
JPEG	.jpg	x	x	No
PICT	.pct, .pict, .pic	x	x	Yes with Windows, no with Mac
PNG	.png	x	x	No
MacPaint	.pntg	x	x	Yes
Photoshop	.psd	x	x	Yes
QuickTime Image	.qtif	x	x	Yes
Silicon Graphics	.sai	x	x	Yes
TGA	.tgf	x	x	Yes
TIFF	.tif, .tiff	x	x	Yes

Note: Macromedia Flash MX will honor the transparency settings of graphics that can have a transparency applied, such as .gif, .png, and .pict files.

Compression in Macromedia Flash MX

One of the most important issues to keep in mind when working with bitmap files is that unless you tell it otherwise, Macromedia Flash MX will always apply its own default compression settings to your bitmap graphics when the movie is exported from the project file. The graphics compression settings are available in two locations. You can set a single compression method and amount for every graphic in the project using the global **Publish settings** (covered in Chapter 16, "*Publishing and Exporting*"), or you can use the **Bitmap Properties dialog box** to set and preview individual compression settings for each file. Any changes you make in the Bitmap Properties dialog box will affect the graphic in the Library and *all* the instances of the bitmap within the project file.

| Lossy (JPEG) compression | Lossless (PNG/GIF) compression |

In the following exercise, you will learn how to compress bitmap images by changing the compression settings in the Bitmap Properties dialog box. There are two different choices for compression: Photo (JPEG), also known as **lossy**, or **Lossless** (PNG/GIF). Generally, an image that is photographic in content will compress better with lossy (JPEG) compression, and images that have a lot of solid colors will compress better as lossless (PNG/GIF). What's nice is that you'll be able to see a preview within this dialog box to determine which choice is best.

When Macromedia Flash MX outputs your finished movie, it takes this individual image compression into account and overrides its default compression settings.

I. ——————— Importing and Compressing Bitmaps

This first exercise will teach you how to import a bitmap into Macromedia Flash MX and then how to adjust its compression settings.

1. Copy the **chap_08** folder from the **Macromedia Flash MX H•O•T CD-ROM** to your hard drive. You must copy the files to your hard drive if you want to save changes to them.

2. Open a new document in Macromedia Flash MX. Save the file as **import.fla** in the **chap_08** folder.

The import dialog box using Windows.   *The import dialog box using a Mac.*

3. Choose **File > Import** or press **Ctrl+R** (Windows) or **Cmd+R** (Mac). This will open the **Import** dialog box. Browse to the **import1.jpg** file located inside the **chap_08** folder. Select the file, and click **Open**.

Note: The file import1.jpg may or may not have the .jpg extension, depending on which platform you are using (Windows or Mac) and whether you have the extensions turned on or off, as shown in the screen shots above. Either way is fine, since the file name, import1, is what is important to locate this file. See the Introduction to learn how to hide or reveal the file name extensions.

When you add a bitmap file to your project using the Import dialog box, you might wonder where the file goes. The file is automatically placed in two locations: on the Stage and in the Library.

4. Press **F11** to open the **Library** window.

5. Select the **import1** image inside the **Library**. Click the **Properties** button at the bottom of the Library window. The **Bitmap Properties** dialog box will open.

TIP | Additional Ways to See the Bitmap Properties

In this exercise, you use the Properties button in the Library window to display the Bitmap Properties dialog box. There are three additional ways to access this dialog box.

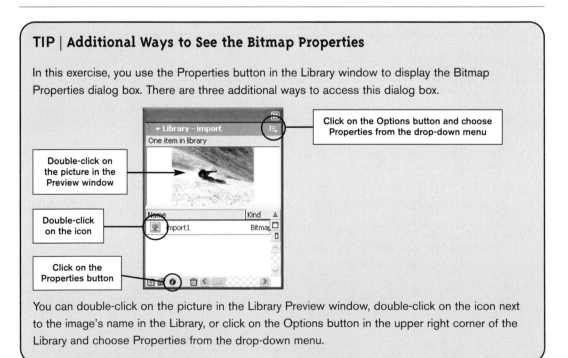

You can double-click on the picture in the Library Preview window, double-click on the icon next to the image's name in the Library, or click on the Options button in the upper right corner of the Library and choose Properties from the drop-down menu.

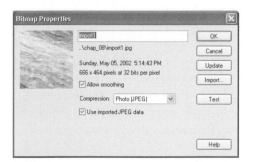

The Bitmap Properties dialog box is where you can set compression for individual images. A chart that describes all of the settings in this dialog box is located at the end of this exercise.

6. In the **Bitmap Properties** dialog box, move your cursor over the **Preview** window. Notice that your cursor changes to a hand. Click and drag the picture until you see the snowboarder in the Preview window. This will give you a much better view of the compression changes you are about to make.

7. Set the **Compression** option to **Lossless (PNG/GIF)** and click the **Test** button. Notice that the new compression information appears at the bottom of the dialog box. You have just changed the compression settings for the **import1** image. The new compressed image size is 791.6 KB, compared to the original, which was 1236.1 KB. If you click OK, this setting will alter the bitmap in the Library and the instance on the Stage. However, don't click OK just yet—you are going to make a couple more changes.

NOTE | Why Is File Size Important?

As you build project files in Macromedia Flash MX, you may have to keep your total .swf file size below a certain number, or you may have to keep all imported files under a certain file size so that playback is optimal for all users viewing a Web site, including people using dial-up connections. With this in mind, it is important to find a good balance between image quality (check the Preview window after you click the Test button) and file size. You may have to experiment with several settings, but the file-size savings will be well worth the time spent!

---

8. In the **Bitmap Properties** dialog box, change the **Compression** setting back to JPEG by choosing **Photo (JPEG)**. **Uncheck** the **Use imported JPEG data** check box, and add your own quality setting by typing **80** (100 is best, while 0 is worst) in the **Quality** box. Click the **Test** button again. Notice that the new compression information appears at the bottom of the dialog box. The new compressed image size is 70.3 KB, significantly smaller than the size obtained using PNG/GIF compression, which was 791.6 KB. Additionally, the image still looks great in the Preview window.

---

9. Click **OK** to keep the last settings you applied.

---

10. Save and close this file.

Bitmap Properties Dialog Box	
Option	**Description**
Preview window	Shows the current properties of the bitmap and allows you to preview any changes applied to the settings in the dialog box.
File Name	Displays the bitmap's Library item name. Clicking in the File Name field and typing a new name will change the bitmap's name.
Image path	Displays the path for the image.
File information	Shows the date the bitmap was last modified, the file's dimensions, and the color depth.
Allow smoothing	Smoothes or dithers the image when checked. If this box is unchecked, the image will appear aliased or jagged.
Compression	Allows you to choose between Photo (JPEG) or Lossless (PNG/GIF) for that particular bitmap in the Library. Photo compression is best used for complex bitmaps with many colors or gradations. Lossless compression is best used for bitmaps with fewer colors and simple shapes filled with single colors.
Use imported JPEG data (Use Document Default Quality)	Allows you to use the original compression settings and avoid double compression when checked. If this box is not checked, you can enter your own values—between 1 and 100—for the quality of the image.
Update	Allows you to update the bitmap image if it has been changed outside of Macromedia Flash MX. It uses the image path to track the original image's location and will update the image selected in the Library with the file located in the original location.
Import	Enables you to change the actual file the image path points to. Clicking this button will change the current image to the new file chosen, and all instances in the project file will reflect the new bitmap.
Test	Allows you to see the changes you make to the settings of the Bitmap Properties dialog box in the Preview window and displays the new compression information at the bottom of the dialog box.

2.——————————**Importing Bitmap Sequences**

One way to create a "mock" video effect in Macromedia Flash MX is to use a sequence of photographs in which each image is just slightly different from the previous image. When these images are placed in keyframes, one right after another, and you test the movie, it will appear as if the camera is rolling! The following exercise demonstrates Macromedia Flash MX's ability to create frame-by-frame animations (or mock video) by importing a series of bitmap graphics all at once.

1. Open **bitmapSequenceFinal.fla** in the **chap_08** folder.

2. You will see a series of images in Frames 1 through 14. Press **Enter/Return** on the keyboard to preview the movie. It seems as though you are watching a video of a snowboarder making a jump. You will create this animation sequence next.

3. Close the file.

4. Open the **bitmapSequence.fla** file from the **chap_08** folder. This is a blank file with a black background.

5. Choose **File > Import** or press **Ctrl+R** (Windows) or **Cmd+R** (Mac). In the **chap_08** folder, open the **sequence** folder. Notice that there are 14 numbered files named **bigair--xx**. Select the file **bigair--01** and click **Open** (Windows) or **OK** (Mac).

6. Macromedia Flash MX will automatically detect that the image you are trying to import is part of a sequence of images, and you will be asked if you want to import the whole series of images. Click **Yes** to import all of the images into Macromedia Flash MX.

If you ever want to import a sequence of images as successive frames and have Macromedia Flash MX recognize it as sequence, be sure to number the images in the order you want the sequence to appear, such as image01, image02, etc. Whenever Macromedia Flash MX sees sequentially numbered images in the same folder, it will ask you whether the images should all be imported at once in a sequence.

When you clicked Yes in the last step, Macromedia Flash MX will import all 14 files in the sequence, place them on the Stage, and create a new keyframe for each one in the Timeline. Pretty suave! Notice that the imported images are not centered on the Stage. Why? By default, Macromedia Flash MX will place the imported sequence in the upper left corner of the Stage. You will change this next.

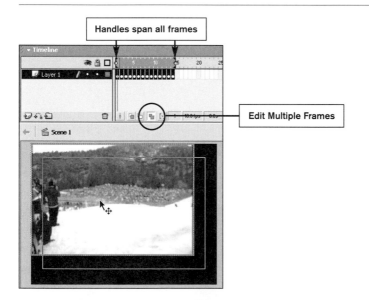

7. In the **Status Bar** on the **Main Timeline**, click the **Edit Multiple Frames** button. Make sure that the Edit Multiple Frames bar in the Timeline spans all the frames. If it doesn't, drag the handles so that it covers all 14 frames. Click to the right of the layer name to select all the frames on the layer. Next, click and drag the bitmap image into the center of the **Stage**. This allows you to reposition all the frames at once.

8. Test the movie (**Control > Test Movie**). Notice that even though each frame holds a separate image, when you test the movie, it appears that you're watching video footage! When you are finished, close the Preview Window.

Note: If your movie doesn't look very realistic, you can make a change that will fix that. You will do that next.

9. In the **Property Inspector**, type **16** for the **Frame Rate**. This will speed up your movie to make the bitmap sequence animation seem more realistic. Choose **Control > Test Movie** to preview it. When you are finished, close the Preview window. Back in the project file, change the Frame Rate to 6 and preview the movie again. **Tip:** You may have to experiment with the frame rate a few times to make your movie appear the most realistic.

10. When you are satisfied with your movie, save this file and keep it open for the next exercise.

3. ———————————**Converting Bitmaps to Vectors**

When you import bitmaps, you are not limited to using the files as they exist in their original form. You can convert imported bitmaps into vector art by using the **Trace Bitmap** feature. This feature traces the shapes of a bitmap graphic and creates a new set of vector shapes that simulate the appearance of the bitmap file. Trace Bitmap is not an exact science, though; it requires a little experimentation to get it just right. This exercise will teach you how to use this feature to turn a bitmap into a vector.

1. You should still have the **bitmapSequence.fla** file open from the last exercise. Make sure the **Edit Multiple Frames** button is not selected.

2. In **Frame 1**, select the image on the **Stage** and choose **Modify > Trace Bitmap**. This will open the **Trace Bitmap** dialog box. You are going to turn the bitmap into a vector next.

NOTE | What Is Trace Bitmap?

The Trace Bitmap feature allows you to convert imported bitmaps into vector art. You might want to do this to create a neat animation effect, reduce the file size of a photo-graphic image, or zoom into a photographic image during an animation (vectors scale when you magnify them, while bitmaps get blurry). The Trace Bitmap feature traces the outlines and internal shapes of a bitmap graphic and simulates the appearance of the bitmap file by creating a new set of vector shapes. You can use the settings in the Trace Bitmap dialog box to control how closely the new vector shapes match the original image.

---

3. To produce a vector that closely resembles the original bitmap, decrease the **Color Threshold** to **80** and the **Minimum Area** to **5**. For **Curve Fit**, select **Very Tight**, and for the **Corner Threshold**, select **Many corners** to create a vector that has outlines with sharp edges that closely match the original bitmap. Click **OK**.

Be aware that the more detail a bitmap contains and the lower your settings in the Trace Bitmap dialog box, the longer it will take to convert the bitmap to a vector. This can increase the file size of the movie. A reference chart describing all the settings found in the Trace Bitmap dialog box is at the end of this exercise.

| Original bitmap | Vector image after using the Trace Bitmap feature |

4. When the conversion process completes, click anywhere outside of the image to deselect it. Notice that the traced bitmap looks very similar to the original.

Note: When you use the Trace Bitmap function, the changes will affect only the selected image on the Stage. The bitmap in the Library will remain unchanged. When you publish your movie, the vector image will appear instead of the original image.

5. Move the **Playhead** to **Frame 14**. On the **Stage**, select the bitmap on **Frame 14** and choose **Modify > Trace Bitmap** to open the **Trace Bitmap** dialog box. You will modify the last image in the sequence next.

6. In the **Trace Bitmap** dialog box, enter **Color Threshold: 200** and **Minimum Area: 10**. For **Curve Fit**, choose **Very Smooth**, and for the **Corner Threshold**, select **Few Corners**. Click **OK**. This will turn the bitmap into a vector shape that has little detail and does not closely resemble the bitmap.

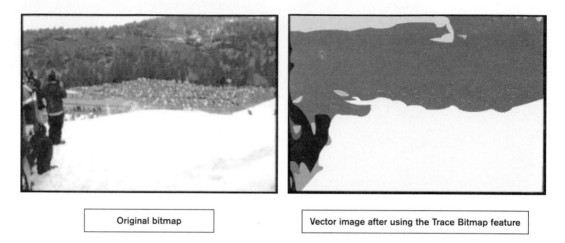

| Original bitmap | Vector image after using the Trace Bitmap feature |

7. When the conversion process completes, you will have an image that is more abstract and does not resemble the original image as closely as the settings you used on the image in Frame 1.

8. Repeat steps 5 through 7, using the **Trace Bitmap** command to trace the remaining 12 images. Go ahead and experiment by applying different settings to each image to see how they change the original image.

Tip: By using the Undo function—Ctrl+Z (Windows) or Cmd+Z (Mac)—you can always return the vector art to the original bitmap version and try it again if you don't like how the new image turned out.

9. When you are finished, choose **Control > Test Movie** to preview the animation. You are now watching vector simulated video footage! This effect produces a stylized version of the video in which the artwork is all vectors. This technique is used often for aesthetic reasons, but a great by-product of it is that the file is often smaller than if you used the bitmap image in its original state. Also, you can zoom into vectors and they remain crisp, while if you scale a bitmap it will look blurry.

10. Save and close the file. You will not need it again in this chapter.

Trace Bitmap Dialog Box	
Option	**Description**
Color Threshold	Sets the amount by which the color of each pixel can vary before it is considered a different color. As the threshold value increases, the number of colors in the image decreases, and the resulting traced bitmap image will have fewer colors than the original. The Color Threshold range is 1 to 500.
Minimum Area	Determines the number of surrounding pixels to consider when calculating the color of a pixel. The Minimum Area range is 1 to 1000.
Curve Fit	Determines how smoothly the outlines in the traced shape are drawn and how closely they match the original image.
Corner Threshold	Determines whether to use sharp edges (**Many corners**) or smoother edges (**Few corners**).

Note: If the desired result of using the Trace Bitmap feature is to conserve file size or create a more abstract image, rather than to match the original image as closely as possible, you can choose a higher Color Threshold, higher Minimum Area, Smooth Curve Fit, and Few Corners. These settings will decrease the final file size.

4. ——————Basic Masking

Masking is another great technique that can be created using bitmaps. A **mask** is a special layer that defines what is visible on the layer below it. Only layers that are beneath the shapes in the mask layer will be visible. This exercise will teach you how to create a text mask that masks a bitmap background. You can also use a mask technique on vector art, but what fun would that be in the bitmap chapter?

1. Open the **mask.fla** file from the **chap_08** folder. This file contains a blue background and one symbol in the Library.

2. Choose **File > Import**. In the **chap_08** folder, double-click the **sideMountain** file to open it (Windows), or double-click the file to add it and then click **Import** (Mac). This places the bitmap on the Stage.

3. In the **Main Timeline**, double-click the **Layer 1** name and rename the layer **mountain**. This layer will become the layer that is masked in the next few steps.

4. Lock the **mountain** layer by clicking on the **dot** under the **Lock** icon for the layer. This way, you won't accidentally move or select the bitmap on the mountain layer.

5. Click the **Insert Layer** button to add a new layer above the **mountain** layer. It's important that the new layer you create is positioned above the mountain layer, so move it there by dragging if it appears below the mountain layer. Name this layer **xboarding** by double-clicking on **Layer 2** and typing the new name.

6. Open the **Library** (**F11**). Notice the symbol named **siteName**. This is a Graphic symbol that has been created for you. Drag an instance of the symbol onto the **Stage** and position the **X** over the snowboarder in the bitmap image, just as you see in the picture above.

This symbol instance of the xboarding.com name is going to end up as the mask for the bitmap. You can think of the text inside the symbol instance as a cookie cutter that will allow you to see what you cut out of the mountain image. **Tip:** *It does not matter what color the mask is—Macromedia Flash MX treats artwork of all colors as a solid mask shape.*

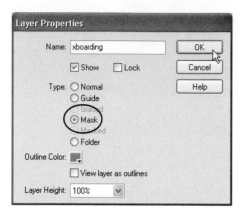

7. Choose **Modify > Layer**. This will open the **Layer Properties** dialog box. For **Type**, select **Mask**. Click **OK**. This will turn the xboarding layer into a Mask layer.

Up to this point, you have a mask layer (xboarding) with a defined mask area. Now you need to create the Masked layer—that is, the layer connected to the Mask layer.

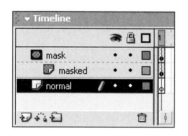

Note: *You can tell whether or not a layer is a mask layer or a masked layer by its icon and indentation. An unmasked (normal) layer has a standard layer icon: a white sheet of paper with the bottom right corner turned up. A mask layer has a blue square with a checkerboard oval inside it, and a masked layer is indented under the mask layer and displays a checkerboard square with the bottom right corner turned up. Additionally, the lines that separate masked layers from the mask layer are dotted rather than solid.*

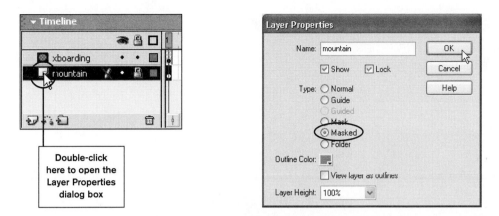

Double-click here to open the Layer Properties dialog box

8. To make the mountain layer become masked by the xboarding mask layer, double-click on the **mountain** layer icon to the left of the **mountain** name. This opens the **Layer Properties** dialog box. For **Type**, select **Masked** and click **OK**. In the Main Timeline, notice that the icon for the mountain layer has changed.

There are two different ways to access the Layer Properties dialog box. You can choose Modify > Layer, as you did in step 7, or you can double-click on the icon next to the layer name, as you did here. Additionally, you can right-click (Windows) or Ctrl+click (Mac) on the layer's name and choose Mask from the drop-down menu, bypassing the Layer Properties dialog box altogether. Any of these options will allow you to declare the layer as a mask, so you can decide which method works better for you!

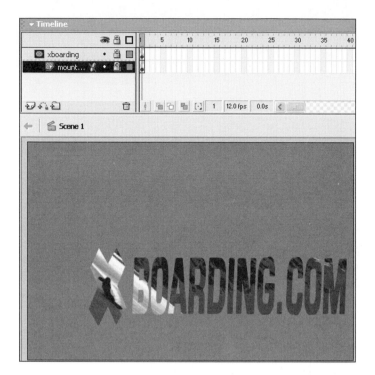

9. Lock the **xboarding** layer so that both layers are locked. You will see the bitmap showing through the text shapes!

Tip: In order to preview what your mask will look like on the Stage, you must have both of the layers locked. To lock the layer, you can either click the Lock column in the layers yourself or right-click (Windows) or Ctrl+click (Mac) on the layer's name and choose Show Masking from the drop-down menu, which will lock both layers for you.

You have just created your first mask! In the next exercise, you are going to animate the mask.

10. Save this file and keep it open for the next exercise.

5. ————————Animated Masks

In the previous exercise, you learned how to create a basic mask out of text. But masks do not have to be static! This exercise will teach you how to create a text mask that moves over a bitmap background.

1. You should still have the **mask.fla** file open from the previous exercise. If you accidentally closed it, open the **mask.fla** file you saved in the **chap_08** folder on your hard drive.

2. On the **xboarding** layer, click on **Frame 20** and press **F6** to add a keyframe.

3. On the **mountain** layer, click on **Frame 20** and press **F5** to add frames.

4. Unlock the **xboarding** layer by clicking on the **Lock** icon. Select the first keyframe and move the **xboarding** symbol instance off the Stage to the left.

5. With the instance still selected in **Frame 1**, choose **Modify > Transform > Flip Vertical**. This will turn the xboarding symbol instance upside down, to serve as the beginning of the mask animation.

6. In the **Timeline**, select one of the frames in the **xboarding** layer between Frame 1 and Frame 20. In the **Property Inspector**, select **Motion** from the **Tween** drop-down menu. This will add a motion tween to the mask.

7. Click on the **Lock** icon to lock the **xboarding** layer. Notice that you can immediately see the masked image on the Stage.

8. Press **Enter/Return** to test your movie. Great job! In just a few steps, you have changed the basic mask from the previous exercise to an animated mask.

9. Save and close this file.

6. _____Breaking Apart Bitmaps

When you import bitmaps, you have many options for how you use the resulting image in your Macromedia Flash MX movie. Often, you may want to use only part of a picture and delete the rest, although with bitmaps, this is not as simple as it sounds. Conveniently, Macromedia Flash MX offers a feature that allows you to convert a bitmap into one simple shape so that you can crop and resize a specific portion of the original bitmap. The following exercise will teach you how to do this.

1. Open the **effectsFinal.fla** file from the **chap_08** folder. This is a finished version of the file you will create over the next three exercises.

2. Choose **Control > Test Movie**, or press **Ctrl+Enter** (Windows) or **Cmd+Return** (Mac) to preview the .swf file. You will see a pencil outline being drawn, the outline being filled with a bitmap that fades in from invisible to visible, and then a background image fading in. In the next three exercises, you will create this effect.

3. Close this file.

4. Open the **breakApart.fla** file from the **chap_08** folder. This is a blank file with a black background that has been created ahead of time to get you started.

5. Choose **File > Import** or press **Ctrl+R** (Windows) or **Cmd+R** (Mac). In the **chap_08** folder, browse to the file named **boarderCloseUp**. Double-click on it to open it (Windows), or double-click on it to add the file to the import list and then click **Import** (Mac). You will see a photo of a snowboarder on the Stage.

Tip: *If you can't see the whole picture, choose View > Magnification > Show All.*

6. In the **Timeline**, rename **Layer 1** to **boarder**.

Original bitmap	Broken-apart bitmap

7. Select the snowboarder bitmap on the **Stage** and choose **Modify > Break Apart**. This option will turn the bitmap into a vector so you can edit it inside Macromedia Flash MX.

Note: Breaking apart a bitmap will affect only the instance on the Stage and not the original in the Library.

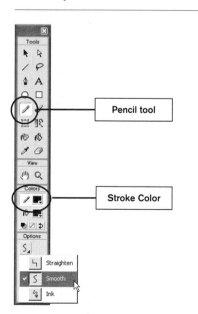

Pencil tool

Stroke Color

8. In the **Toolbox**, select the **Pencil** tool. Make sure the **Stroke Color** is set to **black**, and choose **Smooth** from the **Pencil Mode** options.

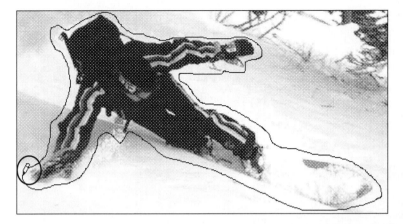

9. Using the **Pencil** tool, draw an outline around the snowboarder similar to the picture above. Make sure that you start and end in the same spot so that the outline is a continuous line, without breaks.

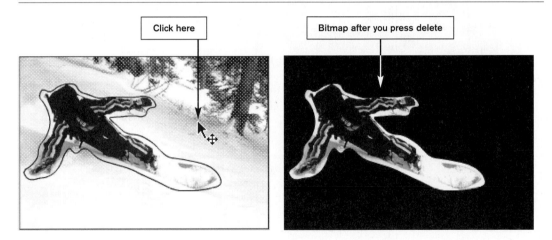

10. Click anywhere off the Stage to deselect the bitmap. Next click on the area outside the outline you drew. This will select the portion of the bitmap that is outside the line. You will see a selection mesh on the image, outside the outline, but notice that there is no selection mesh over the boarder. The mesh indicates the area that has been selected. Press **Delete** on your keyboard. Voila! You have cropped your bitmap!

In this exercise, you were able to crop your bitmap because once a bitmap is broken apart it is considered a shape or a fill. Since a stroke will cut though a fill, as you learned in Chapter 3, you can use a stroke to cut the broken-apart bitmap and then separate the shapes. Neat!

11. Save this file and keep it open for the next exercise.

(7.) ——————————**Stroking a Bitmap**

Once you have broken apart the bitmap, you can use the stroke you drew with the Pencil tool to create some neat animation effects. This exercise will show you how.

1. You should still have the **breakApart.fla** file open from the last exercise.

2. Save this file as **strokeAnim.fla** in the **chap_08** folder.

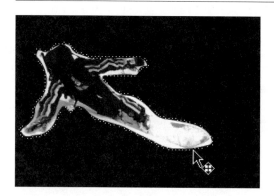

3. Remember the outline you drew around the snowboarder? It is still there—you just can't see it because it is black like the background of the movie. Move your cursor over the edge of the snowboarder shape and click. This will select the outline stroke.

4. In the **Property Inspector**, change the **Stroke Color** to white. Now you will be able to see the stroke better.

5. With the stroke still selected, choose **Edit > Cut**, or press **Ctrl+X** (Windows) or **Cmd+X** (Mac) to cut the stroke out of the frame. You will be pasting the stroke into a different layer in a few steps.

6. In the **Timeline**, lock the **boarder** layer and click the **Insert Layer** button to add a new layer. Rename **Layer 2** to **stroke**. Hide the **boarder** layer by clicking on the **dot** below the **Eye** icon so you can concentrate on the stroke layer for the next few steps.

7. With the **stroke** layer selected, choose **Edit > Paste In Place**. This will position the stroke exactly where it used to be, just in a different frame, so you can work with it separately in the following steps.

Note: Was only part of your outline pasted? If you drew the original outline back in Exercise 6 without selecting the Smooth option for the Pencil mode, or if you drew the outline in several different segments rather than in one continuous segment, you may need to double-click to select all of the outline before you cut it in step 5.

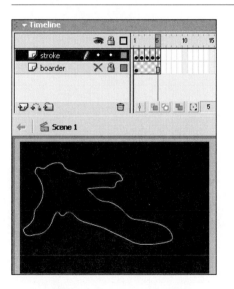

8. Press **F6** four times to add four more keyframes to the **stroke** layer. This will automatically add frames to the boarder layer to match the stroke layer. You are going to create a frame-by-frame animation that simulates a pencil drawing next.

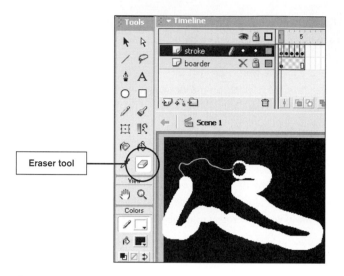

Eraser tool

9. In the **Timeline**, move the **Playhead** back to **Frame 1**. Using the **Eraser** tool, draw over the stroke, leaving only a small portion of the outline, as in the picture above. When you release the mouse, only the portion of the stroke that you did not draw over will remain.

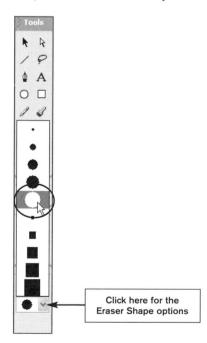

Click here for the Eraser Shape options

Tip: You can change the size of the Eraser tool if you prefer a larger erasing area by clicking on the Eraser Shape drop-down menu.

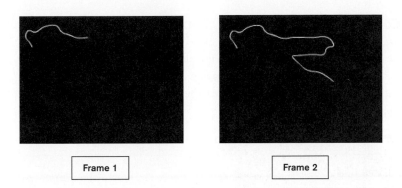

Frame 1	Frame 2

10. Move the **Playhead** back to **Frame 2**. Using the **Eraser** tool again, draw over the stroke in **Frame 2**, but this time allow more of the stroke to remain, as in the picture above. The idea here is to give the illusion that a pencil is drawing the outline, so in each frame, you want to reveal a little more of the outline until you see the full outline in Frame 5.

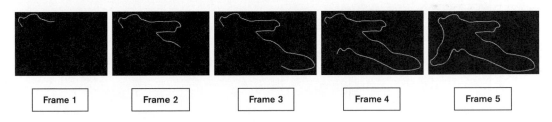

Frame 1	Frame 2	Frame 3	Frame 4	Frame 5

11. Repeat step 10 for Frames 3, 4, and 5, leaving more of the outline each time. When you are finished, the content in each frame should look similar to the pictures above.

12. Press **Enter/Return** on the keyboard to preview the animation. The outline will draw itself.

13. When you are finished, save this file and keep it open for one last exercise.

8. _____ Combining Bitmaps and Vectors

When you are working with bitmaps, you can make them fade in from invisible to visible or vice versa. This handy technique can be accomplished by turning the bitmap into a symbol, creating a motion tween, and applying an alpha to one of the symbols at the end or beginning of the tween. You will learn how to do this in the following steps.

1. You should still have the **strokeAnim.fla** file open from the last exercise.

2. Save this file as **effects.fla** in the **chap_08** folder.

3. Lock the **stroke** layer, and unlock and unhide the **boarder** layer.

You will be creating a motion tween of the boarder changing from invisible to visible in the following steps.

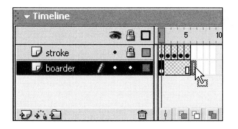

4. On the **boarder** layer, click on **Frame 1** to select it. Next, click and drag **Frame 1** to **Frame 6**. This is how you move frames in the Timeline.

5. Select the **boarder** on the **Stage** and press **F8** to convert the boarder shape to a symbol. In the **Symbol Properties** dialog box, name the symbol **boarder**, and choose **Graphic** for the **Behavior**. Click **OK**. This will be the beginning of the tween animation.

Why am I using a symbol? In the next few steps you will be using alpha to create the fade effect, and you can't apply an alpha effect to an object that is not a Graphic or Movie Clip symbol (which you will learn about in Chapter 10, "Movie Clips").

6. Select **Frame 20** and press **F6** to add a keyframe to Frame 20. This will be the end of the tween animation.

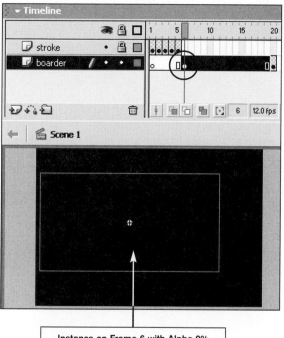

Instance on Frame 6 with Alpha 0%

7. Move the **Playhead** back to **Frame 6** and select the **boarder** symbol instance on the **Stage**. (Be careful to select the instance on the *Stage* and not the *frame* so that the Property Inspector shows you the right attributes.) In the **Property Inspector**, set **Color Style** to **Alpha 0%**.

8. Click anywhere between Frames 6 and 20 to select one of the frames. In the **Property Inspector**, choose **Motion** from the **Tween** drop-down menu.

9. In the **stroke** layer, select **Frame 20** and press **F5** to add frames to match the number of frames on the boarder layer. This will make the outline draw itself and remain visible on the Stage during the tween animation.

10. Press **Enter/Return** on the keyboard to preview the animation. The outline will draw itself, and then the boarder layer will fade from invisible to full color.

You have one more tween animation to create.

11. In the **Timeline**, lock the **boarder** layer and click the **Insert Layer** button to add a new layer. Rename **Layer 3** to **background** and drag it below the **boarder** layer so that it is the bottom layer in the Timeline.

12. Select **Frame 20** and press **F7** to add a blank keyframe to Frame 20 of the **background** layer. Hide the **stroke** and **boarder** layers so that you can see only the background layer for the next few steps.

13. Press **F11** to open the **Library**. Drag an instance of the **boarderCloseUp** bitmap graphic onto the **Stage**.

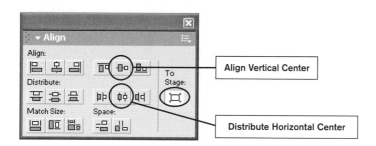

14. Using the **Align** panel, **Ctrl+K** (Windows) or **Cmd+K** (Mac), center the bitmap on the **Stage** by clicking the **To Stage** button and selecting the **Align Vertical Center** and **Distribute Horizontal Center** buttons.

Note: The Align panel allows you to position selected objects relative to the Stage if the To Stage button is selected or relative to one another if several objects are selected.

15. With the snowboarder bitmap still selected on the **Stage**, press **F8** to convert the bitmap to a symbol. In the **Symbol Properties** dialog box, name the symbol **origImage**, and for **Behavior** select **Graphic**. This will convert the bitmap to a symbol so that you can create a motion tween in the following steps.

---

16. Select **Frame 35** and press **F6** to add a keyframe to Frame 35. This will be the end of the tween animation.

---

17. Move the **Playhead** back to **Frame 20** and select the **origImage** symbol instance on the **Stage**. (Be careful to select the instance on the *Stage* and not the *frame* so that the Property Inspector shows you the right attributes.) In the **Property Inspector**, set **Color Style** to **Alpha 0%**. This will be the beginning of the animation on the background layer.

---

18. Click anywhere between Frames 20 and 35 to select one of the frames. In the **Property Inspector**, choose **Motion** from the **Tween** drop-down menu.

19. In the **boarder** layer, select **Frame 35** and press **F5** to add frames to match the number of frames on the background layer. This will make the boarder layer remain visible on the Stage during the background tween animation.

---

20. Click and drag down on **Frame 45** in the **boarder** and **background** layers to select Frame 45 in both layers. Press **F5** to add frames up to Frame 45. This will add frames so that once the background fades up, it will remain for 10 frames before the animation starts over again.

---

21. Press **Enter/Return** on the keyboard to preview the final animation. The outline will draw itself, the boarder layer will fade from invisible to full color, and then the background will fade in. Choose **Control > Test Movie** to see the .swf file all by itself. Great work!

Note: When you press Enter/Return on the keyboard, it is only a preview of the animation inside the editing environment and may not be exactly true to form. A more realistic test of the animation is to choose Control > Test Movie so that you can see the actual .swf file inside the Macromedia Flash Player. In Chapter 16, "Publishing and Exporting," you will learn the most reliable way to see how the file will look in a browser, using the Publish command.

---

22. When you are finished, save and close this file.

That's it! You have conquered another chapter! Take a much-deserved break and get ready to learn about buttons next.

9.

Buttons

| Button States | Button Types |
| Rollover Buttons | Rollover Buttons with Text |
| Duplicating and Aligning Buttons |
| Adding Sound to Buttons | Invisible Buttons |

_____chap_09_____

Macromedia Flash MX
H•O•T CD-ROM

There are three types of symbols in Macromedia Flash MX: Graphic symbols, Button symbols, and Movie Clip symbols. You learned about Graphic symbols in Chapter 6, and this chapter will introduce you to the Button symbol. In the next chapter, you'll learn about Movie Clip symbols.

Buttons are a special type of symbol in Macromedia Flash MX. They can include rollover states and even animated rollover states (which you'll learn about in Chapter 10, "*Movie Clips*"). What you might not realize is that buttons can be programmed to accept "actions" written in ActionScript (covered in Chapter 11, "*ActionScripting Basics*"). But before you can learn how to program the ActionScript for them, you have to learn how to create Button symbols. Learning Macromedia Flash MX involves putting a lot of puzzle pieces together, and Button symbols are an extremely important part of the puzzle. In this chapter, you will build a solid foundation for working with buttons, including how to create, add sound to, test, and preview them.

Button States

When you create or edit a **Button symbol**, you will see that it has its own Timeline, just as Graphic symbols do. The difference with a Button symbol's Timeline is that it displays four frames: **Up**, **Over**, **Down**, and **Hit**. The first three frames of the Button Timeline determine the appearance of the button during three different kinds of mouse interactions. The fourth frame, Hit, determines the clickable area of the button. The terms Up, Over, Down, and Hit are often called **states**, meaning the state of the button interaction. You've already learned that a Timeline must contain keyframes in order to contain changing content. Even though there are slots for the Up, Over, Down, and Hit states, you must insert keyframes in these slots in order to place artwork that changes within each or some of these states.

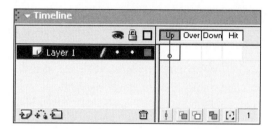

When you create a Button symbol, Macromedia Flash MX automatically adds a blank keyframe in the first frame—the Up state—of the button.

Button States	
State	**Description**
Up	The Up keyframe holds artwork that defines what the button looks like before the user's mouse interacts with the button.
Over	The Over keyframe is what the button looks like when the user positions the mouse over the Hit area of the button. This is also referred to as the **rollover** state of the button.
Down	The Down keyframe defines what the button looks like when it is clicked. This state is usually seen for only a split second, but it can be seen for longer periods of time if the user holds down the mouse.
Hit	The Hit keyframe of the button is always invisible to the user. It defines the area of the button that is reactive to the mouse. This is what makes the button clickable.

Button Types

Fundamentally, all Button symbols are constructed alike. However, you can significantly change their appearance and behavior by altering the frames you use and the keyframes you set to contain artwork. The possibilities are nearly endless, but they will generally fall into the four categories listed in the following chart.

Button Types	
Type	**Description**
Basic Button	A basic button has the same content in the Up, Over, and Down keyframes. Users can click on it, and it can contain actions, but it provides no visual feedback during the user's interaction with it.
Rollover Button	A rollover button has different content in the Up keyframe than in the Over keyframe (and sometimes the Down keyframe). It gives visual feedback about the user's mouse position by changing when the cursor moves over it.
Animated Rollover Button	An animated rollover button is similar to a rollover button, but one or more of its keyframes (usually the Over keyframe) contains a Movie Clip instance. Whenever that keyframe is displayed, a Movie Clip animates. You will learn how to make animated rollover buttons and Movie Clips in the next chapter.
Invisible Button	Invisible buttons contain an empty keyframe in the Up frame and a populated keyframe in the Hit frame. Sometimes they also contain artwork in the Over or Down state, although they never contain artwork in the Up frame, and always contain artwork in the Hit frame. Because there is no artwork in the Up state, the button is invisible to users until they mouse over it. You will learn how to make an invisible button in Exercise 5.

I. ——————————Rollover Buttons

This first exercise will teach you how to create a basic rollover button. You will see how the button's Timeline is different from the Main Timeline, and you will learn about the four different states of buttons. This exercise will also show you how to test and preview the button you created.

1. Copy the **chap_09** folder, located on the **H•O•T CD-ROM**, to your hard drive. You need to have this folder on your hard drive in order to save files inside it.

2. Open **rollOverButton.fla** from the **chap_09** folder. This is a blank file with a gray background that has been created for you.

3. Choose **Insert > New Symbol** to create a new Button symbol. This will open the **Symbol Properties** dialog box. Name the symbol **btnRollo** and set the **Behavior** to **Button**. Click **OK**.

NOTE | Button Naming Conventions

When I do Macromedia Flash development work, I prefer to give symbols names that begin with an abbreviation indicating the type of symbol it is, followed by a meaningful name for the symbol, such as "btnRollo." This way, when I have many symbols in the Library, I can sort my symbols alphabetically and have all the Buttons grouped together, all the Graphic symbols grouped together, and all the Movie Clip symbols (which you will learn about in the next chapter) grouped together. You will have a chance to work with the Library in many of the upcoming chapters.

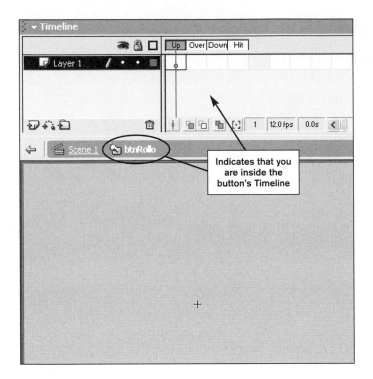

Indicates that you are inside the button's Timeline

As soon as you click OK, you will enter the button's Timeline. Each Button symbol has its own Timeline, which is independent of the Main Timeline. This means that you can place the finished button on the Stage, and even though it contains multiple button states, it will occupy only one frame in the Main Timeline. Notice that the Button Timeline contains four frames: Up, Over, Down, and Hit. Buttons do not automatically "play" as the Main Timeline does or as animated Graphic symbols do. Rather, the Button's Timeline remains paused at the first keyframe (or Up state), showing only the content in the Up state until the cursor comes into contact with the button. The other keyframes in the Button symbol (Over and Down) are shown only in reaction to the cursor position.

4. Choose **View > Grid > Show Grid**. This will cover the Stage with a grid temporarily—the grid will not be exported with your movie. It is visible only in Macromedia Flash MX's editing environment.

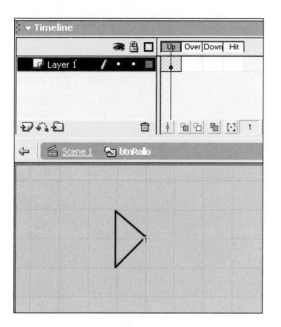

5. In the **Toolbox**, select the **Line** tool. Make sure the **Stroke Color** is set to **black**, and draw a small triangle that spans about two grid boxes in height. The right point of the triangle should be on the center crosshair on the Stage (which is actually the Registration Point of the button), as in the picture above. Placing the triangle on the center crosshair will ensure that the triangle is set to pivot on this point. If you choose to rotate, scale, transform, or position the triangle button, it will always pivot from the Registration Point. You can change the location of this point later, as you learned to do in Chapter 4, "*Animation Basics*."

This will serve as the Up state of the button before the user interacts with it.

Tip: *To make it easier to draw the triangle, you can change the view to 200% in the Information Bar.*

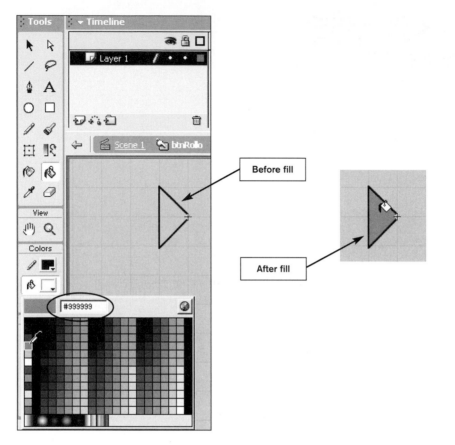

Before fill

After fill

6. Select the **Paint Bucket** tool. Set the **Fill Color** to the fourth color down in the first column of the Fill Color palette in the **Toolbox**, with the value of #999999, as in the picture above. Click once inside the triangle to fill the triangle with gray.

Why do you have to choose that specific gray? The next three exercises will build on one another, and it is important to use the right color in this first exercise so that by the time you get to Exercise 3, the colors will match the interface you will be working with.

7. Select the **Arrow** tool and move the cursor over the black stroke of the triangle; double-click on it to select all three line segments. Press **Delete** on the keyboard to delete the black stroke. You will now have a solid gray triangle without a stroke around it.

8. Press **F6** to add a keyframe to the **Over** frame of the button. This will copy the content—the triangle—from the last keyframe into the **Over** frame.

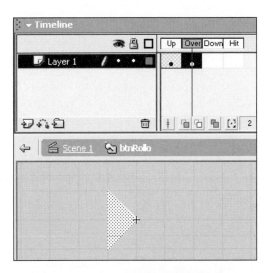

9. Select the **Paint Bucket** tool again, and this time choose **white** for the **Fill Color**. Click once inside the triangle to fill the triangle with white.

10. Press **F6** to add a keyframe to the **Down** state of the button. Set the **Fill Color** to the same color you used in step 6: the fourth gray color swatch down from the top left corner of the Fill Color palette in the Toolbox. Click once inside the triangle to fill it with gray.

11. Move (or scrub) the **Playhead** to see the different states of the button. The Up state triangle should be gray, the Over state triangle should be white, and the Down state triangle should be gray again.

To complete the Button symbol, you need to define the Hit state of the button. You do this next.

12. Press **F6** to add a keyframe to the **Hit** frame of the button. This will define the "hot" area of the button, or the area that will react to the mouse, which in this case is the exact same shape as the button. This is what makes the button clickable.

The Hit keyframe of the button is always invisible to the user. Therefore, it does not matter what color the content in the Hit keyframe is.

NOTE | Hit Me!

The Hit state of the button has one objective: to define an area that will be active when the cursor comes into contact with it. Because the Hit keyframe defines the area of the button that is reactive to the mouse, it is important that it cover the entire area of the button that you want to be active. If the button is tiny and the Hit area is small or smaller, it may be difficult for the user to interact with the button at all. For tiny buttons or buttons that are text only, I suggest using a solid shape that is slightly larger than the button's Up or Over states. You will learn to do this in the next exercise!

You have just created your first button. You will learn to test the button next.

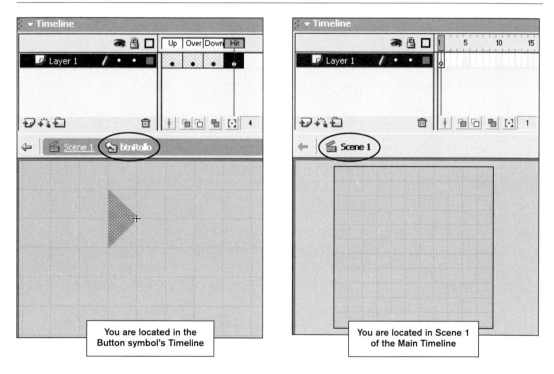

You are located in the Button symbol's Timeline

You are located in Scene 1 of the Main Timeline

13. In the **Information Bar**, click on **Scene 1** to return to Scene 1 of the Main Timeline.

NOTE | Where's the Button?

When you choose **Insert > New Symbol** (as you did in back in step 3), Macromedia Flash MX automatically places the new Button symbol in the Library, so you will not see the button on the Stage of the Main Timeline. If you want to use the new button in your movie, you must drag an instance of the button onto the Stage. In order to test the button you have three options: You can test it in the Library, on the Stage, or by using **Control > Test Movie**. You will try each way next.

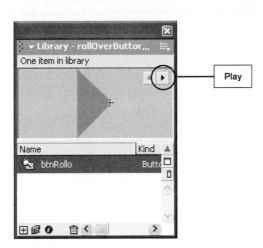

14. Press **F11** to open the **Library**. Click on the **btnRollo** symbol in the Library. Click the **Play** button on the **Controller** in the Preview window to preview the button in the Library.

Notice that the button will play one frame right after the next (Up, Over, Down, and Hit). Although this will give you a very quick preview, it may not be very realistic. The following steps will teach you how to preview the button on the Stage.

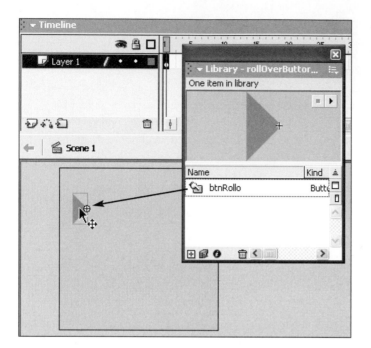

15. Choose **View > Grid > Show Grid** to deselect this option and hide the grid on the Stage. Drag an instance of the button you created onto the **Stage**.

16. Choose **Control > Enable Simple Buttons**. This will allow you to test the button right on the Stage.

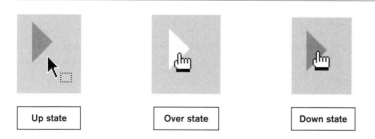

17. Go ahead and move your mouse over the button to see the **Over** state. Click on the button to preview the **Down** state.

18. Choose **Control > Enable Simple Buttons** again to deselect this option. The button will not be active on the Stage anymore.

Although you can still select enabled buttons, it is easier to work with them if they are disabled. You can always enable the buttons again when you want to test their behavior on the Stage.

19. Choose **Control > Test Movie**. This will produce the .swf file (you'll learn more about this in Chapter 16, "*Publishing and Exporting*") that will let you test any of the buttons in the movie. This method of testing will yield the same visual results as choosing **Enable Simple Buttons**; it's just another way to test your work. Go ahead and move the mouse over the button to trigger the Over state to see it working. When you are finished, close the .swf file to return to the editing environment.

20. Save this file and keep it open for the next exercise.

2. _____Rollover Buttons with Text

In the previous exercise, you learned to create and test a button. This exercise will show you how to alter that button by adding text and altering the Hit state of the button. In the steps that follow, you will learn the difference between using text to define the Hit state and using a solid shape to define the Hit state of the button.

1. You should still have the file **rollOverButton.fla** open from the previous exercise. Save this file as **textButton.fla** in the **chap_09** folder.

2. In the **Library**, double-click on the Button symbol's icon to open the button's **Timeline**.

3. Inside the Button symbol's **Timeline**, rename **Layer 1** to **triangle**, and lock the triangle layer.

4. Click the **Insert Layer** button to add a new layer to the button's Timeline. Rename **Layer 2** to **text**.

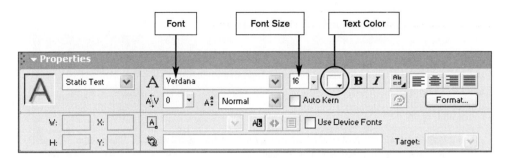

5. In the **Toolbox**, select the **Text** tool. In the **Property Inspector**, choose **Verdana** for the **Font**, **16** for the **Font Size**, and **white** for the **Text Color**.

6. Click on the **Stage** to the right of the triangle and type the word **BACKGROUND** in capital letters. This will automatically add frames so that the word **BACKGROUND** appears across the **Up**, **Over**, **Down**, and **Hit** states.

7. Press **F6** to add a keyframe to the **Over** state of the button.

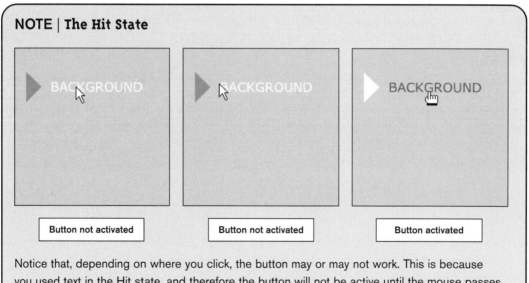

8. Select the text block on the **Stage** in the **Over** frame. In the **Property Inspector**, click on the **Text Color** box and choose the **dark gray** color, three from the top, as in the picture above. This will change the text color for the text in the **Over** frame.

9. Choose **Control > Test Movie** to test the button.

NOTE | The Hit State

| Button not activated | Button not activated | Button activated |

Notice that, depending on where you click, the button may or may not work. This is because you used text in the Hit state, and therefore the button will not be active until the mouse passes directly over the actual text itself (not in between the letter's characters), as shown in the pictures above. This can confuse the end user, because the button will not work unless the user places the mouse cursor directly over a solid part of a letter. A hole in an "O" or even the space between letters can cause the button to flicker on and off. This is why using text to define the Hit state of your buttons is not a good idea. You will learn how to use a solid shape to define the Hit state next.

10. When you test a movie, it opens the results in a separate Preview Window. Close the **Preview Window** to return to the editing environment. Move the **Playhead** to the **Hit** frame.

*To trigger the button, the mouse must move over the area that is defined as the Hit state. In this case, the Hit frame is defined by the content inside it, which consists of the triangle and the text, **BACKGROUND**. As you saw in step 9, the current Hit state causes the button to be triggered only when the mouse rolls exactly over the text or the arrow. This is not the correct way to create a Hit state.*

You will modify the button's Hit state next.

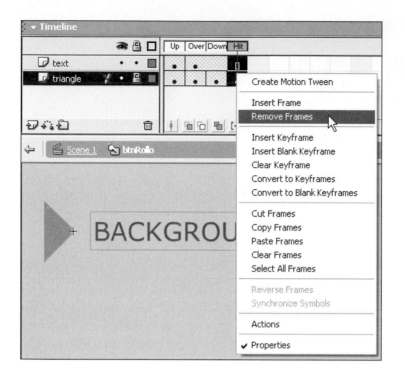

11. In the button's **Timeline**, click and drag down on both layers in the **Hit** frame to select the layers. **Right-click** (Windows) or **Ctrl+click** (Mac) to access the drop-down Options menu. Choose **Remove Frames** to remove both keyframes in the Hit state of the button. You will be adding new content to define the Hit area in the next few steps.

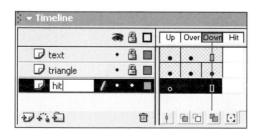

12. Lock the text and click the **Insert Layer** button to add a new layer to the button's **Timeline**. Drag the new layer below the **triangle** layer and rename it to **hit**.

13. Click in the **Hit** frame on the **hit** layer, and press **F7** to add a blank keyframe to the Hit state of the button.

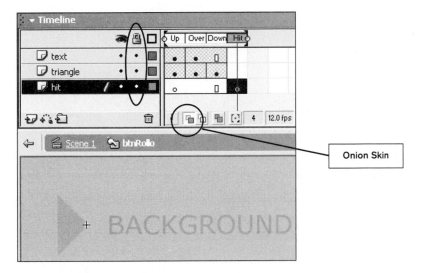

Onion Skin

14. Unlock all the layers and select the **Onion Skin** button. You will be creating the new Hit state next, and you need to be able to see the artwork in the other frames.

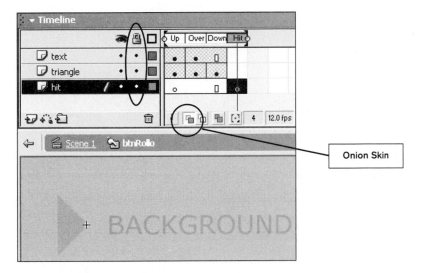

15. In the **Toolbox**, select the **Rectangle** tool. On the **Stage**, draw a rectangle that covers both the triangle and the text. This way, the mouse will only need to move over the rectangle in order for the button to be triggered. After you are finished drawing the rectangle, deselect the **Onion Skin** button to turn off Onion Skinning.

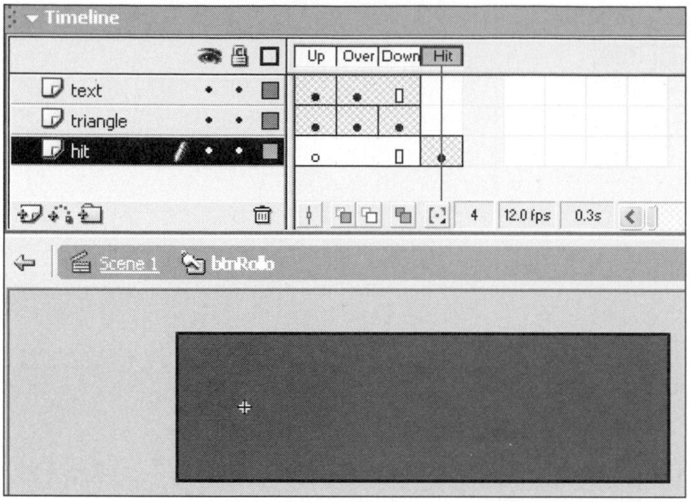

After you draw the rectangle, you will end up with a solid shape that will define the new Hit state for the Button symbol. It doesn't matter what color the Hit state is or if it contains a stroke and a fill. You need to stay focused only on making sure that it covers the appropriate area.

You have just modified the Hit state of your rollover Button symbol! You will test it again next.

---

16. In the **Information Bar**, click on **Scene 1** to leave the Button symbol's Timeline and return to the Main Timeline.

Notice the button instance that you placed on the Stage in the previous exercise. Since you modified the actual symbol itself in this exercise, the button instance on the Stage will automatically be updated with the text and the new Hit state.

NOTE | Understanding the Hit State

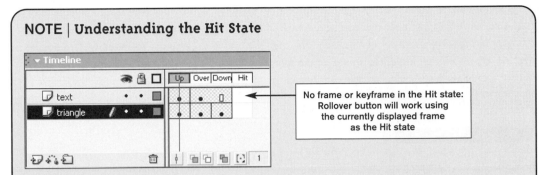

No frame or keyframe in the Hit state: Rollover button will work using the currently displayed frame as the Hit state

If there is no frame or keyframe in the specified Hit state, the Hit shape of the button is set by the currently displayed keyframe of the button. This means that if the Up and Over keyframes contain different shapes, the Hit state will change when the user rolls over the button. This is not an ideal way to create buttons.

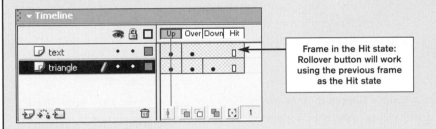

Frame in the Hit state: Rollover button will work using the previous frame as the Hit state

If a frame is specified in the Hit state, it will use the contents of the last set keyframe.

Blank keyframe: Rollover button will not work

Setting a blank keyframe in the Hit state will disable the rollover, since a Hit state is required to trigger the Over and Down states.

If the shape for the button is large enough for the Hit state, you don't have to create a keyframe or new artwork in that frame. In this exercise, however, the text was not an adequate shape or size for the user to trigger the rollover consistently. The best method is to test your rollovers first, to ensure that the Hit state is an adequate shape for the job.

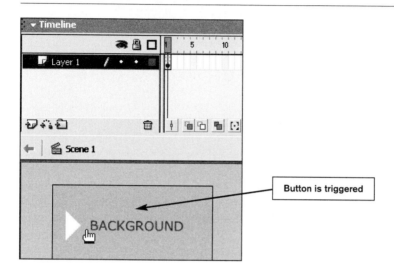

17. Choose **Control > Enable Simple Buttons** to test the button on the Stage. Move your mouse over the button to see the Over state, and click the button to preview the Down state.

Notice how much easier it is to interact with the button now that you've changed the Hit state. This is because you've defined the Hit state as a solid shape that covers the whole Up state of the button (the arrow and the text). Therefore, when you test the button, as soon as you touch the edge of the invisible rectangle shape (the Hit state), the Over state of the button is triggered.

18. Choose **Control > Enable Simple Buttons** again to deselect this option. The button will not be active on the Stage anymore.

19. Save and close this file.

3. —————————Duplicating and Aligning Buttons

You have learned how to create buttons, how to preview the results, and why the Hit state is important in the last two exercises. Now that you know how to make a rollover button, another handy skill is to make copies of the button in the Library. For example, you can change the text in each copy of the Button symbol to create a navigation bar in no time. This exercise will show you how to duplicate buttons in the Library and how to align them on the Stage.

1. Open the file named **duplicateAlign.fla** from the **chap_09** folder. This file contains one layer with a background image.

Tip: Choose View > Magnification > Show All to see the whole background image.

2. Press **F11** to open the **Library**. Notice that there are three items in the Library: the interface Graphic symbol and two bitmaps.

3. Choose **File > Open As Library** and select the **textButton.fla** file from the **chap_09** folder. This will open only the Library (with the Button symbol you created from the last exercise) from the **textButton.fla** file. You will be using the button from that file inside the **duplicateAlign** file in the following steps.

The Open As Library technique can come in handy when you want to use assets such as symbols from one project in another project. This command allows you to open only the Library that is attached to a Macromedia Flash project file. This will keep your computer screen less cluttered than if you had to open a different project file just to use its Library assets.

4. Notice that now the Library looks longer than normal. This is because there are two Libraries in the panel window! On the top is the Library from the **textButton** movie, and below is the Library from the **duplicateAlign** movie.

Note: In some cases the Libraries may be on top of each other but in the reverse order, which is fine. This will not affect the exercise in an adverse way. The important point is that both Libraries are indeed there.

5. In the **Main Timeline**, insert a new layer and name it **buttons**. Make sure the buttons layer is above the background layer.

6. In the **textButton** Library, drag an instance of the **btnRollo** symbol onto the **Stage**, and place it over the gray box on the left side of the Stage, as in the picture above.

After you place the instance on the Stage, something interesting happens. The btnRollo symbol is now located in the duplicateAlign Library also. This is because you have added the symbol from the textButton movie to the duplicateAlign movie, and Macromedia Flash MX adds the symbol to the Library for you.

7. In the **duplicateAlign** Library, **right-click** (Windows) or **Ctrl+click** (Mac) on the **btnRollo** symbol to access the drop-down Options menu. Choose **Duplicate** to make a copy of the Button symbol. This opens the **Duplicate Symbol** dialog box.

8. In the **Duplicate Symbol** dialog box, type **btnSafety** in the **Name** field and make sure **Behavior: Button** is selected. Click **OK**. You have just made an exact duplicate of the button you previously created. Notice the new **btnSafety** symbol in the Library.

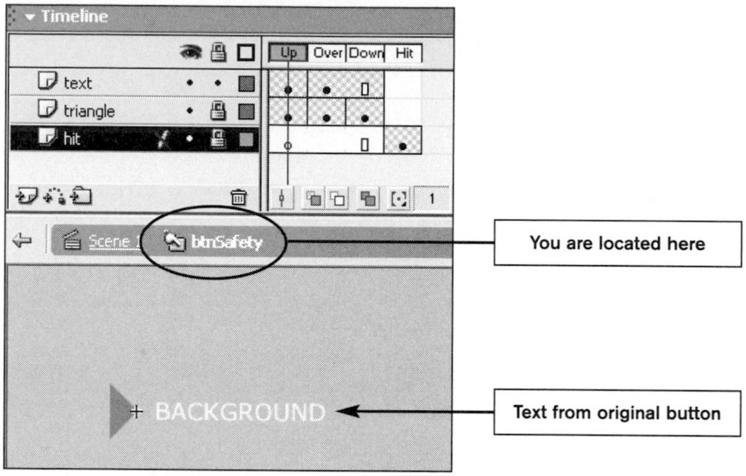

You are located here

Text from original button

9. Double-click **btnSafety** in the **Library** to open the Button symbol's **Timeline**. Notice that the Timeline looks identical to the original button you created. Lock the **triangle** and **hit** layers so you don't accidentally edit anything on those layers. You will be changing the text of this button next.

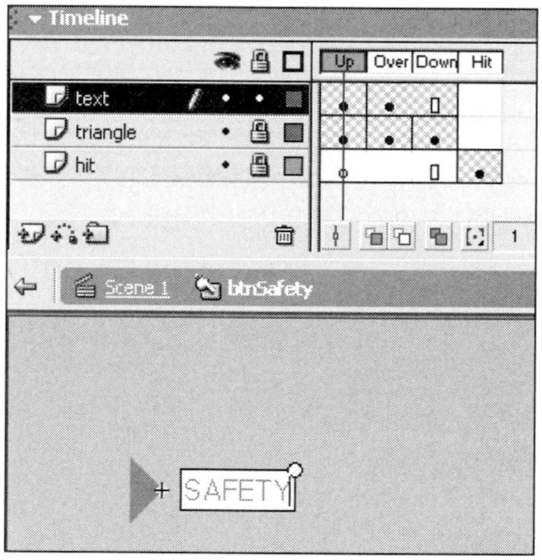

10. On the **text** layer, click in **Frame 1** (the **Up** state of the button). Double-click on the text block on the Stage, highlight the text, and type the word **SAFETY** in capital letters. This will replace the existing text in the first frame with the word **SAFETY**.

11. Click on **Frame 2** in the **text** layer (the **Over** state of the button). Double-click on the text block on the Stage, highlight the text and type the word **SAFETY** in capital letters. This will replace the existing text in the second frame with the word **SAFETY**.

NOTE | Changing the Hit State

The most important things to remember about the Hit state are that it should cover the entire area of the artwork/text and that it should cover the entire area you want to designate as reactive to the mouse.

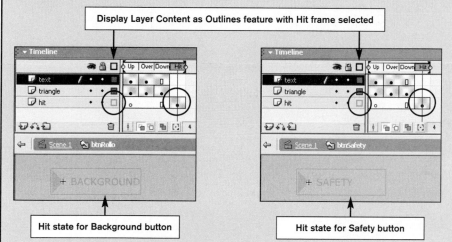

Display Layer Content as Outlines feature with Hit frame selected

Hit state for Background button

Hit state for Safety button

In the last step, the Hit frame contained a rectangle that completely covered the Safety button's triangle and text. Therefore, you did not need to make the rectangle in the Hit state bigger. It is OK if the Hit state is a bit longer than the button text. It is important to make sure that it is not shorter, though. I have turned on Onion Skinning and the Display Layer Content as Outlines feature in the Timeline to illustrate this point. This feature allows you to view the content on the Stage as outlines rather than solid shapes for any layer that is selected. Here it allows you to see the outline of the rectangles in relation to the button text.

You can, however, resize the rectangle in the Hit frame if you want to for any reason by selecting the Free Transform tool and resizing the shape to your liking—just make sure that it covers the entire artwork and text area.

12. In the **Information Bar**, click on **Scene 1** to leave the Button symbol's Timeline and return to the Main Timeline.

13. Drag an instance of the new button, **btnSafety**, onto the **Stage**, just below the background button. Choose **Control > Enable Simple Buttons** and test it. When you are finished testing it, choose **Control > Enable Simple Buttons** again to deselect this feature.

14. Repeat steps 7 through 11 to create three more duplicate buttons. Name them **btnLearning, btnGear**, and **btnWhatsNew**, respectively. Inside each button, the text should read **GEAR, LEARNING**, and **WHAT'S NEW**.

15. When you are finished duplicating and editing the buttons, click on **Scene 1** in the **Information Bar** to return to the Main Timeline.

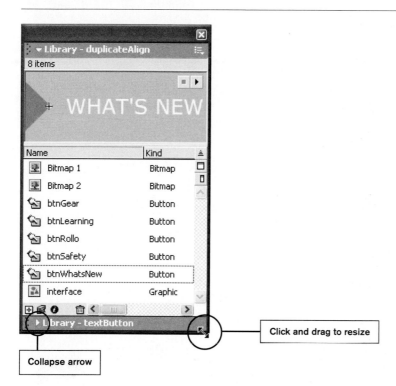

Collapse arrow

Click and drag to resize

16. Click on the **collapse** arrow in the **textButton Library** to collapse that Library, and click and drag down diagonally on the right corner of the **Library** panel to resize the entire panel. This way you will be able to see all the buttons you created at the same time.

NOTE | Closing the Additional Library

In addition to collapsing the textButton Library, you can permanently close the textButton Library by following two easy steps:

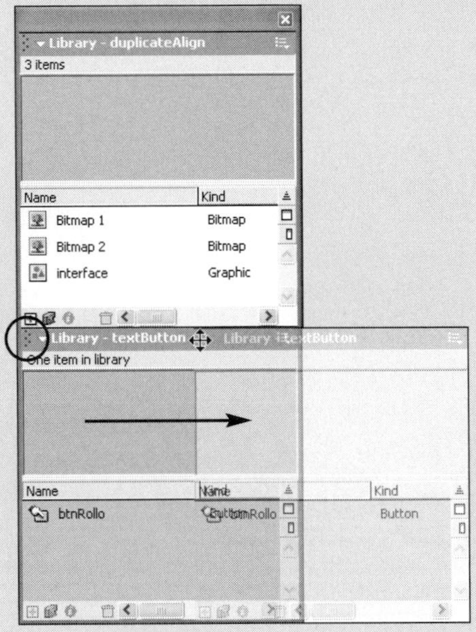

In the textButton Library panel, click on the series of dots in the upper left corner and drag the Library to the right to undock the two Libraries from each other.

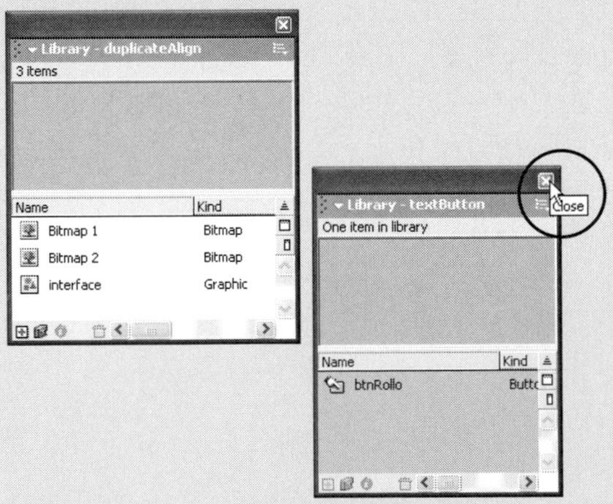

Once the Library is undocked, click the Close button in the upper right corner of the textButton Library window to close it.

Warning: Once you close a Library that was opened using the Open As Library command, you cannot press F11 to open it again. F11 is reserved for the currently open project file (.fla). To open the textButton Library again after you close it, you would need to select File > Open As Library to open it again.

17. Drag the **btnLearning**, **btnGear**,and **btnWhatsNew** buttons onto the **Stage** below the other two buttons.

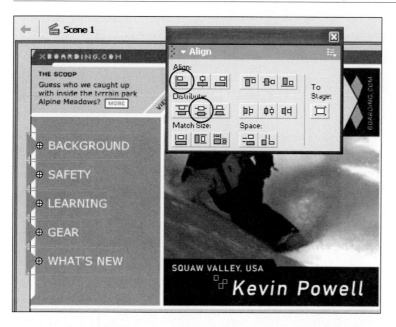

18. Press **Ctrl+A** (Windows) or **Cmd+A** (Mac) to select all five buttons on the **Stage**. Open the **Align** panel (**Window > Align**) and make sure the **To Stage** button is not depressed. Select **Align Left Edge** and **Distribute Vertical Center** to make all the buttons align to the left and be equally spaced.

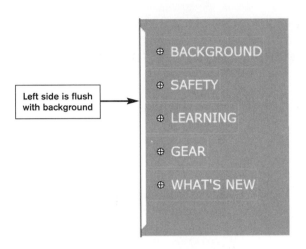

Left side is flush
with background

19. Make sure all the buttons are still selected. Using the **Right Arrow** key on the keyboard, nudge the buttons to the right so that the left side of each button is flush with the gray background, as in the picture above.

20. Choose **Control > Test Movie** to test your rollover buttons. Rather than creating five separate buttons, one at a time, and creating all the artwork inside each button, you have streamlined the process. You have created this simple navigation system by creating the artwork for only one button, duplicating it four more times, and changing only the text inside each button.

21. Save this file and keep it open for the next exercise.

NOTE | Duplicate Versus Instance

In the last exercise, you duplicated the Library item of one button, and created four new buttons based on the original. You might wonder why you couldn't simply drag the button from the Library to the Stage three times and modify the instances. Since the original symbol contains text, you would have to go into the symbol itself to modify the text. If you drag instances onto the Stage, you would not be able to modify the text without changing the actual symbol. You can, however, modify the shape, size, rotation, skew, and color of any instance without affecting the original symbol. Think of it like this: Any time you have to actually go inside the symbol's Timeline to modify something, you are changing the symbol. Any time you change an instance on the Stage in the Main Timeline, you are modifying an instance of the original symbol.

4. _____Adding Sound to Buttons

The different states of the buttons you create can each hold a different sound to give feedback to the user. This exercise will teach you how to add a simple sound to a button.

1. You should still have the **duplicateAlign.fla** file open from the last exercise.

2. Choose **File > Open As Library** and select the **soundz.fla** file from the **chap_09** folder. This will open only the Library of the **soundz.fla** file. You will be using the sound files inside this Library in the following steps.

Note: The sounds were imported into this document in the same way that external artwork is imported—using File > Import or its keyboard shortcut, Ctrl+R (Windows) or Cmd+R (Mac). A list of supported sound formats in Macromedia Flash MX is in Chapter 13, "Sound."

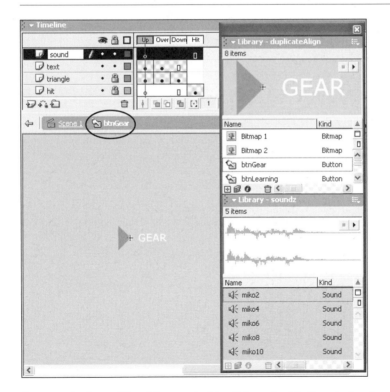

3. In the **duplicateAlign Library**, double-click on the **btnGear** button icon to open the button's **Timeline**. Click the **Insert Layer** button to add a new layer, and make sure it is the topmost layer. Name this layer **sound**.

4. Press **F7** on the **Over** frame in the **sound** layer to add a blank keyframe. You will be adding a sound to this frame.

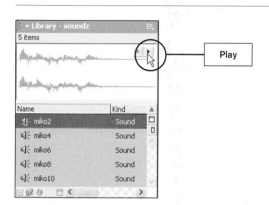

5. In the **soundz Library**, select the **miko2** sound file, and preview the sound by clicking the **Play** button in the Library Preview window.

6. Collapse the **duplicateAlign Library** window so you have more room to work. With the **Over** frame selected in the **sound** layer, drag an instance of **miko2** onto the **Stage**. That's it! You have just added a sound to the button.

Note: You will not see a visual representation of the sound on the Stage. Instead, you will see sound waves in the Over frame of the Timeline. It is OK if the sound extends into the Hit frame in the button's Timeline, because the Hit state is determined by artwork on the Stage, not sound in the Timeline. Therefore, having a sound in the Hit frame will have no effect on the button.

7. In the **Information Bar**, click on **Scene 1** to return to the Main Timeline.

Since you modified the button in the Library, it will update all of the instances on the Stage as well to include the sound you added.

8. Choose **Control > Enable Simple Buttons**. This will allow you to test the button on the Stage. You should hear the sound play when you move the mouse over the **btnGear** button, because you added the sound to the Over state of that button. When you are finished testing it, choose **Control > Enable Simple Buttons** again to deselect this feature. You will add a sound to the Down state of the What's New button next.

Tip: This is a very brief introduction to working with sound. You will learn about sound in depth, including compressing and testing, in Chapter 13, "Sound."

9. In the **Library** panel, expand the **duplicateAlign Library** to see all its contents. Double-click on the **btnWhatsNew** button icon to open the button's Timeline. Collapse the **duplicateAlign Library** to hide it temporarily.

10. Lock the **text** layer, and click the **Insert Layer** button to add a new layer, making sure it's the topmost layer. Name this layer **sound**.

11. Press **F7** to add a blank keyframe on the **Down** frame in the **sound** layer. You will be adding a sound to this frame next.

12. With the **Down** frame selected in the **sound** layer, drag an instance of **miko4** onto the **Stage**. Notice that sound waves appear in the Down frame of the Timeline.

13. Choose **Control > Test Movie** to test your buttons. Notice that the sound in the Gear button will play when the mouse rolls over the button and that the sound in the What's New button will play when you click on the button (because you placed the sound in the Down state).

Tip: You can also choose Control > Enable Simple Buttons in the editing environment to hear the button sounds on the Stage. One method is not better than the other; I just wanted to give you practice using both!

14. Repeat steps 9 through 12 to add sounds of your choice to the remaining buttons: **btnSafety**, **btnLearning**, and **btnRollo** (the Background button).

15. Save and close the file.

5.——————————Invisible Buttons

In previous exercises, you learned about the importance of the Hit state for rollover buttons. The Hit state can also be used to create what are known as invisible buttons. This kind of button comes as an unexpected surprise, because there's no visible display of the button object until the end user passes the mouse over an invisible region. You will learn to change regular buttons into invisible buttons in this exercise.

1. Open the **invisButtonFinal.fla** file from the **chap_09** folder. This is the finished version of the movie you are going to create in this exercise.

2. Choose **Control > Test Movie** to preview this movie. Move your cursor over the lodges in the picture. Notice how the descriptions magically appear. You will be creating this same effect next. When you are finished looking at this movie, close the file.

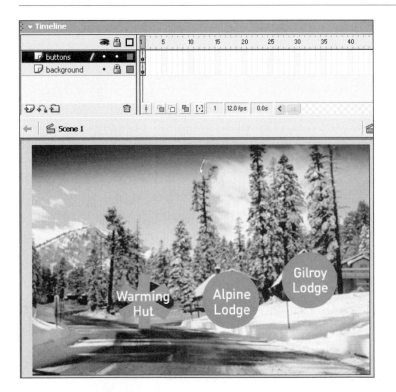

3. Open the **invisible.fla file** located inside the **chap_09** folder. This file was created ahead of time to get you started. Notice that the file contains two layers—one with a background image on it and the other with three buttons on it.

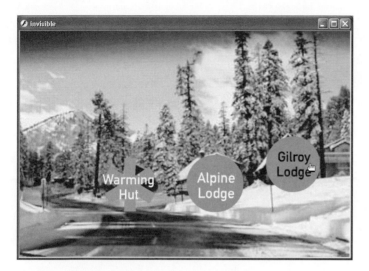

4. Choose **Control > Test Movie** to preview the buttons. Move your mouse over the buttons and notice that they are not invisible. They behave just like normal rollover buttons, with the text changing color when you roll over them with the mouse—not very exciting. You will turn them into invisible buttons to create a surprise rollover effect next.

5. Close the **Preview Window**. Back in the project file, open the **Library**. Double-click on the **alpine** button's icon to open the button's Timeline. Notice that the button has three layers. Scrub the **Playhead** to preview the Up, Over, Down, and Hit states of the button.

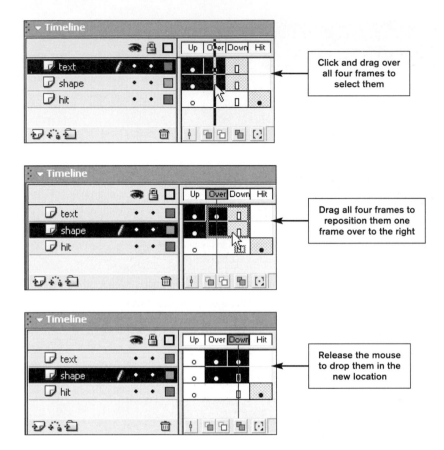

Click and drag over all four frames to select them

Drag all four frames to reposition them one frame over to the right

Release the mouse to drop them in the new location

6. Click on a blank area of the **Stage** to make sure you have nothing selected. In one motion, click and drag to select the first two frames in the **text** and **shape** layers. Drag the four selected frames one frame to the right and release the mouse. This is how you reposition a block of frames at one time.

Why did you move the frames out of the Up state? When you create an invisible button, the Up state needs to be empty so that the user will not know that any button even exists until the mouse moves over the area that is defined in the Hit state. You will test the button next.

7. In the **Information Bar**, click on **Scene 1** to return to the Main Timeline.

Notice that the alpine button looks different on the Stage. Since you modified the button in the Library, any instance on the Stage will be updated. Since the button has no Up state, Macromedia Flash MX will display the shape of the Hit frame in a transparent blue color as visual feedback for where the button is located.

Why not just use a shape with a transparent fill for the Up state when you create a button? That would certainly work as an invisible button, but then it would be hard to see the instances of the button in your work area. When you build an invisible button with a Hit state, Macromedia Flash MX displays the button as a translucent blue, which represents the hot spot of the button. This allows you to easily position and work with the button in the work area.

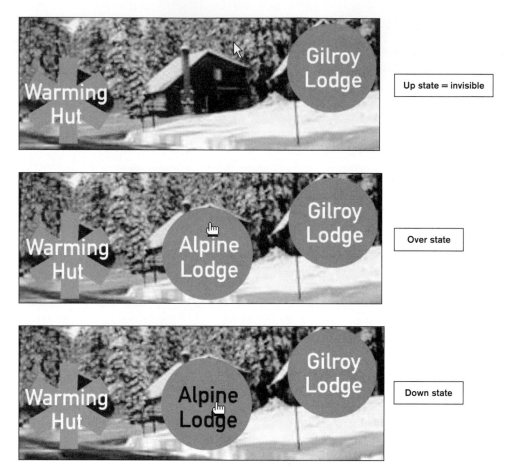

8. Choose **Control > Test Movie** to test the invisible button you just created. Notice the three different states of the button. Since you moved the frames to the right by one frame in step 6, the old Up state of the button (white text, graphic background) is now the Over state, and the old Over state (black text, graphic background) is now the Down state. Test the **gilroy** button and the **warming** button to see the difference between the invisible button and the normal buttons.

You will change the other two buttons into invisible buttons next.

9. Repeat steps 5 and 6 for the other two buttons in the Library: the **gilroy** and **warming** buttons.

10. Choose **Control > Test Movie** to test all three buttons. Neat!

11. When you are finished, save and close this file.

That's it! I hope this chapter gave you a good foundation for working with and understanding the different button states and different kinds of buttons in Macromedia Flash MX. The next chapter will introduce you to Movie Clips. Knowing how to make a Movie Clip will help you learn to make an animated rollover button, so you'll get to add to your new button-making skills soon!

10.

Movie Clips

| What Is a Movie Clip? | Creating a Movie Clip |
| Animated Graphic Symbols Versus Movie Clip Symbols |
| Creating an Animated Rollover Button |
| Animated Rollover Button in Action |

chap_10
_____

Macromedia Flash MX
H•O•T CD-ROM

Understanding Movie Clip symbols is key to producing interactive Macromedia Flash MX movies. This understanding is the last step in building a foundation that will prepare you for Chapter 11, *"ActionScripting Basics."* As you will see, ActionScripting often requires a Movie Clip symbol, so don't underestimate the importance of this chapter.

Up to this point in the book, you've learned how to create both Graphic and Button symbols. At last, you will be introduced to Movie Clip symbols and gain a solid understanding of how they are created and used, compared to—or in combination with— the other two types of symbols you already know.

What Is a Movie Clip?

I saved Movie Clip symbols for last because they can be the most difficult type of symbol to learn to use in Macromedia Flash MX. Let's start with a few vocabulary terms.

Vocabulary Definitions	
Term	**Definition**
Main Timeline	The Main Timeline, introduced in Chapter 6, is the Timeline of the scene (or scenes) in your project file. If you have more than one scene, Macromedia Flash MX will consider them part of the same Main Timeline and will simply add the number of frames inside each scene together to make up one Main Timeline. For example, if Scene 1 contains 35 frames and Scene 2 contains 20 frames, Macromedia Flash will consider the Main Timeline to span 55 frames. You will learn more about managing and naming scenes in Chapter 11, "*ActionScripting Basics.*" As you've seen, Graphic symbols have their own Timeline that has a relationship to the Main Timeline. For example, if your Graphic symbol contains 10 frames of animation, the Main Timeline must also contain 10 frames for the Graphic symbol to play.
Timeline Independent	As you have learned, Graphic (and animated Graphic) symbols have a direct relationship to the Main Timeline. Button and Movie Clip symbols do not have a direct relationship to the Main Timeline. They are referred to as "Timeline independent" objects. Why? Because they can function (play animation, sounds, etc.) regardless of how many frames the Main Timeline contains. For example, if you have a Movie Clip that contains a 10-frame animation of a chair lift moving up a hill, and you place this on the Stage inside the Main Timeline, the chair lift will continue to move up the hill even if the Timeline contains only a single frame. This ability to have different animations and actions occur independently of the Main Timeline is what makes Movie Clips so powerful.
Movie Clips	Movie Clip symbols can contain multiple layers, Graphic symbols, Button symbols, and even other Movie Clip symbols, as well as animations, sounds, and ActionScripting. Movie Clips operate independently of the Main Timeline. They can continue to play even if the Main Timeline has stopped, which, as you will learn, is important when you start to work with ActionScript in the following chapter. A Movie Clip requires only a single keyframe on the Main Timeline to play, regardless of how long its own Timeline is. It's helpful to think of Movie Clips as movies nested in the Main Timeline.

Although Movie Clips are extremely powerful and flexible, they cannot be previewed simply by pressing **Enter/Return**, as is done with Button and Graphic symbol instances. Movie Clips can be previewed only in the Library (out of context of the main movie), by selecting **Control > Test Movie**, or by publishing the final movie (which you will learn about in Chapter 16, "*Publishing and Exporting*"). This is a very important point, because you will find yourself unable to view your work unless you remember this!

I. ——————————Creating a Movie Clip

This exercise will start you off by showing how to make a simple Movie Clip.

1. Copy the **chap_10** folder, located on the **H•O•T CD-ROM**, to your hard drive. You need to have this folder on your hard drive in order to save files inside it.

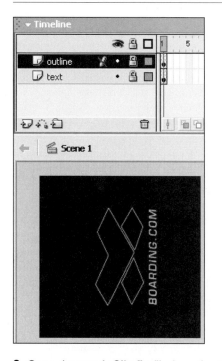

2. Open the **movieClip.fla** file from the **chap_10** folder. This file has been created ahead of time to get you started. Notice that it has two layers: one named **outline**, which contains the outline of the "X," and the other named **text**, which contains the boarding.com letters. You are going to create a simple motion tween next.

3. Click the **Insert Layer** button to add a new layer to the **Timeline**. Name this layer **fillTween**.

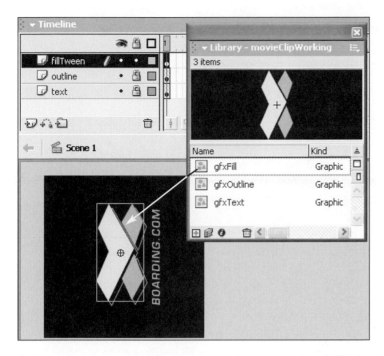

4. Press **F11** to open the **Library**. Drag an instance of the **gfxFill** Graphic symbol onto the **Stage** in the **fillTween** layer. Using the **arrow** keys on the keyboard, position the **gfxFill** instance so that it covers the **X** outline exactly. You will be creating an animation of this outline filling in with color in the next few steps, so it is important that the gfxFill symbol is positioned directly on top of the outline artwork on the Stage.

Tip: You may want to change the magnification in the Information Bar to 200% so that you can see the positioning better.

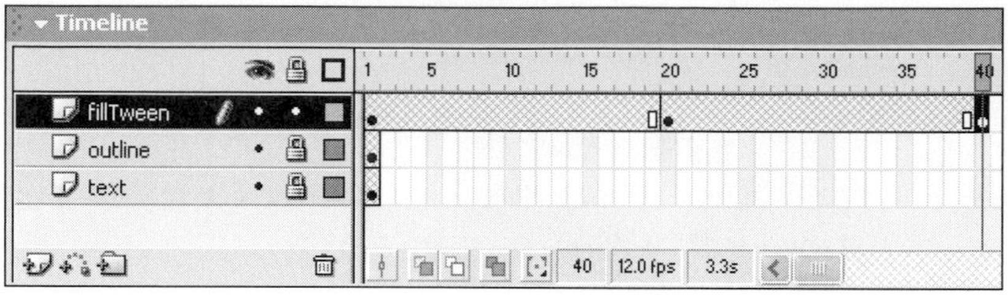

5. Select **Frame 20** and press **F6** to add a keyframe. Select **Frame 40** and press **F6** to add a keyframe.

In the following steps, you will be creating a motion tween in which the gfxFill instance starts off invisible in Frame 1, becomes completely visible in Frame 20, and fades to invisible again in Frame 40.

6. Make sure the **Playhead** is over **Frame 40**, and select the instance on the **Stage**. Using the **Property Inspector**, for the **Color Styles** options, choose **Alpha** and **0%**.

7. Move the **Playhead** to **Frame 1** and select the instance on the **Stage**. Using the **Property Inspector**, set the **Color Styles** options to **Alpha** and **0%**.

8. In the **Timeline**, click to the right of the **fillTween** layer name to select all the frames on the layer. In the **Property Inspector**, choose **Tween: Motion**. This will add a motion tween across all of the frames.

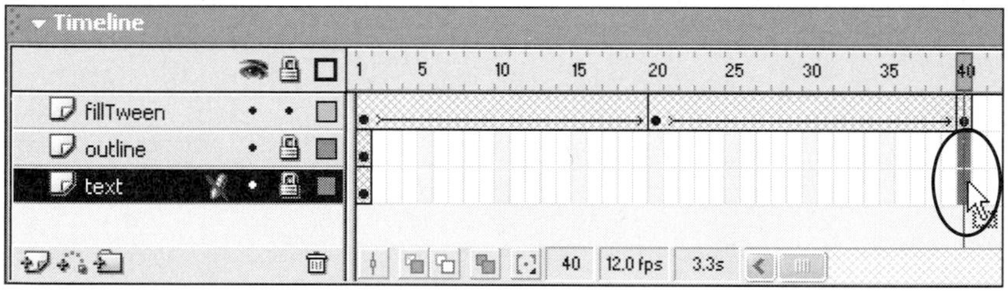

9. In the **outline** layer, click on **Frame 40** and drag down to **Frame 40** of the **text** layer to select Frame 40 in both layers, as shown above. Press **F5** to add frames up to Frame 40. This way the artwork on the outline and text layers will be visible throughout the motion tween on the fillTween layer.

10. Press **Enter/Return** to test the animation. Neat! The "X" outline fills in with color, and then the fill fades away.

What does this all have to do with Movie Clips, you may be thinking. You are going to create a Movie Clip using this animation next!

All frames in all three layers selected

11. Click to the right of the **text** layer name to select all the frames on that layer. Shift+click to the right of the **outline** and **fillTween** layer names to select all the frames on both of those layers as well. With all the frames in all three layers selected, choose **Edit > Cut Frames**. This will cut all the frames you have selected from the Main Timeline.

Don't worry—they won't be gone for long. You will be pasting the frames inside a Movie Clip next. **Note:** *It's important that you choose Cut Frames, and not Cut. Cut Frames allows you to cut multiple frames and layers, while a simple Cut command does not.*

12. Choose **Insert > New Symbol** and type **Name: mcOutlineFill**. Make sure **Behavior: Movie Clip** is selected. Click **OK** when you are finished. This will create a Movie Clip symbol. As soon as you click OK, you will be located inside the Movie Clip symbol's Timeline.

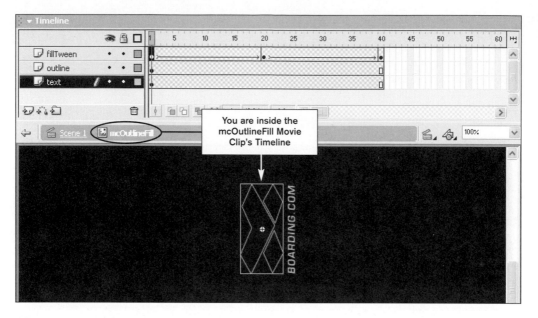

13. After you click OK, notice that you are inside mcOutlineFill's Timeline. Select the first keyframe and choose **Edit > Paste Frames**. This will paste all the frames and all the layers right inside the Movie Clip, maintaining all the layers and layer names just as you had them in the Main Timeline. Neat!

You have just created your first Movie Clip! You will be able to test it in the next steps.

14. Click on the **Scene 1** tab in the **Information Bar** to return to the **Main Timeline**. Notice in the Main Timeline that the three layers you originally had are still there, although they have no content on them. This is because you cut the frames and pasted them into the Movie Clip symbol.

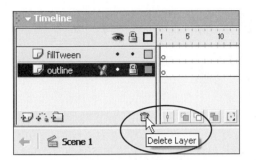

15. Select the **text** layer and click on the **Trashcan** icon in the **Timeline**. This will delete the **text** layer, since you will not need it anymore. Repeat this process to delete the **outline** layer.

What's with all this cutting and pasting and copying? Wouldn't it be easier to just create the content inside the Movie Clip in the first place? Although that would be easier, it may not always be a realistic workflow. Oftentimes, you will find that you create artwork on the Main Timeline first and later decide to turn it into a Movie Clip. Since creating artwork inside a Movie Clip is the easier of the two work-flows, I thought it would help to give you experience in the more difficult method, which is to copy and paste artwork from the Main Timeline into a Movie Clip symbol's Timeline.

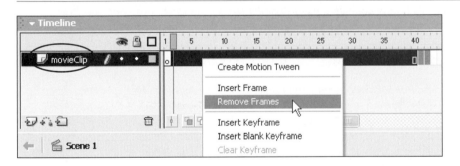

16. Double-click on the **fillTween** layer name and rename this layer **movieClip**. In the **Timeline**, click on **Frame 42** and drag backward to **Frame 2** to select Frames 40 through 2. (Since there are no frames on Frame 41 or 42, only the frames up to Frame 40 will be selected. However, this method of "over-selecting" makes sure you select all the frames and don't miss one.) Right-click (Windows) or Ctrl+click (Mac) on the selected frame to access the drop-down menu. Choose **Remove Frames**. This will remove all the frames you have selected.

Note: When you use Cut Frames, it cuts the content of the layers and frames, but the Timeline still contains the frames. The only way to remove them is to use the Remove Frames command.

17. In the **Information Bar**, make sure you are viewing your movie at **100%** so that you can see the whole Stage.

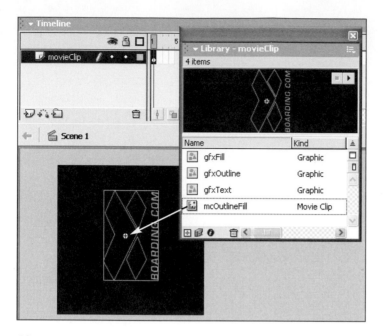

18. Open the **Library** (**F11**), and notice the **mcOutlineFill** Movie Clip symbol you created. Drag an instance of the Movie Clip onto the **Stage**.

19. Choose **Control > Test Movie** to preview the Movie Clip you just made.

Notice that the Movie Clip plays even though there is only one frame in the Main Timeline. This is because the Movie Clip's Timeline is independent from the Main Timeline. Movie Clips need only one keyframe in the Main Timeline in order to play.

20. Save this file and keep it open. You will need it for the next exercise.

TIP | Modifying Movie Clip Instances

Not only do Movie Clips have a Timeline that is independent from the main movie, but, just as you did with Graphic symbols in Chapter 6, you can apply effects to Movie Clip instances on the Stage. You have to create the Movie Clip only once, and then you can change the attributes (such as scale, alpha, skew, and rotation) of each instance on the Stage to achieve very different visual effects. By adding transformations or effects to the instances on the Stage, you can change the appearance of the Movie Clip with just a few clicks of the mouse. The original Movie Clip, however, will remain unchanged in the Library.

2. —————————Animated Graphic Symbols Versus Movie Clip Symbols

In this exercise, you will learn the differences between animated Graphic symbols and Movie Clip symbols. You'll see that the animated Graphic symbol requires multiple frames in the Main Timeline, while a Movie Clip does not. Here you will learn firsthand why I have placed so much emphasis on the Timeline independence of Movie Clips.

1. You should still have the **movieClip.fla** file open from the last exercise. Using **File >
Save As**, save another version of this file as **mcVsGfx.fla** in the **chap_10** folder. This way
you will have two copies of the file: one with everything you have completed up to this point
(**movieClip.fla**) and one that will have everything you will do in this exercise (**mcVsGfx.fla**).

2. Click on the **Stage**. In the **Property Inspector**, click on the **Size** setting button to open the
Document Properties dialog box. For **Dimensions**, change the **width** to **400 px**. This will
change the width of the Stage to 400 pixels, which will give you a little more room to work.

*To understand the difference between an animated Graphic symbol and a Movie Clip symbol,
you need to have one of each type in your project file. Since you already created a Movie
Clip symbol in the last exercise, you can use that same symbol, duplicating it and changing
its behavior, to make an animated Graphic symbol, rather than building a new animated
Graphic symbol from scratch. You will do this in the steps that follow.*

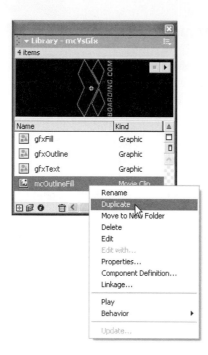

3. Press **F11** to open the **Library** if it isn't already open. Right-click (Windows) or Ctrl+click (Mac) on the **mcOutlineFill** Movie Clip symbol in the Library to access the drop-down menu. Choose **Duplicate** to make a copy of the symbol.

4. In the **Duplicate Symbol** dialog box that opens, name the symbol **gfxOutlineFill** and choose **Graphic** for the **Behavior** option. Click **OK**. This will take all the contents of the Movie Clip symbol and make an exact copy of that symbol. The only difference is that by setting the Behavior option to Graphic, you have changed the way this new symbol functions. Since it contains animation (the fill tween), this kind of symbol is often referred to as an *animated* Graphic symbol.

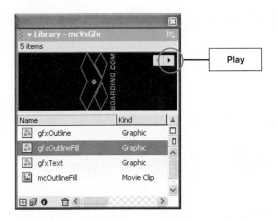

Play

5. In the **Library**, select the **gfxOutlineFill** symbol and click the **Play** button in the **Preview Window** to test the Graphic symbol in the Library. Next, select the **mcOutlineFill** symbol in the **Library** and click the **Play** button to test the Movie Clip symbol. Notice how the animations seem exactly the same?

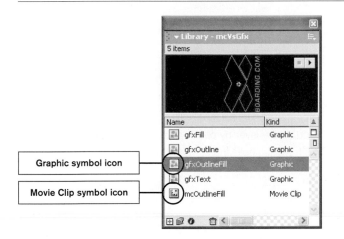

Graphic symbol icon

Movie Clip symbol icon

6. Double-click on the **gfxOutlineFill** Graphic symbol icon to open the symbol's **Timeline**. Notice that it looks exactly like the mcOutlineFill Movie Clip symbol you created in the last exercise. Double-click the **mcOutlineFill** Movie Clip icon to view the Movie Clip's **Timeline**. You will see that the two symbols do, in fact, have the same elements in their Timelines. The only difference between the two symbols is that one is a Movie Clip and the other is a Graphic symbol.

Tip: Double-clicking on the Movie Clip symbol icon in the Library automatically switches the "view" to the Library item you just double-clicked on. No closing of windows necessary!

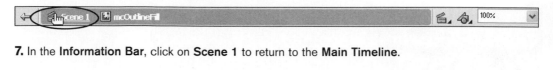

7. In the **Information Bar**, click on **Scene 1** to return to the **Main Timeline**.

Edit Scene button

Tip: You can also return to Scene 1 by clicking the Edit Scene button in the Information Bar and choosing Scene 1 or by choosing Edit > Edit Document.

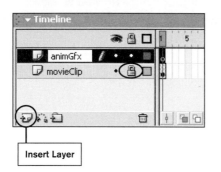

Insert Layer

8. In the **Timeline**, lock the **movieClip** layer. Add a new layer by clicking the **Insert Layer** button in the **Timeline**. Rename the new layer **animGfx**. This layer will hold the animated Graphic symbol that you will create.

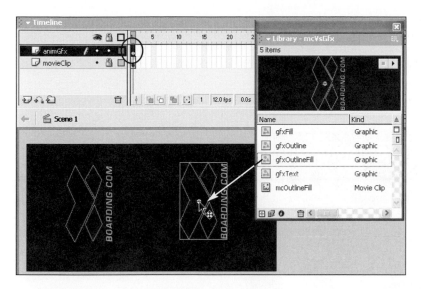

9. Drag an instance of the **gfxOutlineFill** symbol onto the **Stage**, and position it to the right of the **mcOutlineFill** Movie Clip symbol. This adds the animated Graphic symbol to the Main Timeline.

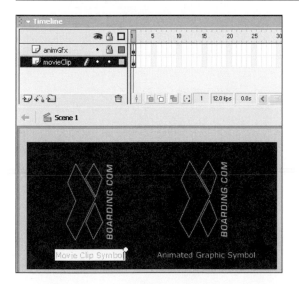

10. In the **Toolbox**, select the **Text** tool. Below the **gfxOutlineFill** instance, click on the **Stage** and add the text **Animated Graphic Symbol**, just like the picture above. Lock the **animGfx** layer, unlock the **movieClip** layer, and add the text **Movie Clip Symbol** below the **mcOutlineFill** instance, also as in the picture above. When you are testing the movie in the following steps, this will help you remember which instance is which.

11. Press **Enter/Return** to test the movie. Notice that nothing happens.

Why? When you press Enter/Return to test the movie, Macromedia Flash MX automatically moves the Playhead across all the frames in the Main Timeline of the movie. In this movie, you have only one frame, so the Playhead has nowhere to go. Therefore, you will see both symbols in their static state only.

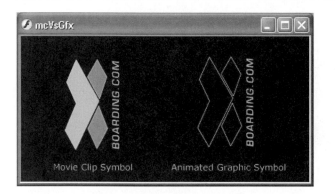

12. Choose **Control > Test Movie** to preview the movie. This time, notice that the Movie Clip symbol plays and the animated Graphic symbol does not. Why?

The main difference between an animated Graphic symbol and a Movie Clip symbol is that the Movie Clip's Timeline is completely independent of the main movie's Timeline. So a Movie Clip's Timeline can play regardless of how many frames the Main Timeline contains. Animated Graphic symbols, on the other hand, play in sync with the Main Timeline. The Timeline of an animated Graphic symbol is tied to the Main Timeline, and therefore at least the same number of frames in the Graphic symbol's Timeline must exist in the Main Timeline in order for the Graphic symbol to play.

13. Close the **Preview Window**. Back on the **Main Timeline**, click and drag to select **Frame 40** in both layers. Press **F5** to add 40 frames to both layers.

Why 40 frames? This is the same number of frames that exist in both the Graphic symbol's Timeline and the Movie Clip's Timeline.

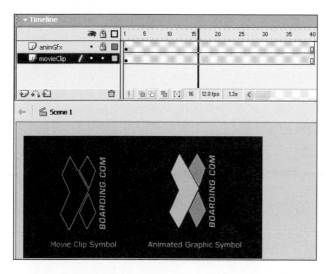

14. Press **Enter/Return** to test the movie.

This time, the animated Graphic symbol will play, although the Movie Clip symbol will not play. This is because there are now enough frames in the Main Timeline so that the animated Graphic symbol can play. However, you will not be able to see the Movie Clip play on the Stage because, as you learned in Exercise 1, in order to preview a Movie Clip, you must view it either in the Library or using Control > Test Movie. This is one of the "rules" of Movie Clips. They don't preview in the editing environment.

15. Choose **Control > Test Movie**. Notice that now both symbols are animating.

To summarize, the animated Graphic symbol will play if there are enough frames in the Main Timeline, but the Movie Clip will play regardless in the Preview window.

16. Save this file, but leave it open for the next exercise.

NOTE | Why Is Timeline Independence Important?

At this point, you probably understand that the Movie Clip can play in its entirety, even though it takes up only one frame in the Main Timeline, while the Graphic symbol needs all 40 frames inserted into the Main Timeline in order to play. You also probably understand that a Movie Clip cannot be previewed inside the editing environment of Macromedia Flash MX, and that you must choose **Control > Test Movie** in order to see the Movie Clip play. Keep in mind that having a symbol be independent of the Timeline is extremely important when programming interactive presentations. ActionScripting, which you'll learn about in the next chapter, can refer to Movie Clips because they have the capacity to be "named" and referenced in scripts, while Graphic symbols do not.

3. ─────────────Creating an Animated Rollover Button

This exercise will demonstrate how to turn a normal rollover button into an animated rollover button by nesting a Movie Clip in the Over state of a Button symbol. If you've been wondering why Timeline independence is important, this example will drive the point home. As you learned when you created buttons in Chapter 9, "*Buttons*," there are only four frames in each Button symbol—Up, Over, Down, and Hit. The only way to put an animation into a single frame for one of these states is to use a symbol that can contain animation yet has an independent Timeline. A Movie Clip symbol is just the ticket.

1. You should still have the **mcVsGfx.fla** file open from the last exercise.

Document Properties

Dimensions: 600 px (width) x 200 px (height)

Match: Printer | Contents | Default

Background Color:

Frame Rate: 12 fps

Ruler Units: Pixels

Help | Make Default | OK | Cancel

2. In the **Property Inspector**, click on the **Size** setting button to open the **Document Properties** dialog box. For **Dimensions**, change the **width** to **600 px**. This will change the width of the Stage to 600 pixels, which will give you more room to work with this exercise. Click **OK**.

When you change the document dimensions, your Stage should look like the picture above.

3. Make sure the **Library** is open (**F11**). To create a new symbol, click on the **New Symbol** button in the bottom left corner of the **Library**. This is another way to open the **Symbol Properties** dialog box.

You will be creating an animated Button symbol in the following steps.

4. In the **Create New Symbol** dialog box, name the symbol **btnAnim**, and set its **Behavior** to **Button**. Click **OK**.

After you click OK, you will be inside the editing environment for the Button symbol's Timeline.

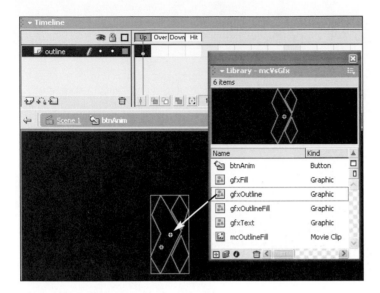

5. Rename **Layer 1** to **outline**. Drag an instance of the **gfxOutline** symbol onto the **Stage**. This symbol is static and contains only the outline of the "X."

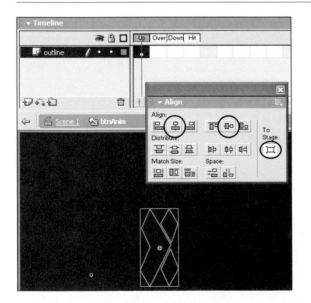

6. With the **gfxOutline** instance still selected on the **Stage**, choose **Window > Align** to open the **Align** panel. Click the **To Stage** button, and then click the **Align Vertical Center** and **Align Horizontal Center** buttons (all circled in the picture above) to perfectly align the instance in the center of the Stage.

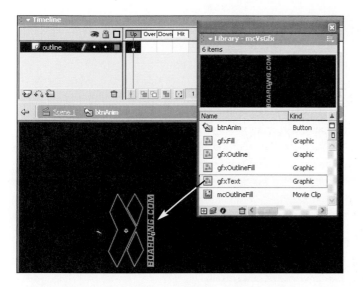

7. From the **Library**, drag an instance of the **gxfText** symbol onto the **Stage**, just to the right of the "X" outline, as in the picture above. This symbol is static and contains the word **boarding.com** on only one frame. The **Align** panel should still be open. If it is not, press **Ctrl+K** (Windows) **or Cmd+K** (Mac). Make sure the **To Stage** button is selected, and click **Align Vertical Center** in the **Align** panel. You have now created the Up state of the button.

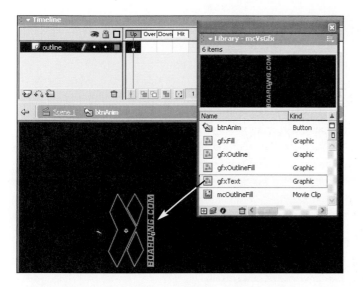

8. Press **F5** in the **Down** frame to add frames in the Over and Down states of the button. Lock this layer so you don't accidentally select anything on it. You will be adding a Movie Clip symbol to the button in the following steps.

9. Click the **Insert Layer** button to add a new layer. Double-click on the **Layer 2** name and change the name of this layer to **movieClip**.

10. In the **Library**, right-click (Windows) or Ctrl+click (Mac) on the **mcOutlineFill** Movie Clip symbol to access the drop-down menu. Choose **Duplicate** to make a copy of the symbol.

11. In the **Duplicate Symbol** dialog box that opens, name the symbol **mcOverAnim** and choose **Movie Clip** for **Behavior**. Click **OK**. This will take all the contents of the Movie Clip symbol and make an exact copy of that symbol. This Movie Clip will be used for the Over state of the button, but first you have to make a modification to the mcOverAnim symbol. You will do this next.

Double-click here to view the Movie Clip's Timeline

12. In the **Library**, double-click on the **mcOverAnim** Movie Clip icon. This will take you into the Movie Clip's Timeline. Notice that it looks exactly like the Timeline for the mcOutlineFill Movie Clip symbol you created in Exercise 1.

You will modify this Movie Clip next.

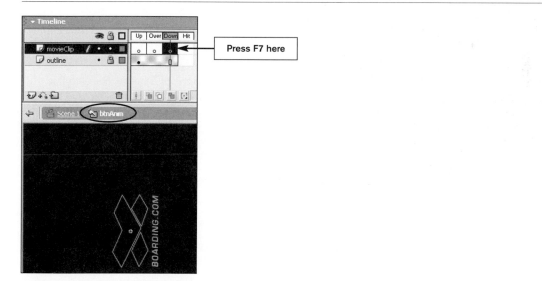

13. Click to the right of the **text** layer name to select the entire text layer. Click on the **Trashcan** icon to delete the **text** layer. Repeat this step for the **outline** layer to delete it also. When you are finished, the Timeline for the mcOverAnim Movie Clip should have only one layer with the fill tween on it, as in the picture above.

You deleted these extra layers because you need only the "X" artwork for the animated Over state you are creating for the button.

14. Scrub the **Playhead** to see the motion tween animation. This Movie Clip will serve as the Over state of the button (once you add it to the button's Timeline).

Tip: *You can also preview the motion tween inside the Movie Clip by selecting mcOverAnim in the Library and clicking the Play button in the Library Preview Window.*

15. In the **Library**, double-click on the **btnAnim** icon to open the Button symbol's **Timeline**. On the **movieClip** layer, press **F7** first in the **Over** frame and again in the **Down** frame to add blank keyframes to both the Over and Down states of the button.

16. With the **Over** state of the button selected, drag an instance of the **mcOverAnim** Movie Clip onto the **Stage**. Use the **Align** panel to center the Movie Clip in the middle of the Stage, just as you did in step 6. When you are finished, lock the **movieClip** layer.

You have just added the Movie Clip to the Over state of the button. You will add the Hit state to the button next to complete the exercise.

17. Click the **Insert Layer** button to add a new layer to the Button symbol's Timeline. Rename this layer **hit**. Click to the right of the layer name, and then drag this layer below the outline layer so that it is the bottom layer.

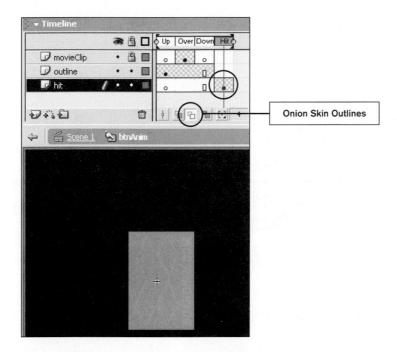

Onion Skin Outlines

18. Press **F7** in the **hit** frame to add a blank keyframe to the Hit state of the button. In the **Toolbox**, select the **Rectangle** tool and draw a rectangle that covers the **X** outline and the **boarding.com** text. You may want to unlock the **outline** layer and select the **Onion Skin Outlines** button to turn Onion Skinning Outlines on. This will help you make sure the rectangle covers the X outline and the boarding.com text.

The rectangle will serve as the Hit state of the button, so when the user's mouse touches any part of the rectangle, the Over state will be triggered.

19. You are finished with the button. In the **Information Bar**, click on **Scene 1** to return to the **Main Timeline**.

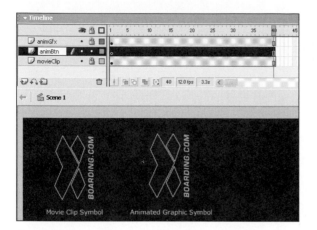

20. In the **Main Timeline**, lock both the **animGfx** and **movieClip** layers. Click the **Insert Layer** button to add a new layer, and rename the layer **animBtn**. You will be placing the button you just created on this layer next.

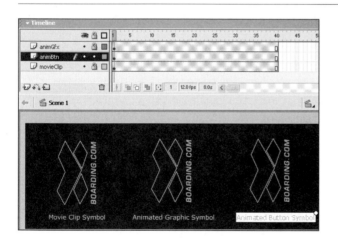

21. Select the **Arrow** tool and drag an instance of the **btnAnim** Button symbol onto the **Stage**, to the right of the animated Graphic symbol. In the **Toolbox**, select the **Text** tool. Below the **btnAnim** instance, click on the **Stage** and add the text **Animated Button Symbol**, as shown in the picture above.

22. Choose **Control > Test Movie** to preview and test all of the symbols.

Notice that the Movie Clip and animated Graphic symbol continue to animate on their own, while the Button symbol waits for you to move the mouse over it in order for the animation to begin. By adding Movie Clips to different states of a button, you can take the rollover button to the next level.

23. Save this file, but keep it open for one last exercise.

4. ——————— Animated Rollover Button in Action

In the previous exercise, you learned how to use a Movie Clip in a button's Over state to create an animated rollover button. In this exercise, you will learn how to use that same button in a different project file and place it in a Web page interface.

1. You should still have the **mcVsGfx.fla** file open from the last exercise. Press **F11** to open the **Library** if it is not already open. It is important that you keep this file (including the Library) open and that you don't close it during the next few steps. You will be taking the animated Button symbol you made in the last exercise from the Library and using it in another file next.

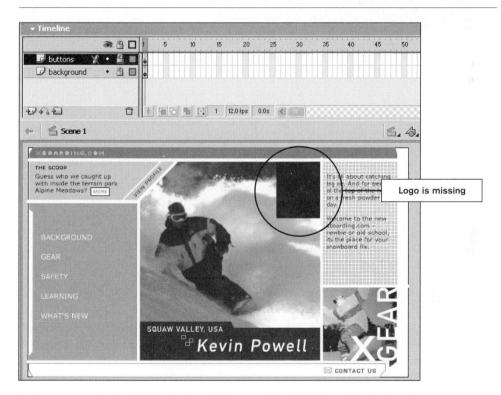

2. Open the **animBtnLive.fla** from the **chap_10** folder. Notice that this file is similar to one you worked on in the last chapter. It contains two layers that are locked, but in this file the logo is missing from the interface. You will be adding the logo in a few steps.

3. Open the **Library** (**F11**) if it is not open. Notice that there are two Libraries in the panel window. On the top is the Library from the **mcVsGfx** movie, and below is the Library from the **animBtnLive** movie.

Since you never closed the mcVsGfx project and you made sure the Library was open before you opened the animBtnLive file, the Library for the mcVsGfx project will stay open until you either close the file or close the Library for that project. In addition to the workflow you learned in Chapter 9, Exercise 3 (File > Open As Library), this is another way you can use assets such as symbols from one project in another project. You will add the Movie Clip symbol from the mcVsGfx movie to the animBtnLive movie next.

4. In the **Main Timeline** of the **animBtnLive** move, insert a new layer and name the layer **logo**.

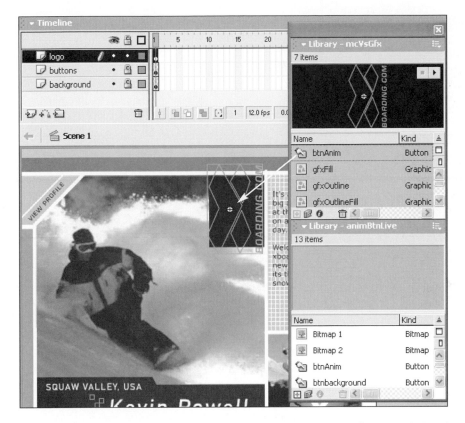

5. In the **mcVsGfx Library**, drag an instance of **btnAnim** onto the **Stage** and place it over the black box, as in the picture above.

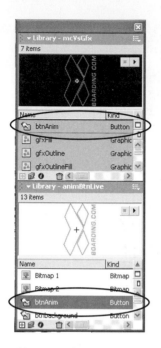

After you place the instance on the Stage, the btnAnim symbol is located in the animBtnLive Library also. This is because you have added the symbol from the mcVsGfx movie to the animBtnLive movie, and Macromedia Flash MX adds the symbol to the Library for you.

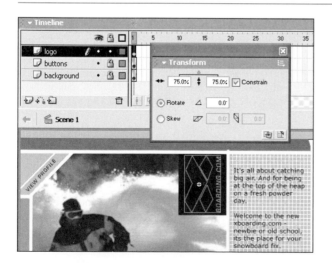

6. Choose **Window > Transform** to open the Transform panel. With the instance still selected, make sure the **Constrain** box is checked, and enter **75.0%** in either the **width** or **height** field. This will change the size of the instance so that it fits in the box in the Interface.

7. Choose **Control > Test Movie** and roll the mouse over the logo to test the animation!

---

8. When you are finished, save and close all the files. You are finished with this chapter.

Congratulations! You have made it through an essential chapter. You now know how to create, modify, and nest Movie Clips inside Buttons. In the next chapter you will use Movie Clips in more advanced ways. Make sure you are well rested before you take on the next chapter, "ActionScripting Basics." It's one of the most challenging chapters in the book.

11.

ActionScripting Basics

| Controlling the Main Timeline |
Controlling Movie Clips	The goto Action to Create a Slideshow
On Mouse Events: getURL	Targeting Scenes
Creating a Drop-Down Menu	Loading Movies

chap_11

Macromedia Flash MX
H•O•T CD-ROM

So far, you've learned how to draw, mask, animate, and create symbols in Macromedia Flash MX. The last step in learning how to make fully interactive presentations is to add ActionScript to your projects. ActionScript is an internal programming language to Macromedia Flash MX, similar to JavaScript. The good news is that you do not have to know JavaScript or be a programmer to add ActionScript to your movies. The Macromedia Flash MX Actions panel assists you so that it is not necessary to write the code from scratch.

Why is ActionScript important? On a basic level, ActionScript enables you to create buttons that control the Main Timeline or Movie Clips, make slideshows with forward and back buttons, link to other URLs on the Internet, or load other movies into a Macromedia Flash MX movie. This is a short list, and covers only some of the possibilities that ActionScripting offers. By the time you are finished with this chapter, you will have a solid understanding of how to add ActionScript to objects and frames and why you would choose one over the other. You will also learn many of the basic ActionScripts to apply in your own projects.

Working with ActionScript code is one of the most technically challenging aspects of Macromedia Flash MX. I hope to give you a solid foundation on which to build later on your own.

Where Do I Place ActionScript?

ActionScript can be attached to a button instance, a Movie Clip instance, or a keyframe in the Timeline. However, ActionScript can *not* be attached to an instance of a Graphic symbol. This chapter will give you a chance to attach ActionScript to each of these elements. You use the Actions panel (described next) to add ActionScript to your project file.

The Actions Panel Defined

In Macromedia Flash MX, you use **Actions** to build ActionScripts that can control your movie. The Actions panel is where you create and edit **object actions** or **frame actions**, which you'll learn about in great detail later in this chapter. This panel has two modes, **Normal mode** and **Expert mode**. You will learn to work in Normal mode; Expert mode is generally used by more advanced users.

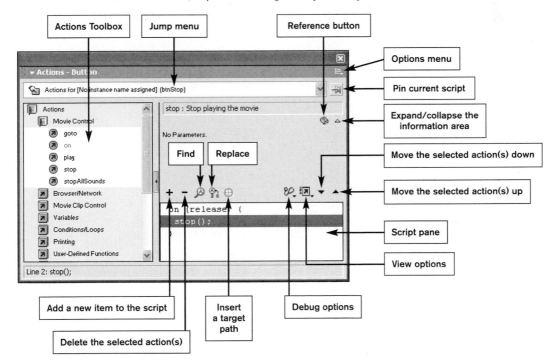

The Normal mode (shown above) allows you to choose items from either the list of code found within the Actions Toolbox or by using the Add (+) button. Once an item is selected, in the Toolbox or in the Script pane, the description of the item appears on the right side of the Actions panel, in the information area. For example, in the picture above, the stop action is selected in the Script pane and the description reads **stop: Stop playing the movie**. When an item is double-clicked in the Actions Toolbox or selected using the (+) button, it will appear in the Script pane on the right side of the Action panel.

You can also enter parameters for actions inside the text boxes that appear above the Script pane for selected items, change the order of statements inside the Script pane, delete selected actions, view script numbers, and keep a script available when you click off of the frame or object using the Pin button. In the exercises in this chapter, you will have a chance to work with many of these features.

The Expert mode allows you to type ActionScript code from scratch directly into the Script pane. For this reason, it is used by intermediate to advanced Macromedia Flash MX users who know how to hand-code actions. Because this book is targeted to beginners, there are no exercises covering Expert mode features. Once you're finished with this book, you will be better prepared to go deeper into ActionScripting.

Macromedia Flash MX will stay in whichever mode you last used to create the ActionScript, so if you need to go back and edit the actions later, the Actions panel will open up in the mode you used.

I. ——————————— Controlling the Timeline

In Macromedia Flash MX, once a movie starts, it will play in its entirety until it reaches the last frame of the Timeline, unless you tell it otherwise. Through the use of ActionScript, you can control when a movie stops and when it starts. This exercise will teach you how to assign **stop** and **play** actions to button instances in order to control animation on the Main Timeline. As well, you will learn to apply actions to frames on the Main Timeline to further control the movie.

1. Copy the **chap_11** folder, located on the **H•O•T CD-ROM**, to your hard drive. You need to have this folder on your hard drive in order to save files inside it.

2. Open the file called **stopAndPlayFinal.fla** from the **chap_11** folder. This is the finished version of the project you'll be building in this exercise.

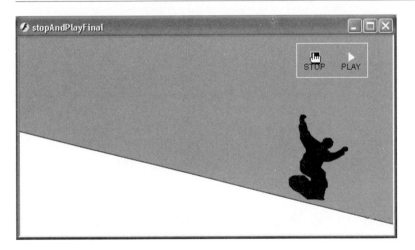

3. Choose **Control > Test Movie** to preview the movie. In the .swf file, click the **Play** button to set the boarder in motion, moving down the mountain. Click the **Stop** button to stop the boarder. You will learn how to add the same functionality to this movie in the following steps.

4. When you are finished stopping and playing this movie, close the **Preview Window** and this file.

5. Open the **stopAndPlay.fla** file from the **chap_11** folder. This is an unfinished version of the movie you just previewed. It contains everything except the ActionScript, which you will add in this exercise.

6. Choose **Control > Test Movie** to preview the movie. Click on the **Stop** and **Play** buttons.

Notice how nothing happens and the movie continues to play. Why? No actions have been added to these buttons yet, and therefore the buttons do not control the movie. You will learn to do this next.

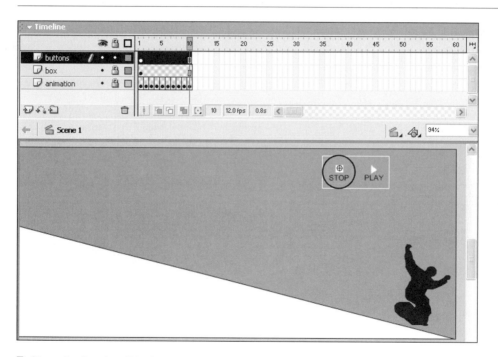

7. Close the **Preview Window** and return to the project file. Click on the **Stop** button instance on the **Stage** to select it.

NOTE | Object or Frame Action Instruction

To add an action to an object, as you will do in the following steps with the Stop and Play buttons, you must select the object and then add the action. *Note:* When you add actions to an object, the object must be either a Movie Clip symbol or a Button symbol. To add an action to a frame in a Timeline, you must place an action in a keyframe. You will have a chance to do this later in the exercise.

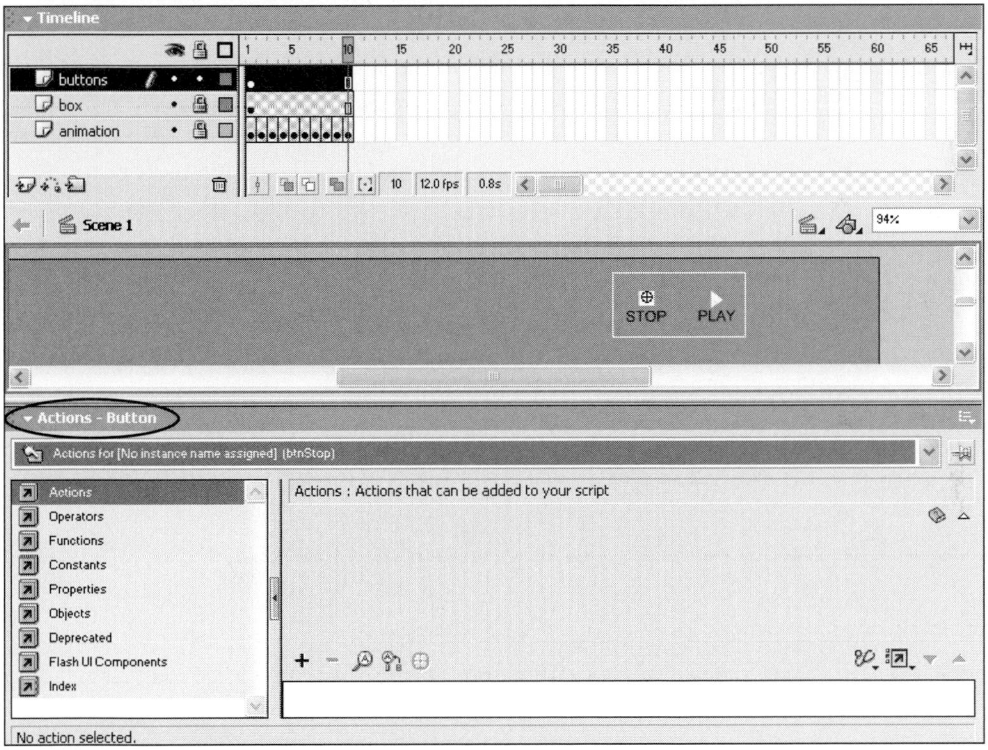

---

8. Choose **Window > Actions** (or use the shortcut key **F9**) to open the **Actions** panel. Notice how the top of the Actions panel reads Actions – Button. Because you have selected the button instance, Macromedia Flash MX knows that you will be adding actions to the button instance on the Stage.

TIP | Undocking the Actions Panel

You are not stuck with working with the Actions panel in the default location. In the Actions panel, you can click on the series of dots (called the gripper) to the left of the Actions – Button text and drag the panel away to undock it. To redock it, click on the same dots again and drag the panel back to the same location.

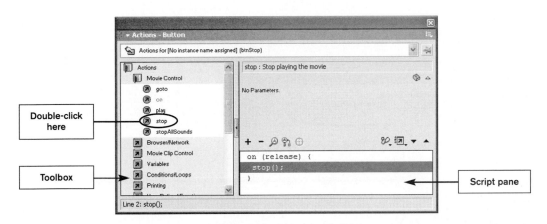

Double-click here

Toolbox

Script pane

9. In the **Actions** panel, click on the **Actions** category in the Toolbox to access a list of all the actions that fall under that category. Click on the **Movie Control** category to expand that category. Double-click on the **stop** action to add it to the Script pane on the right side of the **Actions** panel.

You have just added your first action to the project. The button instance that you selected in step 8 now has the power to stop the Timeline once you test the movie, which you will get to do shortly!

Tip: If you add the stop action, and the on (release) handler does not appear in the Script pane, there may be two reasons for this. First, you may be in Expert mode, rather than Normal mode. If this is the case, click on the Options menu in the upper right corner of the Actions panel and choose Normal mode. Second, you may be adding the ActionScript to a frame, rather than a button. Make sure your Actions panel reads Actions – Button in the upper left corner so that you know you are applying actions to the button and not a frame.

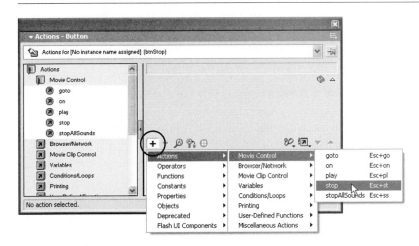

You can also add an action to the list by dragging it from the Toolbox to the Script pane or by selecting the Add (+) button and choosing the action from the pull-down menus, as shown in the picture above.

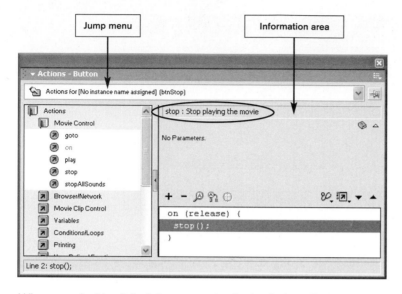

When you double-clicked the stop action in the Actions Toolbox, ActionScript appeared in the Script pane on the right. This Script pane of the Actions panel holds the ActionScript statements and displays all the code for the actions that are applied to an object. Notice also that with the stop action selected in the Script pane, the action's description is displayed in information area.

Located in the white field above the information area is the **Jump menu**, which allows you to quickly move (or jump) to different scripts that you have added to the movie. Notice also that it reads **Actions for [No instance name assigned] (btnStop)**. The Jump menu will display the actions for the selected object or frame, which is great feedback so you can make sure you are adding the ActionScript to the right item.

In this case, you have applied the script to an instance of the btnStop button on the Stage, and since you have not named the instance (which is not necessary in this exercise), the Jump menu field states **[No instance name assigned]**. The reason you would name an instance is so you can use ActionScripting to directly refer to ("talk to") that instance. Unless you need to refer to an instance by its name via ActionScripting, it is not necessary to name each instance in your project file. In later exercises in this chapter, you will need to name an instance in order for the ActionScripting to work; this name will be reflected in the Jump menu.

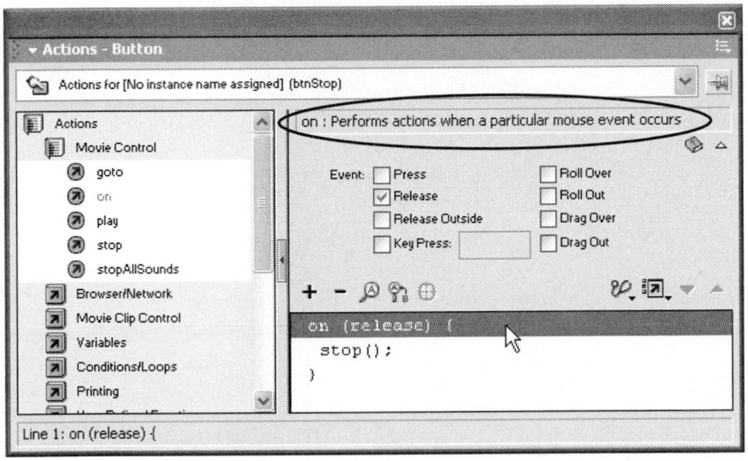

When you click once on any item in the Toolbox or any statement in the Script pane to select it, the Information area will display a description of that item. For example, in the picture above, the first line in the Script pane is selected.

NOTE | Whoa! What's All the Extra Stuff in the Script Pane?

You may also have noticed that when you added the stop action, an on (release) event appeared above it in the Script pane, as well as some parentheses, braces, and a semicolon. In Normal mode, when an action is attached to a button, the action is automatically enclosed in an on (mouse event) handler. Macromedia Flash MX needs to know when to apply the stop action; in this case, the default setting is for Macromedia Flash MX to apply the stop action when the user releases the mouse (on release).

The **parentheses ( )** hold the parameters (called arguments) that apply to an action, the **braces { }** contain statements that should be grouped together, and the **semicolon ;** marks an end of a statement (just as a period marks the end of a sentence). The good news is that you do not have to worry about writing these punctuation marks because in Normal mode, Macromedia Flash MX writes them for you; all you have to do is choose the action.

---

10. Choose **Control > Test Movie** and try out the **stop** action you just added to the button instance. When you click on the **Stop** button, the movie will stop!

Once a movie is stopped, it must be explicitly started again in order to play. You can do this with the play action, which you will do next.

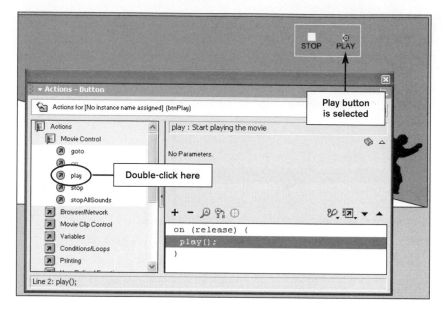

11. Close the **Preview Window** when you are finished. On the **Stage**, click on the **Play** button instance to select it. In the **Actions** panel, double-click on the **play** action under the **Actions > Movie Control** categories to add it to the Script pane.

You have just added a play action to the button instance on the Stage.

12. Choose **Control > Test Movie** and test the movie again. Click on the **Stop** button to stop the movie. Click on the **Play** button to make the movie play again! When you are finished, close the **Preview Window**.

Notice that the movie immediately plays as soon as the Preview Window opens. You'll learn to change this using frame actions next.

13. Back in the **Main Timeline**, click on the **Insert Layer** button to add a new layer to the **Timeline**, and name it **actions**.

NOTE | Adding a Layer for the Frame Action

I *strongly* recommend that you get in the habit of placing all frame actions on their own separate layer in the Timeline. I also recommend that this layer always be located on top of all the other layers in your movie and that you consistently name it the same thing: **actions**. As the movies you create become more and more complex, it will be significantly easier to troubleshoot and debug a movie if you know you can always find the frame actions in the same place: on the first layer of the movie, on the layer named **actions**.

By default, the Main Timeline in the movie will automatically begin to play unless you tell it otherwise. You can keep a movie from playing automatically by adding an action to the Timeline to tell the movie to stop before it begins to play. The movie will then start in a stopped position, and it will not play until the button is clicked. You will do this next.

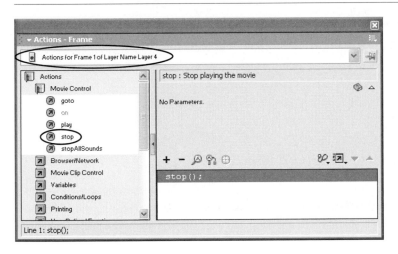

14. Select **Frame 1** of the **actions** layer in the **Main Timeline**, which contains a blank keyframe. In the **Actions** panel, double-click on the **stop** action to add it to the Script pane.

Notice that the Actions panel no longer reads "Actions – Button," but instead it reads "Actions – Frame". Notice also that the Jump menu describes more specifically where the action is being placed. This gives you immediate feedback as to where the action is located and whether you are applying the action to an object, such as a button or Movie Clip, or to a keyframe.

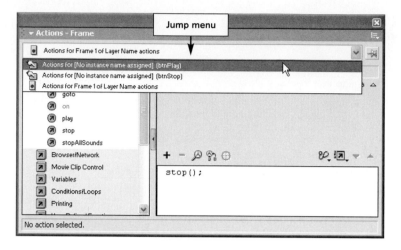

Tip: *You can expand the Jump menu to quickly access any of the actions that have been added to either frames or objects within the movie.*

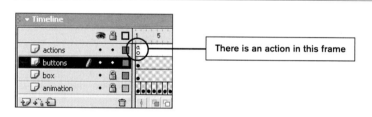

*Once you have added an action to a keyframe, the Timeline will display a small **a** inside the frame as further feedback that there is an action in the keyframe.*

15. Test the movie again (**Control > Test Movie**). The movie will now begin in a static state, waiting for the user to click on the **Play** button. Click on the **Stop** and **Play** buttons to control the animation.

Notice that once the boarder reaches the end of the mountain, it stops. Why? This is because you added a stop action to the first keyframe, so the movie will begin in a stopped state since the first thing the Playhead encounters is a stop action in the first frame, which will stop the movie. When a user clicks on the Play button, it sets the Playhead in motion. The Playhead will play through all the frames and will automatically loop by default, going back to the first frame, where it will encounter that stop action again, which will stop the movie. You can choose to bypass the movie stopping each time it tries to start again; you will do this next.

16. Close the **Preview Window**. In the **Main Timeline**, add a keyframe (**F6**) to **Frame 10** on the **actions** layer. You will be adding actions to Frame 10 next; in order to add an action to a frame, the frame must be a keyframe.

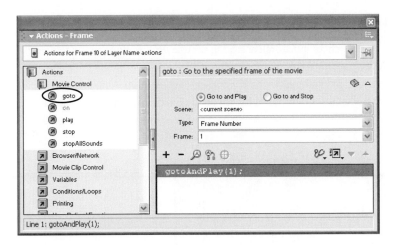

17. Make sure **Frame 10** is selected on the **Main Timeline**. In the **Actions** panel, double-click on the **goto** action to add it to the Script pane.

18. In the **Parameters** pane of the **Action** panel, type **2** in the **Frame** field. This tells Macromedia Flash MX that when the Playhead hits Frame 10, send the Playhead to Frame 2 and play. This creates a small loop because each time the Playhead hits Frame 10, it will go to Frame 2, play the rest of the frames, and then return to Frame 2, etc., each time bypassing Frame 1, which has the stop action on it.

19. Choose **Control > Test Movie** and test the movie again. Click on the **Stop** and **Play** buttons to control the animation. The movie will begin in a stopped state. As soon as you click the **Play** button, the movie will play and continue to play over and over, without stopping, until you click the **Stop** button.

20. When you are finished, save and close this file.

Interactivity and Actions: Events and Event Handlers

When a movie plays, certain actions, such as a user releasing the mouse on a button, are considered an **event** in Macromedia Flash MX. The events fall into one of the following categories: mouse events, Movie Clip events, keyboard events, and time-based events. For every event, there must be something that manages the event. In Macromedia Flash MX, this is known as an **Event Handler**. You can think of the Event Handler as the event's manager because the Event Handler is in charge of (manages) the event. I describe the four types of basic events in the following sections.

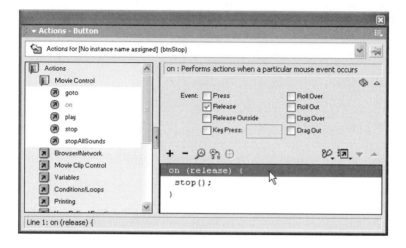

*When you add an action to an object (either a Button symbol or a Movie Clip symbol) in Macromedia Flash MX, it will introduce an event. In the illustration above, the event is a mouse event. It states **on (release)**, meaning that when the user clicks the button, the action is triggered after the mouse has been released. The Event Handler is the **on** action, which handles button events.*

Mouse Events

Mouse events occur when the user interacts with a button instance. When an action (such as a stop action) is added to a button instance, an **on** Event Handler is automatically added, as you saw in Exercise 1. The default **on** event is **release** (shown in the preceding illustration).

The following table defines each possible mouse event.

Mouse Events Defined	
Event	When It Occurs
press	When the mouse pointer is moved over the Hit area of the button, and the mouse is pressed.
release	When the mouse pointer is moved over the Hit area of the button, and the mouse is pressed and then released.
releaseOutside	When a press occurs on the Hit area of a button, then the mouse pointer is moved outside of the Hit area and released.
rollOver	When the mouse pointer moves over the Hit area of a button.
rollOut	When the mouse pointer moves off the Hit area of a button.
dragOver	When the mouse is pressed on the Hit area of a button, then rolls out of the Hit area, and reenters the Hit area with the mouse still pressed.
dragOut	When the mouse is pressed on the Hit area of a button, then the mouse pointer rolls out of the Hit area with the mouse still pressed.
keyPress	When the specified key is pressed on the keyboard.

Keyboard Events

Keyboard events are similar to mouse events, except that they occur when the user presses a key on the keyboard rather than interacting with the mouse. For example, you might want to make a slideshow move forward and backward by pressing the arrow keys on your keyboard instead of having physical buttons on your Stage. This kind of functionality is great when using Macromedia Flash MX as a substitute for a PowerPoint presentation. To change the mouse event to a keyboard event, select the **Key Press** box (circled in the illustration). Press any key on the keyboard or type a letter into the **Key Press** field to assign a keypress to the button. This example was created by pressing **Enter** on the keyboard. Macromedia Flash MX will execute the play action when the user presses the **Enter** key.

Note: If you assign a capital letter for a keypress, the user *must* type in a *capital* letter. Likewise, if you assign a lowercase letter, the user *must* type in a *lowercase* letter. Also, use caution when assigning a keyboard event to a movie that will be displayed on the Web: Keypresses will not be executed in a browser unless the user has already clicked inside the movie at some point. And further, your end users might not intuitively know to use their keyboards unless they are instructed to do so.

Movie Clip Events

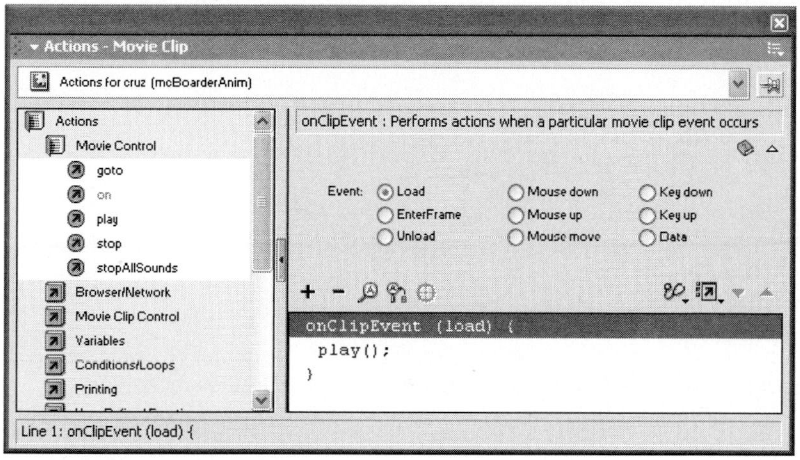

Movie Clip events occur when something happens with a Movie Clip instance. When an action (such as play) is added to a Movie Clip instance, an **onClipEvent** Event Handler will automatically be added. The default **onClipEvent** is **load** (shown above). **Note:** You can also create a Movie Clip that receives button events; this will automatically have the **on** (rather than the **onClipEvent**) Event Handler.

The following table defines each possible Movie Clip event.

Movie Clip Events Defined	
Event	**When It Occurs**
load	When the Movie Clip is inserted and appears in the Timeline.
unload	When the Movie Clip is removed from the Timeline.
enterFrame	When the Playhead hits a frame, the action is triggered continually at the frame rate of the movie.
mouseDown	When the mouse button is pressed.
mouseUp	When the mouse button is released.
mouseMove	Every time the mouse is moved.
keyDown	When a key is pressed.
keyUp	When a key is released.
data	When data is received in a **loadVariables** or **loadMovie** action.

Time-Based Events

Unlike mouse events, keyboard events, and Movie Clip events, time-based events are located in keyframes as frame actions. Time-based events occur when the Playhead reaches a keyframe containing actions.

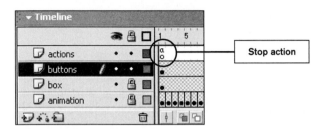

In the last exercise, you added a time-based event by adding the stop action to the first keyframe. Time-based events can exist on the Main Timeline or in any Graphic or Movie Clip instance's Timeline.

2. ——————————Controlling Movie Clips

In the last exercise, you attached the stop and play actions to button instances to control an animation on the Main Timeline. You can also use the stop and play actions to control the Timeline of any Movie Clip or loaded movie. In order to control a Movie Clip, you must give it an instance name and it must be present in the Timeline. This exercise will show you how.

1. Open the file called **stopAndPlayMC.fla** from the **chap_11** folder. This file was created to get you started.

Original stopAndPlay project file

stopAndPlayMC project file

2. Notice that this project file looks very similar to the original project file from Exercise 1, with two exceptions: In the **stopAndPlayMC** project file, there is a **movie clip** rather than an **animation** layer in the Main Timeline, and there is only one frame in the Main Timeline.

Because this exercise will show you how to use actions to control a Movie Clip rather than the Main Timeline, the frames from the animation layer in the stopAndPlay project file were converted into a Movie Clip in the stopAndPlayMC project file for you.

3. Choose **Control > Test Movie** to preview the movie. Click on the **Stop** and **Play** buttons. Notice that nothing happens and the movie continues to play. This is because no actions have been added to these buttons yet, and therefore the buttons do not control the movie. You will add actions to control the Movie Clip in the steps that follow. When you are finished previewing the movie, close the **Preview Window**.

Click here to select the
Movie Clip instance

Instance Name

4. On the **Stage**, click on the snow to select the Movie Clip instance. In the **Property Inspector** (**Window > Properties**), type **boarder** in the **Instance Name** field. This will assign an instance name to the Movie Clip on the Stage.

In Exercise 1, the stop and start actions you added to the buttons automatically controlled the Main Timeline. Conversely, in order to control a Movie Clip, (make it start or stop, for example) you have to refer to the Movie Clip by its instance name when you apply actions to the buttons in the next steps.

5. Select the **Stop** button instance on the **Stage** to select it.

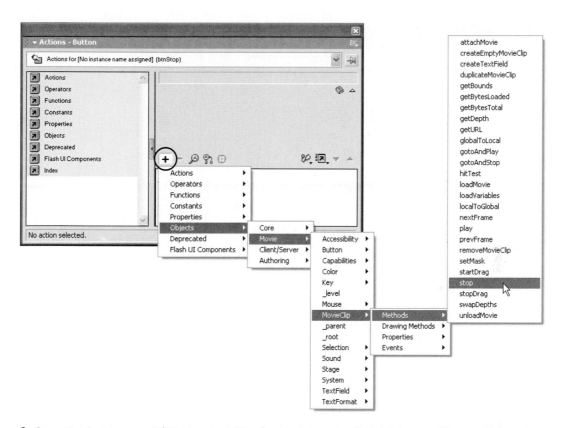

6. Open the **Actions** panel (**Window > Actions**) and click on the **Add** (+) button. Choose **Objects > Movie > MovieClip > Methods > stop**.

This is a little different than simply choosing Actions > stop as you did in Exercise 1, because this time, you want to select an action that corresponds with controlling a Movie Clip, rather than the Main Timeline.

Note: You can also select the same stop action using the path described above inside the Toolbox rather than using the Add (+) button. Both paths will lead you to the same stop action, I just want to give you practice using another method for choosing an action.

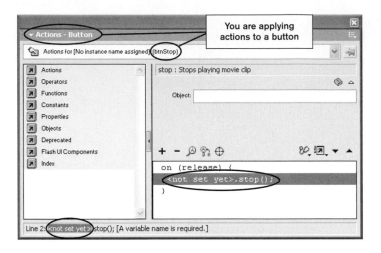

Once you select the stop action, the Actions panel should look like this. Notice that the Actions panel provides feedback that you are applying actions to a button. As you learned in Exercise 1, when an action is attached to a button, the action is automatically enclosed in an on (mouse event) handler. Notice also that the Script pane looks a bit different than it did in the last exercise because after you select the stop action, the words **<not set yet>** are highlighted in red before the stop action and also in the status bar at the bottom of the Actions panel. This is an indication that the syntax is not correct yet, and Macromedia Flash MX is looking for the name of the object you want to stop. You will add this next.

NOTE | Syntax Errors

Any time your ActionScripts are incomplete or incorrect, Macromedia Flash MX will automatically highlight the error or the incomplete part of the script in red. If you move your mouse pointer over the red highlighted area, a ToolTip displays the associated error message.

7. In the **Object** field, type **boarder**. This is the instance name that you gave the Movie Clip in step 4. This ActionScript tells Macromedia Flash MX that when a user releases the mouse, make boarder (which is the Movie Clip instance) stop.

Note that because you are applying the ActionScript to a button that will control the Movie Clip, the on Event Handler is automatically added for you.

Controlling Movie Clips

Why can't you just choose **Actions > stop** to add the stop action to the button rather than all these steps? If you choose **Actions > stop**, you are controlling the Main Timeline, not a specific Movie Clip. To control the Movie Clip, the way to choose a stop action is different. Here's why: In Macromedia Flash MX, Movie Clips can be controlled using either actions or methods. In ActionScripting, methods are functions that are assigned to an object. Because some actions and methods yield the same behavior, you can control a Movie Clip by either one. For example, to make a Movie Clip stop, you need the instance name, a dot, and then the method, such as `boarder.stop();` as you did in the last step. In other words, the stop *method* halts the Playhead in the boarder Movie Clip instance.

---

8. Choose **Control > Test Movie** and try out the **stop** action you just added to the button instance. When you click on the **Stop** button, the Movie Clip will stop! When you are finished, close the **Preview Window**.

---

9. Back in the project file, click on the **Play** button on the **Stage** to select it.

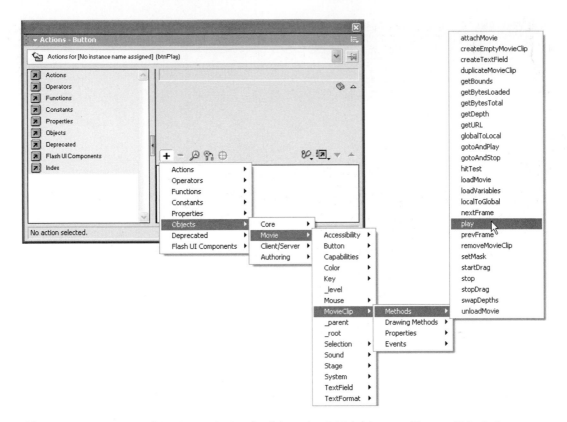

10. In the **Actions** panel (**Window > Actions**), click on the **Add (+)** button. Choose **Objects > Movie > MovieClip > Methods > play**. This will add the **play** action to the Script pane, along with the **on** Event Handler.

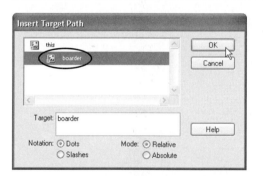

11. After you select the **play** action, click in the **Object** field and then click on the **Insert a Target Path** button above the Script pane, as pictured above. This will open the **Insert Target Path** dialog box.

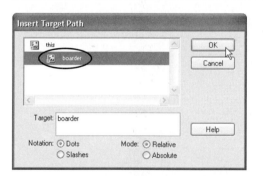

12. In the **Insert Target Path** dialog box, select the **boarder** icon and click **OK**. This adds the word "boarder" to your statement in the Script pane.

NOTE | What Are Target Paths?

Target paths are hierarchical addresses that display Movie Clip instance names, variables, and objects inside your movie. After you name a Movie Clip instance in the Property Inspector, as you did in step 4, you can use the Insert a Target Path button to find all the Movie Clip instance names in the movie (you have only one in this exercise) and select the one you want to direct the action to. Using the Insert a Target Path button to find the boarder instance name is the same as typing the boarder name in the Object field, as you did in step 7. Oftentimes, you may forget exactly how you spelled an instance name; the target path feature is a quick and surefire way to find the instance you want to refer to.

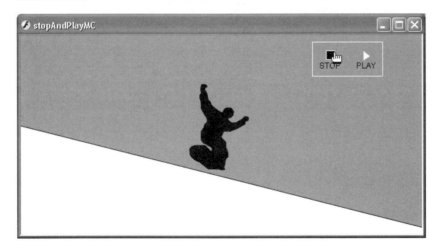

After you select boarder in the Insert Target Path dialog box, your Actions panel should look like this.

13. Choose **Control > Test Movie** and try out the **stop** and **play** actions you just added to the button instances. You have just added actions to button instances that control a Movie Clip.

NOTE | Starting the Movie in a Stopped Position

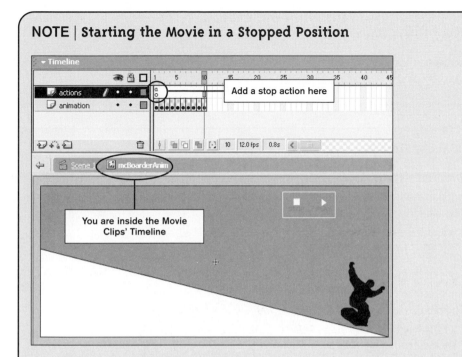

If you want the movie to start in a stopped position, as it did in the last exercise, you can add a stop frame action. However, you would need to add that stop frame action inside the Movie Clip's Timeline and not on the Main Timeline, as you did in Exercise 1. The reason for this is that, as you learned in Chapter 10, Movie Clips play independently of the Main Timeline, so in order for the Movie Clip to start in a stopped state, you must add a stop frame action to the first frame inside the Movie Clip's Timeline.

To access the Movie Clip's Timeline, you can either double-click the Movie Clip on the Stage, double-click on the Movie Clip in the Library, or select the Movie Clip symbol on the Stage and use the menu command **Edit > Edit Symbols** or **Edit > Edit Selected** or **Edit > Edit in Place**, all of which will open the Movie Clip symbol's Timeline. As well, in Frame 10, you can also add the **gotoAndPlay** Frame 2 ActionScripting to send the Playhead to Frame 2 to create a loop.

14. When you are finished, save and close this file.

MOVIE | controlMC.mov

To see this exercise performed, play the **controlMC.mov** located in the **movies** folder on the **H•O•T CD-ROM**.

Dot Syntax Made Simple

You may have noticed that there was a dot (.) added between the instance name and the stop and play methods in the last exercise: **boarder.stop();** In ActionScripting, the dot indicates the properties or methods that relate to a Movie Clip or other object. This is part of the ActionScript syntax, also referred to as **dot syntax**.

You may have heard of this term before. In Macromedia Flash MX, dot syntax simply refers to the convention that is used to create ActionScripting. Dot syntax is used to construct statements that consist of objects, properties, methods, and variables. Each dot syntax statement begins with the name of the object followed by a dot (.) and ends with the property, method, or variable you want to identify. For example, in the statement **boarder.play ( );**, the object is the Movie Clip named **boarder**, and the method is **play**. The **parentheses ( )** hold the parameters (called arguments) that apply to an action; in this case, no parameters are required. The **semicolon ;** marks an end of a statement (just as a period marks the end of a sentence).

3. ——————The goto Action to Create a Slideshow

In addition to the stop and play actions, you can be even more specific and add actions that tell the Playhead not just to play, but *exactly* where to start and stop on the Timeline. This exercise will demonstrate how ActionScript can be used to create a Macromedia Flash MX movie that can be navigated one frame at a time, similar to a slideshow. You will use the goto action—which can be used to send the Playhead to a frame you specify—to do this.

1. Open the **slideShowFinal.fla** file from inside the **chap_11** folder. This is the finished version of the slideshow you are going to create.

2. Choose **Control > Test Movie** to preview the movie. Click the right arrow button to advance the slideshow forward. Click the left arrow button to display the previous slide. You will be creating this same slideshow in the steps that follow.

3. When you are finished, close the **slideShowFinal.fla** file.

4. Open the **slideShow.fla** file from the **chap_11** folder. This is an unfinished version of the movie you just previewed, containing only the slideshow images. You will add new layers, buttons, and the necessary ActionScripting in this exercise.

5. Choose **Control > Test Movie** to preview the movie. Notice that the frames go by very fast, one after another. This is because, by default, the movie will automatically play through the frames unless you tell it otherwise. You will add a stop action to Frame 1 to change this so that the movie starts in a stopped state. Close the **Preview Window** when you are finished.

6. In the **Main Timeline**, click the **Insert Layer** button to add a new layer to the Timeline. Name the new layer **actions**. Make sure the new layer is above the **images** layer. If it is not, click on the layer name and drag it above the **images** layer so that the **actions** layer is on top.

7. Select the first keyframe in the **actions** layer, Frame 1, and open the **Actions** panel (**Window > Actions** or **F9**).

8. In the **Actions Toolbox**, choose **Actions > Movie Control** and double-click on **stop** to add a stop action to the Script pane on the right side of the Actions panel. Because you are adding the stop action to the Main Timeline, this will cause the movie to stop when it first appears on the screen.

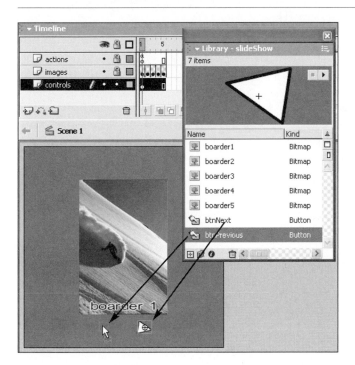

9. Click on the **Insert Layer** button to add another new layer to the Timeline. Name the new layer **controls**. Drag the **controls** layer below the other two layers, as shown in the picture above.

10. Lock the **actions** and **images** layers so that you don't accidentally select anything in either of those layers. Select the first keyframe in the **controls** layer.

11. Open the **Library** (**F11**). Drag an instance of **btnNext** and **btnPrevious** onto the **Stage**. Position them side by side. Select both of the button instances using **Ctrl+A** (Windows) or **Cmd+A** (Mac), then choose **Ctrl+K** (Windows) or **Cmd+K** (Mac) to open the **Align** panel and align the bottom edge of the buttons.

12. Click on the **btnNext** instance and make sure that the **Actions** panel is still open. You will be adding actions to the button instance next. (You may have to click off the Stage to deselect both buttons and then click on the btnNext instance to select only that instance.)

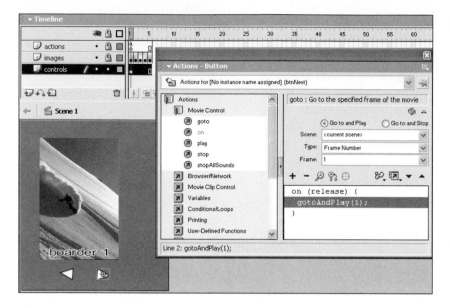

13. Choose **Actions > Movie Control** and double-click on the **goto** action to add it to the Script pane. Notice that once you add the **goto** action, additional information appears above the Script pane. This is where you can change the parameters attached to the action. You will do this next.

14. In the **Type** field, select **Next Frame** from the drop-down list.

When you are finished, your ActionScript should look like this:

```
on (release) {
    nextFrame ();
}
```

You have just added ActionScript to the right button. Now when the user clicks on this button and releases the mouse, the Playhead will advance to the next frame and stop. **Tip:** *Part of the description in the nextFrame action will send the Playhead to the next frame and automatically stop, so you do not need to add an additional stop action.*

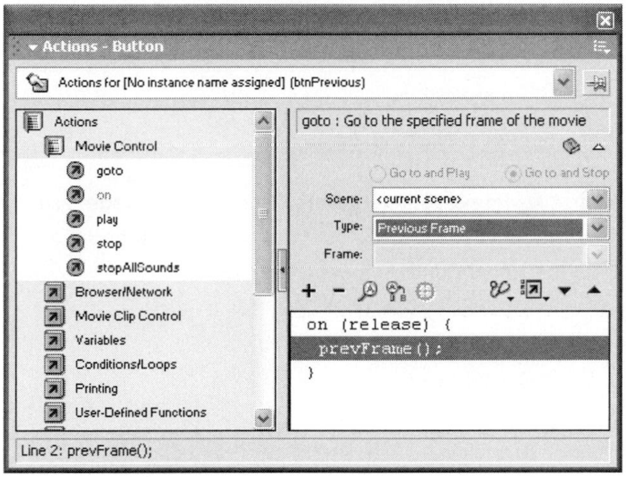

15. Click on the button instance on the **left** to select it. Choose **Actions** > **Movie Control** and double-click on the **goto** action to add it to the Script pane. In the **Type** field, select **Previous Frame** from the drop-down list.

When you are finished, your ActionScript should look like this:

```
on (release) {
    prevFrame ();
}
```

This time, you have added ActionScript to the left button. Now when the user clicks on this button and releases the mouse, the Playhead will move to the previous frame and stop.

16. Choose **Control** > **Test Movie** to test your movie. Click on the **right arrow** button several times to advance the slideshow to the next picture and click on the **left arrow** button to reveal the previous picture. Neat!

Notice that when you continue to click on the right arrow the slideshow stops at boarder 5 (the last frame) and never starts over at Frame 1. Likewise, notice that when you continue to click on the left arrow, the slideshow stops at boarder 1 (the first frame) and never loops to Frame 5. You can fix this to make the slideshow loop back to the beginning or to the end by adding a few keyframes and changing some of the ActionScript, which you will do next.

17. On the **controls** layer, add keyframes to **Frames 2** and **5** by selecting each frame and then pressing **F6**. Your **controls** layer should look like the picture above. This will copy all the contents of Frame 1, including the actions attached to the buttons, to Frames 2 and 5.

18. Move the **Playhead** so that it is over the **first** keyframe of the **controls** layer. On the **Stage**, select the **left** button instance. (You may have to click off the Stage to deselect both buttons first and then select the left button.) You are going to change the ActionScript in this button next.

```
▾ Actions - Button                                              ▣  ≡
┌──────────────────────────────────────────────────────────────┐
│ ⬚  Actions for [No instance name assigned] (btnPrevious)   ⌄ 🔾│
├────────────────────┬───────────────────────────────────────── │
│ ⬈ Actions        ⌃ │ goto : Go to the specified frame of the movie │
│ ⬈ Operators        │                                    🔾 △   │
│ ⬈ Functions        │       ○ Go to and Play   ● Go to and Stop │
│ ⬈ Constants        │ Scene: <current scene>              ⌄     │
│ ⬈ Properties       │  Type: Frame Number                 ⌄     │
│ ⬈ Objects          │ Frame: 5                            ⌄     │
│ ⬈ Deprecated       │                                            │
│ ⬈ Flash UI Components │ + − 🔎 🎬 ⊕          💯 📑 ▾ ▲        │
│ ⬈ Index            │ ┌────────────────────────────────────────┐│
│                    │ │ on (release) {                         ││
│                    │ │    gotoAndStop(5);                     ││
│                    │ │ }                                      ││
│                    │ └────────────────────────────────────────┘│
│                  ⌄ │         ↑                                 │
│                    │   ┌──────────────────────┐               │
├────────────────────┤   │ Select this line in  │               │
│ Line 2: gotoAndStop(5); │ order to change it   │               │
└────────────────────┴───┴──────────────────────┴───────────────┘
```

19. In the **Actions** panel, select the line in the Script pane that reads **prevFrame ();**. This line needs to be changed to direct the Playhead to the last frame of the slideshow, Frame 5. In the **Type** field, select **Frame Number** from the drop-down list. In the **Frame** field, type **5**. Lastly, select the **Go to and Stop** radio button. When you are finished, your Script pane should look like the picture above.

You have just changed the ActionScript on the left button instance appearing in the first keyframe of the movie. Instead of the script telling the Playhead to go to the previous frame (which it can't do because this is Frame 1, the first frame), you have now changed the script to tell Macromedia Flash MX: When the user releases the mouse on this button in the first frame of the movie, just go to Frame 5 and stop there!

20. Move the **Playhead** so that it is over the last keyframe of the **controls** layer. On the **Stage**, select the **btnNext** instance. You are going to change the ActionScript in this button and then you are done!

21. In the **Actions** panel, select the line in the Script pane that reads **nextFrame ();.** In the **Type** field, select **Frame Number** from the drop-down list. In the **Frame** field, type **1.** Lastly, select the **Go to and Stop** radio button.

You have just changed the ActionScript on the right button instance appearing in the last keyframe of the movie. Instead of the script telling the Playhead to go to the next frame (which it can't do because this is Frame 5, the last frame), you have now changed the script to tell Macromedia Flash MX: When the user releases the mouse on this button in the last frame of the movie, just go to Frame 1 and stop there!

22. Test the movie again. This time, the movie should never be "stuck" on boarder 1 or boarder 5. Instead, it should loop when either the first or last frame is reached.

23. When you are finished testing the movie, save and close this file.

4. ————————On Mouse Event: getURL

You can also use ActionScripting to open other Web sites from within a Macromedia Flash MX movie. This exercise will introduce the **getURL** action, which is used to create links to other documents on the Web. The following steps will teach you how to use the getURL action to link to an external Web site and to generate a preaddressed email message.

1. Open the **getURL.fla** file from the **chap_11** folder. This file has been created to get you started.

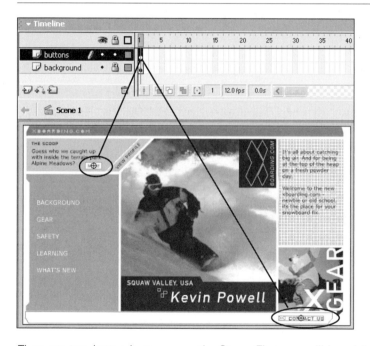

There are two button instances on the Stage. First, you will be adding ActionScript to the ***More*** *button that will open up an HTML page in a new browser window. Later in the exercise, you will add ActionScript to the* ***Contact Us*** *button to create an email message.*

2. On the **Stage**, select the **More** button and press **F9** to open the **Actions** panel. You have to select the button instance first in order to be able to add actions to it. In the **Actions Toolbox**, click **Actions > Browser/Network** and double-click on the **getURL** action to add it to the Script pane.

3. In the Parameters pane, type **thescoop.html** in the **URL** field. This will open **thescoop.html** Web page in a browser window when the user clicks on the **More** button. The HTML file **thescoop.html** is located in the **chap_11** folder.

NOTE | Relative and Absolute Addresses

The addresses that you use in a getURL command can be either relative or absolute addresses. Relative addresses describe the file's location in relation to another. Relative addresses can refer to local HTML files that are located in the same directory as the .swf file, such as **thescoop.html**. Absolute addresses are the complete address that specifies the name of the server on which the file resides. Absolute addresses can refer to files located on other Web servers, such as **http://www.xboarding.com**.

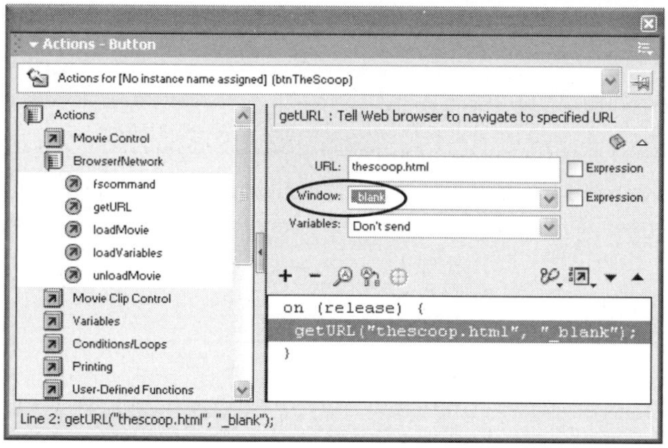

---

4. In the **Parameters** pane, select **_blank** in the **Window** field. This setting tells Macromedia Flash MX to open the link you specified in step 3 in a new browser window.

You have the ability to control the window or frame that displays the linked file by changing the parameters in the Window field. The following chart explains each of the four options: _blank, _self, _parent, and _top.

Get URL Window Parameter Options	
Option	**Description**
_blank	Opens the link in a new browser window.
_self	Opens the link in the same browser window that is occupied by the current Macromedia Flash MX movie.
_parent	Opens the link in the parent window of the current window.
_top	Opens the link in the same browser window and removes any existing framesets.

5. The Variables option allows Macromedia Flash MX to send variable values to a server. Leave the **Variables** option at the default setting because sending variables is beyond the scope of this exercise.

NOTE | What Is a Variable?

In Macromedia Flash MX, a variable is simply a container that holds information. A variable can hold such information as a name, a number, or even a Movie Clip. This information can then be retrieved via ActionScripting. You will have a chance to work with variables in the next chapter, "*Working with Text.*"

6. Choose **Control > Test Movie** to preview the link you just created. When you use **Control > Test Movie**, the getURL action will automatically launch your machine's default browser and load the HTML Web page you specified into a new window. When you are finished, close the browser window and the Preview Window.

*Like an HREF tag in HTML, the **getURL** action can be used as an email link by adding "mailto" to an email address. In the steps that follow, you will add ActionScript to the second button to create an email link that will produce a preaddressed email message,* `mailto:flashmxhot@lynda.com`.

---

7. Back in the project file, select the **Contact Us** button on the **Stage**. In the **Actions Toolbox**, choose **Actions > Browser/Network** and double-click on the **getURL** action to add it to the Script pane.

---

8. In the Parameters pane, type **mailto:flashmxhot@lynda.com** in the **URL** field. This will preaddress the email message to **flashmxhot@lynda.com** when the user clicks on the **Contact Us** button.

9. Select **_blank** in the **Window** field. This setting will tell Macromedia Flash MX to open the email message in a new window, leaving the Macromedia Flash MX movie still visible in the background. Leave the **Variables** option at the default setting.

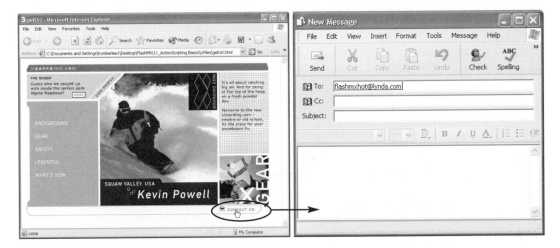

10. Choose **File > Publish Preview > HTML**. This will open the .swf file in a browser window so that you can test the email link. Once the browser window opens, click the **Contact Us** button to test the link. A new email message window will open when you click on the button!

Note: On some computers, you may be able to choose Control > Test Movie and have this file work, although I have found this not always to be the case. Therefore, if you test it in a realistic environment by viewing the .swf file inside a browser, it will work on all machines. You will learn about the Publish settings in depth in Chapter 16, "Publishing and Exporting."

11. When you are finished, close the open windows and save and close this file.

What Are Scenes?

In Macromedia Flash MX, you are not limited to only the frames in the Timeline of the main movie. You can have several timelines, which play one right after another. Macromedia Flash MX calls these multiple Timelines **scenes**. Scenes allow you to break up large projects into smaller, more manageable pieces, much as a Web site is broken up into individual Web pages. By default, Macromedia Flash MX will play all the scenes in order, unless you use ActionScript to tell it otherwise. If no ActionScript is present in the Main Timeline to stop the movie, the Playhead will continue on to the next scene and continue to play the frames until the end is reached or a stop action is encountered. The Macromedia Flash Player treats all the scenes in a movie as one long Timeline. Therefore, if the first scene contains 30 frames and the second scene contains 20, the Macromedia Flash Player will see that as one Timeline of 50 consecutive frames and will play the scenes in the order in which they appear in the Scene panel. You can use scenes to break up a Web site into different sections, to structure a project where many smaller movies get loaded on demand, or even as a way to organize different stages of a project. The next exercise will teach you how to work with scenes.

5. ————————Targeting Scenes

Up to this point in the book, you have been working with one scene, Scene 1, in the Main Timeline. In the following exercise, you will learn how to create additional scenes in Macromedia Flash MX as well as to rename, duplicate, and target them using ActionScript.

1. Open the **gotoSceneFinal.fla** file from the **chap_11** folder. This is the finished version of the file you are going to create. At first glance, the interface may look similar to the file you created in the last exercise, although as you will see in the next step, this is an entire Web site.

> ## NOTE | Missing Fonts
>
> When you open **gotoSceneFinal.fla**, you may see a dialog box that reads "One or more of the fonts used by this movie are unavailable. Substitute fonts will be used for display and export. They will not be saved to the Macromedia authoring document." This simply means that your computer does not have some of the fonts that were used to create the artwork in this file. Go ahead and choose **Use Default** so that your computer will pick a default font to replace the unrecognizable fonts in the movie.

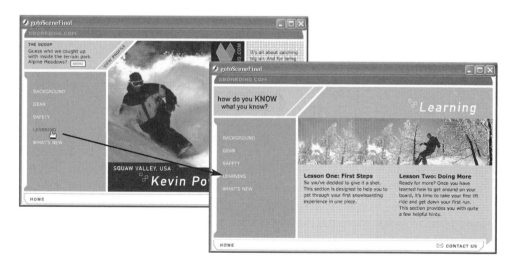

2. Choose **Control > Test Movie** to preview the movie. Click on each of the navigation buttons to view a different section of the Web site. What is happening behind the scenes (pun intended) is that when you click the button, the Playhead is moving to the appropriate scene in the movie. You will learn how to re-create this Web site next. When you are finished previewing the movie, close the Preview Window and then close the project file.

3. Open the **gotoScene.fla** file from the **chap_11** folder. This is an unfinished version of the movie that you just previewed; you just need to add the ActionScript to recreate the movie.

4. Choose **Control > Test Movie** to preview the movie. Notice that the navigation buttons don't go anywhere when you click on them. This is because there are no actions on the buttons telling them where to go. You will be adding ActionScript to the buttons in the steps that follow. When you are finished previewing the movie, close the Preview Window.

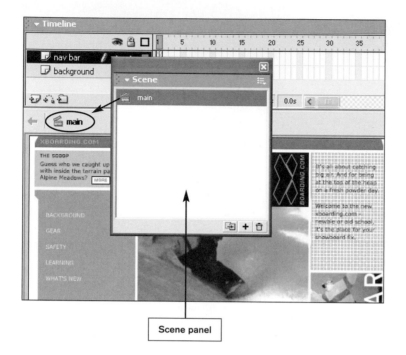

Scene panel

5. In the **Main Timeline**, choose **Window > Scene** to open the **Scene** panel. The Scene panel displays a list of the scenes in this movie. At this point, you have only one scene named Scene 1 by default. Double-click inside the **Scene 1** name in the **Scene** panel and rename the scene **main**. As soon as you press **Enter/Return**, the name **Scene 1** will change to **main** in the Scene panel and also in the Information Bar of the project window.

Tip: You can also access the Scene panel by choosing Modify > Scene. This method of choosing Window > Scene will yield the same result: The Scene panel will open. I just want you to be aware of all your workflow options!

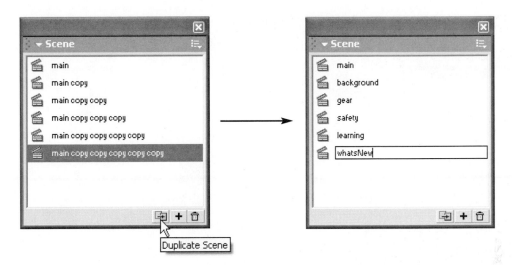

Duplicate Scene

6. In the **Scene** panel, click on the **Duplicate Scene** button (located at the bottom of the Scene panel) five times to duplicate the main scene five times. Next, double-click on each of the duplicate scenes in the **Scene** panel and rename them to match the navigation buttons on the Stage: **background**, **gear**, **safety**, **learning**, and **whatsNew**, as shown in the picture above.

Note: When you name the scenes in your movie, try to keep the names short and descriptive. Because you will be using ActionScripting to target the scenes, it is important that scene names reflect the content inside them.

You have just added five new scenes to the movie, although they will all look exactly the same because you just duplicated the main scene. You will change the content inside each scene next. You'll soon realize the value of duplicating scenes as you learn to align new artwork from scene to scene.

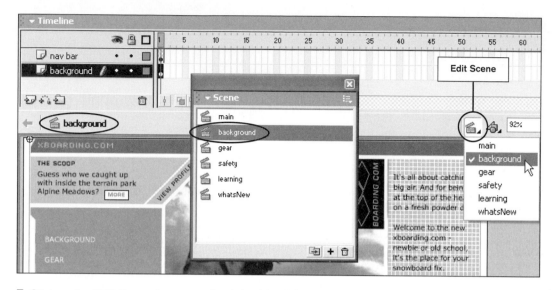

7. Click on the **Edit Scene** button on the right side of the **Information Bar**. A menu will appear with the list of scenes that you just made in this project. From the menu, select the scene named **background**. This will take you into the Timeline of that scene. Notice that the scene name changed in the Information Bar, the background scene is highlighted in the Scene panel, and there is a check mark next to the background scene drop-down menu from the Edit Scene button. These are all cues that tell you which scene you are currently inside within the project. When you are finished, close the **Scene** panel.

Note: The Edit Scene button is useful to move quickly from scene to scene. The Scene panel can also be used to jump from scene to scene, but additionally, this is where you can add, delete, name, and copy scenes in your movie.

8. Click anywhere on the **Stage** to select the artwork. Open the **Property Inspector** if it isn't already open (**Window > Properties**), and notice that it says "Instance of: mcMain." This means that the artwork on the Stage is contained in an instance of the mcMain Movie Clip. Because you are now located in the background scene, you need to change the artwork to reflect the correct scene; you can do this with a few clicks of the mouse. Make sure the **mcMain** instance is still selected, and in the **Property Inspector**, click on the **Swap Symbols** button.

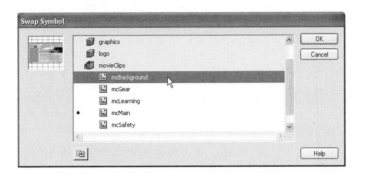

9. In the **Swap Symbol** dialog box, select the **mcBackground** Movie Clip and click **OK**. This will swap (or change) the mcMain Movie Clip with the mcBackground Movie Clip.

Tip: In the Swap Symbol dialog box, you can also double-click on the symbol you want to swap rather than selecting it and clicking OK. By swapping a symbol, you keep it in perfect alignment with the symbol that was there before. Keep in mind that this is true only if both symbols have the same dimensions, which is the case in this exercise.

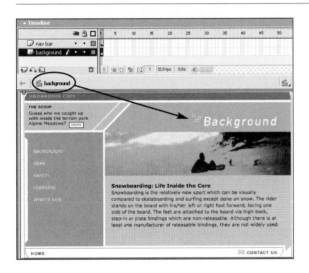

As soon as you click OK, notice that the artwork has changed in the background scene. This artwork was created ahead of time and saved as a Movie Clip. It is the same size as the main scene Movie Clip; the difference is in the colors, the photo, and the text. Swapping symbols is a good technique to use, for example, when you mock up several pages for a Web site and need to show a client how the Web site will work. You can create the artwork, save each page as a Movie Clip or Graphic symbol in Macromedia Flash MX, make one scene, duplicate it, and switch out the artwork in each scene. This helps keep all the artwork registered in the same place. It's not easy to register artwork from scene to scene any other way, because you don't have Onion Skinning between scenes, only between frames on the Timeline.

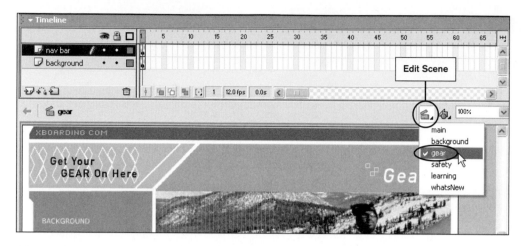

10. Using the **Edit Scene** button again, choose the scene named **gear** to open the **gear** scene's Timeline.

11. Select the artwork on the **Stage**, and in the **Property Inspector**, select the **Swap Symbols** button again. This time double-click on the **mcGear** Movie Clip in the **Swap Symbol** window.

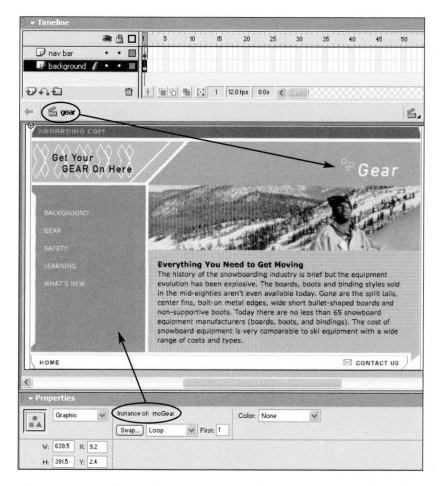

*After you double-click on the mcGear Movie Clip, your Stage should look like the picture above.
Notice also that the Property Inspector reflects the name of the new Movie Clip you chose.*

12. Repeat steps 10 and 11 for the remaining scenes: in **safety**, swap the **mcSafety** Movie Clip; in
learning, swap the **mcLearning** Movie Clip; in **whatsNew**, swap the **mcWhatsNew** Movie clip. When
you are finished, you can use the **Edit Scene** button to quickly check each scene and make sure the
scene name in the Information Bar matches the artwork.

*Next, you will add the ActionScripting to the buttons to tell Macromedia Flash MX to go to a specific
scene when the user clicks on a button.*

13. In the **Information Bar,** click on the **Edit Scene** button and choose **main** to open the **main**
scene's **Timeline.**

14. Select the **Background** button on the **Stage** by clicking on it. Open the **Actions** panel (**Window >
Actions**). In the **Actions Toolbox**, choose **Actions > Movie Control** and double-click on **goto** to add it
to the Script pane.

15. In the **Parameters** pane, select the **Go to and Stop** radio button and choose **background** from
the **Scene** drop-down menu. (This drop-down list will automatically contain all the scenes you have
created in your movie.) Leave the **Type: Frame Number** and the **Frame: 1** fields at the defaults. This
ActionScript will tell Macromedia Flash MX that as soon as the user releases the mouse on the
Background button it should go to the scene named background and stop there.

```
on (release) {
    gotoAndStop("gear", 1);
}
```

Line 2: gotoAndStop("gear", 1);

16. Repeat steps 14 and 15 for the **Gear**, **Safety**, **Learning**, and **What's New** buttons. The only differences are these: In the **Parameters** pane in the **Actions** panel, choose **Scene: gear** for the **Gear** button; **Scene: safety** for the **Safety** button; **Scene: learning** for the **Learning** button; and **Scene: whatsNew** for the **What's New** button.

You now have five buttons, each with ActionScript that instructs Macromedia Flash MX to go to the appropriate scene when the user releases the mouse on each button. You will add ActionScript in each of the scenes next.

17. Select **Frame 1** in the **nav bar** layer to select all the content in Frame 1. Choose **Edit > Copy Frames**.

18. Using the **Edit Scene** button again, choose the scene named **background** to open its Timeline. Select **Frame 1** in the **nav bar** layer and choose **Edit > Paste Frames**. This will paste the content, including the buttons and all the ActionScripting, from the main scene in Frame 1 of the nav bar layer into the background scene, replacing any content that was previously in that frame.

Why I am copying the buttons into a scene that already has buttons? There are many ways to do this, but the idea is to be efficient as possible in your workflow. So rather than recode each button in every scene, copying and pasting frames is a quick and easy way to copy all the buttons with their attached ActionScripting into another scene.

19. Repeat step 18 for the **gear**, **safety**, **learning**, and **whatsNew** scenes.

Be sure to select Frame 1 in the nav bar layer inside each scene before you paste the frames so that you paste the buttons into the right location!

20. Choose **Control > Test Movie** to test the movie. Notice that all the scenes play, one right after another. By default, the movie will continue to play, one scene after another, unless you tell the Playhead to stop by adding a stop action to a frame in the Timeline. You will do this next. When you are finished testing the movie, close the **Preview Window**.

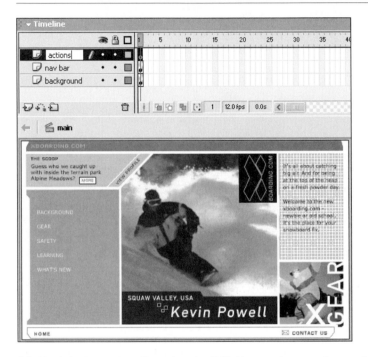

21. Back in the project file, using the **Edit Scenes** button, choose the **main** scene. Inside the **main** scene's **Timeline**, click on the **Insert Layer** button to add a new layer, and rename it **actions**. Make sure the **actions** layer is above all the other layers; if it is not, click on the layer name and drag it above all the other layers.

Note: Ideally, as you create projects that use scenes to separate pages of a Web site, you will want to do as much work as possible on the main scene before duplicating it. This will save you from having to edit sections of each scene as you continue to work on the project file. In the real world, although this is the ideal situation, you may find that you still have to go back and alter parts of each scene, but the more you do in the beginning, the more efficient your workflow will be.

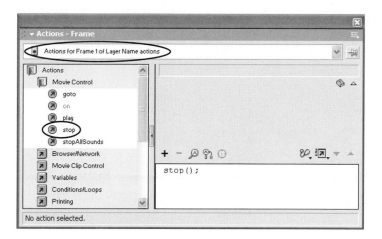

22. Select **Frame 1** in the **actions** layer, and in the **Actions** panel, choose **Actions > Movie Control** in the **Actions Toolbox**, and double-click on **stop** to add a stop action to the Script pane. This will cause the movie to stop when the Playhead reaches the first frame in the main scene.

23. Repeat steps 21 and 22 to add stop frame actions to the **background**, **gear**, **safety**, **learning**, and **whatsNew** scenes. This will force the Playhead to stop as soon as it reaches each of the scenes.

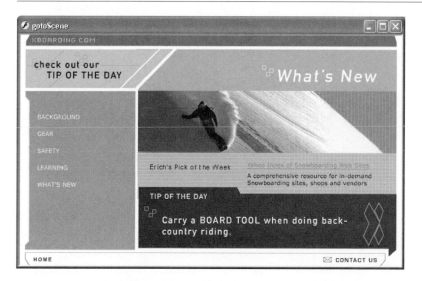

24. Choose **Control > Test Movie** to test the movie. Preview the scenes by clicking on each navigation button. Notice that once you click on a button to advance to a different scene, there is no visual feedback on the button to let you know which scene you are in. You will change this last element of the movie next. When you are finished, close the **Preview Window**.

25. Back in the project file, using the **Edit Scene** button, choose the **background** scene. Inside the **background** scene's **Timeline**, choose the **Background** button on the **Stage**.

26. Make sure the **Background** button is selected and, in the **Property Inspector**, choose **Graphic** from the **Symbol Behavior** drop-down list. This will convert the behavior of the Background button instance in this scene to become a Graphic symbol, which cannot be clicked on and cannot have actions applied to it. For **Color**, choose **Tint**, select **white** for the **Tint color**, and choose **100%**.

Because the Up state of this button contains a triangle next to the word "Background," changing the tint to white will turn the triangle white and provide visual feedback to the user regarding where he/she is located. So when you are in the background scene, the Background button will be white and you will not be able to click on it because you are already in the background scene. Cool!

NOTE | Why Do I Need to Change the Behavior and Color of My Button?

There are many different ways to give the user visual feedback that a button has been selected. In good user interface design, you should make it as easy as possible for the user to know where he/she is at all times. By changing the behavior of the button to a graphic, the button instance (not the original Button symbol in the Library) will turn into a Graphic symbol, using the button's Up state as the graphic. When the button is a graphic, the user will not be able to click on it because it is no longer a button. Further, by also changing the color of the button-turned-graphic, you provide the user with extra visual feedback that he/she is located in a particular section of the Web site.

27. Repeat steps 25 and 26 for the **gear**, **safety**, **learning**, and **whatsNew** scenes. Inside the **gear** scene, select the **Gear** button and change its behavior to **graphic** and tint to **white** at **100%**. Likewise, inside the **safety** scene, select the **Safety** button; inside the **learning** scene, select the **Learning** button; and in the **whatsNew** scene, select the **What's New** button. Make the same changes for each in the **Property Inspector**.

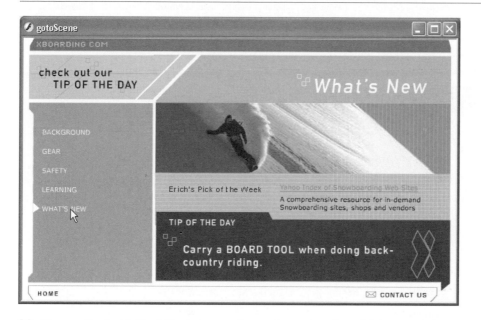

28. Choose **Control > Test Movie** to test the movie one last time! Click on each button to go to the appropriate scene. Notice that once you are inside a scene, the button with the same name of the scene will now reflect the current scene by showing the white arrow and will not allow you to click on it. By using scenes, you can separate different sections of the project and target those sections on demand using ActionScript.

29. When you are finished testing the movie, save and close the file.

6. _____Creating a Drop-Down Menu

There are many ways to create interactive menus in Macromedia Flash MX. From scrolling menus to animated menus to draggable menus, all you need is a little creativity and a few bits of ActionScripting to develop all kinds of different navigation systems for your users. This exercise will start you on your way to creating interactive navigation schemes by teaching you how to develop a basic drop-down menu.

1. Open the **menuFinal.fla** file from the **chap_11** folder. This is the finished version of the menu you are going to create.

2. Choose **Control > Test Movie** to preview the movie. Click on the different navigation buttons and notice that some of them will reveal a drop-down menu. When you are finished, close the **Preview Window** and **menuFinal.fla**.

In this exercise, you will be adding frame labels and ActionScript to make this drop-down menu work. In the following exercise, you will add functionality to the buttons on the menu to load different .swf files into the interface by using the loadMovie action.

3. Open the **menu.fla** file from the **chap_11** folder. This is an unfinished version of the movie you just previewed, containing everything you need to create a drop-down menu.

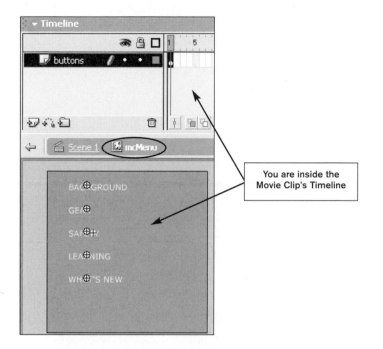

You are inside the
Movie Clip's Timeline

Frame Label

4. Double-click on the menu on the **Stage** to open the Movie Clip's **Timeline**. Notice that there is one layer with five buttons. Choose **Control > Test Movie** to preview the menu. As you click on each button, you will see that there are no drop-down menus; however, you will be creating them next. When you are finished previewing the menu, close the **Preview Window**.

5. Back in the project file, inside the **mcMenu** Movie Clip, click on the **Insert Layer** button to add a new layer to the **Timeline**. Rename this layer **labels**. Make sure this layer is above the **buttons** layer.

6. Select the first keyframe selected in the **labels** layer. In the **Property Inspector**, type the name **begin** in the **Frame Label** field. This will add the frame label **begin** to **Frame 1**, where the menu is in the starting position.

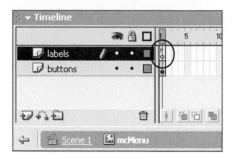

*As soon as you add the label name, notice the hollow circle and the flag in the Timeline. This is feed-back to show you that a label exists on this frame. **Note:** You will not be able to see the begin frame label name just yet, because there are not enough frames in the Timeline, but you will see it after the next step.*

NOTE | What Is a Frame Label?

Frame labels identify a frame by a name, rather than by a number. As you add and delete frames in the movie, the frame numbers will change, which can cause problems if you are referring to a frame number in your ActionScript. When you reference a frame label, if frames are added or deleted, the frame label will remain constant, and Macromedia Flash MX will be able to find the correct frame.

Just like ActionScripting that has been added to the movie, frame labels are also exported with the rest of the movie, so it is a good idea to keep the frame labels short in order to minimize overall file size. Also, shorter frame labels are much easier to work with.

---

7. On the **labels** layer, select **Frames 5**, **10**, **15**, **20**, and **25**, one at a time, and press **F7** on each of them to add a blank keyframe to each of the frames.

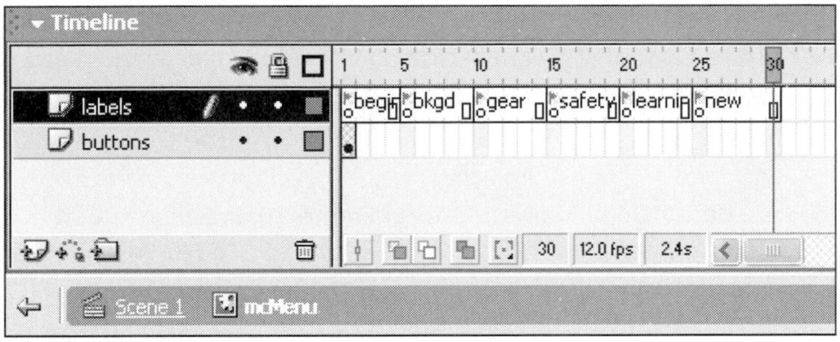

8. In the **Property Inspector**, add the Frame labels **bkgd**, **gear**, **safety**, **learning**, and **new** to **Frames 5**, **10**, **15**, **20** and **25**, respectively. Select **Frame 30** and press **F5** to add frames up to Frame 30 so that you can see the **new** label. When you are finished, your Timeline should look like the picture above.

Tip: In order for a frame label to be visible in the Timeline, there must be enough frames to display the entire name; so by pressing F5, you can add frames and see the name. **Note:** *Even if you can't see the whole name, the label is still there; you can always tell that by looking for the flag on the frame in the Timeline or by looking at the frame label in the Property Inspector.*

9. Click the **Insert Layer** button to add another layer to your movie. Name this new layer **actions**. Make sure the new layer is above the **labels** layer. If it is not, click on the layer name and drag it above all the other layers so that the actions layer is on top.

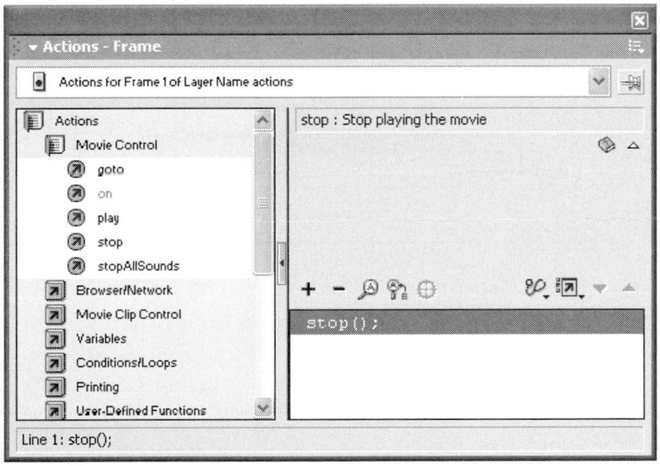

10. Select **Frame 1** in the **actions** layer and open the **Actions** panel. In the **Actions Toolbox**, choose **Actions > Movie Control** and double-click on the **stop** action to add a stop action to the first keyframe. This action will tell the Playhead to stop on this frame.

11. On the **actions** layer, select **Frame 5** and press **F7** to add a blank keyframe. In the **Actions** panel **Actions Toolbox**, choose **Actions > Movie Control** and double-click on the **stop** action to add a stop action to the first keyframe. This action will tell the Playhead to stop on Frame 5 until another action tells Macromedia Flash MX to do something else.

12. With **Frame 5** still selected, choose **Edit > Copy Frames**. Click in **Frame 10** and choose **Edit > Paste Frames**. This will copy the contents of Frame 5 to Frame 10. Choose **Edit > Paste Frames** on **Frames 15**, **20**, and **25** to copy the contents into those frames, adding a stop action to each of them.

Now that you have set up the frame labels and added stop frame actions, it is time to add the ActionScripting to the buttons. You will do this next.

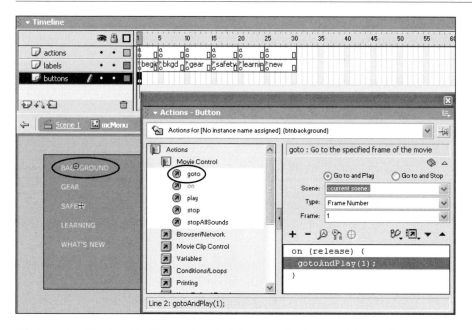

13. Drag the **Playhead** to **Frame 1** and click on the **Background** button instance on the **Stage** to select it. In the **Actions** panel, in the **Actions Toolbox**, choose **Actions > Movie Control** and double-click on **goto** to add the goto action to the Script pane.

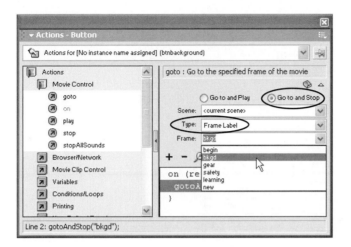

Line 2: gotoAndStop("bkgd");

14. In the Parameters pane of the **Actions** panel, select the **Go to and Stop** radio button and leave the **Scene** field set to **<current scene>**. In the **Type** field, select **Frame Label** from the drop-down menu. In the **Frame** field, select **bkgd** from the drop-down menu. This ActionScript will tell Macromedia Flash MX that as soon as the user releases the mouse on the Background button, go to the frame label **bkgd** and stop there.

15. Repeat steps 13 and 14 to add ActionScripting to the four remaining navigation buttons. For the **Gear** button, select the **gear** frame label; for the **Safety** button, select the **safety** frame label; for the **Learning** button, select the **learning** frame label; and for the **What's New** button, select the **new** frame label in the Parameters pane of the **Action** panel.

16. In the **Timeline**, on the **buttons** layer, select each frame first and press **F6** on **Frames 5, 10, 15, 20,** and **25** to add keyframes to each frame. This will copy the buttons, including all the ActionScripting, into each frame. Select **Frame 30** and press **F5** to add frames up to **Frame 30** on the **buttons** layer.

17. Test the movie (**Control > Test Movie**) and click on each of the buttons. Notice that nothing much happens.

By pressing F6 in the previous step, you copied all the contents of the last keyframe into the next keyframe; although the ActionScripting is working to send the Playhead to a different frame label, all the content will look the same. In the steps that follow, you will slightly modify the buttons in each keyframe so that the menu changes at each keyframe.

18. Move the **Playhead** to **Frame 5**. Select the **Background** button on the **Stage** and open the **Property Inspector**. Just as you did in the last exercise, choose **Graphic** from the **Symbol Behavior** drop-down menu. For **Color Styles**, choose **Tint**, select **white** for the **Tint** color, and choose **100%**.

This will change the behavior of the Background button instance in this frame only to a Graphic symbol, which cannot be clicked on and cannot have actions applied to it. So when the Playhead hits the background label, the Background button will be white and you will not be able to click on it because you are already in the Background section.

You are on Frame 10 with the Gear button selected

19. Move the **Playhead** to **Frame 10**. Select the **Gear** button on the **Stage**, and in the **Property Inspector**, choose **Graphic** from the **Symbol Behavior** drop-down menu. For **Color Styles**, choose **Tint**, select **white** for the **Tint** color, and choose **100%**.

This will change the behavior of the Gear button instance in this frame only to a Graphic symbol, which cannot be clicked on and cannot have actions applied to it. So when the Playhead hits the gear label, the Gear button will be white and you will not be able to click on it because you are already in the Gear section.

20. Repeat step 19 and modify the **Safety** button on **Frame 15**, the **Learning** button on **Frame 20**, and the **What's New** button on **Frame 25**.

Make sure you move the Playhead to the correct frame first, select the appropriate button on the Stage next, and then make the changes in the Property Inspector to make sure you are changing the right button on the right frame.

21. Test the movie (**Control > Test Movie**). Click on each of the buttons. Notice that when you do, the arrow will appear to indicate where you are located. All you have left to do is to add the subnavigation menus, which you will do next. When you are finished testing the movie, close the Preview Window.

22. In the project file, move the **Playhead** to **Frame 10**. Open the **Library** (**F11**) and notice two buttons named btnGearSubBGCL and btnGearSubBoards. These are subnavigation buttons that have been created for you.

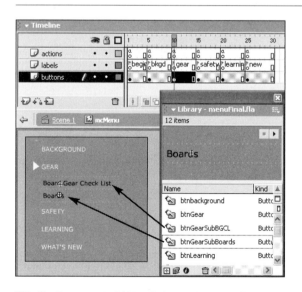

23. On **Frame 10**, Shift+click to select the **Safety**, **Learning**, and **What's New** buttons on the **Stage** all at once. With those three buttons selected, use the **down** arrow key on your keyboard to move them down toward the bottom of the **Stage** to make room for two subnavigation buttons under the **Gear** button. Drag an instance of **btnGearSubBGCL** and **btnGearSubBoards** onto the **Stage** and position them as shown in the picture above.

These will serve as the subnavigation buttons for the Gear section.

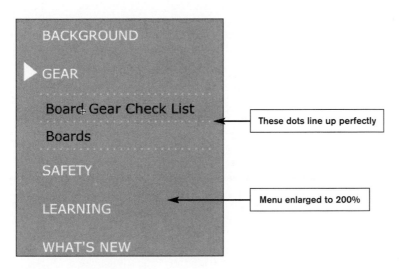

Note: *In this example, I positioned the two subnavigation buttons so that the bottom dotted line of one button lines up and overlaps the top dotted line on the other button, so that it appears as if there is only one dotted line between the two buttons. You can use the Zoom button in the Information Bar to get a close-up view to make lining up the buttons easier.*

24. Choose **Control > Test Movie**. When you click on the **Gear** button, the arrow and the subnavigation buttons will appear. When you are finished, close the **Preview Window**.

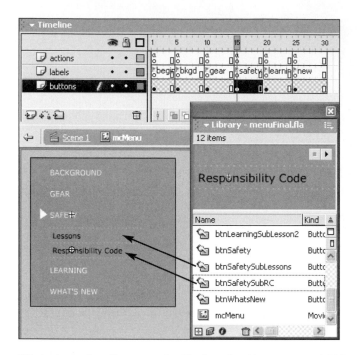

25. In the project file, move the **Playhead** to **Frame 15** and Shift+click to select the **Learning** and **What's New** buttons on the **Stage**. With those two buttons selected, use the **down** arrow key on your keyboard to move them down toward the bottom of the **Stage** to make room for two subnavigation buttons. From the **Library**, drag an instance of **btnSafetySubLessons** and **btnSafetySubRC** onto the **Stage** and position them as shown in the picture above.

These will serve as the subnavigation buttons for the Safety section. You have one last subnavigation section to add next.

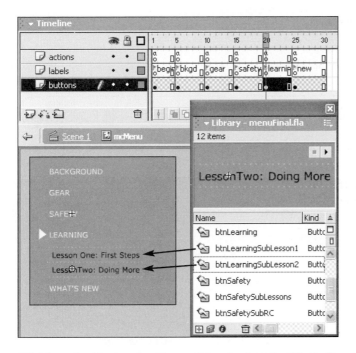

26. Move the **Playhead** to **Frame 20** and select the **What's New** button on the **Stage**. Use the **down** arrow key on your keyboard to move the **What's New** button down toward the bottom of the Stage to make room for two subnavigation buttons under the **Learning** button. From the **Library**, drag an instance of **btnLearningSubLesson1** and **btnLearningSubLesson2** onto the **Stage** and position them as shown in the picture above.

These will serve as the subnavigation buttons for the Learning section.

27. Choose **Control > Test Movie** to test your drop-down menu! Click on each of the buttons to make sure they are all working correctly. When you are done testing the menu, close the **Preview Window**.

28. When you are finished, save and close this file.

In the next exercise, you are going to use a menu similar to the one you just created, and you will add more ActionScripting to create a finished Web site using a new technique with the loadMovie action.

MOVIE | menu.mov

To see this exercise performed, play the **menu.mov** located in the **movies** folder on the **H•O•T CD-ROM**.

What Is loadMovie?

In earlier chapters, I described the difference between the project file (.fla) and the movie file (.swf). In this chapter, you will learn that the .swf file has the capability to load other .swf files into itself. This idea is similar to links on an HTML page, which replace content with other HTML pages when clicked.

Why would you want to do this in Macromedia Flash MX? If you have a large project with lots of graphics and navigation, it can take a long time to download all the content to the user's browser before he/she can access the finished result. If you instead learn to structure your projects so that many smaller movies are loaded on demand, it can create a better user experience for your audience.

This process is called Load Movie in Macromedia Flash MX, because it requires the loadMovie action.

As you begin to stack .swf files on top of one another, their arrangement simulates layers. In ActionScripting, the layers are called levels. The Main Timeline (named Scene 1 by default) is always located at Level 0, and when you load an additional movie, you can specify a level number for that movie, such as 5 or 20. The number of levels is infinite, and as you load movies into different levels, any movies that are currently in different levels will still be visible, and the movies that are loaded into higher levels will be placed in front of movies in lower levels. If this sounds abstract, it will become more clear as you work through the next exercise. The stacking order of loadMovie is similar to the stacking order of layers in the Timeline. Additionally, if you load a movie into a level that is already occupied by another movie, the new movie will replace the previous one. You will learn to program the loadMovie action in the following exercise.

7. ───────────Loading Movies

Loading multiple .swfs into the main .swf is an efficient way to present large Macromedia Flash MX documents, because the visitor doesn't have to download the entire Macromedia Flash MX movie. Instead, with the Load Movie ActionScript, multiple .swfs can be downloaded in the Macromedia Flash Player on demand. This exercise will show you how this is done.

1. Open the **loadMovie** folder inside the **chap_11** folder. Inside you will see many .swf files and one .fla file.

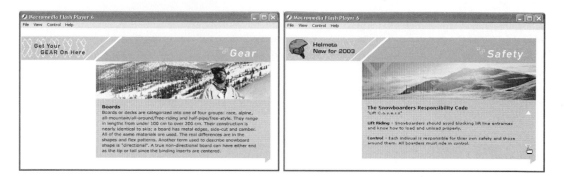

2. Double-click on any of the .swf files to open and preview the artwork inside them. These are the .swf files that you will be loading into the .fla file holding the main interface in the steps that follow. When you are finished, close the .swf files.

3. Open the file named **loadMovie.fla**, from the **loadMovie** folder. This file has been created to get you started.

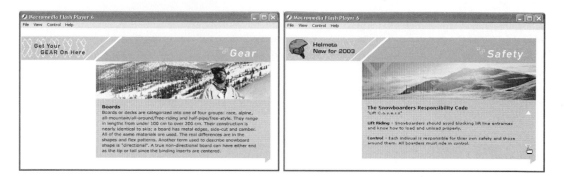

4. Choose **Control > Test Movie** to preview the movie. Notice that all you see is an empty interface with the navigation menu. This will serve as the main movie file. You will load the external movies (the .swf files that you previewed in step 2) into levels above the main movie, using the **loadMovie** action in the steps that follow. When you are finished previewing the movie, close the **Preview Window**.

Note: *If you get an error message telling you to check if the file destination is locked, or to check if the file name is not too long, try removing the <Read only> option to both chap_11 and its sub-folder, loadMovie.*

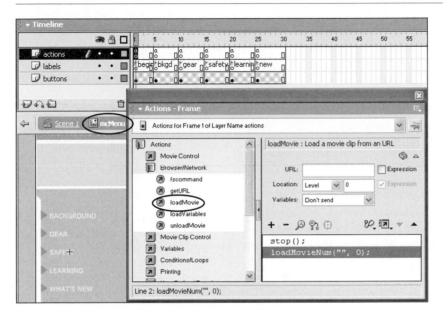

5. In the project file, double-click on the **menu** to open the Movie Clip's **Timeline**. (This menu is identical to the one you built in the last exercise.) Select **Frame 1** of the **actions** layer in the **Timeline** and open the **Actions** panel (**Window > Actions**). In the **Actions Toolbox**, choose **Actions > Browser/Network** and double-click on the **loadMovie** action to add it to the Script pane.

TIP | Why Add the Actions to a Frame Rather Than an Object?

You can add the loadMovie action to either a frame or an object. Which one you choose will largely depend on how you set up your movie. By adding the actions to a keyframe, as you did in the previous step, the ActionScript will be executed as soon as the Playhead hits the keyframe with the action in it. In the following steps, you will also add the loadMovie ActionScript to objects as well.

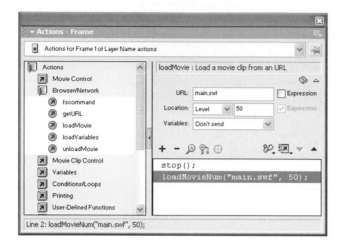

6. In the Parameters pane, type **main.swf** in the **URL** field. (**Note:** You must type the **.swf** extension after **main** in order for the script to work.) In the **Location: Level** field, type **50**. This will tell Macromedia Flash MX to load the .swf file you specified (**main.swf**) into Level 50, above the main movie. Leave the **Variables** field at the default because variables are beyond the scope of this exercise.

NOTE | Movie Levels

Why Level 50? Because you can specify any level (up to an infinite amount) to load a movie into, I choose 50 so that you have plenty of other "open" levels under 50 and over 50 that you can load additional content into. The Main Timeline is always located at Level 0; when you load an additional movie at a level higher than 0, it will appear above the Main Timeline. As you load movies into different levels, any movies that are currently in other levels will still be visible and the movies that are loaded into higher levels will be placed in front of movies in lower levels.

NOTE | Load Movie and Addressing

When you use the loadMovie ActionScript, the URL field in the Actions panel will specify the path to the file you are loading above the main movie. This path can be either relative or absolute. In this example, the relative path is used; therefore, all the .swf files you will be loading into levels above the main movie must be located in the same folder or directory as the main movie; otherwise, Macromedia Flash MX will not know where to find these files.

Use caution! Whenever you use a relative address for the loadMovie command, Macromedia Flash MX will always look for the files in the same folder as the main project file.

7. Choose **Control > Test Movie** to test the ActionScript you added. You will now see content inside the interface. Notice that you added the **main.swf** file, but the menu is still visible on the left side. This is because you loaded the **main.swf** file into Level 50, which is above the original interface, so **main.swf** will sort of float above the original interface, and anywhere there is no artwork in the loaded movie, those sections will be transparent, allowing the original interface to show through. When you are finished, close the **Preview Window**.

The Main Timeline is always located at Level 0 and, as additional movies are loaded above it, their corresponding level counts upward. Because there is no such thing as a negative level, you can't load movies below Level 0. When you load movies into different levels, any movies that are currently in other levels will still be visible, and the movies that are loaded into higher levels will be placed above movies in lower levels. Further, the loaded movies will have transparent Stages. So here, the original interface is at Level 0 (the lowest level) and all other movies with their transparent backgrounds will stack above the original interface.

NOTE | The File Cabinet Analogy

As you begin to stack .swf files on top of one another, their arrangement simulates layers. In ActionScript, the layers are called levels. The concept of loading movies into layers can be a bit confusing, so I will use the likeness of a file cabinet to explain this more clearly.

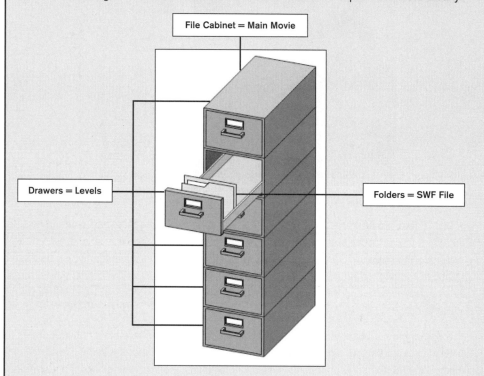

Imagine a file cabinet. This file cabinet is analogous to the main movie. Inside the cabinet, you have empty drawers, which are similar to levels within the main movie. Let's say that each drawer can contain only one thing, a folder, which is analogous to the .swf file. You can place one folder (.swf file) into any drawer (level) that you want to, but each drawer can hold only one folder. If you want to place a purple folder (.swf file) into a drawer (Level 4) that already has a green folder (.swf file) in it, you have to take out the green folder first before you put the purple one in, because you can have only one folder (.swf file) in a drawer (level) at a time. However, if you have the green folder (.swf file) already in a drawer (Level 4), you can add a blue folder (.swf file) to a drawer above it (Level 5, for example). If you did this, you would have the file cabinet, a green folder in drawer 4, and a blue folder in drawer 5. Or, in Macromedia Flash MX terminology you would have the main movie at Level 0, with the .swf file loaded into Level 4, above both the main movie and another .swf file loaded into Level 5, above both the main movie and the .swf file in level 4.

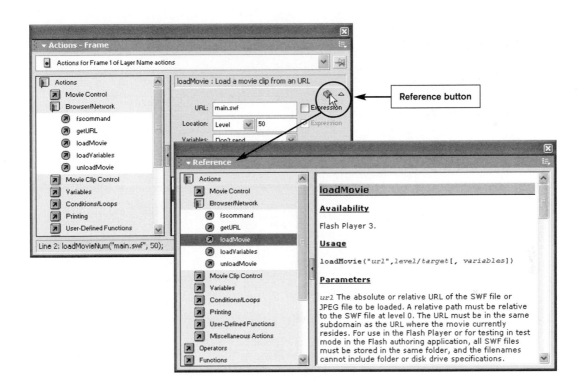

Reference button

8. In the project file, select the line in the Script pane with the **loadMovie** action. Click on the **Reference** button to open the **Reference** panel. Notice that the Reference panel automatically displays information about the loadMovie action. If you select an action or a line of code, the Reference panel will display information about that action.

Tip: You can also access the Reference panel by choosing Window > Reference or by using the shortcut key Shift+F1.

NOTE | The Reference Panel

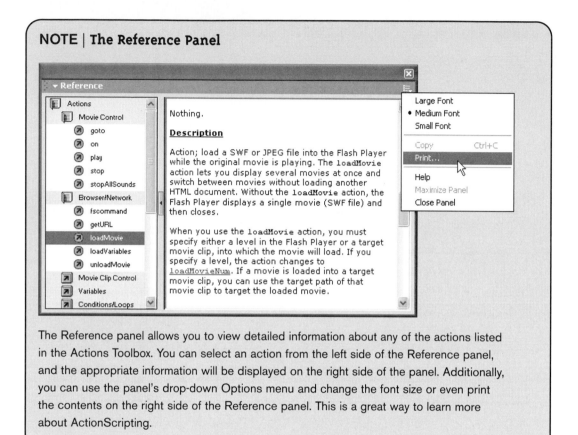

The Reference panel allows you to view detailed information about any of the actions listed in the Actions Toolbox. You can select an action from the left side of the Reference panel, and the appropriate information will be displayed on the right side of the panel. Additionally, you can use the panel's drop-down Options menu and change the font size or even print the contents on the right side of the Reference panel. This is a great way to learn more about ActionScripting.

9. You should still be inside the **menu** Movie Clip's **Timeline**. Select **Frame 5** of the **actions** layer in the **Timeline** and open the **Actions** panel (**Window > Actions**). In the **Actions Toolbox**, choose **Actions > Browser/Network** and double-click on the **loadMovie** action to add it to the Script pane.

10. In the Parameters pane, type **background.swf** in the **URL** field. In the **Location: Level** field, type **50**. This will tell Macromedia Flash MX to load the .swf file you specified (**background.swf**) into Level 50, above the main movie. Leave the **Variables** field at the default.

11. Choose **Control > Test Movie** and click on the **Background** button. As soon as you do, notice that the main content is switched out for the background content. How did this happen? Each time you use the loadMovie command to load a movie into a level (such as 50) that already had content in it, the new content will replace the old content. When you are finished previewing the file, close the window.

TIP | Loading into an Already Occupied Level

A movie doesn't have to be loaded into the next *empty* level; you can load a movie to any level you wish. However, if a movie is loaded into a level that is already occupied by another file, the old file is kicked out and replaced by the new movie.

12. Repeat steps 9 and 10 for **Frames 10**, **15**, **20**, and **25**. For **Frame 10**, type **gear.swf** in the **URL** field; for **Frame 15**, type **safety.swf** in the **URL** field; for **Frame 20**, type **learning.swf** in the **URL** field; and for **Frame 25**, type **whatsNew.swf** in the **URL** field. Choose **50** In the **Location: Level** field for each of the frames. This will load the appropriate content into Level 50, kicking out any content that was previously loaded into that level, each time the Playhead hits the appropriate frame.

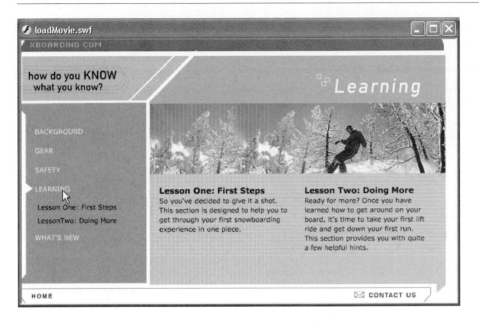

13. Choose **Control > Test Movie**. Click on each of the top-level navigation buttons to test the movie. When you are finished, close the **Preview Window**. You will add ActionScript to the subnavigation buttons in the steps that follow.

14. Back in the project file, move the **Playhead** to **Frame 10**. On the **Stage**, select the **Board Gear Checklist** button.

You will be adding the loadMovie action to this button next.

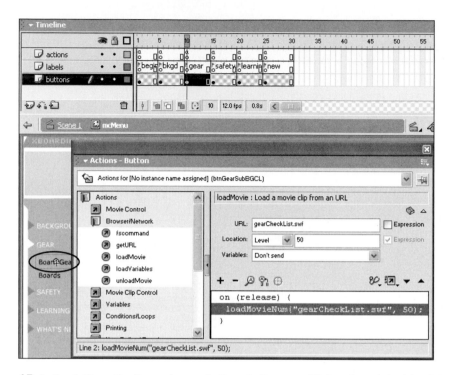

15. In the **Actions Toolbox**, choose **Actions > Browser/Network** and double-click on the **loadMovie** action to add it to the Script pane. In the Parameters pane, type **gearCheckList.swf** in the **URL** field. In the **Location: Level** field, type **50**. Leave the **Variables** field at the default. This will tell Macromedia Flash MX to load the **gearCheckList.swf** file into Level 50 when the user clicks on this button.

16. On the **Stage**, select the **Boards** button. In the **Actions Toolbox**, choose **Actions > Browser/Network** and double-click on the **loadMovie** action to add it to the Script pane. In the Parameters pane, type **gearboards.swf** in the **URL** field. In the **Location: Level** field, type **50**. Leave the **Variables** field at the default. This will tell Macromedia Flash MX to load the **gearBoards.swf** file into Level 50 when the user clicks on this button.

17. Repeat step 16 for the four remaining subnavigation buttons: two buttons on **Frame 15** and two buttons on **Frame 20**. This will add the loadMovie action to each of the subnavigation buttons.

For each of the buttons, the ActionScript should look like the following:

Frame 15—Lessons button:

```
on (release) {
    loadMovieNum("safetyLessons.swf", 50);
}
```

Frame 15—Responsibility Code button:

```
on (release) {
    loadMovieNum("safetyRC.swf", 50);
}
```

Frame 20—Lesson One: First Steps button:

```
on (release) {
    loadMovieNum("learningL1.swf", 50);
}
```

Frame 20—Lesson Two: Doing More button:

```
on (release) {
    loadMovieNum("learningL2.swf", 50);
}
```

You have one last button to add ActionScript to. You will do this next.

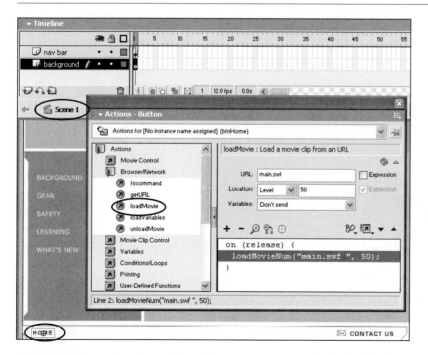

18. In the **Information Bar**, click on **Scene 1** to return to the **Main Timeline**. Unlock the background layer and select the **Home** button in the bottom left corner of the **Stage**. In the **Actions** panel, add one last loadMovie action, and for **URL**, choose **main.swf** and a **Location: Level** of **50**. When a user clicks on the Home button, **main.swf** will be loaded into Level 50, replacing any other .swf file that was previously occupying Level 50.

19. Test the movie! Try all the buttons, including the subnavigation buttons, to see how they work. When you are finished, close the **Preview Window**.

Now that you are intimately familiar with loading movies into the same level, you have a chance to see the results of loading a movie into a different level next.

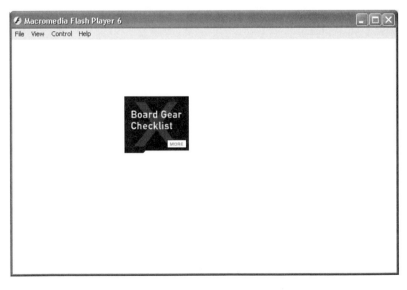

20. Open the **loadMovie** folder inside the **chap_11** folder again. Double-click on the **gearExtra.swf** file to preview the file. Notice that there is only one small button in the Preview Window. You will be loading this file in the main movie next. When you are finished, close the .swf file.

Why is there so much extra space around the button? When you load movies into levels, Macromedia Flash MX automatically places the loaded movie flush top left in the Macromedia Flash Player. Up to this point in the exercise, you have loaded movies into levels that all had the same dimensions. If you load a new movie that has much smaller dimensions into a level, it will automatically be registered in the top left corner and therefore might not be placed where you want it.

There are two ways around this issue. In this case, the button in the gearPopUp.swf has been strategically placed where it should "land" in the interface, but the movie dimensions in the gearPopUp.swf file match each of the other .swf files you have worked with in this exercise. Because all loaded movies will be transparent except for the content, you will see the button only when you load it in. Another way to have precision control over where a movie lands when it is loaded is to load it into a target that would be a Movie Clip, rather than a level. For this exercise, you will concentrate on loading movies into levels, and you will load the gearPopUp.swf file into a different level in the next steps.

21. Back in the project file, double-click on the **menu** to open the Movie Clip's **Timeline**. Select **Frame 10** of the **actions** layer in the **Timeline**. In the **Actions** panel, choose **Actions > Browser/ Network** and double-click on the **loadMovie** action to add it to the Script pane.

This will add a new script below the previous loadMovie script you created.

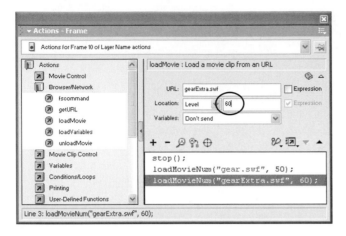

22. In the Parameters pane, type **gearExtra.swf** in the **URL** field. In the **Location: Level** field, type **60**. This will tell Macromedia Flash MX to load the .swf file you specified (**gearExtra.swf**) into Level 60, above the main movie (at Level 0) and also above the gear.swf file in Level 50.

What is really going on behind the scenes? When the user clicks on the Gear button, the Playhead will be sent to the gear label inside the menu Movie Clip's Timeline. (You already programmed this ActionScripting when you built the menu in the last exercise.) When the Playhead hits the gear label in the Timeline (which is Frame 10), first it will stop (because you have a stop action) and then it will load the gear.swf file into Level 50 and then load the gearExtra.swf file into Level 60.

23. *Choose* **Control > Test Movie** *and click on the* **Gear** *button in the menu. Notice that the button from* **gearExtra.swf** *file is there! This is because you loaded the gear.swf file into Level 60, above any content loaded into Level 50. As far as stacking order goes with loaded movies in Macromedia Flash MX, the higher the level number, the closer to the top of the stacking order; so in this case, the* **gearExtra.swf** *file is loaded just above the* **gear.swf** *file. Close the* **Preview Window** *when you are finished.*

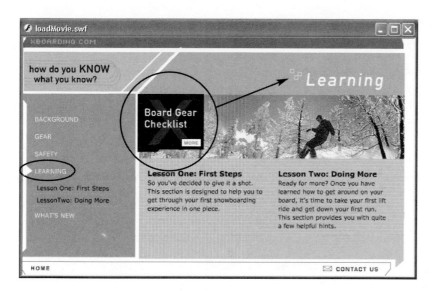

When you click on any of the other buttons in the menu, notice that the *gearExtra.swf* file appears, no matter what section you are in. Why? This is because the *gearExtra.swf* file has been loaded into Level 60, and it will stay there (no matter what else is going on in other levels, such as Level 50) until you tell it otherwise. Speaking of which, you will tell it otherwise next.

Note: You may have noticed that if you click on the *gearExtra* button, the Board Gear Checklist page shows up. Why? This is because inside the project file that created the *gearExtra.swf* there is a button with the following ActionScript attached to it:

```
on (release) {
    loadMovieNum("gearCheckList.swf", 50);
}
```

This means that when a user clicks on the button, it should load the *gearExtra.swf* file into Level 50.

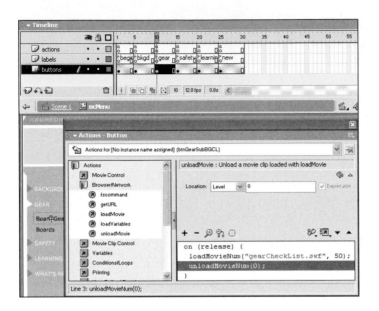

24. In the project file, the **Playhead** should still be over **Frame 10**. This time, select the **Board Gear Checklist** button on the **Stage** and in the **Action** panel's **Script** pane, select the `loadMovieNum ("gearCheckList.swf", 50);` line of code. Double-click on the **unloadMovie** action in the **Actions Toolbox** (**Actions > Browser/Network > unloadMovie**) to add it to the Script pane.

The reason you select the loadMovie line of code first is so that when you select the unloadMovie action from the Toolbox, it will add the unloadMovie action inside the on Event Handler right under the loadMovie action.

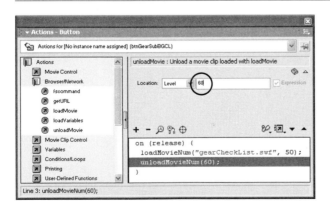

25. In the Parameters pane, type **60** for **Location: Level**. This ActionScripting tells Macromedia Flash MX that when a user clicks on the Board Gear Checklist button, it should unload whatever movie is currently in Level 60 (this happens to be gearExtra.swf).

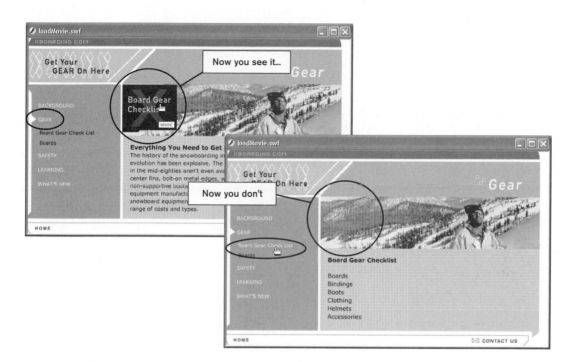

26. Choose **Control > Test Movie** and click on the **Gear** button in the menu. Notice that the button from the **gearExtra.swf** file is there! Click on the **Safety** and **Learning** buttons and notice that the **gearExtra.swf** content remains in place. Now click on the **Board Gear Checklist** button and notice that the **gearExtra.swf** content is gone. This is because you unloaded the **gear.swf** file from Level 60 when the user clicks on the button.

In summary, by using the loadMovie action, you can keep the main movie small, and you can load additional movies into levels above the main movie as you wish or as they are needed.

27. When you are finished, save and close this file.

MOVIE | loadMovie.mov

To see this exercise performed, play the **loadMovie.mov** located in the **movies** folder on the **H•O•T CD-ROM**.

That's a wrap on this chapter. I covered a lot of information in the exercises, and if anything isn't crystal clear, you can always go back and do a review. Take a well-deserved break and then get ready for the Text chapter, which comes next.

12.
Working with Text

| Text Block Types | Text Options |
| Static Text and Device Fonts |
| Loading Dynamic Text Fields | Dynamic Text and HTML |
| Scrollable Text Fields | Input Text |

---
chap_12

Macromedia Flash MX
H•O•T CD-ROM

When working with text, you have many options that go far beyond simply selecting the Text tool and typing on the Stage. In Macromedia Flash MX, you can create horizontal or vertical text, you can change the text attributes such as kerning (spacing between characters) and line spacing, and you can apply transformations such as rotation and skew. However, that is only the beginning. As this chapter will show you, you can also create text fields that bring in text from an external document, make text scroll, and create text fields where users can enter information themselves.

Macromedia Flash MX allows you to create three different types of text elements: Static Text, Dynamic Text, and Input Text. You'll learn about these different types of text treatments and try them out with hands-on exercises.

Text Block Types

When you select the Text tool in Macromedia Flash MX, you can choose from three types of text fields: **Static Text**, **Dynamic Text**, or **Input Text**, each of which will be explained in the context of the exercises in this chapter. When you add one of these text fields to the Stage, a text block is created with a corner handle to identify the type of text block you are creating. A chart follows to identify the different types of text blocks.

Types of Text Blocks					
Text Type	**Orientation**	**Defined or Extending**	**Handle Shape**	**Handle Position**	
Static	Horizontal	Extending	Round	Upper right corner	xboarding.com
Static	Horizontal	Defined	Square	Upper right corner	xboarding.com
Static	Vertical (right to left)	Extending	Round	Lower left corner	x b o a r d
Static	Vertical (right to left)	Defined	Square	Lower left corner	x b o a r d
Static	Vertical (left to right)	Extending	Round	Lower right corner	x b o a r d
Static	Vertical (left to right)	Defined	Square	Lower right corner	x b o a r d
Dynamic or Input	Horizontal only	Extending	Round	Lower right corner	xboarding.com
Dynamic or Input	Horizontal only	Defined	Square	Lower right corner	xboarding.com

---

TIP | Changing the Text Box Type

You can switch a text block from an extending text block to a defined text block and back again simply by double-clicking on the handle.

TIP | Fixing a Text Block That Extends Too Far

If, by accident, you do create a text block that continues off the Stage, don't worry: You can choose **View > Work Area** and reduce the magnification to make the entire line of text visible. You can then force the text to wrap downward by placing the cursor inside the text block and adding your own line breaks or returns.

Creating, Modifying, and Formatting Text

In Macromedia Flash MX, you have a lot of control over the attributes of type. By using the Property Inspector, you can change, preview, and adjust text in a few easy clicks of the mouse. The next section will give you a close look at each of the available settings.

Text Options in the Property Inspector

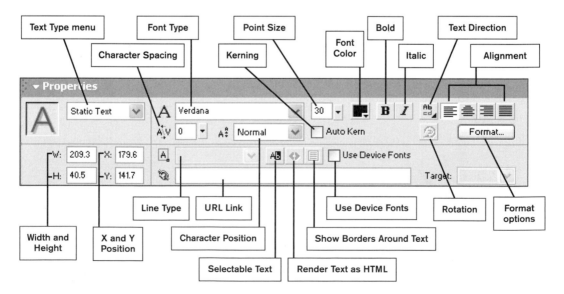

As soon as you select the Text tool, the Property Inspector will display the text attributes available to you. A chart follows detailing each of the items labeled on the preceding page.

Text Attributes Defined	
Attribute	**Description**
Text Type menu	Allows you to choose from one of three behaviors (Static Text, Dynamic Text, or Input Text) for the text box. Each Text Type has its own associated options that will appear in the Property Inspector when that text behavior is selected. Static Text is the default behavior.
Font Type	Displays the name of the current font. Click the arrow to the right of the font name to view a list of all the available fonts. As you scroll through the font list, Macromedia Flash MX displays a preview of what each font will look like.
Character Spacing (Tracking)	Allows you to adjust the space between characters in selected text. Click the arrow next to the Character Spacing field and use the slider to increase or decrease the amount of space between characters.
Character Position (Baseline Shift)	Normal: Resets characters to the baseline. Superscript: Shifts characters above the baseline. Subscript: Shifts characters below the baseline.
Point Size (Font Height)	Displays the current font point size. Click the arrow to the right of the Point Size field and use the slider to adjust the size of the font.
Auto Kern	Controls the spacing between pairs of characters. Checking this box will automatically use the font's built-in kerning information. (See the note below for more information on kerning.)
Font (Fill) Color	Allows you to change the color of the type by presenting you with a palette of available colors. Note: For text blocks, you can use only solid colors, not gradients. If you want to use gradients, you have to break the text apart, which will convert it to a shape, and then you can apply a gradient.
Bold	Bolds the selected type.
Italic	Italicizes the selected type.
	continues on next page

Text Attributes Defined *continued*

Attribute	Description
Text Direction	New to Macromedia Flash MX. Changes the direction of the text. You can choose from Horizontal; Vertical, Left to Right; and Vertical, Right to Left.
Alignment	Controls how the selected text will be aligned: Left Justified, Center Justified, Right Justified, or Full Justified.
Rotation	Allows you to have more control over vertical text and change its rotation. x xboarding b o a r d i n g This option is available only for vertical text.
Format	Launches a pop-up window with options for formatting text blocks where you can specifically set the values. For horizontal text, the options are Indent, Line Spacing, Left Margin, and Right Margin. For vertical text, the options are Indent, Column Spacing, Top Margin, and Bottom Margin. **Format Options** Indent: 0 px [Done] Line Spacing: 2 pt Left Margin: 0 px Right Margin: 0 px [Help] Indent controls the distance between the margin of a paragraph and the beginning of the first line of a paragraph. Line/Column Spacing (Leading) controls the spacing between lines of type (horizontal text) or between vertical columns (vertical text). Left/Top Margin determines the amount of space between the characters and the left side (horizontal text) or top (vertical text) of the text box. Even if text is centered or right-aligned, increasing the amount of space in the left/top margin will create the space you specify from the left side/top of the text box to the leftmost/first character within the text box. Right/Bottom Margin determines the amount of space between the characters and the right side (horizontal text) or bottom (vertical text) of the text box.

continues on next page

Text Attributes Defined *continued*	
Attribute	**Description**
Width and Height	Displays the width and height of a selected text box.
X and Y Position	Displays the X and Y position of a selected text box, relative to the Stage, where 0, 0 is the top left of the Stage.
URL Link	Creates a hyperlink that is attached to selected text. In effect, this creates a Button that will link to an internal or external HTML file, without the need to create a Button symbol. Using this option will automatically add a dotted line under the linked text in the .fla file. Note, however, that hyperlinks created using this feature will not carry any visual feedback (such as an underline) in the .swf file, although when previewed in a browser, the hand icon will appear when the user moves his or her mouse over the linked text. You learned a better way to create a hyperlink in Chapter 11, "*ActionScripting Basics*."
Line Type	Allows you to choose from Single line (displaying the text on one line), Multiline (displaying the text in multiple lines with word wrap), Multiline No Wrap (displaying the text in multiple lines), and Password. This option is available only for Dynamic and Input Text.
Selectable	Allows a user to select text within a block and either copy it or cut it.
Render Text as HTML	Preserves Rich Text Formatting, including fonts, hyperlinks, and bold with the appropriate HTML tags. You will learn to use this option in Exercise 3 of this chapter.
Show Border Around Text	When selected, displays a white background with a black border for the text field.
Use Device Fonts	If this box is not checked, Macromedia Flash MX will embed font information for any fonts used within the text block. When the movie is exported, this font will appear antialiased (not jaggy). If this box is checked, Macromedia Flash MX will prevent the font information from being embedded. You will learn more about device fonts in Exercise 1 of this chapter.

NOTE | To Kern or Not to Kern?

When font sets are created, the individual characters might look great all by themselves, but some letters might not look very good next to each other or may not be spaced very well. To solve this issue, many fonts are created with additional instructions about spacing between specific characters. This is known as kerning information.

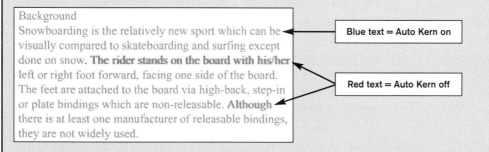

To illustrate this point, I created two text blocks (one blue and one red) and placed them in the exact same position, with the blue text on top of the red text. I selected the Auto Kern feature in the Property Inspector for the blue text and left the red text at its default spacing. Notice how the red text shows through in some spots. This indicates that the Auto Kern feature has changed the spacing of the blue text.

When you create horizontal text, kerning sets the horizontal distance between characters. As you may have guessed, when you create vertical text, kerning sets the vertical distance between characters.

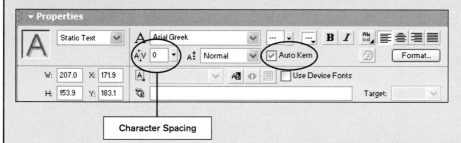

Macromedia Flash MX will not automatically add this special kerning information to your text unless you tell it to by checking the Auto Kern check box in the Property Inspector. You can use this option, especially when typing paragraphs of text, in order to achieve the best-looking text Macromedia Flash MX is capable of producing.

You can also select the Character Spacing option (shown circled above) if you wish to adjust the space between selected individual characters or blocks of characters.

WARNING | **Text in Macromedia Flash MX and Search Engines**

When you create text in Macromedia Flash MX, it is important to note that unlike HTML, Macromedia Flash MX text is not searchable by search engines. Therefore, if you need key words within your movie to be seen by search engines, I suggest you add Meta tags to the HTML document that the .swf file resides in. You will learn more about embedding .swf files in HTML documents in Chapter 16, "*Publishing and Exporting.*" For further information about Meta tags, a good resource book is *HTML 4 for the World Wide Web Visual QuickStart Guide*, from Peachpit Press.

I. ────────── Working with Static Text and Device Fonts

When you add text to your Macromedia Flash MX project, it is important to be aware of what the end user will see when looking at the text on a live Web site. Often this will differ from what you see on your Stage–at first glance the text on the Stage might seem fine, but when you preview the movie in a browser, it can look fuzzy or out of focus. There is an option called **Use Device Fonts** that allows your text to appear sharper in a Web browser. This exercise will teach you the difference between embedded and device fonts. You will work with predeveloped Static Text blocks and then export the blocks of text using both options to see the difference between checking and not checking the Use Device Fonts box.

1. Copy the **chap_12** folder, located on the **H•O•T CD-ROM**, to your hard drive. You need to have this folder on your hard drive in order to save files inside it.

2. Open the **staticText.fla** file from the **chap_12** folder. This file has been created to get you started. Notice the two text blocks side by side. Both of these text blocks have the same text attributes.

3. Using the **Arrow** tool, select the left block of text and make sure the **Property Inspector** is open (**Window > Properties**). In the Property Inspector, notice that the **Font** setting applied to that text block is _serif. Click on the right text block and you will notice the same Font setting.

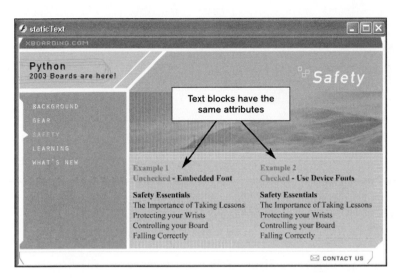

4. Choose **Control > Test Movie** to preview the text blocks. Notice that nothing is different between the two blocks of text. When you are finished, close the Preview Window.

In the following steps, you will modify the right block of text to use a device font while leaving the left block of text at the default setting, which is to use an embedded font.

Note: *At the end of this exercise, you will find an explanation detailing the difference between embedded fonts and device fonts.*

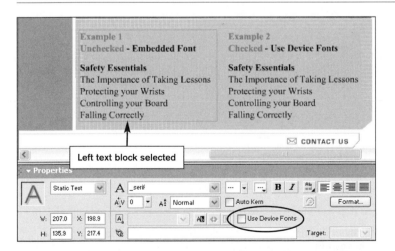

5. Select the left block of text. In the **Property Inspector**, notice that the **Use Device Fonts** box is unchecked. This is the default setting when you create a Static Text block. In effect, it will create an embedded font.

6. Click on the right block of text to select it on the **Stage**. In the **Property Inspector**, check the **Use Device Fonts** box.

When you preview this file next, the right block of text will use the device fonts feature and the left block of text will not.

7. Choose **Control > Test Movie** to preview the movie. Notice that the Embedded Font text block on the left is fuzzier, whereas the text on the right is sharper? This is because the text block on the right is using a device font, which is a quick way to keep the file size down and allow the text to be readable even at smaller font sizes.

8. Save and close this file.

Embedded Fonts Versus Device Fonts

When you select a font for a text block, Macromedia Flash MX automatically takes all the font information (the description of how the font will look, whether aliasing or antialiasing and kerning are in effect, etc.) and embeds it in the exported movie. This is what is known as an **embedded font**. This ability to embed fonts makes Macromedia Flash MX a great platform for using unusual fonts in movies because when viewing the .swf file or a projector file, the end user doesn't have to own the fonts to see the results, since the Macromedia Flash Player embeds all the necessary information.

The down side to using embedded fonts is that they can increase the file size of the movie. Also, it is important to know that some fonts, although displayed in your project file, cannot be exported with the movie because Macromedia Flash MX does not recognize the font's outline. You can select **View >** **Antialias Text** to preview the text. If it appears rough or jagged, this indicates that the text will not be exported because Macromedia Flash MX does not recognize the font outline.

Missing Font Warning

One or more fonts used by this movie are not available. Substitute fonts will be used for display and export. They will not be saved to the Macromedia Flash authoring document.

☐ Don't warn me again.

[Choose Substitute...] [Use Default]

Another indication that Macromedia Flash MX does not recognize the font's outline is the Missing Font Warning message, shown above, displayed when you try to preview the movie in the Macromedia Flash MX Player. For example, you might see this message if you are working on a project file that was originally created by someone else who used fonts that you don't have installed on your machine. You may be able to see the font on the Stage, but when you try to test or publish the movie, you'll get this alert to let you know that the font cannot be exported with your movie, and instead a substitute font will be used.

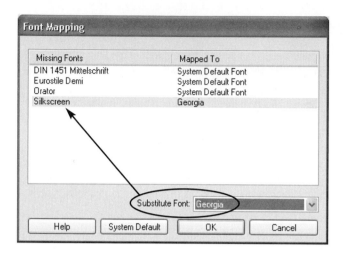

When you receive the Missing Font Warning message, you have the option of using the program's default substitute font, or you can choose your own substitute for each unrecognized font, as in the picture above.

Device fonts were created as a way around this issue. They are special fonts that will not be embedded in the exported movie and therefore create a smaller file size. Rather than use an embedded font, the Macromedia Flash MX Player displays the text using the closest match on the user's computer to the device font. Generally, at smaller type sizes below 10 points, device fonts are sharper and easier to read.

The drawback to device fonts is that if a user doesn't have a font installed on his/her system that is similar to the device font; he or she might see text that bears little resemblance to the text you see on your machine. To combat this concern, Macromedia Flash MX includes three built-in device fonts to help produce results closer to what you expect:

• **_sans**–similar to Helvetica or Arial

• **_serif**–similar to Times Roman

• **_typewriter**–similar to Courier

2. Loading Dynamic Text Fields Using External Files

Oftentimes you may want to add functionality to your Macromedia Flash MX movie, so that it displays current information such as news, weather reports, or company information that will get updated often. Macromedia Flash MX allows you to do this using a Dynamic Text field, a variable, and an external file that holds the text. This allows Macromedia Flash MX to be a robust program for handling dynamic content. The following exercise will take you through these steps and teach you how to load a pre-created .txt file right into a Dynamic Text block.

1. Open the **chap_12** folder, and double-click on the **textFileLearning.txt** file to open it. This is not a Macromedia Flash MX file, it is a .txt file, and it will open in the default text editor on your computer. This .txt file has been created to get you started.

```
content=Renting the Board
Nearly, all resorts have rental facilities. When
purchasing your lift ticket, check for beginner packages
which include the lift ticket, rental and lessons - all
for a reduced price. Boards are measured in centimeters.
For example, I board a "163"(meaning 163 centimeters
long). When selecting a board, you will typically want a
board that comes up to your chest when standing. Once
you find the optimum board size remember its
measurements for the next time.
Next determine if you are goofy or regular. (Right foot
forward or left foot forward?) If you have experience
with skateboarding or surfing then use the same stance.
Otherwise it doesn't really matter, but once you start
one way it is very hard to switch. There are various
techniques designed to determine the whether someone is
regular or goofy. Some say, have someone push you from
behind, which ever foot you catch yourself with should
be your front foot on the snowboard. Others say that if
you run real fast on a waxed kitchen floor then stop and
slide, the foot that naturally extends forward is the
one that you should lead with. Probably a few more
boarders are regular than goofy.
Before leaving the rental facility, make sure:
1. Your board has a leash.
2. There are no loose screws on the bindings.
3. You are able to strap or step your feet securely into
the bindings.
```

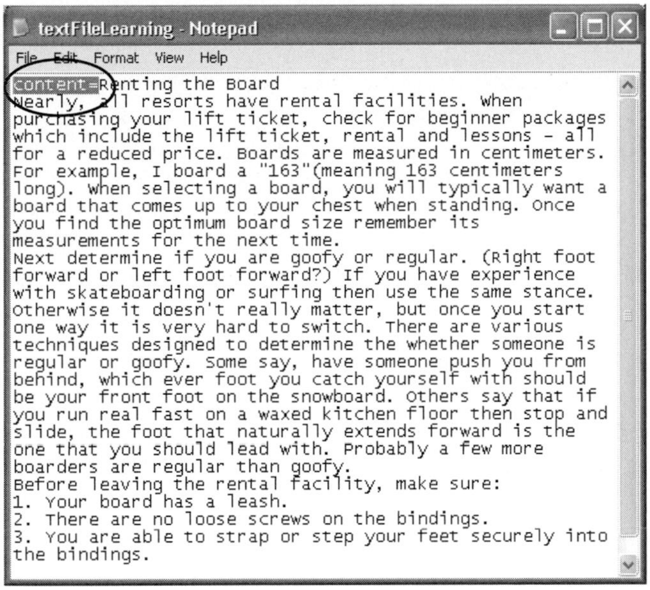

2. In order for Macromedia Flash MX to recognize the information in this file, you need to give it a variable name. Place your cursor at the very beginning of the paragraph and type **content=**, just as you see in the picture above. You have now declared that the text within the text file will be assigned to the variable name **content**.

NOTE | What Is a Variable?

A variable is simply a container that holds information, such as a name or number.

For example, in the following ActionScript,

```
author=''Kymberlee'';
```

the variable name (or container) is **author** and everything after the equal sign between the quotes is the value of the variable, which, in this example, is **Kymberlee**.

NOTE | URL-Encoded Text

When you use the loadVariables action (which you will add in step 11) to load an external text file, the data in the text file must be in a special format called **URL-encoded**. This format requires that each variable travel in a pair with its associated value. The variable and the associated value are separated by the = symbol. In step 2 on the preceding page, the variable name is *content* and the associated value is all the text that immediately follows the = symbol.

---

3. Save and close the text file. Make sure you save it in the **chap_12 folder**, because Macromedia Flash MX will be referring to this file in later steps.

4. In Macromedia Flash MX, open the **dynamicText.fla** file from the **chap_12** folder. Notice that this file contains one layer with a background image.

You will add the Dynamic Text box next.

5. In the **Timeline**, add a new layer by clicking the **Insert Layer** button, and rename this layer **holder**.

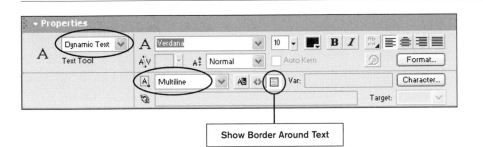

6. Select the **Text** tool from the **Toolbox**. In the **Property Inspector**, choose **Dynamic Text, Multiline,** and **Show Border Around Text**. Make sure the **Font Color** is set to **black** and the **Font Type** is set to **Verdana** with a **Point Size** of 10.

When you draw the text field on the Stage (next), these settings will create a Dynamic Text field with a white background and a black border that can support multiple lines of text that will wrap.

7. With the **holder** layer selected, click and drag on the **Stage** to create a text field that looks just like the picture above.

Tip: After you draw the text field, you can drag the handle of the Dynamic Text box to resize the text field, if necessary.

8. In the **Property Inspector**, type the word **content** in the **Var** (variable) field. This will be the variable name that is assigned to the text field. This has to be the same variable name you assigned to the text inside the .txt file in step 2.

TIP | Loading External Data into a Project File

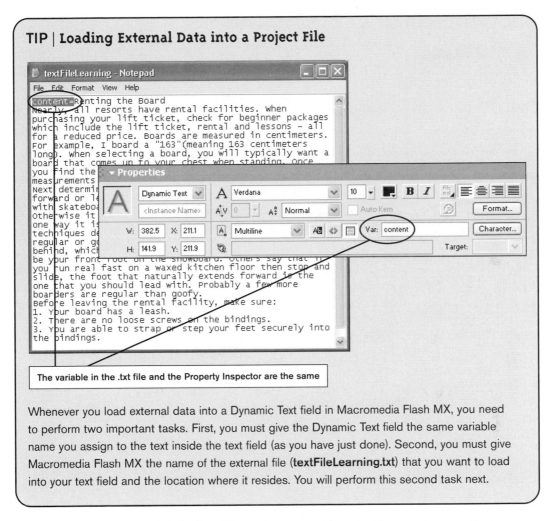

The variable in the .txt file and the Property Inspector are the same

Whenever you load external data into a Dynamic Text field in Macromedia Flash MX, you need to perform two important tasks. First, you must give the Dynamic Text field the same variable name you assign to the text inside the text field (as you have just done). Second, you must give Macromedia Flash MX the name of the external file (**textFileLearning.txt**) that you want to load into your text field and the location where it resides. You will perform this second task next.

9. On the **Main Timeline**, click the **Insert Layer** button to add one last layer, and rename the layer **actions**. Make sure the actions layer is above all other layers.

10. Select the first frame on the **actions** layer of the **Timeline** and open the **Actions** panel (**Window >
Actions**, or use the shortcut key **F9**).

Script pane

11. Inside the **Actions** panel Toolbox, choose **Actions > Browser/Network** and double-click on the **loadVariables** option to add it to the **Script** pane.

```
Line 1: loadVariablesNum("textFileLearning.txt", 0);
```

12. For the **URL**, type **textFileLearning.txt** (this is the text file you modified in step 2), using lower-case and capital letters exactly as you see here. You can leave the other settings at their defaults. This ActionScripting command tells Macromedia Flash MX to look for **textFileLearning.txt** and to load the variables from that file into the movie (level 0). Since you assigned the variable name **content** to both the Dynamic Text field and the text within the **textFileLearing.txt** file, the text field will be populated with the text from the .txt file.

Note: Since the .txt file is in the same folder as the project file and the .swf file, you can simply type the name of the file (the relative address) in the URL field. If, however, the .txt file was located in a different folder, you would have to specify the path to that folder (the absolute address) in the URL field, such as ../projectSnow/learning/textFileLearning.txt.

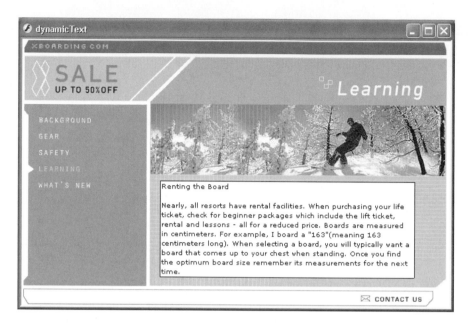

13. Choose **Control > Test Movie** to test your movie! When you are finished, close the Preview Window.

Troubleshooting tip: *If you don't see any text when you test the movie, select the text field back in the project file and make sure the Font Color is set to black. Also click in Frame 1 on the actions layer in the Actions panel, and check the spelling of the .txt file name to make sure you have the name spelled exactly as the document is named. The URL field in the Actions panel is case sensitive, so you must type the word exactly as the .txt document is named:* textFileLearning.txt.

NOTE | Changing Character Attributes

The Dynamic Text field will take on all the character attributes that are set in the Property Inspector. You can quickly change the way the text is displayed in the .swf file by making some slight modifications to the text box using the Property Inspector. First, select the Dynamic Text field. Then go ahead and try changing the font name, the font height, and the font color. You can even deselect the Show Border Around Text option to remove the white background from the text. Test the movie again and you will see a completely different look for your text field!

14. Save the file and keep it open for the next exercise.

3. —————Working with Dynamic Text and HTML

In the last exercise, you created a Dynamic Text field in your project file that displayed the data of an external text file. In this exercise, you will take it one step further and change one setting of the Dynamic Text field to allow Macromedia Flash MX to recognize and preserve HTML formatting applied to the content inside the external text field.

1. Open the **textFileLearning.txt** file from the **chap_12** folder. This is the same .txt file you worked with in the last exercise.

NOTE | Dynamic Text HTML Support

Macromedia Flash MX supports the following HTML tags in Dynamic and Input Text fields:

\<A\> = anchor, **\<B\>** = bold, **\<FONT COLOR\>** = font color, **\<FONT FACE\>** = typeface, **\<FONT SIZE\>** = font size, **\<I\>** = italic, **\<P\>** = paragraph, **\<U\>** = underline, and **\<a href="..."\>** = hyperlinks.

Macromedia Flash MX supports the following HTML attributes in Dynamic and Input Text fields:

LEFTMARGIN, **RIGHTMARGIN**, **ALIGN**, **INDENT**, and **LEADING**.

You will add some of these tags in the next few steps.

---

2. Add bold HTML tags around the words **Renting the Board**. It should read **\<B\>Renting the Board\</B\>**.

```
textFileLearning - Notepad                        _  □  X
File  Edit  Format  View  Help
content=<B>Renting the Board</B>
Nearly, all resorts have rental facilities. when
purchasing your lift ticket, check for beginner packages
which include the <FONT COLOR="#3399ff"> lift ticket,
rental and lessons</FONT> - all for a reduced price.
Boards are measured in centimeters. For example, I board
a "163"(meaning 163 centimeters long). when selecting a
board, you will typically want a board that comes up to
your chest when standing. once you find the optimum
board size remember its measurements for the next time.
Next determine if you are goofy or regular. (Right foot
forward or left foot forward?) If you have experience
with skateboarding or surfing then use the same stance.
otherwise it doesn't really matter, but once you start
one way it is very hard to switch. There are various
techniques designed to determine the whether someone is
regular or goofy. Some say, have someone push you from
behind, which ever foot you catch yourself with should
be your front foot on the snowboard. others say that if
you run real fast on a waxed kitchen floor then stop and
slide, the foot that naturally extends forward is the
one that you should lead with. Probably a few more
boarders are regular than goofy.
Before leaving the rental facility, make sure:
1. Your board has a leash.
2. There are no loose screws on the bindings.
3. You are able to strap or step your feet securely into
the bindings.
```

3. Add font color HTML tags around the words **lift ticket, rental and lessons**. It should read **<FONT COLOR="#3399ff"> lift ticket, rental and lessons</FONT>**.

```
textFileLearning - Notepad                        _  □  X
File  Edit  Format  View  Help
content=<B>Renting the Board</B>
Nearly, all resorts have rental facilities. when
purchasing your lift ticket, check for beginner packages
which include the <FONT COLOR="#3399ff"> lift ticket,
rental and lessons</FONT> - all for a <I>reduced</I>
price. Boards are measured in centimeters. For example,
I board a "163"(meaning 163 centimeters long). when
selecting a board, you will typically want a board that
comes up to your chest when standing. once you find the
optimum board size remember its measurements for the
next time.
Next determine if you are goofy or regular. (Right foot
forward or left foot forward?) If you have experience
with skateboarding or surfing then use the same stance.
otherwise it doesn't really matter, but once you start
one way it is very hard to switch. There are various
techniques designed to determine the whether someone is
regular or goofy. Some say, have someone push you from
behind, which ever foot you catch yourself with should
be your front foot on the snowboard. others say that if
you run real fast on a waxed kitchen floor then stop and
slide, the foot that naturally extends forward is the
one that you should lead with. Probably a few more
boarders are regular than goofy.
Before leaving the rental facility, make sure:
1. Your board has a leash.
2. There are no loose screws on the bindings.
3. You are able to strap or step your feet securely into
```

4. Add italic HTML tags around the word **reduced**. It should read **<I>reduced</I>**.

5. Save and close this file.

6. If it isn't still open from the last exercise, open the **dynamicText.fla** file from the **chap_12** folder.

All you need to do is change one setting and you will see the HTML-based text file loaded into the same Dynamic Text box.

7. Select the Dynamic Text field on the **Stage**, and in the **Property Inspector** check the **Render text as HTML** button. This will allow the Dynamic Text block to interpret the HTML code and dynamically display any of the supported HTML tags within the external text file.

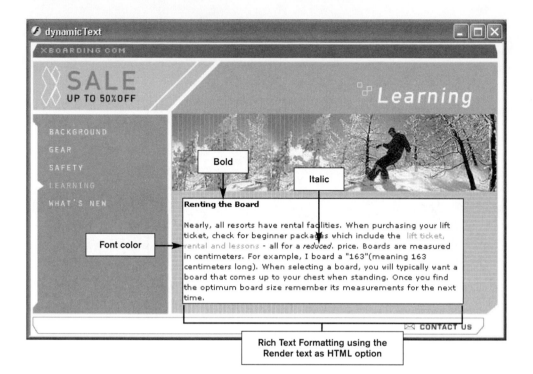

8. Test your movie! You will notice that Macromedia Flash MX recognized all the HTML formatting you made in the text file!

9. Save this file and keep it open for one more exercise.

4. ────────Scrollable Dynamic Text Fields

In the previous two exercises, you have been working with Dynamic Text fields. This exercise will take the project file one step further: You will learn to make the Dynamic Text scroll.

1. You should still have the **dynamicText.fla** file open from the last exercise.

2. Select the Dynamic Text field on the **Stage**. In the **Property Inspector**, type **learnText** in the **Instance Name** box. This will assign the instance name **learnText** to the Dynamic Text field.

NOTE | Why Do I Need an Instance Name and a Variable Name?

In Macromedia Flash MX, text is its own ActionScript object, so now (this is new in Flash MX) a text field (Dynamic and Input Text) can have both a variable name and an instance name. As you learned in Exercise 2, you need a variable name to be able to load the external text file into a Dynamic Text field. In this exercise, you need to give the text field an instance name so that ActionScripting on the Buttons can control the text field. You will do this next.

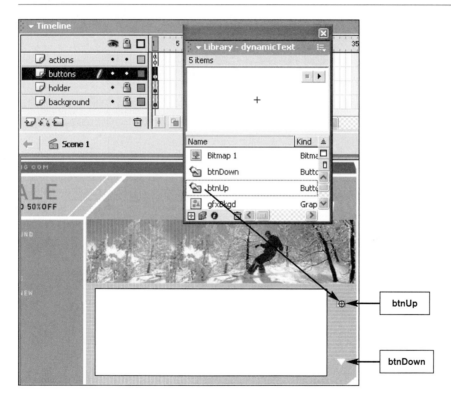

btnUp

btnDown

3. On the **Main Timeline**, lock the **holder** layer and click the **Insert Layer** button to add a new layer. Rename the layer **buttons**. Position the buttons layer below the actions layer.

4. Open the **Library (F11)** and notice that it contains two Buttons: **btnDown** and **btnUp**. Drag an instance of each Button onto the **Stage**. Position the **btnDown** Button under the **btnUp** Button, as in the picture above.

5. Select the **btnUp** Button on the **Stage** and press **F9** to open the **Actions** panel.

6. In the **Actions** panel Toolbox, choose **Objects > Movie > TextField > Properties**. Double-click on the **scroll** property to add it to the **Script** pane.

7. In the **Expression** box, place your cursor before **.scroll** and type the instance name of the Dynamic Text field: **learnText**. After the word **scroll**, type **-= 1**. The expression should now read **learnText.scroll -= 1**. This tells Macromedia Flash MX that, when a user clicks on the Up Button, it should take the learnText instance (the Dynamic Text field) and scroll it down 1 line.

Tip: You can change the number of lines that scroll at one time by changing the number after the -= 1. For example, learnText.scroll -= 5 will scroll the Dynamic Text field down five lines for each click on the Button.

8. Select the **btnDown** Button on the **Stage** and press **F9** to open the **Actions** panel. Choose **Objects >**
Movie > TextField > Properties and double-click on the **scroll** property to add it to the **Script** pane.

9. In the **Expression** box, inside the **Parameters** pane, place your cursor before **.scroll** and
type **learnText**. After the word **scroll**, this time type **+= 1**. The expression should now read
learnText.scroll += 1. This will tell Macromedia Flash MX that, when a user clicks on the Down
Button, it should take the learnText instance (the Dynamic Text field) and scroll it up one line.

10. Choose **Control > Test Movie** to try out your new scroll buttons!

Troubleshooting tip: *If your scroll buttons don't work, go back and check the ActionScripting on the*
buttons and make sure that all the text is spelled correctly and that you used the correct lowercase
and uppercase letters, since the ActionScript you applied to the Buttons is case sensitive.

11. When you are finished, save and close this file.

5. ——————Working with Input Text

Some projects that you develop in Macromedia Flash MX will require that the user be able to enter a special code or password in order to gain access to a Web site. The following steps will show you how to use **Input Text** blocks and check whether the user has entered a correct user name and password. This exercise will teach you what Input Text is and how it differs from Dynamic or Static Text.

1. Open the **inputText.fla** file from the **chap_12** folder. Notice that this file has one layer with a background image on it.

2. Click the **Insert Layer** button and add **five** new layers above the **background** layer. You will be adding content, actions, and labels to these layers in the next few steps.

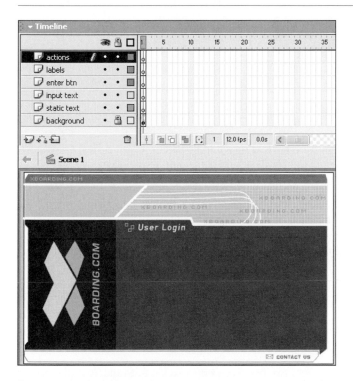

3. Name the layer above the background layer **static text**. Continuing from bottom to top, name the remaining layers **input text**, **enter btn**, **labels**, and **actions**, respectively. Your layers should look like the picture above.

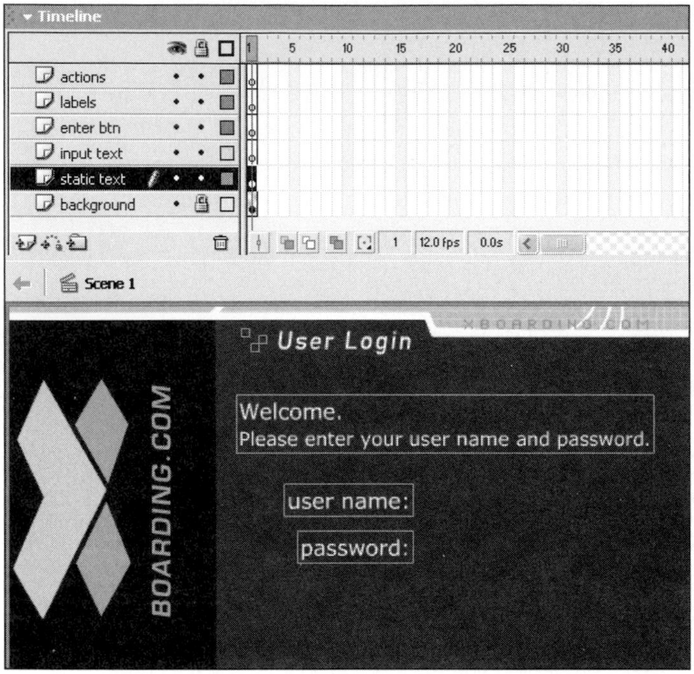

4. Select the **static text** layer and, with the **Text** tool, add **three** Static Text boxes, one at a time, to the Stage. In the first text block, add the text **Welcome. Please enter your user name and password.** In the second block, add the text **user name:**. In the third block, add the text **password:**. Your Stage should look similar to the picture above. Feel free to use any character attributes you wish for each of these Static Text boxes (font, font height, etc.).

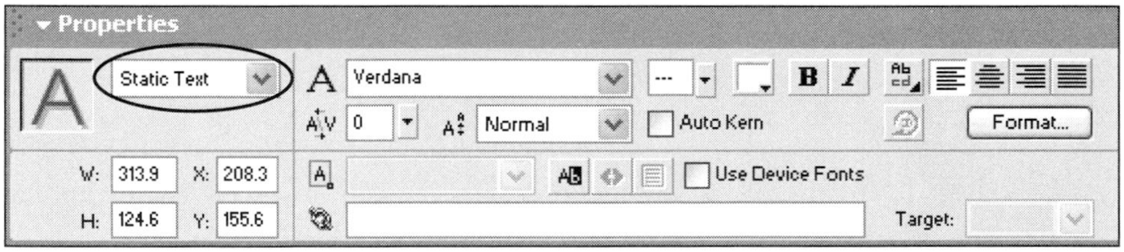

5. In the **Property Inspector**, make sure the **Text Type** option is set to **Static Text** (the default setting) for each text block that you added in step 4. Lock the **static text** layer to avoid editing anything on that layer by accident.

Input Text box

6. Click on the **input text** layer to select it. Select the **Text tool**. In the **Property Inspector**, choose **Input Text** for the **Text Type**. Create a text box to the right of the **user name** text on the **Stage**.

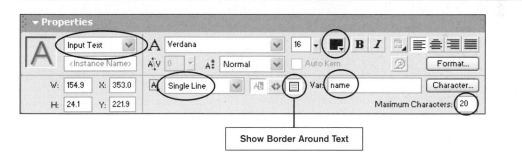

Show Border Around Text

7. Using the **Arrow** tool, select the Input Text box on the **Stage**. In the **Property Inspector**, make sure **Input Text** is selected and select **black** for the **Font Color** and **Single Line** for the **Line Type**. Click the **Show Border Around Text** button, and set the **Maximum Characters** to **20**. In the **Var** field, type the word **name** to give this Input Text box the variable name **name**. The Property Inspector should look just like the picture above.

NOTE | Naming Variables

According to the ActionScript Coding Standards, variable names can contain only letters, numbers, and underscores. However, when you name variables in Macromedia Flash MX, they should begin with a lowercase letter and cannot begin with numbers or underscores. Additionally, words that are used by ActionScript, such as "scroll," should not be used as variable names.

NOTE | Input Text Options

Clicking the **Show Border Around Text** button creates a border and background around the Input Text box. If the button is not selected, a dotted line will surround the text box in the .fla file, although when you publish the movie, there will be no border or background.

The **Maximum Characters** setting allows you to set the maximum number of characters that can be typed in the text box. The default is set to 0, meaning that there is no maximum number of characters. This allows the user to type forever in this box, so entering a value here is usually a good idea.

The **Line Type** option allows you to set the text box to either Single Line (displaying the text on one line), Multiline (displaying the text in multiple lines), or Password (automatically turns all characters into asterisks as they are typed in the field of either the .swf file or the executable).

The **Variable** setting (Var) enables you to assign a variable name to the text box.

8. Make sure you still have the **input text** layer selected and, using the **Text** tool, create a text box to the right of the **password** text on the **Stage**.

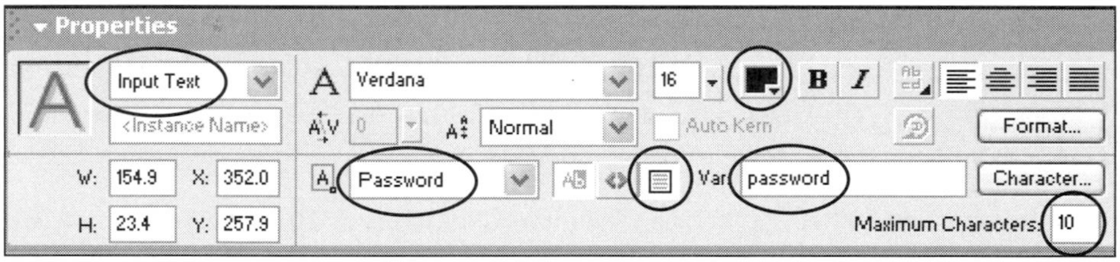

9. Using the **Arrow** tool, select the Input Text box on the **Stage**. In the **Property Inspector**, choose **Input Text** and select **black** for the **Font Color** and **Password** for the **Line Type**. Click the **Show Border Around Text** button, and set the **Maximum Characters** to **10**. In the **Var** field, type the word **password** to give this Input Text box the variable name **password**. The Property Inspector should look just like the picture above.

You have just created two Input Text fields, which will allow users to enter their user name and password. In a few steps, you will add ActionScript to have Macromedia Flash MX check to see if the user name and password are correct.

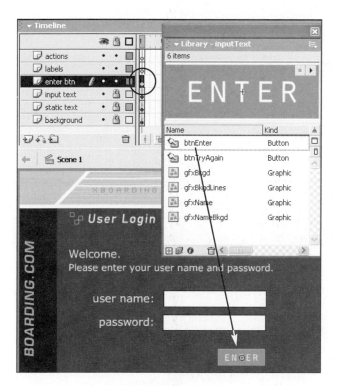

10. Lock the **input text** layer and select the **enter btn** layer. Open the **Library** and, with the **enter btn** layer selected, drag an instance of the **btnEnter** symbol onto the **Stage**. When you are finished, lock the **enter btn** layer so you don't accidentally edit anything.

11. On the **labels** and **actions** layers, add a keyframe (**F6**) at **Frames 10** and **20**.

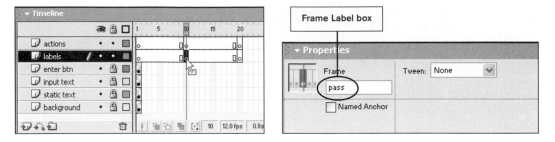

12. Select **Frame 10** on the **labels** layer. In the **Property Inspector**, type **pass** in the **Frame Label** box. Select **Frame 20** on the **labels** layer and type **fail** in the **Frame Label** box in the Property Inspector.

NOTE | The Hidden Label

In the Timeline, you can clearly see the pass label, although the fail label seems to be hiding. Why?

This is the frame label that is hiding

This is the frame label visible after frames are added after the label

This is because there are no frames after the fail label. To see the whole label, you can add frames if you wish. Doing so will not affect your movie; it will simply allow you to see the whole word "fail." You can also use the Frame View drop-down menu in the Timeline to change the frame view to Large. This will allow you to see the whole fail label in the Timeline.

Even if you can't see the whole frame label in the Timeline, the label does exist, and you can always check it by selecting the frame label in the Timeline and making sure the label name appears in the Property Inspector.

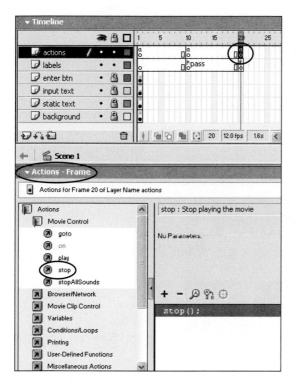

13. On the **actions** layer, add a **Stop** frame action (in the **Actions** panel, choose **Actions > Movie Control > stop**) to **Frames 1, 10,** and **20.** When you are finished, lock the **labels** and **actions** layers.

14. Select **Frame 20** on the **background** layer and press **F5** to add frames. This way you will be able to see the background of the movie for all of the frames.

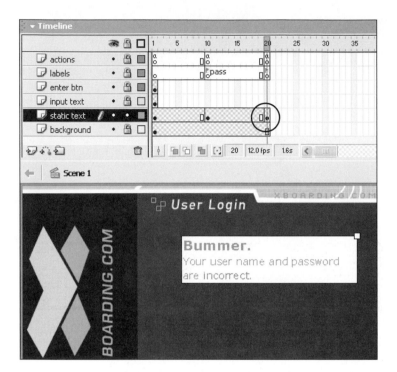

15. Unlock the **static text** layer and add a blank keyframe (**F7**) to **Frames 10** and **20**. On **Frame 10** of the **static text** layer, create a Static Text box that reads **Enjoy the ride! Your user name and password are right on the money**. On **Frame 20** of the **static text** layer, create a Static Text box that reads **Bummer. Your user name and password are incorrect**. Don't forget to select **Static Text** in the **Property Inspector** for both of these new text blocks. Feel free to adjust the settings in the Property Inspector, such as font name and font color. When you are finished, lock the **static text** layer.

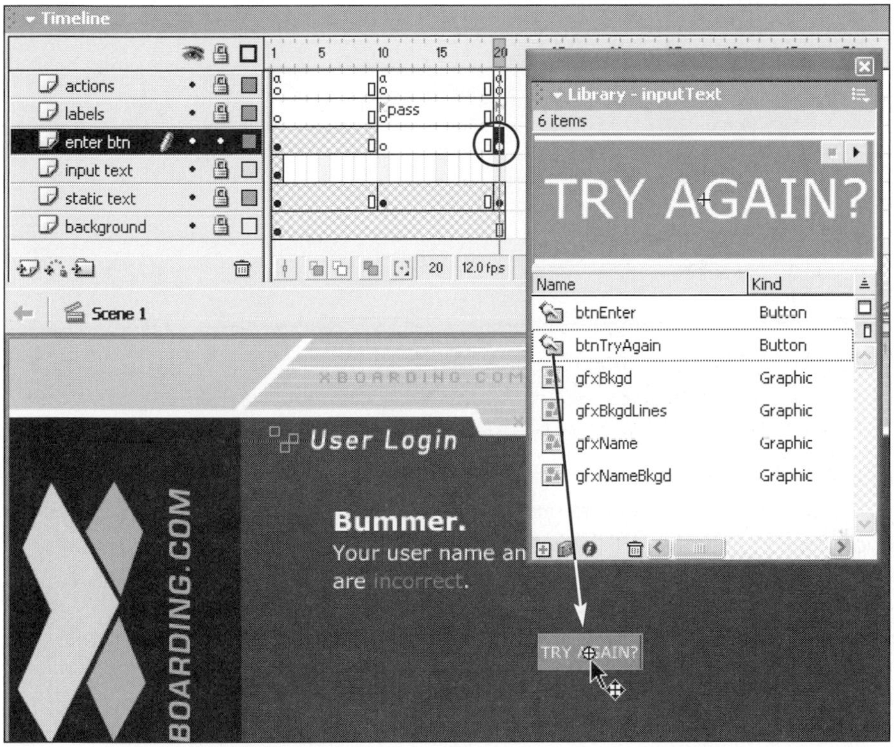

16. Unlock the **enter btn** layer, and add a blank keyframe on **Frames 10** and **20**. Select **Frame 20** and drag an instance of the **btnTryAgain** button onto the **Stage**, as in the picture above.

You have just added messages and a button that your movie will display, depending on whether the user name and password are correct or not. You will add ActionScript shortly that will send the user to Frame 10 if the user name and password are correct and to Frame 20 if they are incorrect.

17. With the **enter btn** layer still unlocked, click on the **Enter** button on the **Stage** in **Frame 1** to select it. Choose **Window > Actions** or press **F9** to open the **Actions** panel if it is not already open.

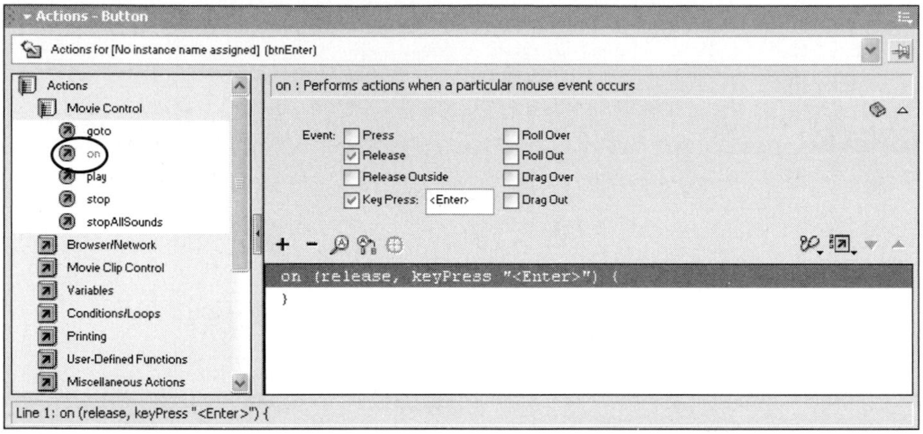

18. In the **Actions** panel, choose **Actions > Movie Control** and double-click on the **on** action to add it to the **Script** pane. Select the events **Release** and **KeyPress**. As soon as you select the KeyPress event, notice that your cursor is blinking in the empty field next to this option. Press the **Enter** button on your keyboard. This will add <Enter> to the empty field for you.

Tip: This will work with many other keys on the keyboard, such as the Backspace key or Tab key. The ActionScripting you added tells Macromedia Flash MX that when the user clicks on the button and releases the mouse, or presses Enter/Return on the keyboard, something is about to happen.

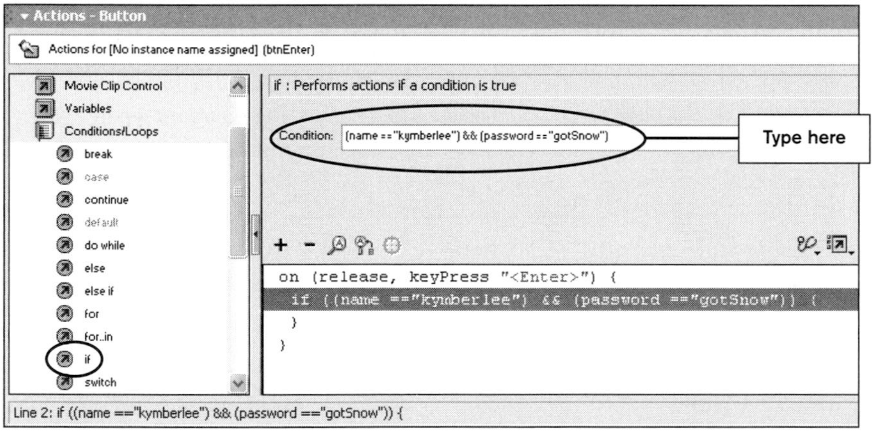

19. Choose **Actions > Conditions/Loops** and double-click on the **if** action to add it to the **Script** pane. In the **Condition** field, type the following: **Condition: (name =="kymberlee") && (password == "gotSnow")**. Your Script pane should look similar to the picture above.

This step tells Macromedia Flash MX that if the user name is equivalent to kymberlee and the password is equivalent to gotSnow, it should do something. You will add the "something" in the next step.

TIP | Using the = or == Signs

In ActionScripting, when you use **name="kymberlee"**, it means that the variable **name** becomes **kymberlee**. When you use **name == "kymberlee"**, it means that Macromedia Flash MX will check for equivalency—that is, it will check whether the value that is entered matches the value given after the == symbol.

Actions - Button

Actions for [No instance name assigned] (btnEnter)

Actions
  Movie Control
    goto
    on
    play
    stop
    stopAllSounds
  Browser/Network
  Movie Clip Control
  Variables
  Conditions/Loops
  Printing
  User-Defined Functions
  Miscellaneous Actions

goto : Go to the specified frame of the movie

○ Go to and Play   ⊙ Go to and Stop

Scene: <current scene>
Type: Frame Label
Frame: pass

```
on (release, keyPress "<Enter>") {
  if ((name =="kymberlee") && (password =="gotSnow")) {
    gotoAndStop("pass");
  }
}
```

Line 3: gotoAndStop("pass");

---

20. Choose **Actions > Movie Control**, and double-click on the **goto** action. For **Type**, select **Frame Label**; for **Frame**, select **pass** from the drop-down menu; and select **Go to and Stop**. This will tell Macromedia Flash MX that if the user name and password are correct, it should go to the frame labeled "pass."

Tip: In order for the user name and password to be correct when the user enters them, they must be typed exactly as they appear inside the quotes in the Script pane, since these values are case sensitive.

21. Choose **Actions > Conditions/Loops** and double-click on **else** to add it to the **Script** pane. Then choose **Actions > Movie Control** and double-click on **goto** to add it to the Script pane. For **Type**, choose **Frame Label**; for **Frame**, type **fail**; and select **Go to and Stop**. This tells Macromedia Flash MX that if the user name and password are *not* correct, it should go to the frame labeled "fail."

This is what your ActionScript should look like:

```
on (release, keyPress "<Enter>") {
    if ((name =="kymberlee") && (password =="gotSnow")) {
        gotoAndStop("pass");
    } else {
        gotoAndStop("fail");
    }
}
```

You have only one more ActionScript to create.

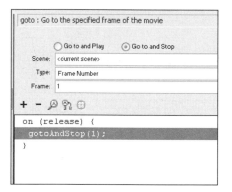

22. In **Frame 20**, on the **enter btn** layer, select the **Try Again?** button on the **Stage**. In the **Actions** panel, choose **Actions > Movie Control** and double-click on the **on** action to add it to the **Script** pane. Select the event **Release**. Choose **Actions > Movie Control** and double-click on **goto** to add it to the Script pane. For **Type**, select **Frame Number**; for **Frame**, type **1**; and select **Go to and Stop**. This tells Macromedia Flash MX that when the user clicks on the button and releases the mouse, it should go back to Frame 1 and stop.

23. Select **Control > Test Movie** to preview the movie.

Caution! If you don't see any text as you type in the user name or password field, check and make sure that the Text Color in the Input Text boxes is set to black. If it is set to white, you will not be able to see your text!

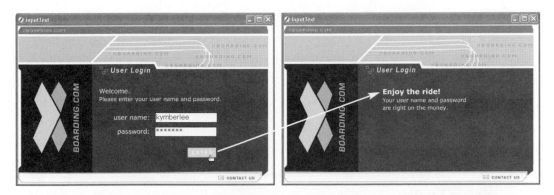

If you type in the user name and password correctly, you will get the "Enjoy the ride" message.

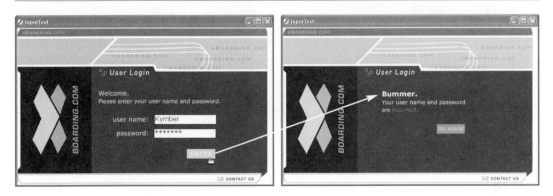

If you type in the user name and password incorrectly, you will get the "Bummer" message.

24. When you are finished, save and close this file.

You have successfully made it though the text chapter! Time to take a quick break and get amped up (pun intended) for the sound chapter next!

I3.
Sound

| Importing Sounds | Compressing Sound |
| Creating Background Sound with Sound Effects |
| Sound Settings | Controlling Sound with On/Off Buttons |
| Synchronizing Sound to Narration |

chap_13

Macromedia Flash MX
H·O·T CD-ROM

In Macromedia Flash MX, sound can be used for many purposes—including narration, background soundtracks, rollover noises, and for sound effects that complement animation effects. You also have the ability to work with a variety of sound formats, including .wav files (Windows users), .aiff files (Mac users), and MP3 files, which work on both the Windows and Macintosh platforms. The advantage of MP3 files is that they allow the file size to be small while providing high sound quality.

This chapter will give you a solid understanding of how to work with sounds in Macromedia Flash MX, including how to import sounds and compress sound files. You will learn how to change the format of a sound using MP3 compression settings, how to create background sounds, and how to control sound using buttons. You will also learn how to synchronize voice sound clips with an animation.

I. ———————Importing Sounds

In this exercise, you will learn how to import sound files into Flash. The following steps will teach you which kinds of sounds can be imported into Flash and will show you where the sound files go when you import them.

1. Copy the **chap_13** folder, located on the **H•O•T CD-ROM**, to your hard drive. You need to have this folder on your hard drive in order to save files inside it.

2. Open a new file and save it as **basicSound.fla** inside the **chap_13** folder.

3. Choose **File > Import**. Navigate to the **soundFiles** folder (also inside the **chap_13** folder) and browse to the folder named **soundsPC** if you are using a Windows machine or **soundsMac** if you are using a Macintosh.

TIP | I Don't See Any Files!?

If you don't see any sounds in the list, make sure you select **Files of type: All Files** in the Import dialog box rather than **Files of Type: All Formats**.

NOTE | What Kinds of Sounds Can I Import?

In Macromedia Flash MX, you can import a variety of sound files, depending on which platform you use and whether you have QuickTime 4 or later installed on your machine. The chart that follows lists the types of file you can import. You will learn about compressing sounds for export in the next exercise.

Import Sound File Types Supported by Macromedia Flash MX

Sound File Format	Windows	Mac
WAV	Yes	Yes, with QuickTime 4 or later installed
AIFF	Yes, with QuickTime 4 or later installed	Yes
MP3	Yes	Yes
Sound Designer II	No	Yes, with QuickTime 4 or later installed
Sound Only QuickTime Movies	Yes, with QuickTime 4 or later installed	Yes, with QuickTime 4 or later installed
Sun AU	Yes, with QuickTime 4 or later installed	Yes, with QuickTime 4 or later installed
System 7 Sounds	No	Yes, with QuickTime 4 or later installed

4. To import the sound files from inside the **soundsPC/soundsMac** folder:

- **Windows users: Ctrl+click** on the files to select **Breakout7**, **Miko_Big_Beatz**, and **Miko_Boardgrinder**, and click **Open** to import the sounds into Macromedia Flash MX.

- **Mac users: Cmd+click** on the files named **Breakout7.aif**, **Miko_Big_Beatz.aif**, and **Miko_Boardgrinder.aif**, and click **Open**. The sound files will be imported into Macromedia Flash MX.

TIP | Where Did the Sounds Go?

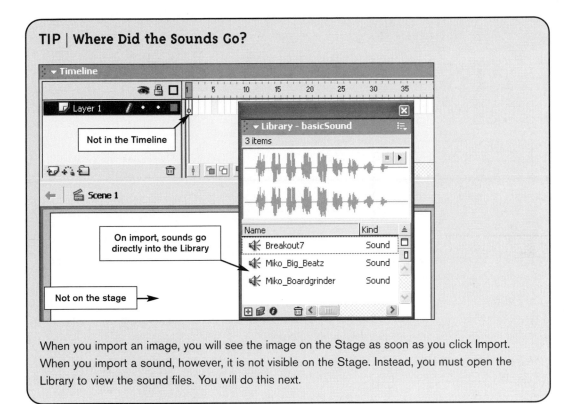

When you import an image, you will see the image on the Stage as soon as you click Import. When you import a sound, however, it is not visible on the Stage. Instead, you must open the Library to view the sound files. You will do this next.

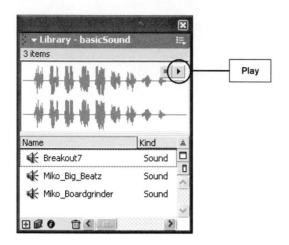

5. Press **F11** to open the **Library**. You will see all three of the sounds you just imported in the Library. Select the sounds, one at a time, and click the **Play** button to listen to each one.

That's all there is to it! Importing sounds is the simple part. Working with them in the Timeline can be a bit more challenging. By the end of this chapter, you will have experience working with sounds, the Timeline, and sound integration in Macromedia Flash MX.

Note: *The sounds inside these folders were donated generously by Patrick Miko and Michet Orthier for use in your own projects. Visit the* **http://www.ultrashock.com** *and* **http://www.breakout4u.com** *for access to even more sounds to use in your Macromedia Flash MX projects.*

---

6. Save this file and keep it open for the next exercise.

$\textbf{2.}$———————**Compressing Sound**

Now that you know how to import sounds into Macromedia Flash MX, the next step is to learn how to compress them. Compressing sounds is especially important when you need to keep your file size down, because uncompressed sounds can increase your file size drastically. In this exercise you will learn how to control sound compression settings and how to alter one of the sounds using the MP3 compression settings and the Sound Properties dialog box.

1. You should still have the **basicSound.fla** file open from the last exercise.

2. In the **Library**, click on the **Miko_Big_Beatz** sound to select it. Click the **Properties** button, located at the bottom of the **Library** panel, to open the **Sound Properties** dialog box.

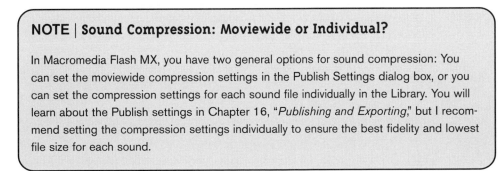

NOTE | Sound Compression: Moviewide or Individual?

In Macromedia Flash MX, you have two general options for sound compression: You can set the moviewide compression settings in the Publish Settings dialog box, or you can set the compression settings for each sound file individually in the Library. You will learn about the Publish settings in Chapter 16, "*Publishing and Exporting*," but I recommend setting the compression settings individually to ensure the best fidelity and lowest file size for each sound.

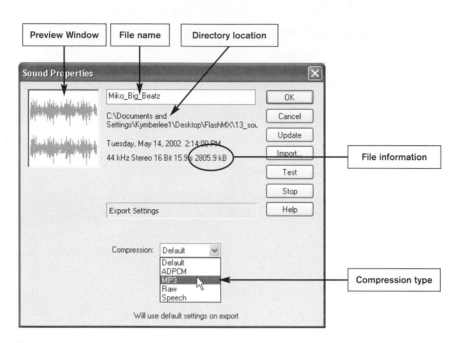

3. Notice that the sound is large at its default compression setting: 2805.9 KB. Click to see the **Compression** drop-down menu. You'll see five settings: Default, ADPCM, MP3, Raw, and Speech. Select **MP3**.

Sound Compression Defined	
Option	**Description**
Default	This option uses the global compression settings in the Publish Settings dialog box. You will learn about the Publish settings in Chapter 16, "*Publishing and Exporting*."
ADPCM	This compression model is the "old" method of compression from Macromedia Flash 3. It sets compression for 8-bit and 16-bit sound data. You may want to consider using this format if you need to author back to the Flash 3 Player.
MP3	This compression model can be heard only by users with the Macromedia Flash 4, Flash 5, or Flash 6 Player, but it offers the best compression rates and sound fidelity.
Raw	This format will resample the file at the specified rate but will not perform any compression.
Speech	This option is new to Macromedia Flash MX, and it uses a compression method designed specifically for speech sound files. You will have a chance to work with this compression type in Exercise 5 in this chapter.

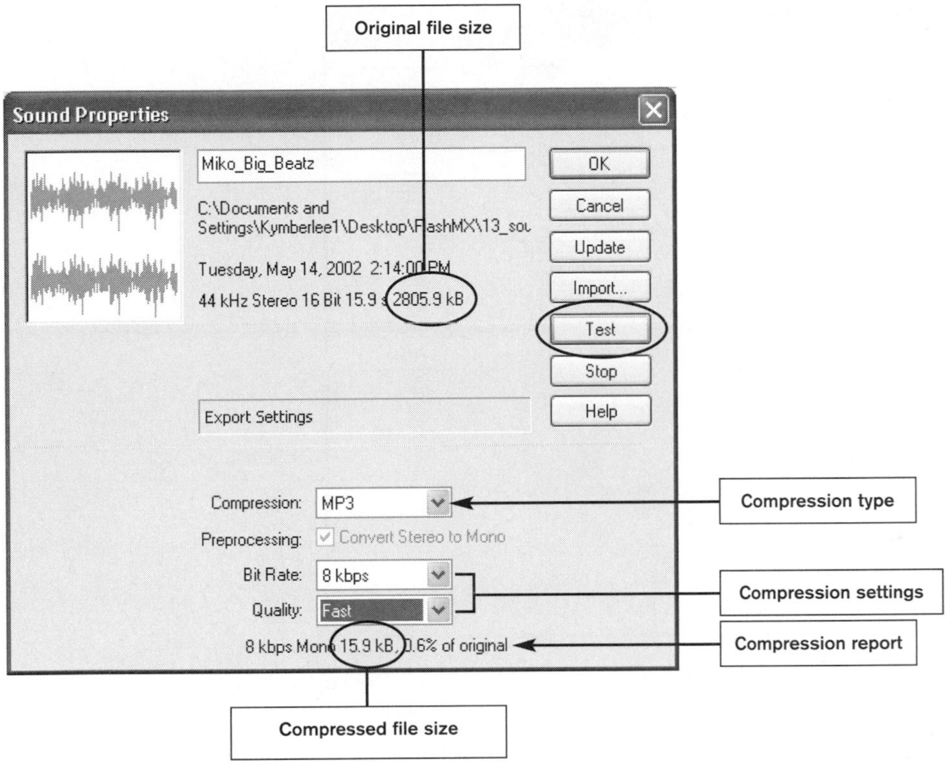

Original file size

Compression type

Compression settings

Compression report

Compressed file size

4. Choose **Bit Rate: 8 kbps**. Click the **Test** button to hear the sound with the new compression applied. Notice that the file size has drastically decreased from the original 2805.9 KB to 15.9 KB with the compression settings you applied.

Note: The lower the bit rate, the lower the sound quality and the lower the file size. The higher the bit rate, the higher the sound quality and the larger the file size.

5. Choose **Bit Rate: 160 kbps** and uncheck the **Preprocessing: Convert Stereo to Mono** box. Click the **Test** button to hear the sound again. Notice how much better the sound quality is at 160 kbps. However, look at the file size: It has increased to 318.1 KB. Although this is smaller than the original 2805.9 KB, it is more than 20 times the size of the file at the 8 kbps bit rate.

Note: The Preprocessing option is available only for bit rates of 20 kbps or higher. This feature converts mixed stereo sounds to mono sound if selected.

6. Choose **Bit Rate: 24 kbps** and uncheck the **Preprocessing: Convert Stereo to Mono** box. Click the **Test** button to preview the sound. Notice that the sound quality is very good and the file size has dropped to 47.7 KB.

When you are working with sound files in Macromedia Flash MX, you will find that you will want to test several bit-rate settings to determine which one offers the lowest file size without sacrificing sound quality.

7. Click to see the **Quality** drop-down menu and choose **Best**. Click the **Test** button and notice that it takes much longer to convert the file to an MP3. The sound file will sound better and the file size will be the same; the only trade-off is that it will take longer to convert the file inside Macromedia Flash MX. That's not a bad price to pay for better sound. **Note:** The longer conversion time for the Best setting occurs inside the Macromedia Flash MX project file, and since the file size is the same (between Best and Fast), you will not notice a difference in download time on a user's computer, although the Best sound will sound better. When you are finished, click **OK** to close the Sound Properties dialog box.

To summarize, you will find that choosing the best compression settings is often a process of selecting and testing several different options before you settle on the best setting to meet your needs. I recommend using the MP3 compression setting whenever possible because of its superior compression capabilities. You have the best of both worlds using this compression method: small file size with good sound quality.

8. Save and close this file.

Note: Once you produce the .swf file, the sound in your Macromedia Flash MX movie can be heard by users on both Windows and Mac machines, and it will not matter which format the sound was in when it was originally imported. This is because the sound is compressed as either ADPCM, MP3, Raw, or Speech when you create the .swf file, and these options are platform independent.

3. ──────────Creating Background Sound with Sound Effects

As you develop certain projects in Macromedia Flash MX, you may find that adding background sound that plays continuously will help the interface come to life. This exercise will show you how to create a background soundtrack, including how to fade the sound in and stop the sound in the Timeline. You will also be introduced to the **Edit Envelope dialog box**, which can be used to customize effects applied to the sound files.

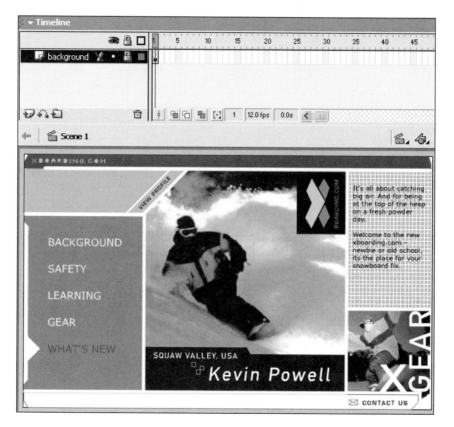

1. Open the file named **bkgdSound.fla** from the **chap_13 folder**. Choose **View > Magnification > Show All** to see the whole image on the Stage. Notice that it contains one layer with a background image.

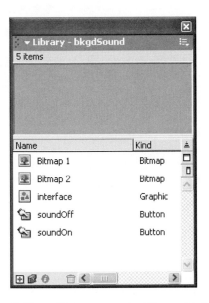

2. Press **F11** to open the **Library**. Notice that there are bitmaps, a Graphic symbol, and some buttons but no sounds ... yet.

3. On the **Main Timeline**, click the **Insert Layer** button to add a new layer. Rename the layer **sound**.

TIP | Why Am I Making a New Layer for the Sound?

Ideally, sound files, like frame actions, should be placed on their own separate layer. This will separate the sound from other artwork and animation, allowing you to view the waveform (the picture of the sound) better and to work with the sound more easily.

---

4. Choose **File > Import**. Inside the **sounds** folder, open the **mp3** folder and select the sound file named **X-tacy-groove**. Click **Open** to import the MP3 sound file.

MP3 sounds will work on both Macintosh and Windows machines, so no matter which platform you are using, this file will work for you.

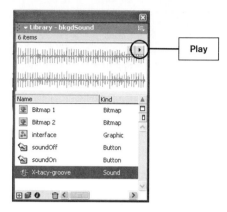

5. After you select **Import**, notice that the sound is added to the Library. Click the **Play** button to test the sound. You will be adding this sound to the movie next.

NOTE | When Sound Exists

Although the sound file has been successfully imported into the Macromedia Flash MX project file, it does not officially exist in the movie yet—it exists only in the Library. In order for it to be a part of the movie, you must add it to a keyframe in the Timeline.

---

6. With the first frame in the **sound** layer selected, drag the **X-tacy-groove** sound out of the **Library** and drop it anywhere on the **Stage**. After you drop the sound, you will not see a representation of that sound anywhere on the Stage. However, the sound will appear in the Timeline in the form of a blue waveform. This is visual feedback to you that the sound is located there.

NOTE | **Adding Sounds to Keyframes**

Each sound file must be tied to a keyframe. The simplest way to do this is to drag a sound out of the Library and drop it onto the Stage at the point in your Timeline that you want it to start playing. Make sure that you have a keyframe at the point where you want your sound to begin, and that you have selected that keyframe. Otherwise, you will not be able to add the sound at all, or the sound will attach itself to the last keyframe prior to the location of the Playhead at the time you drag and drop.

---

7. Choose **Control > Test Movie** to preview the movie with the new sound added. You will hear the sound play once and stop. When you are finished, close the **Preview Window**.

NOTE | **Testing Sounds**

All sounds can be tested using **Control > Test Movie**, since you are creating the .swf file when you use that method. You can also test sounds in the editing environment by pressing **Enter/Return** on the keyboard, but this method has its limitations, since certain conditions must be met in order for the sound to play. The list that follows defines when you can test sounds in the editing environment.

• When the Main Timeline has only 1 frame, no sound can be tested using Enter/Return on the keyboard.

• When the Main Timeline has more than 1 frame, you *can* test Event and Start sounds using Enter/Return on the keyboard, and they will play in their entirety (even if there are 2 frames in the Timeline but the sound takes 100 frames to play). Event and Start sounds play independently of the Main Timeline. (You will see what Event, Start, and Stream sounds are as you follow the steps of the exercise.)

• When the Main Timeline has more than 1 frame, Stream sounds *can* be tested using Enter/Return on the keyboard. Use caution, however, because if the number of frames in the Timeline is fewer than the length of the sound, or if another keyframe is encountered before the sound finishes, the sound will stop (it will be cut short) when the Timeline stops or encounters another keyframe. Stream sounds are tied directly to the Main Timeline.

Sound name

8. Click on the first frame in the **sound** layer to select the sound. Notice the settings in the **Property Inspector**, including the name of the sound displayed in the **Sound** box. This section of the Property Inspector is where you control the behavior of the sound.

9. In the **Property Inspector**, notice that the **Sync** option is set to **Event**. The Event setting causes the sound to start playing when the Playhead hits the frame that contains it. The sound will continue to play all the way to the end, independently of whatever is happening on the Main Timeline—even if the Main Timeline stops or is only 1 frame in length, as the last step showed.

10. In the **Property Inspector**, choose **Sync: Stream**.

11. Choose **Control > Test Movie** to preview the movie with the Stream sound setting. You will not hear the sound at all. Why? Unlike the Event setting, the Stream setting stops the sound when the movie stops. So if you have only 1 frame in your movie, and you apply a Stream setting to a sound in the Main Timeline, the sound will not play.

Stream sounds also have many benefits. These will be discussed in the chart at the end of this exercise and again in Exercise 4, where you will work with Stream synchronization sounds.

12. Close the **Preview Window** and choose **Sync: Start** in the **Property Inspector**. This setting is most often used for background sounds. The Start setting is very similar to the Event setting: It causes the sound to begin playing as soon as the keyframe holding it is reached, and the sound will play to the end, independently of the Main Timeline, just as an Event sound will. The only difference between the Event and Start settings is that if a Start sound is already playing, no new instance of the sound can be played. With the Event setting, if an instance of the sound is playing and another instance is triggered, the sounds will overlap.

If the previous description seems a little abstract, you might be wondering when you would use the Start sound setting. This setting is often used if you have a layer with a sound that is already playing, and you don't want the new sound to begin until the currently playing sound has stopped. The Start setting prevents the sound from overlapping itself. For a detailed explanation of all the sound settings available to you, see the "Modifying Sound Options" section following this exercise.

13. Choose **Control > Test Movie** to preview the movie with the Start sound setting. The sound will play just as it would with the Event setting. When you are finished, close the **Preview Window**.

14. In the **Property Inspector**, click to see the **Effect** drop-down menu and choose **Fade In**. This will make the sound start out soft and gradually become louder.

15. Type **Loop: 3**. This will make the sound repeat three times before it stops. This setting will not affect the overall file size, since Macromedia Flash MX downloads the file only once.

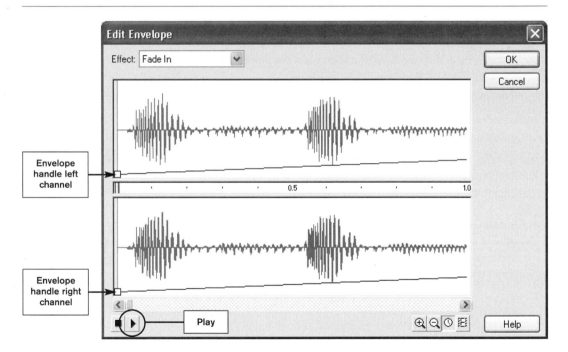

16. Click the **Edit** button in the **Property Inspector**. This opens the **Edit Envelope** dialog box.

When you click the Edit button in the Property Inspector's Sound panel, Macromedia Flash MX will open the Edit Envelope dialog box, where you can edit your sound. Notice that the Effect option shows Fade In selected. This effect was created when you selected it from the drop-down list in the Sound panel.

17. In the **Edit Envelope** dialog box, click the **Play** button to test the sound. Move the **right** and **left Envelope** handles. This will change the way the sound fades into the right and left speakers. Click the **Play** button again to test it.

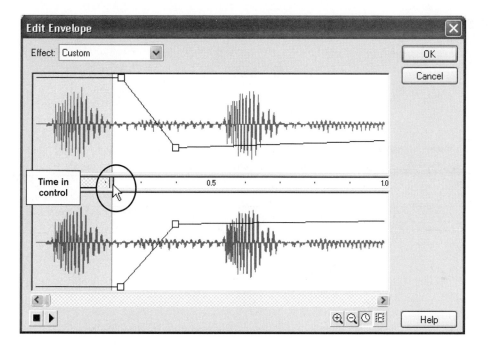

18. Drag the **Time In** control in the **Edit Envelope** dialog box. This will change the start point of the sound. Click the **Play** button again to test it. When you are happy with the way your adjustments sound, click **OK** in the **Edit Envelope** dialog box.

19. Choose **Control > Test Movie** to preview the movie again. You will hear the sound with your custom effects applied to it.

Tip: If you don't like the custom effects you created, you can either click Cancel rather than OK in the Edit Envelope dialog box or you can choose an Effect option other than Custom in the Property Inspector to reset the sound to the effect you choose.

20. Save this file and keep it open for the next exercise.

You will learn how to control the sound with On and Off buttons in the next exercise.

Modifying Sound Settings

After you place an instance of a sound in the Timeline, you can use the settings in the Property Inspector to control the behavior of the sound, as you learned in this exercise. The following sections provide an in-depth look at the sound settings options.

Effect Option

The **Effect option** in the Property Inspector allows you to choose from a drop-down list of preset effects that you can apply to your sound. Choosing the **Custom** setting will allow you to create your own sound effects.

Effect Options Explained	
Option	**Description**
Left Channel	Plays only the left channel of a stereo sound.
Right Channel	Plays only the right channel of a stereo sound.
Fade Left to Right	Creates a panning effect by playing a stereo sound from the left channel to the right channel (or left speaker to right speaker).
Fade Right to Left	Creates a panning effect by playing a stereo sound from the right channel to the left channel (or right speaker to left speaker).
Fade In	Makes the sound gradually become louder as it begins to play.
Fade Out	Makes the sound gradually become softer as it nears the end.
Custom	Allows you to create your own effects for the sound.

Sync Option

The **Sync option** in the Property Inspector allows you to set the synchronization of the sound file in the movie. Each option controls the behavior of the sound in the Timeline. The following chart explains the various Sync options.

Sync Options Explained	
Option	**Description**
Event	Begins playing the sound when the Playhead reaches the frame that holds the sound in the Timeline. Event sounds will continue to play independently, even if the Timeline stops. If a different instance of the same sound is started, the sounds will overlap. This option is good for button sound.
Start	Behaves similarly to an Event sound, except that a second instance of the sound cannot be started until any currently playing instances have finished. This prevents the sound from overlapping itself. This option is good for background sound.
Stop	Stops the indicated sound. You might use this feature, for example, if you have a sound in the Main Timeline that spans 50 frames and is set to Start. The sound will play in its entirely no matter what happens in the Main Timeline. If you need the sound to stop at Frame 30, you can add the same sound to a keyframe in Frame 30 and set that sound to Stop. This will stop the Start sound (or an Event sound) from playing.
Stream	Forces the movie to keep pace with the sound. If the movie cannot download its frames fast enough to keep pace, Macromedia Flash MX forces it to skip frames. Stream sounds stop when the Timeline stops or when another keyframe is encountered on the same layer. One advantage to Stream sounds is that they begin to play before the entire sound file is downloaded, so the user does not have to wait for the whole file before the sound begins to play. This is not the case for Event and Start sounds. Stream sounds are great for narration and animation.

Loop Option

The **Loop option** in the Property Inspector sets the number of times that the sound will repeat. There is no limit to the number of times the sound can loop. However, use caution when you have Sync: Stream selected because looping a Stream sound will cause Macromedia Flash MX to add frames for each loop, thereby increasing the file size significantly. Looping Event or Start sounds has no effect on file size.

Edit Button

When you click the **Edit button** in the Property Inspector, Macromedia Flash MX will open the Edit Envelope dialog box, where you can edit your sound.

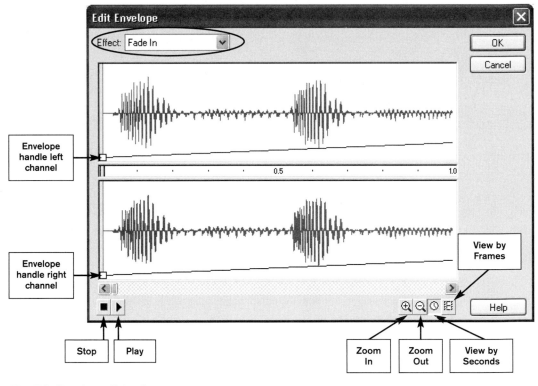

The Edit Envelope dialog box

Inside the Edit Envelope dialog box, you can change the effect of the sound, change the start and end points of a sound, modify the Envelope handles to change the volume of the sound, test the sound, view the sound using seconds or frames, and zoom in and out to see more or less of the sound wave.

4. Controlling Sound with On/Off Buttons

Even though you might choose a sound that you love for the background sound of your movie, certain users may simply not want to listen to it. This exercise will show you how to give them control of the sound in a movie, using sound off and sound on buttons.

1. Open the **soundOnOffFinal.fla** from the **chap_13** folder.

2. Choose **Control > Test Movie** to preview the movie. Click the **sound off** button to stop the sound. Click the **sound on** button to start it again. You will be creating this movie in the steps that follow. When you are finished, close this file.

3. You should still have the **bkgdSound.fla** file open from the last exercise. Save the file as **soundOnOff.fla** inside the **chap_13** folder.

4. In the **Property Inspector**, choose **Effect: Fade In** and **Sync: Start**. Type **Loop: 5**. These actions will make the sound fade in, play independently of the Timeline, and repeat five times.

Tip: If you want a sound to play continuously, looping over and over, enter a number in the Loop box large enough to make the sound play for an extended amount of time. If you have a 10-second sound clip that you want to play for at least 100 minutes, for example, you would enter Loop: 600, since 10 minutes = 60 seconds × 100 minutes = 6000, and 6000/10 = 600.

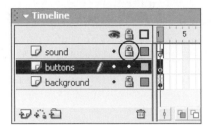

5. In the **Timeline**, lock the **sound** layer and click the **Insert Layer** button to add a new layer. Click and drag the new layer below the **sound** layer, and rename the new layer **buttons**.

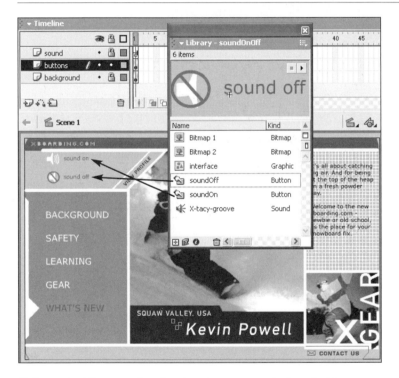

6. Open the **Library** and notice that there are two buttons inside: one named **soundOn** and one named **soundOff**. These are basic rollover buttons that have been created ahead of time for you. Drag an instance of each of the buttons onto the **Stage**, as shown in the picture above.

Now that you have added the buttons to the movie, you will learn to add ActionScripting that will control the button's ability to start and stop the sound file in the sound layer.

7. Select the **sound off** button on the **Stage**. You have to select the button instance in order to be able to add actions to it.

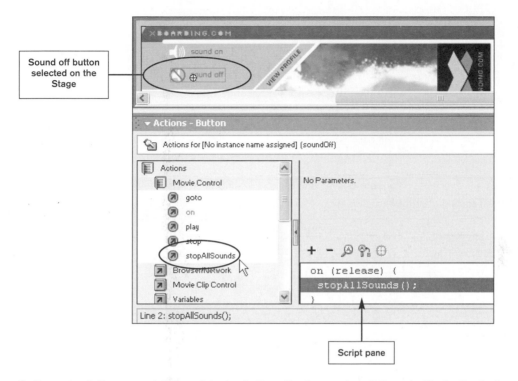

Sound off button selected on the Stage

Script pane

8. Open the **Actions** panel (**F9**) and, in the **Actions Toolbox**, select **Actions > Movie Control** to expand those folders. Double-click on the **stopAllSounds** action to add it to the **Script** pane. This action tells Macromedia Flash MX to execute the stopAllSounds action when the user releases the mouse button. This will stop any sounds that are currently playing in the Timeline.

9. Choose **Control > Test Movie** to preview the movie again. Click the **sound off** button. Look Ma, no sound!

Now that you have the sound off button working, you will make the sound on button work. Since there is no playAllSounds action, getting the sound to play again is a little more tricky, but if you follow the steps below, your sound on button will work in no time!

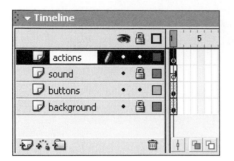

10. Add a new layer above the **sound** layer, and rename it **actions**. You are going to add a stop action to the Main Timeline after the next step.

11. Click and drag down on **Frame 2** in the **Timeline** to select Frame 2 on all the layers at once. Press **F5** to add a frame to each layer in the Timeline.

You need to have a least two frames in the Timeline for this technique to work.

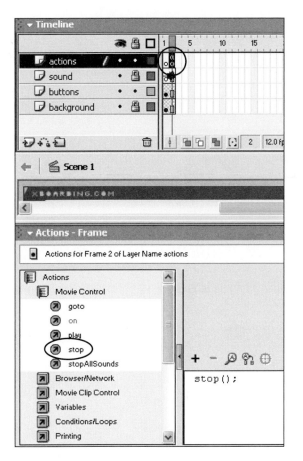

12. Click in **Frame 2** of the **actions** layer and press **F7** to add a blank keyframe. In the **Actions** panel, select **Actions > Movie Control** to expand those folders in the **Actions Toolbox**. Double-click on the **stop** action to add it to the **Script** pane. This action tells Macromedia Flash MX to execute the stop action when the Playhead hits Frame 2. This will stop the Playhead from moving any further in the Timeline.

Why add the stop action in the Timeline? Even though you have added ActionScript to stop all sounds, the Main Timeline is still going to loop by default. To prevent it from doing this, you add a stop action to Frame 2. Keep in mind that the sound file will not stop, since Event and Start sounds are independent of the Main Timeline. So even though you stop the Timeline, the sound will keep playing until you click the sound off button.

13. In the **buttons** layer, click the **sound on** button to select it. A thin blue line will appear around the button when it is selected.

Line 2: gotoAndPlay(1);

14. In the **Actions** panel, double-click the **goto** action inside the **Movie Control** folder. Make sure that **Go to and Play** is selected and that **Type** is set to **Frame Number** and **Frame** is set to **1**. This action tells Macromedia Flash MX to go to Frame 1 and then play the movie when the user releases the mouse on the sound on button. This will start the movie over from the beginning, and the sound will start over from Frame 1. Neat!

This is why you needed to add the frames in step 11. You have to have more than one frame in the Timeline so that, as the Playhead begins to play (in unison with the sound file), you can stop the sound using your stopAllSounds action on the sound off button. In order to start the sound playing again, you use the goToAndPlay action to send the Playhead back to Frame 1. When this happens, the sound will play automatically. It does this because, as you learned in the last exercise, Event and Start sounds play as soon as the Playhead hits the frame that the sound file is located in.

15. Choose **Control > Test Movie** to preview the movie one last time. Click the **sound off** button and then click the **sound on** button. Notice how the sound immediately stops when you click the sound off button and starts over again when you click the sound on button.

16. Save and close this file.

MOVIE | soundControl.mov

To see this exercise performed, play the **soundControl.mov** file, located in the **movies** folder on the **H•O•T CD-ROM**.

5. ——————Compression Settings for Narration

Sound in Macromedia Flash MX can also be controlled so that it synchronizes with animation, such as narration or a sound effect that is synchronized with a character's movement. This exercise will show you how to import and compress sounds using a feature new to Macromedia Flash MX: **Speech compression**. You will also learn how to modify the Timeline for easier editing. As well, you will learn to use the Stream option so that voice sound files synchronize with animation.

1. Open the **soundSyncFinal.fla** file from inside the **chap_13** folder. This is a finished version of the file you will create in the next two exercises.

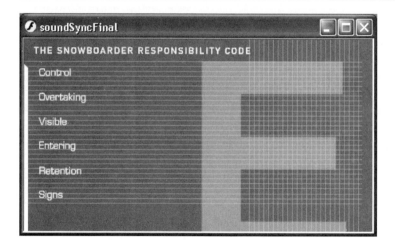

2. Choose **Control > Test Movie** to preview the movie. Notice that the narration voice is synchronized perfectly with the animation. You will create this same effect next. When you are finished previewing the movie, close this file.

3. Open the **soundSync.fla** file from the **chap_13** folder. This file has been created to get you started. Notice the seven layers in the Main Timeline. The top six layers hold different parts of the animation, and the bottom layer holds a background image. Scrub the **Playhead** back and forth to see the letters animate. In a few steps, you will be adding the voice sound clips to the Timeline, and you'll decide where each sound should begin in the Timeline.

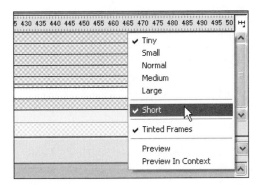

Tip: *Since there are a lot of frames in the Main Timeline, you can change the frame view temporarily by clicking on the Frame View pop-up menu and choosing Tiny and Short. This will allow you to see more frames at once on the Timeline.*

Click and drag to expand the Timeline

You can also expand the Timeline by clicking and dragging on the bottom of the Timeline, so that you can view all the layers.

4. On the **Main Timeline**, click the **Insert Layer** button to add a new layer. Rename the layer **sounds**. Drag the new **sounds** layer so that it is on top of all the other layers.

5. Choose **File > Import**. Inside the **sounds** folder, open the **codeSounds** folder. Shift+click to select all the sounds and click **Open** to import the sounds into Macromedia Flash MX.

6. Press **F11** to open the **Library**. Notice that the six sounds are now in the Library. Select the **control** sound and click the **Play** button to test it. Select the other sounds in the Library and click the **Play** button to test those as well.

You will change the compression setting of the sounds next.

7. Select the **control** sound again and click on the **Properties** button, located at the bottom of the **Library** panel, to open the **Sound Properties** dialog box, as you learned in Exercise 2.

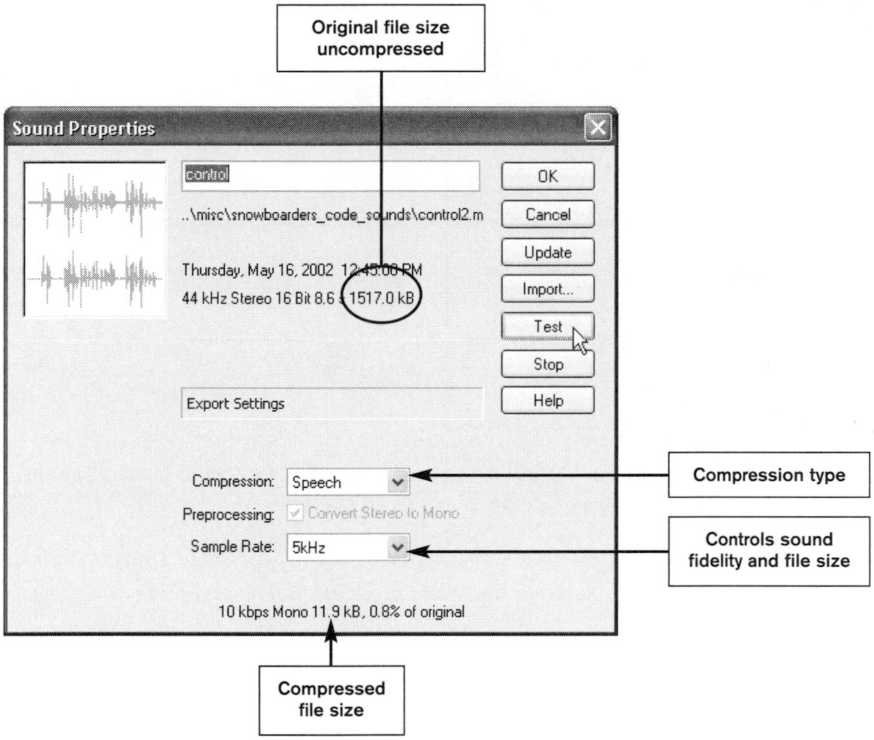

Original file size
uncompressed

Sound Properties

control

..\misc\snowboarders_code_sounds\control2.m

Thursday, May 16, 2002 12:45:00 PM

44 kHz Stereo 16 Bit 8.6 s 1517.0 kB

OK
Cancel
Update
Import...
Test
Stop
Help

Export Settings

Compression: Speech

Compression type

Preprocessing: ☑ Convert Stereo to Mono

Sample Rate: 5kHz

Controls sound
fidelity and file size

10 kbps Mono 11.9 kB, 0.8% of original

Compressed
file size

8. Notice that the sound is large at its default compression setting: 1517.0 KB. Click to see the **Compression** drop-down menu. Select **Speech**. Click to see the **Sample Rate** drop-down menu. Select **5kHz**. Click the **Test** button to test the sound. Notice that it does not sound very good.

9. Select **Sample Rate: 11kHz** and click the **Test** button again. Notice that the sound is much better at 11KHz, and the file size has been reduced to only 23.7 KB! Click **OK**.

Speech compression is new to Macromedia Flash MX, and it is specifically adapted to speech sounds. The sample rate controls sound fidelity and file size. The lower the sample rate is, the lower the file size and the lower the sound quality. However, 11 KHz is the recommended sample rate for speech.

10. In the **Library**, choose each of the remaining five sounds, one at a time, and change each sound's compression settings using the **Sound Properties** dialog box. For each sound, select **Compression: Speech** and **Sample Rate: 11kHz**. Click **OK**.

Note: If you have multiple sounds in your project that will all have the same compression settings, you can set them globally all at once using Macromedia Flash MX's Publish settings, which you will learn about in Chapter 16, "Publishing and Exporting." A drawback to setting sounds globally is that you can't test (listen to) the different sound settings when you use Publish settings. For that reason, I showed you how to set them individually in this exercise.

11. Save this file and keep it open for the next exercise.

6. ——————————Synchronizing Sound to Narration Cues

In the previous exercise, you learned to compress sounds using the Speech compression setting. This exercise will show you how to use the Stream option and to work with the Main Timeline so that voice sound files synchronize with animation.

1. You should still have the **soundSync.fla** file open from the last exercise.

2. Select **Frame 1** in the **sounds** layer of the **Main Timeline**. From the **Library**, drag an instance of the **control** sound onto the **Stage** in the **sounds** layer. Notice the waveform in the Timeline. The control sound will be located in Frame 1, since all sounds must be placed in a keyframe.

3. Double-click on the **Layer** icon next to the **sounds** layer name. This will open the **Layer Properties** dialog box. From the **Layer Height** drop-down menu, choose **200%** and click **OK**. This will make the sounds layer taller than all the rest of the layers in the Timeline.

*Increasing the layer height allows you to view the waveform more easily. Notice that you can see the waveform in more detail now. **Tip:** You can also access the Layer Properties dialog box by choosing Modify > Layer.*

4. Click on **Frame 1** to select it in the **Timeline**. In the **Property Inspector**, select **Sync: Stream**. The Stream setting forces the movie to keep pace with the sound. If the movie cannot download its frames fast enough to keep pace, Macromedia Flash MX forces it to skip frames.

5. Choose **Control > Test Movie** to test the sound and the animation. The voice sound will play in synchronization with the animation.

You will add the remaining sounds to the Timeline next.

TIP | Streaming and Looping

Be careful about setting your sound's **Sync** to **Stream** and adding loops. Unlike the Event and Start settings, Stream causes the file size to increase for each loop you specify. If you can avoid it, try not to loop sounds that are set to the Stream setting.

Current frame the Playhead
is located on

6. Scrub the **Playhead** back and forth to identify where the next animation of the **O** begins on the **Overtaking** layer. Notice that this happens at about Frame 101. You want to start the **overtaking** sound clip to start where the **O** animation begins. You will do this next.

---

7. Click on the **Frame View** pop-up menu on the right side of the **Timeline**, and choose **Normal** and **Short**. This will allow you to select the frames in the Timeline more easily.

---

8. On the **sounds** layer, select **Frame 101** and press **F7** to add a keyframe to that frame, because sound files must be tied to a keyframe.

---

9. In the **Property Inspector**, with **Frame 101** selected, choose **overtaking** from the drop-down **Sound** list. This will add the overtaking sound to Frame 101. Also in the Property Inspector, select **Sync: Stream**, if it is not already selected.

Macromedia Flash MX automatically allows you to access all the sounds inside the movie's Library from the Sound drop-down list in the Property Inspector. This way, you can access all the sounds in your Library quickly and can even switch the sound located in a keyframe by selecting a different sound from the drop-down list.

NOTE | Adding Sound to the Timeline

In this chapter, you have learned two ways to add sounds to the Timeline. You can drag an instance of the sound onto the Stage, or you can first select the frame in the Timeline and then choose a sound from the drop-down Sound list. Both workflow methods yield the same result—you can decide which is best for you!

---

10. Repeat step 8 to add keyframes to the appropriate frames in the Timeline on the **sounds** layer where you want each new sound to begin.

Hint: Each animation is 100 frames long, so you will want to place keyframes at the beginning of each new animation: Frames 201, 301, 401, and 501.

---

11. Repeat step 9 for each of the keyframes you just added to attach the appropriate sound to each keyframe.

Hint: Frame 201 (visible sound), frame 301 (entering sound), frame 401 (retention sound), and frame 501 (signs sound).

12. Test the movie again. Notice that some of the sounds are cut short when a new animation begins. Why? This is because some sound files are longer than others, since some of the narration takes longer to say, and Stream sounds will stop as soon as another keyframe is encountered in the same layer.

You will fix this so the sound files don't get cut short next.

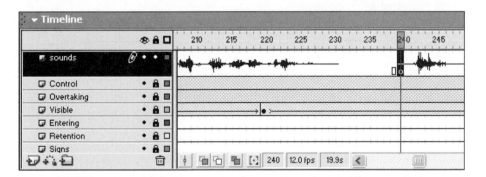

13. In the **Timeline**, on the **sounds** layer, click and drag **Frame 201** (with the **visible** sound) to the right to **Frame 240**. Notice that as you do, the sound wave in the previous frame (the overtaking sound) continues until Frame 231. This means that the overtaking sound is not 100 frames long, as the animation is. Instead, it is 131 frames long. Therefore, in order for the animation and the sound file to span the same duration, you need to make them match. You can do this by altering the frames in the Timeline, which you will do next.

14. Click and drag **Frame 240** back to **Frame 232**, just after the **overtaking** sound wave ends in the **Timeline**. This will start the next sound (visible) after the overtaking sound ends, without cutting it off.

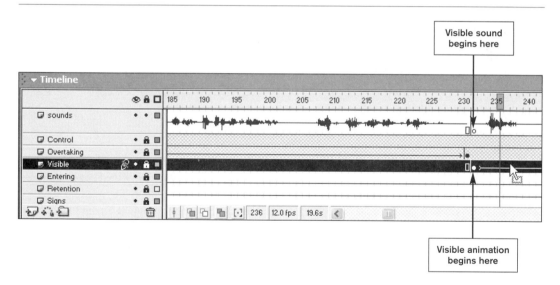

15. Click and drag the last keyframe in the **Overtaking** layer to **Frame 231**. This will make the overtaking animation and the sound narration end together.

Visible sound
begins here

Visible animation
begins here

16. Click to the right of the layer name on the **Visible** layer to select all the frames on that layer, including the entire tween. Click and drag all the frames to the right at once, so that the tween that started on Frame 201 now begins on Frame 232, at the same point that the visible sound begins.

17. Test the movie again. Notice that the sounds and the animations of the first few letters are now harmonized and the sounds are not cut short! This is synchronization at its finest!

18. Repeat steps 14 through 16, so that the remaining sounds have enough frames to play and the animations end when the sounds end. Test the movie as you go to see how the changes you make affect the movie. When you are done, you will have a movie with perfectly synchronized narration and animation!

19. When you are finished, save and close this file.

MOVIE | soundSync.mov

To see this exercise performed, play the **soundSync.mov** located in the **movies** folder on the **H•O•T CD-ROM**.

Congratulations! You have conquered another chapter. You should now feel comfortable working with sound in Macromedia Flash MX. If you feel you need more practice, you can always review the exercises again. Next stop: working with components and forms!

14.

Components and Forms

| What Are Components? | Creating a Form |
| Configuring and Modifying Components|

_____

chap_14
_____

Macromedia Flash MX
H•O•T CD-ROM

In past versions of Macromedia Flash MX, creating complex forms for your users to fill out was not an easy task. The sheer thought of developing a scrollable text box would make many a Macromedia Flash developer shiver. The introduction of components in Macromedia Flash MX has been a breath of fresh air. The purpose of components is to make your life easier. Rather than build a scrollable list box from scratch that offers the user many choices that are highlighted when the mouse rolls over them, you can drag and drop the ListBox component onto the Stage and presto: You have a scrollable ListBox and all you have to do is add the words you want to appear in the list. Components can be used for a variety of purposes, including creating collapsible menus and easy Tool Tips, working with XML, and even handling dynamic data. This chapter teaches you how to work with components to create a form. In the following exercises, you will add components to a project file, configure them to display the correct information for the user, and then modify them so that they match the interface design.

What Are Components?

Components are like Movie Clip symbols on steroids—they are a special type of Movie Clip that has a predefined appearance and functionality. You can use components in your movie to add simple interface elements such as check boxes and scroll bars that have already been built for you. Macromedia Flash MX ships with seven components, including a check box, a combo box, a list box, a push button, a radio button, a scroll bar, and a scroll pane. You can use the components individually or together to create user interface elements such as forms or surveys. As well, you can even modify the appearance of each component by changing such aspects as the color, size, or even shape of the component. A chart detailing each of the seven components that ship with Macromedia Flash MX follows.

Component Types	
CheckBox	Allows users to select or deselect this check box.
ComboBox	Displays a single choice with a drop-down menu revealing additional choices.
ListBox	Seems similar to the ComboBox, although this component offers a list of all choices in a scrollable menu.
PushButton	Accepts standard mouse and keyboard interactions. This component can be programmed to carry out a specific command when the user clicks on it or presses Enter/Return.
RadioButton	Allows you to add several instances of the radio button to your project file and prevents more than one choice in a group of radio buttons from ever being selected at one time.
ScrollBar	Adds a scroll bar to any text field (dynamic or input text field) that you create.
ScrollPane	Allows the user to view Movie Clips through a scrollable window.

Working with Components

There are four general phases when working with components: adding them to your Macromedia Flash MX project file, configuring the components with the correct information for the user to see and select from, modifying the component skins to change the appearance of the components, and writing ActionScript to gather and submit the data for the form. This chapter concentrates on the first three phases because phase four involves more complicated ActionScripting and is outside the scope of this book.

I. ——————Creating a Form

The first step in working with components is to add them to your Macromedia Flash MX project file. This exercise will show you how.

1. Copy the **chap_14** folder, located on the **H•O•T CD-ROM**, to your hard drive. You need to have this folder on your hard drive in order to save files inside it.

2. Open the file called **orderFormFinal.fla** from the **chap_14** folder. Chose **Control > Test Movie** to preview the file. This is the finished version of the form you'll be creating in this exercise. Test out the different form elements to see how they work. When you are finished, close the preview window.

Note: If you click the Submit button, nothing happens because this form is not set up to submit the data to a server.

3. Close the **orderFormFinal.fla** file and open the **orderForm.fla** from the **chap_14** folder. This file was created to get you started.

4. In the Main Timeline, click on the **Insert Layer** button to add a new layer. Rename the new layer **components**. Make sure the components layer is on top, above the other two layers.

Tip: You can choose View > Magnification > Show All to see all of the Stage at one time.

5. If the **Components** panel isn't already open, choose **Window > Components** to open it. This is where all the components are stored.

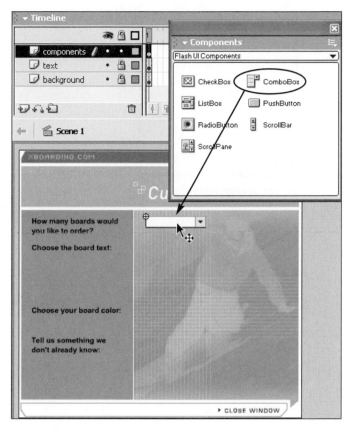

6. In the **Components** panel, click on the **ComboBox** to select it and drag an instance of it onto the Stage, to the right of the **How many boards would you like to order?** text, as shown in the picture above. The ComboBox displays a single choice with a drop-down menu revealing additional choices. You will configure the ComboBox choices in the next exercise. You have just added your first component to your movie!

Tip: You can also double-click on a component in the Components panel to add it to your project file. However, doing so adds the component to the center of the Stage; you then have to drag it to the desired position.

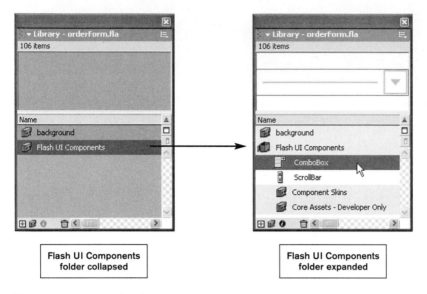

Flash UI Components
folder collapsed

Flash UI Components
folder expanded

7. Open the **Library** (F11). Notice that it contains two folders: **background** and **Flash UI Components**. The background folder was created ahead of time; it contains all the files that make up the interface of this project file. The Flash UI Components folder was automatically added to the Library as soon as you dragged the ComboBox component onto the Stage. Double-click on the **Flash UI Components** folder to see the contents inside. These are all the elements that are needed to make up the ComboBox component. *Aren't you glad you didn't have to create all these yourself?*

Note: *For each additional component you add to your project, Macromedia Flash MX will add the necessary additional assets inside the Flash UI Components folder, adding to whatever components assets are already inside. The items added to the Library include the component Movie Clip or Movie Clips (including the icon that shows the component's type), the Component Skins folder (the graphic elements that control the appearance of the component), and the Core Assets folder (for advanced developers who want to make changes to the component).*

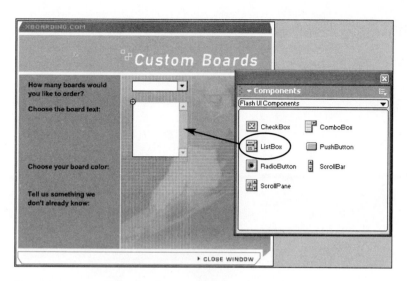

8. From the **Components** panel, click on the **ListBox** to select it and drag an instance of it onto the Stage, to the right of the **Choose the board text:** text, as in the picture above. The ListBox component offers a list of all choices in a scrollable menu.

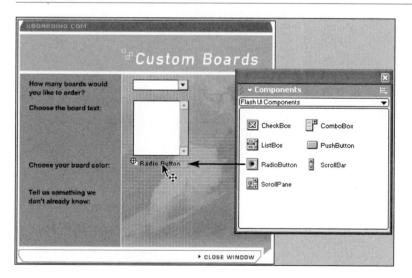

9. From the **Components** panel, click on the **RadioButton** to select it and drag an instance of it onto the Stage, to the right of the **Choose your board color:** text. The RadioButton component allows you to add several instances of the radio button to your project file (which you will do in the next step) and prevents more than one choice in a group of radio buttons from ever being selected at one time.

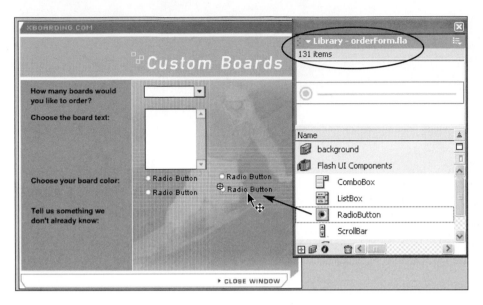

10. Using the **Library**, drag three more instances of the **RadioButton** onto the Stage and position them as shown in the picture above. You don't have to worry about naming them differently or aligning them precisely because you will align all the components a few steps from now.

Note: Why do you have to use the Library? Once you add a component to your project file, the component is added to the Library. Each time you add additional instances of the same component (just like added additional instances of a symbol), you use the Library to add them to the Stage.

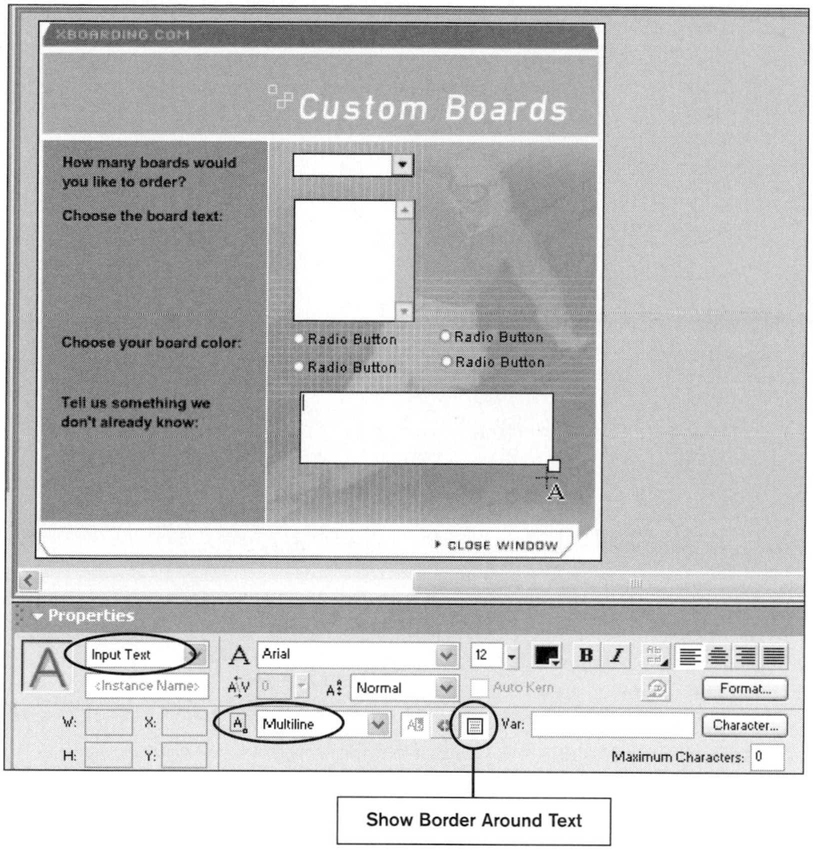

Show Border Around Text

11. Select the **Text** tool in the **Toolbox**. In the **Property Inspector** (**Window > Properties**), choose **Input Text** for the **Text Type**, select **Multiline** for the **Line Type**, and click the **Show Border Around Text** button. Make sure the **Font** is set to **Arial**, the **Font Size** is set to **12**, and the **Font Color** is set to **black**. Click and drag to create a text box on the stage, similar to the picture above. This will serve as the text field where the user can type comments inside of. You will add a ScrollBar component to the text box next.

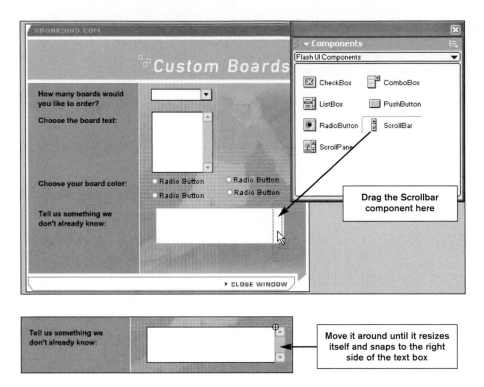

Drag the Scrollbar
component here

Move it around until it resizes
itself and snaps to the right
side of the text box

12. From the **Components** panel, click and drag the **ScrollBar** component onto the right edge of the text box on the Stage. Notice that the ScrollBar component automatically resizes itself to match the height of the text box and attaches itself to the right side. *Note:* You *may* have to reposition the ScrollBar component several times to get it to snap in place and if you do, just keep moving it around the right side of the text box until it does. *You have now added a scrolling text box to your form!*

Tip: In addition to placing the scrollbar vertically, you can also drop it on the bottom of the text box to create a horizontally scrolling text box.

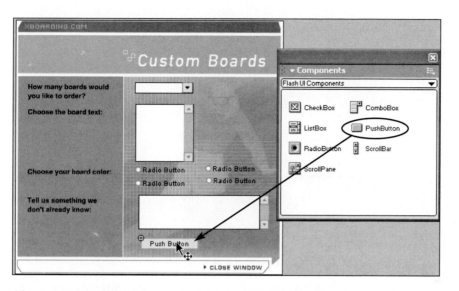

13. From the **Components** panel, click on the **PushButton** to select it and drag an instance of it onto the Stage, just below the scrolling text box, as shown in the picture above. The PushButton component accepts standard mouse and keyboard interactions, and it can be programmed to carry out a specific command when the user clicks on it or presses Enter/Return.

After you add the PushButton in the last step, take another look at the Library. Notice that each of the components you have placed on the Stage is also located in the Library. You can add additional instances of each of these components by dragging them from the Library onto the Stage.

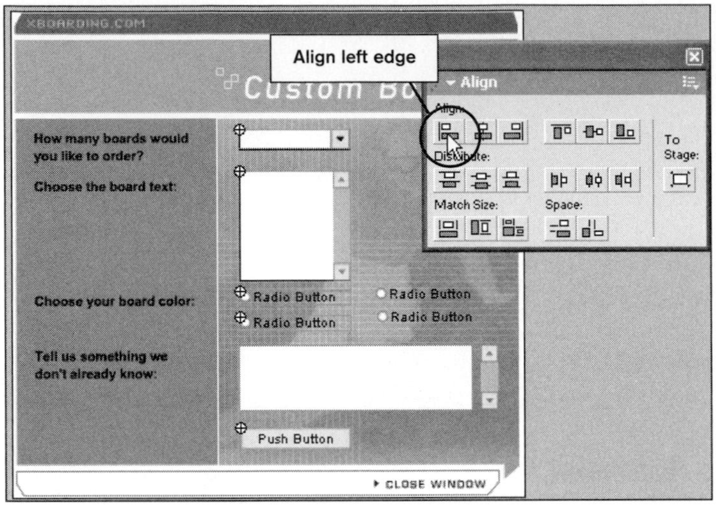

14. Choose **Window > Align** to open the **Align** panel. Select all the components that are nearest the white vertical interface line, as shown in the picture above. To select multiple components at once, Shift+click each of the components. In the **Align** panel, click on the **Align left edge** button so that all of the selected components will be aligned vertically.

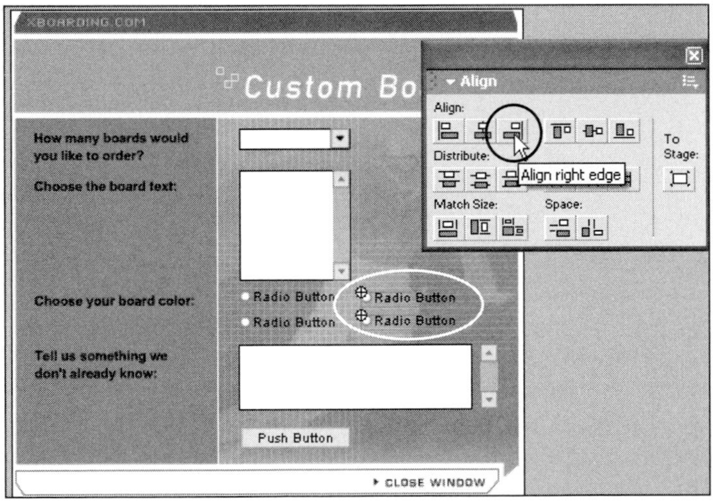

15. Click off the Stage to deselect everything and then Shift+click on the two **right-most** Radio Buttons, as shown in the picture above. In the **Align** panel, choose **Align right edge** to align the two components.

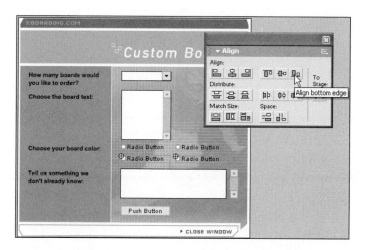

16. Click off the Stage to deselect everything. Shift+click on the **top two RadioButton** components and select **Align top edge** in the **Align** panel. This will align the top of the two RadioButtons to each other. Click off the Stage to deselect everything again. Shift+click on the **bottom two RadioButton** components to select both of them and choose **Align bottom edge** in the Align panel. This will align the bottom of the RadioButton components to each other.

17. On the Stage, notice how the ScrollBar component is not attached to the text box anymore. Although the ScrollBar component snaps to the text box when you drag it onto the text box, it does not remain attached if you move the text box (as you did when you aligned it in step 14). Click on the **ScrollBar** component on the Stage to select and drag it back onto the right side of the text box. It will snap back to the right edge again.

18. When you are finished, save this file and keep it open for the next exercise.

2. —————————Configuring Components

Now that you have the components in place in the project file, you need to make adjustments to each component so that they display the correct information to the user. This exercise will show you how to do this by setting the parameters for each component.

1. You should still have the **orderForm.fla** file open from the last exercise. On the Stage, click on the **ComboBox** to select it. Open the **Property Inspector** (**Window > Properties**)–if it is not already open–and make sure the **Parameters** tab is selected in the upper right corner. Notice that the Property Inspector looks a little different than normal. This is part of the built-in functionality of the component: It already has parameters assigned to it, and these are displayed in the Property Inspector.

Note: *For a detailed description of each of the parameters available for each of the components, see the Using Macromedia Flash MX manual.*

Note: *In addition to using the Property Inspector, you can also view the parameters for a component by using the Component Parameters panel. To do this, choose Window > Component Parameters to open the panel. Select a component instance on the Stage to view the parameters associated with that component. Using the Component Parameters panel will give you the same information as choosing the Parameters tab in the Property Inspector, so whichever workflow works better for you is fine to use. In this exercise, you will be using the Property Inspector to modify the component parameters.*

2. In the **Property Inspector**, click inside the **Instance Name** text box and type **quantityCB**. This will give the ComboBox on the Stage an instance name of quantityCB so that it can be referred to via ActionScript.

3. Click on the **Labels** parameter to select it. The Labels parameter contains a list of values that the user can choose from in a scrollable drop-down menu. Notice the magnifying glass that appears at the end of the Labels row. Click on the **magnifying glass**. This will open the **Values** dialog box, where you can enter the values that will appear for the user to select from.

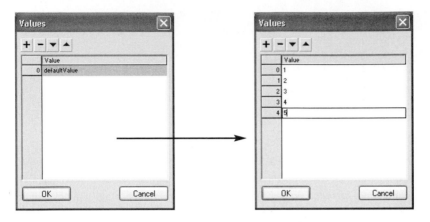

4. In the **Values** dialog box, click on the **Plus** (+) button to enter a new value. Click in the default field and type **1**. This will set the first value as **1**. Click on the **Plus** (+) button again to enter the next value. Click in the default field and type **2**. This will set the second value as **2**. Repeat this step to add **3**, **4**, and **5** to the list, as shown in the second picture above. When you are finished, click **OK**.

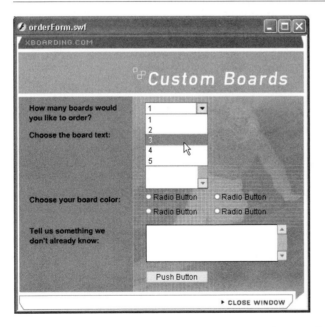

5. Choose **Control > Test Movie** to test out your first functioning ComboBox component. Cool! When you are finished, close the preview window.

Note: Although you can see the component on the Stage, you can not test how it works in the editing environment. In order test a component's functionality, you must choose Control > Test Movie.

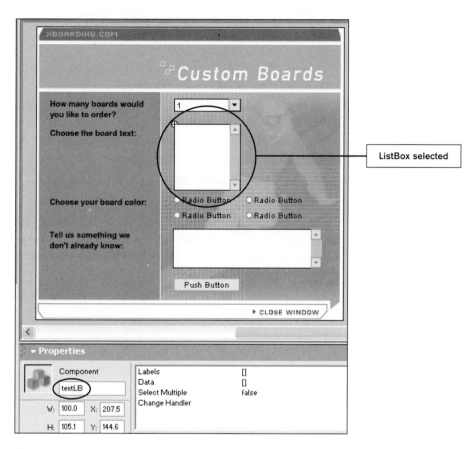

6. Back in the project file, click on the **ListBox** component to select it. In the **Property Inspector**, click inside the **Instance Name** text box and type **textLB**. This will give the ListBox on the Stage an instance name of textLB so that it can be referred to via ActionScript.

7. Click on the **Labels** parameter to select it. The Labels parameter contains a list of items that the user can choose from in a scrollable single or multiple selection list box. Click on the **magnifying glass** that appears at the end of the Labels row. This will open the **Values** dialog box, where you can enter the values that will appear for the user to select from.

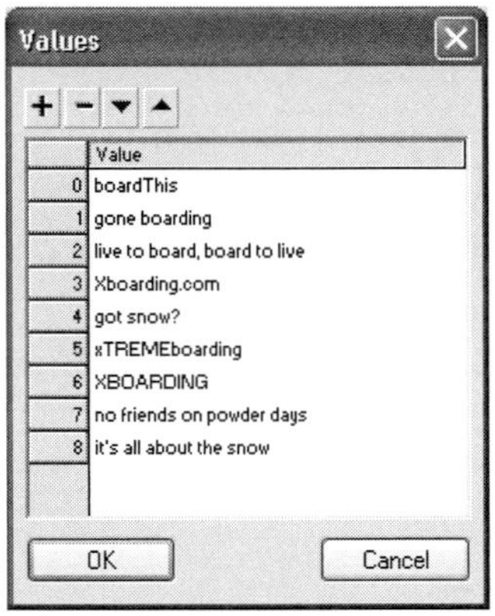

8. In the **Values** dialog box, click on the **Plus** (+) button to enter a new value. Click in the default field and type **boardThis**. This will set the first value for the user to select from inside the ListBox as **boardThis**. Click on the **Plus** (+) button again to enter the next value. Click in the default field and type **gone boarding** to set the second value. Repeat this step six more times to add text for the user to choose from that will appear on the snowboard, as shown in the picture above. You can either use the board text options I used in the picture above, or you can be creative and create you own board text. Just make sure that you add a total of eight values. When you are finished, click **OK**.

Tip: If you want to move any of your entries higher or lower in the list, you can click on the number to the left of the Value text and use the up or down arrows at the top of the Value dialog box to move them where you want them.

9. Choose **Control > Test Movie** to test out the ListBox component. Move the scroll bar inside the ListBox to see all the options you created for the user. Notice, however, that the longer text is cut off in the List Box. You will change this next. When you are finished, close the preview window.

10. Back in the project file, select the **Free Transform** tool in the Toolbox and click on the **ListBox** on the Stage to select it. Click on the **right-hand middle handle** on the Free Transform bounding box and drag to the right to resize the ListBox, making all text entries visible.

Note: You can modify the width and height of ListBox components in your project file by using the Free Transform tool. However, you can only modify the width of ComboBox components by using the Free Transform tool. This is because the height of ComboBox component is set by the font size that displays the menu choices and the Row Count parameter that determines the number of choices visible in the drop-down menu at one time.

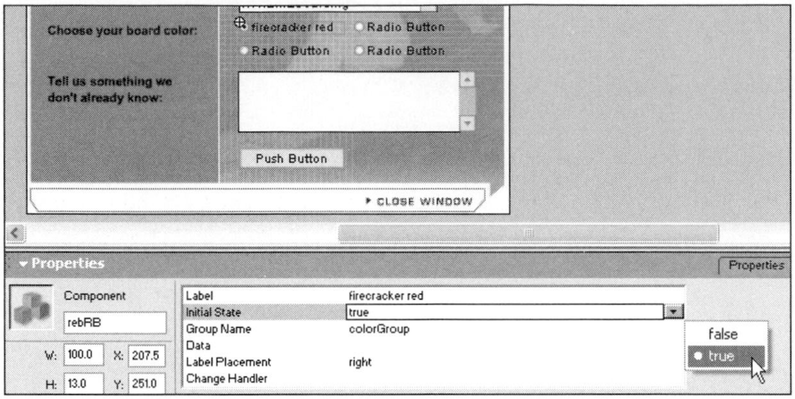

11. Select the **top left RadioButton** on the Stage. In the **Property Inspector**, type **redRB** for the **Instance Name**. Select the **Label** parameter and type **firecracker red**. This is the text that will appear to the right of the RadioButton in the form. Select the **Group Name** parameter and type **colorGroup**. This will make this RadioButton part of a group of RadioButtons. Select the **Initial State** parameter and choose **true** from the drop-down menu. A value of true for the Initial state of the RadioButton will make it selected by default. *Note:* Only one radio button in a group can have the Initial State as true. Leave the **Label Placement** parameter set to **right** (the default value). The Label Placement parameter sets the location of the RadioButton label text to either the right of the left of the RadioButton. When you are finished, the Property Inspector should look just like the picture above.

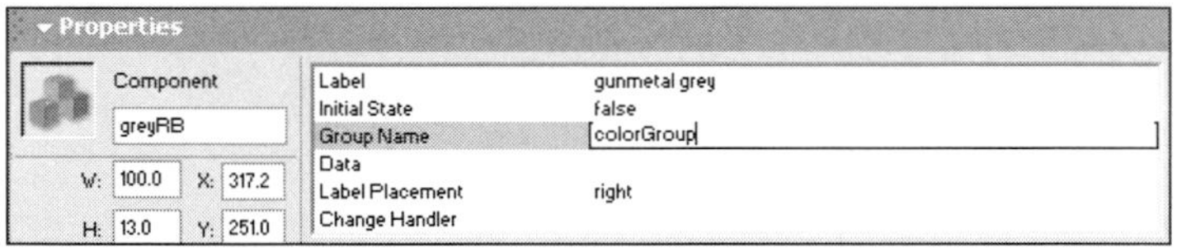

12. Select the **top right RadioButton** on the Stage. In the **Property Inspector**, type **greyRB** for the **Instance Name**; for **Label**, type **gunmetal grey**; set **Initial State** to **false**; and for **Group Name**, type **colorGroup**. When you are finished, the Property Inspector should look just like the picture above.

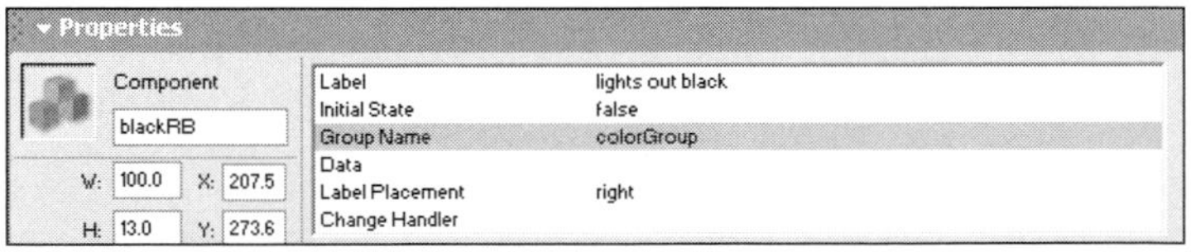

13. Select the **bottom left RadioButton** on the Stage. In the **Property Inspector**, enter the following parameters: type **blackRB** for the **Instance Name**; for **Label**, type **lights out black**; set **Initial State** to **false**; and for **Group Name**, type **colorGroup**. When you are finished, the Property Inspector should look just like the picture above.

14. Select the **bottom right RadioButton** on the Stage. In the **Property Inspector**, enter the following parameters: type **blueRB** for the **Instance Name**; for **Label**, type **midnight blue**; set **Initial State** to **false**; and for **Group Name**, type **colorGroup**. When you are finished, the Property Inspector should look just like the picture above.

15. Choose **Control > Test Movie** to test out the RadioButton components. Notice that the **firecracker red** RadioButton is selected by default, although you can click to select any of the other RadioButton components and only one can be selected at any time. This is an example of components in action at their finest—all of the behind-the-scenes work was done for you. By simply modifying some of the component parameters, you have a fully functional group of RadioButton components. Sweet! When you are finished, close the preview window.

16. Back in the project file, click on the **text box** on the Stage to select it. In the **Property Inspector**, type **messageTxt** in the **Instance Name** text box. The text box needs an instance name so that the ScrollBar component can refer to it. You will configure the ScrollBar component next.

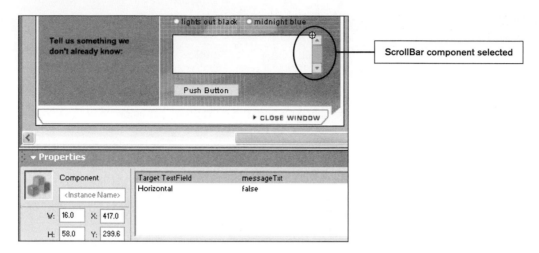

ScrollBar component selected

17. Select the **ScrollBar** component that is attached to the text box on the Stage. In the **Property Inspector**, type **messageTxt** for the **Target TextField** parameter. This needs to be the same name as the instance name of the text field that you created in step 16 because the ScrollBar component needs to know what text field (the target) to scroll. You can leave the **Horizontal** parameter set to **false**, which sets the scroll bar as vertical. *Note:* Setting the Horizontal parameter to true means that the scroll bar is horizontal.

Note: Although you gave the text box an instance name, you don't need to give the ScrollBar component an instance name in the Property Inspector.

18. Choose **Control > Test Movie** to test the scrolling input text box. Try typing a large amount of text and notice that the text box automatically will allow you to keep adding text as it scrolls. Cool! When you are finished, close the preview window. *You have one last component to configure next.*

19. Back in the project file, click on the **PushButton** to select it. In the **Property Inspector**, type **submitPB** in the **Instance Name** text box. For the Label parameter, type **Submit**. This will be the text that appears on the PushButton component. For the **Click Handler** parameter, type **onSubmit**. This will name the function that is called when a user clicks on the Submit button. *Note:* A function is a block of ActionScript code that can be reused anywhere in a movie. You can pass values as parameters to a function, and the function will operate on those values and can also return values.

Why do I name the function? In ActionScripting, a function is a set of statements that you define to perform a certain task. Although working with functions is beyond the scope of this book, naming the function in the preceding step above will allow you to have the entire form set up and capable of collecting and submitting data once more advanced ActionScripting is applied to the movie.

20. In order to test the functionality of the Submit button, including collecting all the data entered on the form and actually sending it to a server, you need to add more complex ActionScripting to the movie, which is outside the scope of this book. You can, however, visit the Macromedia Flash Support Center at **http://www.macromedia.com/support/flash/applications_building.html** to find articles and resources that will teach you how to use ActionScripting to gather and submit data entered in a form.

21. When you are finished, save this file and keep it open for the next exercise.

3. ───────Modifying Components

Fortunately, you are not stuck with the bland appearance of the components. You can modify the color and shape of components with a few clicks of the mouse. This exercise will teach you how to change the appearance of the component by changing the color of the component skins.

1. You should still have the **orderForm.fla** file open from the last exercise. Choose **Control > Test Movie** to preview the form you have created up to this point in the chapter.

2. Notice how the background of the scroll bars of the ListBox and ScrollBar components are grey. You will change this next. When you are finished, close the preview window.

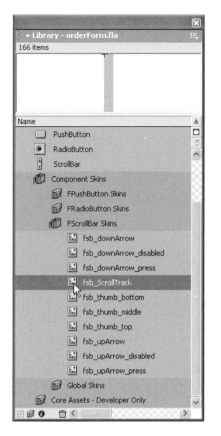

3. In the **Library**, double-click on the **Component Skins** folder to expand it. Inside the **Component Skins** folder, double-click on the **FScrollBar Skins** folder to expand that folder. Notice that there are many Movie Clip symbols inside the folder. These are all parts and pieces of the components and are automatically added to the Library when you add a component to your project file. Double-click on the **fsb_ScrollTrack** Movie Clip to open that Movie Clip symbol's Timeline. This symbol represents the scroll track or the actual background of the scroll bar in the ListBox and the ScrollBar components on the Stage.

NOTE | What is a Component Skin?

A component skin is made up of the graphic elements that determine how the component looks. All components use the skins inside the Global Skins folder. Individual components also use skins folders that are specific to their component type, such as the FScrollBar Skins folder. You will learn more about skins in the Library in the steps that follow.

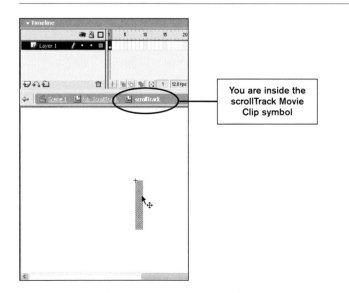

4. After you double-click on the **fsb_ScrollTrack** Movie Clip symbol in the Library, notice that you are inside the Movie Clip symbol's Timeline. Double-click on the artwork on the Stage to open the scrollTrack symbol's Timeline.

You are inside the scrollTrack Movie Clip symbol

5. Inside the **scrollTrack** Movie Clip symbol, select the shape on the Stage.

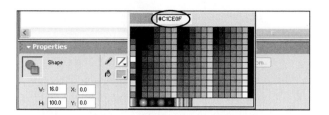

6. In the **Property Inspector**, click on the **Fill Color** box to open the Fill color palette. Inside the text field at the top of the Color palette, type **#C1CE0F** (the 0 is a zero and not the letter "O") and press **Enter/Return**. This will change the color of the scroll track to a green color that matches the header of the form.

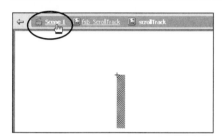

7. In the **Information Bar**, click on **Scene 1** to return to the Main Timeline.

Tip: The changes you make to component skins can not be seen on the Stage. You have to choose Control > Text Movie to see the changes. You will do this next.

8. Choose **Control > Test Movie** to preview the changes. Notice that both the backgrounds of the scroll bars of the ListBox and ScrollBar components are now green. When you are finished, close the Preview window.

Modifying Skins in the Library

I changed only one symbol in the Library, why did two different components change? The ListBox and the ScrollBar components share the same skins in the FScrollBar Skins and Global Skins folders with all the other components that also use scroll bars. If you modify any of the skins in the FScrollBar Skins folder, as you did in step 6, you will be modifying all the ComboBox, ListBox, ScrollBar, and ScrollPane component instances on the Stage.

9. In the **Library**, double-click on the **FRadioButton Skins** folder to expand that folder. Notice that there are many Movie Clip symbols inside the folder. Double-click on the **frb_frame** Movie Clip to open that Movie Clip symbol's Timeline. This symbol represents the circles you see in the RadioButton component.

10. In the **Information Bar**, change the **magnification** to **800%** so that you can see the artwork inside the **frb_frame** Movie Clip more clearly.

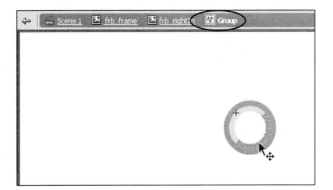

11. Double-click on the lower right edge of the inner circle. This will place you inside the **frb_rightIn** Movie Clip. Double-click again in the same spot to open the group inside that Movie Clip.

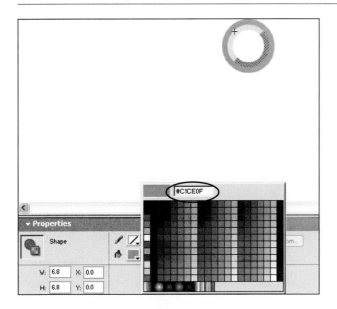

12. In the **Property Inspector**, click on the **Fill Color** box to open the Fill color palette. Inside the text field at the top of the Color palette, type **#C1CE0F** (the 0 is a zero and not the letter "O") and press **Enter/Return**. This will change the color of half of the inner circle that frames the radio button to a green color that matches the header of the form.

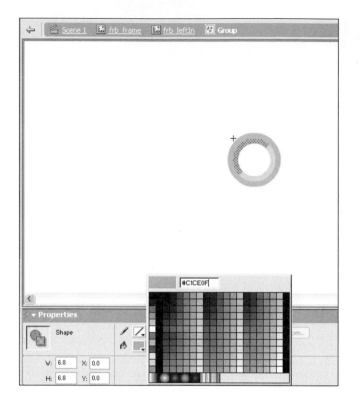

13. On the Stage, double-click four times on the upper right side of the inner circle to leave the group inside the **frb_rightln**, leave the **frb_rightln**, open the **frb_leftln** Movie Clip, and open the group inside it. In the **Property Inspector**, click on the **Fill Color** box to open the Fill color palette. Inside the text field at the top of the Color palette, type **#C1CE0F** and press Enter/Return on the keyboard. This will change the color of the other half of the inner circle that frames the radio button to a green color that matches the header of the form.

---

14. In the **Information Bar**, click on **Scene 1** to return to the Main Timeline. Change the magnification to **100%** in the **Information Bar**.

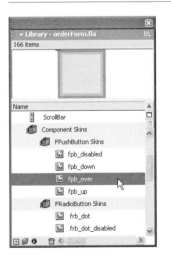

15. Choose **Control > Test Movie** to preview the changes you made to the RadioButton components. Notice that all the RadioButtons changed. Why? When you make modifications to the component skin in the Library, you are changing the actual symbol, which in turn changes all instances of the symbol on the Stage. When you are finished, close the preview window.

You have one last component skin to modify.

16. In the **Library**, double-click on the **FPushButton Skins** folder to expand that folder. Double-click on the **fpb_over** Movie Clip to open that Movie Clip symbol's Timeline. This symbol represents the over state of the PushButton component, which you will modify next.

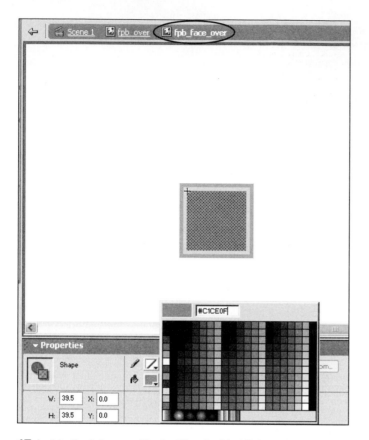

17. Inside the **fpb_over** Movie Clip, double-click on the side of the square. This will place you inside the **fpb_face_over** Movie Clip. Click once on the inside square to select the **Fill** of the square. In the **Property Inspector**, you guessed it: Click on the **Fill Color** box to open the Fill color palette. Inside the text field at the top of the color palette, type **#C1CE0F** and press **Enter/Return**. This will change the color of the of the inner square that will appear when a user rolls over the PushButton to a green color that matches the header of the form.

18. In the **Information Bar**, click on **Scene** 1 to return to the Main Timeline.

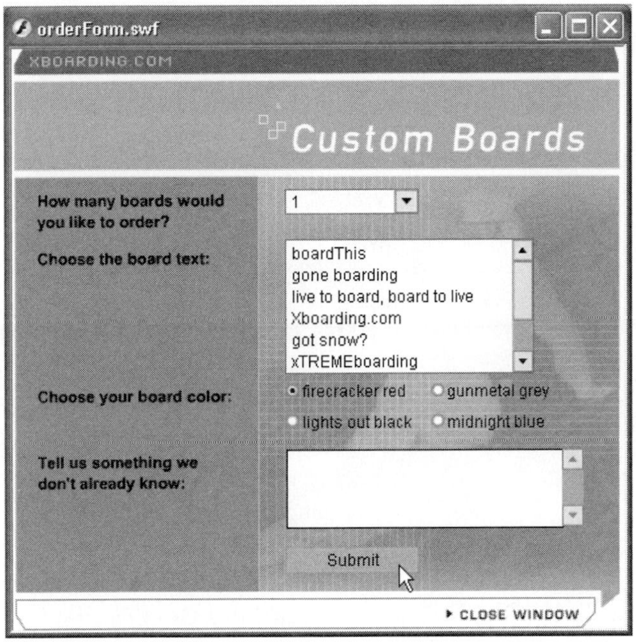

19. Choose **Control > Test Movie** to preview the changes you made to the PushButton component when you roll over it. When you are finished, close the preview window.

With a few clicks of the mouse, you made the appearance of a dull component come to life!

---

20. Save and close this file.

Note: You may have noticed the "Close Window" text at the bottom right corner of the Stage. In Chapter 17, you will learn how to make this button work because this form will be a pop-up window in the xboarding.com Web site.

Great work! Now that you are more familiar with working with components to create forms, take a quick break and get ready for the next action-packed (pun intended) chapter: Video.

15.

Video

| Acceptable Video Import Formats | Importing Video |
| Controlling Video with stop and go Actions |
| Controlling Video Targeting Frame Labels |
| Applying Effects to Video | Linking to QuickTime Video |

chap_15

Macromedia Flash MX
H•O•T CD-ROM

With the release of Macromedia Flash MX, you can now include video inside your .swf files. This opens up many types of opportunities for Macromedia Flash developers. Once you import video into Macromedia Flash MX, you can control it using very basic ActionScripting, target different points in the video to allow users to jump from point to point, transform video clips on the Stage, apply effects such as tinting and skewing, or publish a QuickTime file from Macromedia Flash MX. The exercises in this chapter will teach you these techniques and will lay the groundwork for working with video inside Macromedia Flash MX.

Importing Video into Macromedia Flash MX

Macromedia Flash MX can import a variety of different file formats. This largely depends on what software you have installed you're your machine: QuickTime 4 or higher or DirectX 7 or higher. A chart follows detailing each of the acceptable video file formats.

Acceptable Video Import Formats				
File Type	Extension	Windows	Macintosh	Software
Audio Video Interleaved	.avi	x	x	QuickTime 4 or higher or DirectX 7 or higher installed
Digital Video	.dv	x	x	QuickTime 4 or higher installed
Motion Picture Experts Group	.mpg, .mpeg	x	x	QuickTime 4 or higher or DirectX 7 or higher installed
QuickTime Movie	.mov	x	x	QuickTime 4 or higher installed
Windows Media File	.wmv, .asf	x		DirectX 7 or higher installed
Flash Video File	.flv	x	x	Neither needed

Sorenson Spark Video Compression

Video is imported and exported using the Sorenson Spark codec, which now ships with Macromedia Flash MX. A codec is an algorithm that controls the way video files are compressed and decompressed during import and export. Sorenson Spark is a video encoder and decoder that controls how video files are compressed when they are imported into Macromedia Flash MX and decompressed so that they can be viewed in the Macromedia Flash Player.

There are two different methods that are used to compress video: spatial and temporal. Spatial compression compresses the data in each frame of video, similar to the way a JPEG image is compressed. The frames that are compressed using spatial compression are called *intra*frames. Temporal compression compares data between each frame and stores only the frame differences between them. The frames that are compressed using temporal compression are called *inter*frames.

Sorenson Spark uses a combination of both spatial and temporal methods. It primarily uses temporal compression, which allows it to use a low data rate but produce good quality video. Sorenson Spark also uses spatial compression so that the intraframes (spatial compression) can be used as a reference for the interframes (temporal compression). Therefore with Sorenson Spark, you have the best of all worlds because many other codecs use only intraframe compression.

Now that you have a background for how video is compressed and what Sorenson Spark is, it is time for the hands-on exercises.

I.————————————Importing Video

The first step in working with video is importing it into Macromedia Flash MX. This exercise will teach you how to import a video clip into Macromedia Flash MX as an embedded video.

1. Copy the **chap_15** folder, located on the **H•O•T CD-ROM**, to your hard drive. You will need to have this folder on your hard drive in order to save changes to the files inside it.

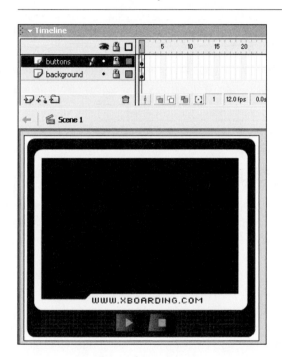

2. Open the **importVideo.fla** file from the **chap_15** folder. This file was created to get you started.

3. Click the **Insert Layer** button to add a new layer to the Timeline. Rename the layer **video** and make sure it is above all the other layers.

4. Choose **File > Import** and select the **jumps.mov** file from the **chap_15** folder. Click **Open**. *Note: This is a QuickTime video clip.*

5. The **Import Video** dialog box will appear. Make sure the **Embed video in Macromedia Flash document** option is selected. Click **OK**.

Note: You will see the Import Video dialog box only if you choose to import a QuickTime (.mov) file into Macromedia Flash MX. By default, all other video file types are automatically embedded.

To Embed or Not to Embed?

When you import a video clip, you can choose to embed it or link it. If you choose to embed a video clip, the video becomes part of the movie, just as a bitmap does when you import it into Macromedia Flash MX. The embedded video clip will then play in the .swf file inside Macromedia Flash Player. This is wonderful because users do not need any special player to view the video—all they need is the Macromedia Flash 6 Player installed on their browsers. When you import video, you can also choose to link to an external video file. In this case, the video will not be stored inside the Macromedia Flash MX document, and when you export the file from Macromedia Flash MX, you can not export it as a .swf file—instead, you have to export it as a QuickTime file (.mov). This means that the resulting file will not play in the Flash player, but will in the QuickTime player. The "Link vs. Embed" note near the end of this chapter compares the advantages and disadvantages between embedded and linked video files. You will learn about linked video in Exercise 5, but for now, the next few exercises concentrate on embedded video.

6. The **Import Video Settings** dialog box will appear. For **Quality**, move the slider to **100**. This setting will compress the video at the highest quality: 100. As you lower the quality setting, the file size will decrease, which will also cause the video to appear blocky.

Note: You may have noticed the audio note at the bottom of the Import Video Settings dialog box. This note will appear if either the audio codec used in the audio track is not supported on your system or if there is no audio attached to the video file, which is the case in this exercise.

7. For **Keyframe interval**, move the slider to **12**. This will create video keyframes inside the video at every 12 frames. See the following Note for further information on keyframe intervals.

NOTE | Keyframe Intervals

Keyframe intervals are different than the kind of keyframes you've learned about in the Macromedia Flash MX timeline. When you set the keyframe interval, you are determining how often a full frame of video will play back in the event that the computer cannot play all the frames due to slow processing speed. The computer playback will skip frames if it has to until it reaches a keyframe. If it can keep up with all the frames, it will play them all.

A setting of 12 instructs the video playback to play every 12th frame, no matter what. The lower you set the keyframe interval, the better, because you could compromise the playback of your project if you force a slow computer to play every frame.

You will not see the video keyframes in the Main Timeline inside Macromedia Flash MX. Instead, the video keyframes are part of the compression settings that compress the actual video file itself. Video keyframes are invisible to you in the project file; they simply affect the playback quality of the embedded video.

Import Video Settings

Path: C:\Documents and Settings\Kymberlee1\Desktop\FlashMX\15_video\chap_15\jumps

Movie size: 180x120 pixels, 1910.3 Kb
Length: 21.56 secs, 24.0 frames/sec

Quality: 100
0   100

Keyframe interval: 12
0   48

Scale: 100 %
1   100

Sorenson Spark

For expanded video capabilities, see Sorenson Spark Pro www.sorenson.com/sparkpro

☑ Synchronize video to Macromedia Flash document frame rate

Number of video frames to encode per number of Macromedia Flash frames   1:1

⚠ The audio in this file can not be imported.

Output properties:
Size: 180 x 120 pixels
Length: 21.56 secs
Frames/sec: 12.00

Help   OK   Cancel

8. For **Scale**, move the slider to **100%**. This will size the video to 100% of the original.

9. Check the **Synchronize video to Macromedia Flash document frame rate** box. Leave the **Number of video frames to encode per number of Macromedia Flash frames** at the default: 1:1. This will match the playback rate of the imported video to the Macromedia Flash project file's frame rate. The ratio of Macromedia Flash MX frames to video frames will match one frame for every one frame. When you are finished applying these settings, click OK.

A chart at the end of the exercise details the Import Video Compression options.

10. As soon as you click OK in the last step, you will see the Import progress bar. Then you will be presented with one last dialog box. This dialog box allows you decide if you want Macromedia Flash MX to automatically expand the Timeline to accommodate the length of the video file. In most cases you will always want to allow Macromedia Flash MX to do this. Go ahead and click **Yes**.

Just like you learned in Chapter 13, "Sound," when you work with Stream sound on the Main Timeline, the Timeline must be as long as the sound file in order to play the entire sound file. This also holds true for video—you must make the Timeline as long as the video file in order to see all the video. Otherwise, the video clip will be cut short.

11. As soon as you clicked Yes in the last step, the video clip will appear on the Stage. When you chose File > Import back in step 4, by default, the video clip was placed in the Library, and an instance of it was placed centered on the Stage. Click on the video clip to select it and move it slightly higher so that it is centered inside the background window, as shown in the picture above.

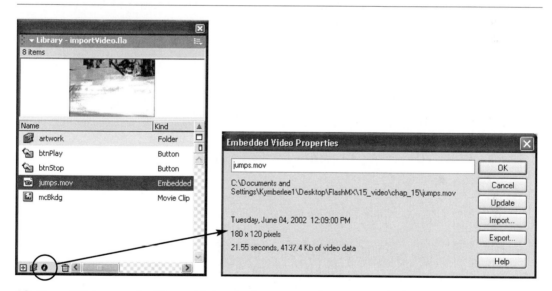

12. In the Timeline, notice that the video layer is filled with many frames. This is because you chose to allow Macromedia Flash MX to automatically expand the Timeline to accommodate the length of the video file in step 10. Move the **Playhead** to **Frame 259** in the Timeline. Click and drag down on the buttons and background layers to select **Frame 259** in both layers. Press **F5** to add frames up to Frame 259 so that you can see the background and the buttons throughout the video.

13. Press **F11** to open the Library. Notice the **jumps.mov** file. This is the video clip that you imported. Macromedia Flash MX has automatically placed it in the Library. Select the **jumps.mov** file in the Library and click on the **Properties** button. This will open the **Embedded Video Properties** window, where you can see the dimensions, duration in seconds, and size in kilobytes of video data. Click **OK** when you are finished.

14. Choose **Control > Play** to preview the video inside the project file. You will see the video play right on the Stage.

Tip: To preview your video inside the project file, you can either scrub the Playhead of the Timeline where the video resides or choose Control > Play. However, if your video contains sound, you must use Control > Test Movie to hear the sound.

15. Choose **Control > Test Movie** to see your movie in action in the .swf file! *Note:* The buttons will not work yet—you will learn to program these in the next exercise.

16. When you are finished, close the **Preview Window** and save this file but keep it open for the next exercise.

Compression Options	
Option	**Description**
Quality	Determines the image quality applied to the video. The values range from 0 to 100. Higher values will yield better image quality and larger file sizes. Lower values will yield smaller file sizes and lower image quality.
Keyframe interval	Controls how frequently a full frame of the source video is displayed on playback of the video, if the processor is slow and has to skip frames. The values range from 0 to 48. The lower the value, the more keyframes will be inserted. Note: If you set the Keyframe Interval to 0, a single keyframe will be added at the beginning of the video stream. For example, if you set the Keyframe interval to 12, Macromedia Flash MX will insert a video keyframe every 12th frame in the Timeline.
Scale	Controls the video's dimensions proportionally as it will appear on the Stage.
	continues on next page

Compression Options *continued*

Option	Description
Synchronize video to Macromedia Flash document frame rate	Matches the playback rate of the imported video to the Macromedia Flash MX project file's frame rate if this option is selected. For example, if the imported video has a faster frame rate than the Macromedia Flash MX project file, frames will be dropped from the video on import to synchronize both frame rates. If this option is not selected, Macromedia Flash MX will assign each frame of video to one frame in the Macromedia Flash MX Timeline. If the video has a faster frame rate than the Macromedia Flash MX project file, the imported video will play back slower than the original video because it is keeping the number of frames the same but playing back at a slower rate.
Number of video frames to encode per number of Macromedia Flash frames	Establishes the ratio of imported video frames to frames in the Macromedia Flash MX Timeline. For example, a 1:1 ratio will play one imported video frame for every one Macromedia Flash MX frame. A 2:1 ratio will play two imported video frames for every one Macromedia Flash MX frame. If frames are dropped from the imported video, the video will display fewer frames per second and will appear more choppy. Generally, a 1:1 ratio will work fine when you are first learning how to work with video. As you gain experience, you can test other ratios to see the effect on the final movie.
Import Audio	Includes the audio track in the imported video clip if the video clip has one. If this option is deselected, the audio track will be deleted from the imported video. The audio track in a video file is imported in its original form (uncompressed) and then compressed during export to a .swf file. You can use the Flash Publish settings (described in the next chapter) to control the compression applied to the imported video's audio track. Note: Be sure to use the Audio Stream settings inside the Flash Publish Settings because audio that is linked to an embedded video is considered a Stream sound so that it will sync with the video.

2. ———————Controlling Video with stop and go Actions

Now that you know how to import video and work with the compression settings, you need to learn how to control the video playback. This exercise will teach you how to control video on the Main Timeline by adding ActionScripting to buttons to control the video clip.

1. You should still have the **importVideo.fla** file open from the last exercise.

2. In the **Timeline**, move the **Playhead** back to **Frame 1**. Lock the **video layer** and unlock the **buttons** layer.

3. On the **Stage**, select the **play** button—the one with the right pointing triangle. Open the **Actions** panel (F9).

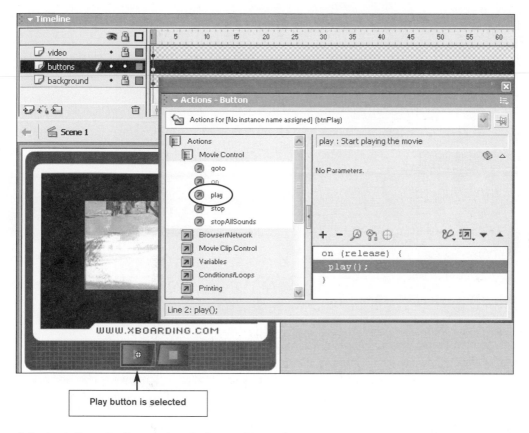

Play button is selected

4. In the **Actions Toolbox**, select **Actions > Movie Control** and double-click on the **play** action to add it to the **Script** pane. Because you are adding the action to a button, the **on** event handler will automatically be added to the Script pane as well. This ActionScript tells Macromedia Flash MX the following: When a user clicks on the play button, let the Playhead play through the frames in the Timeline.

5. On the **Stage**, select the **stop** button—the one with the square.

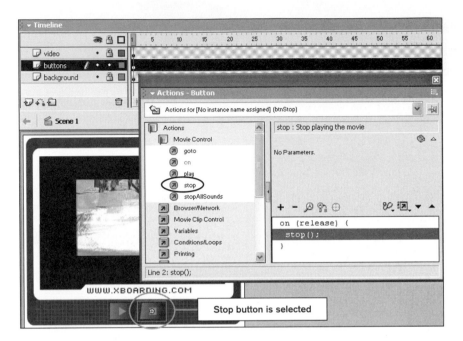

6. In the **Actions Panel**, select **Actions > Movie Control** and double-click on the **stop** action in the **Actions Toolbox** to add it to the **Script** pane. Because you are adding the action to a button, the on event handler will automatically be added to the Script pane as well. This ActionScript will tell Macromedia Flash MX the following: When a user clicks on the stop button, stop the Playhead in the Timeline.

7. Choose **Control > Test Movie** to preview the video. Click on the **stop** button to stop the video and click on the **play** button to play the video again. Cool! When you are finished, close the Preview Window.

You may have noticed that as soon as you test the movie, it begins to play. You will add one more action so that the movie starts in a stopped position, next.

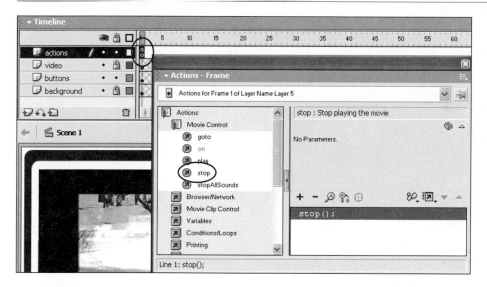

8. In the **Timeline**, click on the **Insert New Layer** button to add a new layer to the Timeline. Name this layer **actions** and make sure it is above all the other layers in the Timeline.

9. Select **Frame 1** on the **actions** layer. In the **Actions** panel, double-click on the **stop** action (Actions > Movie Control > stop) to add it to the **Script** pane. This will stop the Playhead at Frame 1 of the Timeline until you tell it otherwise.

10. Choose **Control > Test Movie** to preview the video again. Notice that the video is stopped. Click on the **play** button to set the video in motion and click on the **stop** button to stop the video again. By adding a few basic actions, you can allow the user to have complete control over you video. When you are finished, close the Preview Window.

11. Save and close this file, you won't be needing it again.

3. ———————————Controlling Video Targeting Frame Labels

Not only do you have the ability to start and stop the video using ActionScripting, you can also use ActionScripting to target specific points, in the video. This exercise will teach you how use the goto action to target different frames within the video sequence. Additionally, you will learn how to use named anchors to navigate through the video.

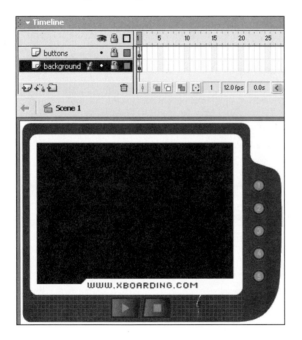

1. Open the **targetVideo.fla** file from the **chap_15** folder. This file was created to get you started.

2. Click the **Insert Layer** button to add a new layer to the Timeline. Rename the layer **video** and make sure it is above all the other layers.

3. Choose **File > Import** and select the **catchingAir.mov** file (*Note:* This is a QuickTime video clip) from the **chap_15** folder. Click **Open**. You will be presented with the **Import Video** dialog box.

4. As soon as you click on the Open button in the last step, you will be presented with the **Import Video** dialog box as in the picture above. Make sure the **Embed video in Macromedia Flash document** option is selected. Click **OK**. You will be presented with the **Import Video Settings** dialog box.

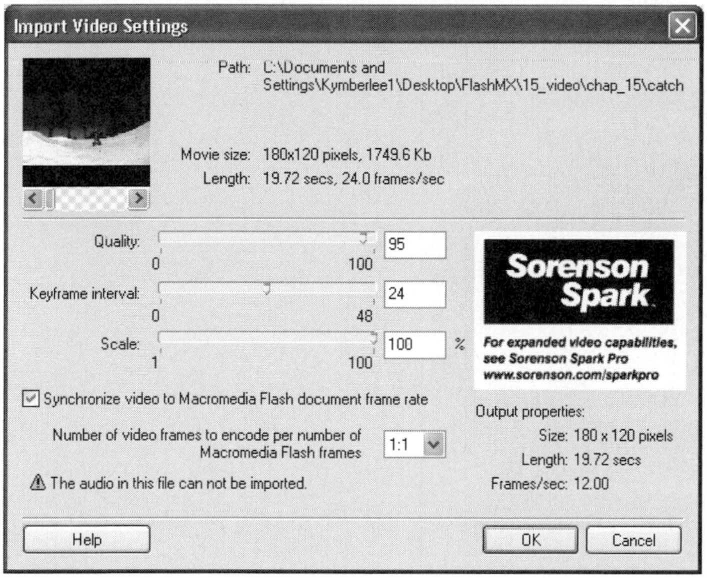

5. For **Quality**, choose **95**, for **Keyframe interval**, choose **24**, and for **Scale** choose **100**. Make sure the **Synchronize video to Macromedia Flash document frame rate** box is selected. For the **Number of video frames to encode per number of Macromedia Flash frames**, choose **1:1**. These settings will compress the video to a high quality (95), create a video keyframe every 24 frames, and scale the video to 100% of the original video. The playback rate of the imported video will be matched to the Macromedia Flash project file's frame rate. The ratio of Macromedia Flash MX frames to video frames will match one frame for every one frame. When you are finished, click **OK**.

6. The Import progress bar will appear, and then you will be presented with the last dialog box asking if you want Macromedia Flash MX to automatically expand the Timeline to accommodate the length of the video file (237 frames). Click **Yes**.

7. The video clip will be placed centered on the Stage. Click on the video clip to select it and move it so that it is centered inside the background window, as shown in the picture above.

8. In the **Timeline**, move the **Playhead** to **Frame 225** and scrub the **Playhead** between Frame 225 and where the video frames stop at 237. Notice how the video fades out at about Frame 233. The rest of the frames from 233 to 237 are not necessary because the video has faded to black. Click on **Frame 237** in the video layer to select it. Highlight **Frame 233 through 237** by dragging backwards from 237 to 233. Right-click (Windows) or Ctrl+click (Mac) to access the drop-down menu and choose **Remove frames** to remove the unnecessary frames from the Timeline.

Why remove the frames? In Macromedia Flash MX, video in the Timeline is treated just like Stream sound is treated in the Timeline. Only the frames that exist in the Timeline will be exported with the Macromedia Flash movie (.swf file). To reduce file size of the .swf file, you can remove frames from the Timeline to trim the video and save file size. In this example, the .swf file will be reduced from 1421KB to 1415KB by removing those five frames in the Timeline. **Note:** *Although you deleted frames from the video clip on the Main Timeline, the original full video clip is still in the library.*

9. In the **Timeline**, click and drag down on the buttons and background layers to select **Frame 232** in both layers. Press **F5** to add frames up to Frame 232 so that you can see the background and the buttons throughout the video.

10. Move the **Playhead** back to **Frame 1** and click the **Insert New Layer** button to add a new layer to the Timeline. Name this layer **labels**. Make sure it is above all the other layers.

```
▼ Properties
┌──────────────┬──────────────────────┬─────────────────────────────┐
│  Frame       │ Tween:  None      ▼  │ Sound:  None            ▼   │
│ (boarder1)   │                      │ Effect: None        ▼  Edit...│
│ □ Named Anchor│                     │ Sync:  Event ▼ Loop: 0  times│
│              │                      │     No sound selected.      │
└──────────────┴──────────────────────┴─────────────────────────────┘
```

11. Select **Frame 1** on the **labels** layer in the **Timeline**. In the **Property Inspector** (Window > Properties), type **boarder1** in the **Frame Label** field. This will mark the place where the first snowboarder is shown.

```
▼ Timeline
                    🐝 🔒 ▢  1    5    10   15   20   25   30   35   40   45   50   55
   📄 labels      / • • ▢  ▸boarder1                                    ▸boarder2
   📄 video       • 🔒 ▢  ●
   📄 buttons     • 🔒 ▢  ●
   📄 background  • 🔒 ▢  ●
   🗐 🕂 🗐            🗑   |  🔳 🔳 🔳 [·] 47  12.0 fps  3.8s ◀ ▥
```

12. Scrub the **Playhead** to see where a transition occurs and a new snowboarder appears in the video. Notice that a new snowboarder appears at Frame 47. Click on **Frame 47** on the **labels** layer and press **F7** to add a blank keyframe to Frame 47. In the **Property Inspector**, type **boarder2** in the **Frame Label** field. This will mark the place where the second snowboarder is shown.

```
▼ Timeline
                    🐝 🔒 ▢  95   100  105  110  115  120  125  130  135  140  145  150
   📄 labels      / • • ▢    ▸boarder3       ▸boarder4                 ▸boarder5
   📄 video       • 🔒 ▢
   📄 buttons     • 🔒 ▢
   📄 background  • 🔒 ▢
   🗐 🕂 🗐            🗑   |  🔳 🔳 🔳 [·] 146  12.0 fps  12.1s ◀  ▥
```

13. Repeat step 12 to add blank keyframe and frame labels for three more snowboarders. Hint: boarder3 = Frame 96, boarder4 = Frame 118, and boarder5 = Frame 146.

In the following steps, you will add the ActionScripting to target these frame labels.

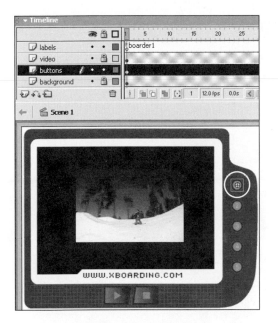

14. Move the **Playhead** back to **Frame** 1 in the **Timeline**. Unlock the **buttons** layer and click on **button 1** on the right side of the Stage to select it, as shown in the picture above.

15. In the **Actions** panel, choose **Actions > Movie Control** and double-click on the **goto** action to add it to the **Script** pane. In the **Parameters** pane, for **Type**, select **Frame Label** and for **Frame** select **boarder1** from the drop-down menu. This ActionScripting will tell Macromedia Flash MX that when a user clicks on button 1, send the Playhead to the frame labeled boarder1 and then play.

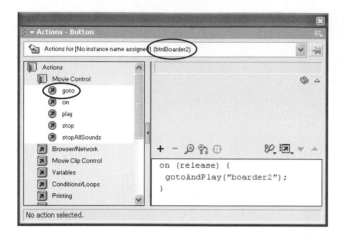

16. On the **Stage**, click on **button 2** on the right side of the Stage to select it. In the **Actions** panel, choose **Actions > Movie Control** and double-click on the **goto** action to add it to the **Script** pane. In the **Parameters** pane, choose **Type: Frame Label** and **Frame: boarder2**. This ActionScripting will tell Macromedia Flash MX to send the Playhead to the frame labeled boarder2 and play when a user clicks on button 2.

17. Repeat step 16 for the remaining three buttons. For button 3, choose **Type: Frame Label** and **Frame: boarder3**. For button 4, choose **Type: Frame Label** and **Frame: boarder4**. For button 5, choose **Type: Frame Label** and **Frame: boarder5**.

18. Choose **Control > Test Movie** and click on each of the buttons to the right of the video clip to test the buttons. Each button will play a different snowboarder segment of the video. When you are finished, close the Preview Window. You will learn to apply named anchors to your movie next.

Note: *You may have noticed that the stop and go buttons worked as well. These were programmed for you using the exact same ActionScripting that you applied in Exercise 2.*

19. Back in the project file, in the **labels** layer, click on the **boarder1** frame label in the **Timeline** to select that frame (Frame 1). In the **Property Inspector**, notice that under the Frame Label text box is a **Named Anchor** check box. Select this box. As soon as you select the Named Anchor box, notice that the icon next to the frame label in the Timeline changes. This is an indication that a named anchor is attached to that frame.

NOTE | What Is a Named Anchor?

New in Macromedia Flash MX is the capability to create movies that work with the Forward and Back buttons in a browser. This feature is called a Named Anchor. A Named Anchor is a special frame label that resides on the Main Timeline and has a unique anchor icon. Once the Named Anchor is played in a browser window, it is registered in a browser's history. Then, when a user clicks on the Back button in the browser window, the browser will play the previous named anchor position on the Timeline.

The Named Anchor feature will work in the Macromedia Flash 6 Player on browsers that support the FSCommand with JavaScript, including Internet Explorer (Windows) or Netscape 3.x to 4.x (Windows and Mac). You will learn about FSCommands in the next chapter, "*Publishing and Exporting*."

20. Repeat step 19 by selecting each of the remaining four **frame labels** (boarder2, boarder3, boarder4, and boarder5) and then selecting the **Named Anchor** check box in the Property Inspector.

21. Select **Frame 232** on the **actions** layer and press **F7** to add a blank keyframe. In the **Actions** panel, double-click on the **stop** action (Actions > Movie Control > stop) to add it to the **Script** pane. This will stop the Playhead at Frame 232 of the Timeline until you tell it otherwise.

22. Choose **File > Publish Settings** to open the **Publish Settings** window. Click on the **HTML** tab at the top, and in the **Template** drop-down list, choose **Flash with Named Anchors**. Leave the rest of the settings at their defaults and click **OK**. This will add JavaScript into the HTML document that will catch the named anchors as they play in the browser.

Note: You will learn all about the Publish Settings in detail in Chapter 16, "Publishing and Exporting."

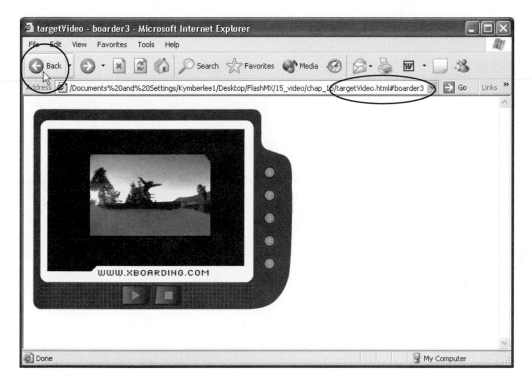

23. Choose **File > Publish Preview > HTML**. This will allow you to preview the Macromedia Flash MX movie in an HTML document so that you can test the Named Anchors. As the video plays, notice the URL in the browser window: The end will change to reflect the Named Anchor that is currently playing. When the movie reaches the end and stops, test the **Back** button in the browser—it will jump back one anchor to boarder4. Click it again and it will jump back to boarder3. Now click the **Forward** button in the browser and the movie will advance forward to the next Named Anchor. Neat! When you are finished, close the browser window.

Tip: You can use Named Anchors with video or with any content on the Main Timeline. Because many users will not be accustomed to using the Forward and Back buttons with Macromedia Flash movies, you may have to add some text to your movie, instructing the users that they can navigate using the browser Forward and Back buttons. Note: You will learn all about the Publish Preview Options in Chapter 16, "Publishing and Exporting."

NOTE | Other Uses for Named Anchors

In the past, Macromedia Flash movies could never utilize the Back button of a browser. Because many people built entire Web sites using the Macromedia .swf file format, this created a usability problem. Using the Named Anchors technique, you could build back browser functionality into any Macromedia Flash MX Web site. You learned from this exercise how easy it is to add this feature, so consider this technique for any complete Web sites that you build in the future. Just make sure that the Named Anchors exist on the Main Timeline because they have to be placed there in order to work correctly.

---

24. When you are finished, save and close this file.

---

4. ——————Applying Effects to Video

When you work with video, you are not limited to working only with the video object on the Stage. You can place video inside a Movie Clip and add multiple instances of that Movie Clip to the Stage without significantly increasing the file size of the .swf file. Once inside a Movie Clip, you can transform the video by applying such effects as Tint and Skew. This exercise will show you how.

1. Open the **videoMC.fla** file from the **chap_15** folder. This file was created to get you started.

2. Choose **File > Import to Library** and select the **shortJump.mov** file from the **chap_15** folder. Click **Open**. You will be presented with the **Import Video** dialog box.

NOTE | Importing Video

There are two ways to import video into Macromedia Flash MX. The first way is to choose File > Import, as you have done up to this point in the chapter. This will import the video clip into the Library and add an instance of it to the Stage. The second way is to choose File > Import to Library. This command will import the video clip directly into the Library without placing an instance on the Stage.

---

3. As soon as you click on the Open button in the last step, you will be presented with the Import Video dialog box as in the picture above. Make sure the **Embed video in Macromedia Flash document** option is selected. Click **OK**.

Import Video Settings

Path: C:\Documents and
Settings\Kymberlee1\Desktop\FlashMX\15_video\chap_15\shortJ

Movie size: 180x120 pixels, 183.3 Kb
Length: 1.95 secs, 150.0 frames/sec

Quality: 100
0   100

Keyframe interval: 8
0   48

Scale: 100 %
1   100

Sorenson Spark

*For expanded video capabilities,
see Sorenson Spark Pro
www.sorenson.com/sparkpro*

☑ Synchronize video to Macromedia Flash document frame rate

Number of video frames to encode per number of
Macromedia Flash frames   1:1

⚠ The audio in this file can not be imported.

Output properties:
Size: 180 x 120 pixels
Length: 1.95 secs
Frames/sec: 12.00

Help   OK   Cancel

4. As soon as you click OK in the last step, you will be presented with the Import Video Settings dialog box. For **Quality**, choose **100**, for **Keyframe interval**, choose **8**, and for **Scale**, choose **100**. Make sure the **Synchronize video to Macromedia Flash document frame rate** box is selected. For the **Number of video frames to encode per number of Macromedia Flash frames**, choose **1:1**. These settings will compress the video at the highest quality (100), create a video keyframe every eight frames, and scale the video to 100% of the original video. The playback rate of the imported video will be matched to the Macromedia Flash project file's frame rate. The ratio of Macromedia Flash MX frames to video frames will match one frame for every one frame. When you are finished, click **OK**.

5. As soon as you click OK in the last step, notice that no Movie Clip appears on the Stage. Why? This is because you chose the File > Import to Library command in step 2, which will place the video clip in the Library only, and not on the Stage. Press **F11** to open the Library. Notice that the **shortJump.mov** file is there.

6. Choose **Insert > New Symbol**. Name the new symbol **mcVideoHolder**. For **Behavior**, choose **Movie Clip**. Click **OK**. You will be placed inside the Movie Clip's Timeline.

7. From the **Library**, drag the **shortJump.mov** file onto the **Stage**.

8. You will be presented with a dialog box asking if you want Macromedia Flash MX to automatically expand the Timeline to accommodate the length of the video file (24 frames). Click **Yes**.

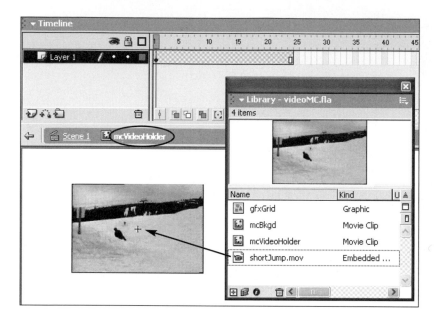

After you clicked Yes in the last step, notice that the video clip was placed on the Stage and the frames in the Timeline of the mcVideoHolder were extended to match the number of frames in the video (24).

9. Click on **Scene 1** in the **Information Bar** to return to Scene 1 in the Main Timeline.

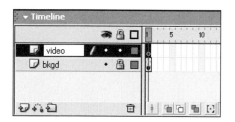

10. On the **Main Timeline**, click the **Insert Layer** button to add a new layer to the Timeline. Rename the layer **video** and make sure it is above the bkgd layer.

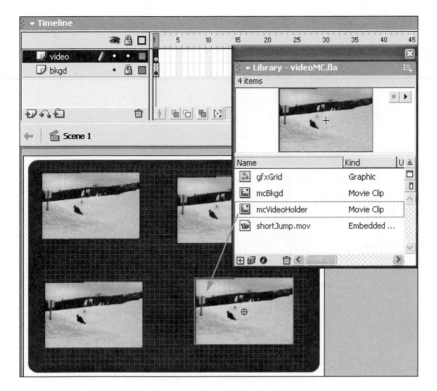

11. In the **Main Timeline**, select **Frame 1** of the **video** layer and drag four instances of the **mcVideoHolder** Movie Clip onto the **Stage**, as shown in the picture above.

Tip: As with other symbols in the Library, you can reuse embedded video by creating several instances of it on the Stage, without a significant increase in file size.

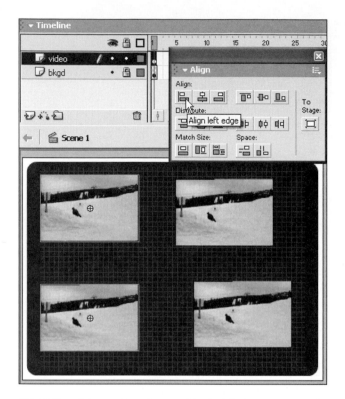

12. Shift+click to select the two Movie Clip instances on the left side of the **Stage**. Open the **Align** panel (Window > Align) and choose **Align left edge**. Click off the Stage to deselect everything.

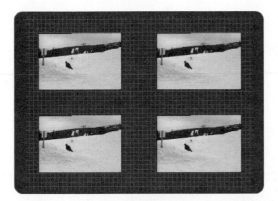

13. Repeat Step 12 but this time select the two Movie Clip instances on the right side of the Stage and choose **Align right edge** in the **Align** panel. Next, select the two Movie Clip instances on the top of the **Stage** and choose **Align top edge** in the Align panel. Lastly, select the two Movie Clip instances on the bottom of the **Stage** and choose **Align bottom edge**. When you are finished, close the **Align** panel. Additionally, you can also select two of the Movie Clips and use the arrow keys on your keyboard to nudge them higher or lower once they are aligned. When you are finished, all of the Movie Clips should be aligned and positioned similar to the picture above.

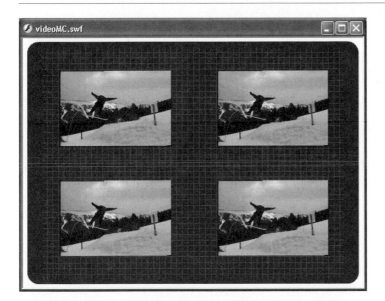

14. Choose **Control > Test Movie** to test the Movie Clips. They will all play in unison because they are each instances of the same Movie Clip. When you are finished, close the Preview Window.

You will be applying effects to the Movie Clip instances next.

Color Styles menu

15. Back in the project file, click on the Movie Clip instance in the upper left corner of the **Stage** to select it. In the **Property Inspector**, choose **Tint** from the **Color Styles** drop-down menu. In the **Tint Color** box, select a blue color from the color palette. Move the **Tint amount** slider to **60**. This will give a blue tint to the selected instance of the Movie Clip that contains the video inside.

Tip: In order to apply color effects to a video object, the video must be placed inside a Movie Clip or Graphic symbol.

16. Click on the Movie Clip instance in the upper right corner of the **Stage** to select it. In the **Property Inspector**, choose **Brightness** from the **Color Styles** drop-down menu. Move the **Brightness amount** slider to **80**. This will give the selected instance an 80% Brightness color.

Tip: *The Brightness amount ranges from 100% (pure white) to −100% (pure black).*

17. Go ahead and apply different **Color Styles** to the remaining two Movie Clip instances. You can experiment with Tint and Brightness or even Alpha, if you wish.

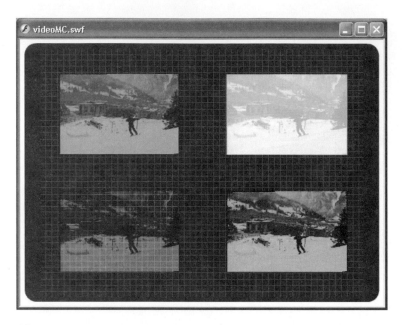

18. When you are finished, choose **Control > Test Movie** to preview your changes. Close the Preview Window when you are done.

Note: In the picture above, I used Alpha: 30% on the instance on the bottom left and a Red Tint of 20% on the instance on the right. By adding a few different Color Styles, including Tint, Brightness, and Alpha, you can dramatically change the appearance of the instances.

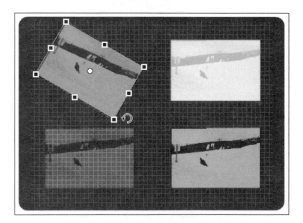

19. In the project file, select the **Free Transform** tool in the **Toolbox**. Click on the instance in the upper left corner of the **Stage** to select it. Move the cursor over a corner handle until it turns into a **curved arrow** and drag to rotate the instance, as shown in the picture above.

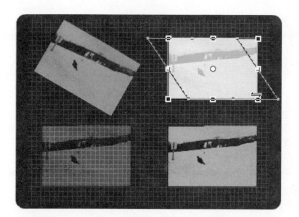

20. Click on the instance in the upper right corner of the **Stage** to select it. Move the cursor between the bottom middle and corner handles until it turns into a **double arrow** and drag to the right to skew the instance, as shown in the picture above.

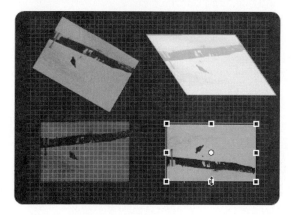

21. Click on the instance in the lower right corner of the **Stage** to select it. Move the cursor over the top middle handle and drag all the way to the other side of the instance to flip it upside down, as shown in the picture above.

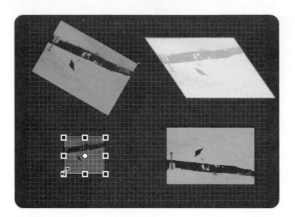

22. Click on the instance in the lower left corner of the **Stage** to select it. Click and drag inwards on a corner handle to scale down the size of the instance, as shown in the picture above.

23. Choose **Control > Test Movie** to see all the modifications you made.

Note: Although this file has four instances of the Movie Clip with the video clip inside on the Stage, the .swf file is only 389KB. If you delete all but one of the instances on the Stage and test the movie again, the .swf file will still be 389KB. Why? This is because once a video clip is in the Library, you can use multiple instances of it on the Stage without having a significant impact on file size. Cool!

24. When you are finished, save and close this file.

WARNING | Color Effects or Stream?

In this exercise, you placed the video inside a Movie Clip symbol so that you were able to apply color effects to it. It is important to note that movie clips have to be downloaded first before they will play back in the Macromedia Flash Player. Therefore, if you want a Movie Clip to play right away using Macromedia Flash's streaming capabilities, the video must reside on the Main Timeline and not inside a symbol. If the video is not inside a symbol, you will lose the ability to apply color effects. Ultimately, you must decide which is the most important objective of your project: to use color effects or to stream.

5.————————Linking to QuickTime Video

In addition to embedding a video inside a Macromedia Flash file, you can link to a QuickTime video clip from the Macromedia Flash movie. In the following steps, you will learn about the integration between Apple QuickTime and Macromedia Flash MX. This exercise will show you how to use a linked QuickTime movie with a custom Macromedia Flash MX interface. You need to have a current version of QuickTime to complete this exercise. A full version of Apple QuickTime 6 is included on the **H•O•T CD-ROM**. It is located inside the software folder.

1. Open the **linkingToQT.fla** file inside the **chap_15** folder. This file was created to get you started.

2. Click the **Insert Layer** button in the **Timeline** to insert a new layer. Rename the layer **video** and make sure it is above the existing layers.

3. Select **Frame 1** of the **video** layer and choose **File > Import**. Select the **linking.mov** file from the **chap_15** folder and click **Open**. You will be presented with the **Import Video** dialog box.

4. Select the **Link to external video file** radio button. Click **OK**.

5. As soon as you click OK in the last step, you will be presented with a dialog box asking if you want Macromedia Flash MX to automatically expand the Timeline to accommodate the length of the video file (108 frames). Click **Yes** to expand the number of frames in the Timeline to match the number of frames in the video.

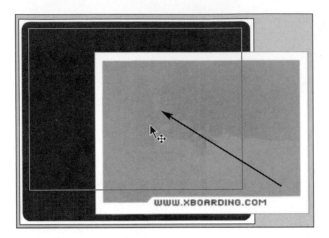

6. As soon as you click Yes in the last step, the video clip will be placed in the center of the work environment. Click on the linked video clip to select it and move it so that it is positioned inside the background window, near the top, as shown in the picture above.

7. Press **F11** to open the Library. Notice the **linking.mov** file. This is the video clip that you imported. Macromedia Flash MX has automatically placed it in the Library, as well as an instance of it on the Stage.

8. In the **Timeline**, notice that the video layer is filled with many frames (108 to be exact). This is because you chose to allow Macromedia Flash MX to automatically expand the Timeline to accommodate the length of the video file in step 5. Move the **Playhead** to **Frame 108** in the **Timeline**. Click and drag down on the **buttons** and **background** layers to select **Frame 108** in both layers. Press **F5** to add frames up to Frame 108 so that you can see the background and the buttons throughout the video.

9. Scrub through the movie with your **Playhead** to see the QuickTime content playing. Move your **Playhead** back to **Frame 1** and choose **Control > Play** to preview the movie inside the project file.

Note: You can not preview linked QuickTime video files using the Test Movie command because you can not export a linked QuickTime movie as a .swf. Instead, you need to export it as a QuickTime movie (.mov). You will do this later in this exercise.

10. Move the **Playhead** to **Frame 1** and lock the **video** layer and unlock the **buttons** layer. In the following steps, you will add ActionScripting to one button to tell the movie to play and the other to tell the movie to stop.

11. On the **Stage**, select the button on the left. Open the **Actions** panel (F9).

Play button is selected

12. In the **Actions Toolbox**, select **Actions > Movie Control** and double-click on the **play** action to add it to the **Script** pane. Because you are adding the action to a button, the on event handler will automatically be added to the Script pane as well. This ActionScript will tell Macromedia Flash MX the following: When a user clicks on the play button, let the Playhead play through the frames in the Timeline.

13. On the **Stage**, select the button on the right.

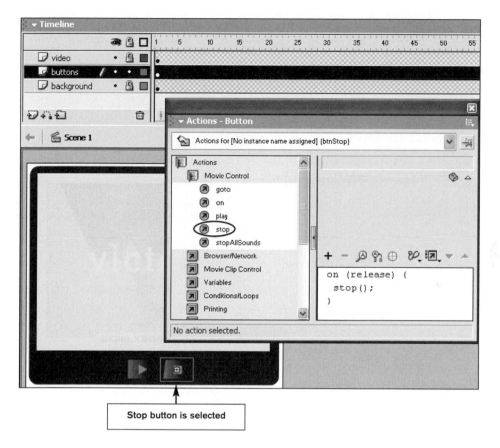

Stop button is selected

14. In the **Actions Panel**, select **Actions > Movie Control** and double-click on the **stop** action in the **Actions Toolbox** to add it to the **Script** pane. Because you are adding the action to a button, the **on** event handler will automatically be added to the Script pane as well. This ActionScript will tell Macromedia Flash MX the following: When a user clicks on the stop button, stop the Playhead in the Timeline.

Publish Settings

Formats | Flash | HTML

Version: Flash Player 4

- Flash Player 1
- Flash Player 2
- Flash Player 3
- Flash Player 4
- Flash Player 5
- Flash Player 6

Load Order:

Options:

☐ Omit Trace actions
☐ Debugging Permitted
☐ Compress Movie

Password:

JPEG Quality: [80]
0   100

Audio Stream: MP3, 16 kbps, Mono [Set]
Audio Event: MP3, 16 kbps, Mono [Set]
☐ Override sound settings

[OK]
[Publish]
[Cancel]

[Help]

15. Choose **File > Publish Settings** to open the Publish Settings window. Click on the **Flash** tab at the top, and in the **Version** drop-down list, choose **Flash Player 4**. Leave the rest of the settings at their defaults and click **OK**. Because the current version of the QuickTime Player will play only Macromedia Flash 4 content, you have to change the version of the Macromedia Flash file to Flash 4 before publishing the file as a QuickTime movie, as you will do next.

Note: You will learn all about the Publish Settings in detail in Chapter 16, "Publishing and Exporting."

16. Choose **File > Export Movie**.

17. From the **Export Movie** dialog box, name the movie **flashQT.mov** and select **QuickTime** as the file format and click **Save**. Although you will notice many file format options here, the only way to view the QuickTime content is to save the file in the QuickTime format. **Note:** You can't import a linked QuickTime file and export out the .swf file because a *linked* QuickTime movie simply will not play as a .swf.

Note: QuickTime uses "tracks" to separate and store different forms of multimedia. In version 4 of QuickTime, the Flash track was added. A Flash track allows you to include content that you built in Macromedia Flash (limited to include Flash 4 level ActionScript.) Many people build QuickTime movies that have Flash controllers (CNN has a lot of content on their site that is created this way). The advantage to this kind of movie is that it requires only the QuickTime player to view the content, but it has the advantage of being able to employ cool-looking Macromedia Flash–created navigation buttons.

18. You will be presented with the **Export QuickTime** dialog box. Select the **Paused At Start** Playback option and leave the rest of the settings at their defaults. Click **OK** and Macromedia Flash MX will export this file as a QuickTime movie. The Paused At Start option will force the movie to start in a stopped position and wait for instructions to begin playing the movie (such as a user clicking on the play button).

A chart follows at the end of this exercise detailing the different QuickTime export options.

19. To check the results, go to the **chap_15** folder and double-click on the file titled **flashQT.mov** file to open your file inside the QuickTime movie player. Notice that the movie is stopped. Click on the **play** button to start it; click on the **stop** button to stop it again.

20. When you're done, close the **flashQT.mov** file. **Save** and **close** the **linkingToQT.fla** file.

Note: To recap: You can not export a linked QuickTime movie as a .swf. Instead, you need to export it as a QuickTime movie (.mov). If you want to export a .swf file that has a QuickTime movie inside, choose to have the QuickTime movie embedded (rather than linked) when you import the video.

The QuickTime Dialog Box

The following chart explains all of the QuickTime features.

QuickTime Dialog Box	
Setting	**Description**
Dimensions	This option controls the size of the movie. If the Match Movie box is checked, a QuickTime movie will be created that will have the same dimensions as those you set in the Document Properties dialog box.
Alpha	This option controls transparency of Flash background on top of QuickTime. The Auto option sets the Flash track to transparent if the Flash track appears over the other tracks, and opaque if it is at the bottom or is the only track in the movie. Alpha Transparent makes the Flash track transparent so that you can see content under it. Copy sets the Flash track to opaque.
Layer	This option controls where Flash plays in the stacking order of QuickTime tracks. Top places the Flash track on top of all other tracks. Bottom places the Flash track below other tracks in the QuickTime movie. Auto detects where the Flash content is located and places the Flash track on top if it has been positioned in front of an imported QuickTime movie.
Streaming Sound	If this box is checked, Macromedia Flash MX will export streaming sound to a QuickTime sound track.
Controller	This option allows you to choose which QuickTime controller will be used to play back your exported QuickTime movie.
Playback	This option allows you to choose how your movie is played. Loop will play your movie from start to finish and will keep playing over and over. Paused At Start will not play your movie until a button is pressed within your movie to initiate it, or until the play button is pressed on the QuickTime control panel. Play every frame will allow every frame to be viewed, no matter the effect on playback, and all sound will be disabled in the exported QuickTime movie if this option is selected.
File	If this box is checked, Macromedia Flash MX content will be combined with the imported video content into a single QuickTime file.

NOTE | Link vs. Embed

Why choose **Link** instead of **Embed**, or vice-versa?

This can depend largely on which type of file you want as the end result (in other words, which file you want to export). If you want a Macromedia Flash .swf file, you would have to choose to embed the video because you can not create a .swf file that contains linked video—the video will not show up inside a .swf file. If you want a QuickTime file (.mov), you can either link to the video or embed the video.

When you import video, if you choose embed it, the video will become part of the Macromedia Flash project file and will result in an increase (sometimes very significant) in file size in the project file (.fla). On the other hand, a linked file is not part of the Macromedia Flash file, and instead, Macromedia Flash maintains a pointer to the linked file so this can keep your project file (.fla) file size smaller. For example, in this exercise, if you link to the video, the .fla will be 39KB. If you embed the video, the .fla will be 1,376KB—quite a difference.

There is one more point to consider when deciding to embed or to link to the video file. When you embed a file, you compress it on import into Macromedia Flash MX. However, when you link to a file, you do not compress the native file at all—you simply point to it, which can result in a larger file size. Keep in mind that I am now referring to the exported file—not the project file. It is important to note that if you use relative addressing when you specify the location of the video you are linking to, you can't move the video file. If you do move the video file, the link will be broken, and Macromedia Flash will not be able to find it. Therefore, when using relative addressing, make sure you leave the video file in the same folder you specified, or if you move it, make sure to update the ActionScripting to reflect the new location.

As a test, I created an exercise just as you did using a *linked* video file inside Macromedia Flash. I exported the file out as a QuickTime file and the resulting file size was 19,070KB. In the second test, I re-created the exercise, this time choosing to *embed* the video. I exported out a QuickTime file resulting in a 1,323KB file size. And just for fun, I also exported out a .swf file resulting in a 1,322KB file size. In conclusion, the exported .mov file with the linked video was almost 15 times the size of the exported .mov file and .swf file with the embedded video.

What Is Sorenson Squeeze?

In addition to using Macromedia Flash MX's built-in program (the Sorenson Spark Standard Edition) to compress video files as you have done in this chapter, you can also use more sophisticated technology to compress your videos outside Macromedia Flash MX for higher quality video compression. Sorenson Squeeze is a separate product available at **http://www.sorenson.com**. Sorenson Squeeze allows you to compress video files using Sorenson Spark Pro, which is a more advanced product than the standard edition of Sorenson Spark that comes built into Macromedia Flash MX. As of this writing, Sorenson Squeeze is available for $119 on the Sorenson Web site at **http://www.sorenson.com**. A trial version of Sorenson Squeeze is included on the **H•O•T CD-ROM** inside the software folder.

Compressed inside Macromedia Flash MX;
.swf file size = 2,048KB

Compressed using Sorenson Squeeze;
.swf file size = 292KB

The same file was compressed using Sorenson Spark inside Macromedia Flash MX and Sorenson Squeeze outside Macromedia Flash MX. The squeezed .swf file is seven times smaller than the file compressed inside Macromedia Flash MX! It also looks quite a bit better.

Sorenson squeeze is surprisingly easy to use; Macromedia has a great tutorial at **http://www.macromedia.com/desdev/tip/017.html**. You can also see a demo of the Sorenson Squeeze product at **http://www.sorenson.com/sparkpro.html**.

Nice job! You have made it through another chapter. Get ready for the next chapter—it is filled with useful information on how to publish your movies using Macromedia Flash MX's Publish and Export Settings.

16.
Publishing and Exporting

Publishing Choices	HTML Files
Projector Files	Modifying Projectors with FSCommands
Exporting Image Files	Publish Settings
Optimizing Movies

chap_16

Macromedia Flash MX
H•O•T CD-ROM

Prior to this chapter, you tested your movies in Macromedia Flash MX by choosing Control > Test Movie, in order to see your work and generate the .swf file. This chapter will show you how to publish your movies using the Publish settings instead. Testing and publishing are two different methods of producing the .swf file. You'll learn that publishing your movie instead of testing it offers many more options and greater control over the final output. As well, you'll learn how to generate an HTML file and a projector file from Macromedia Flash MX. This chapter will also teach you how to export an image from a project file.

At the end of this chapter, you will find a reference guide that explains what all the Publish settings do, so that you can try settings that are more advanced than those covered by the exercises in this chapter. In addition, a chart is provided listing the file types you can export. The chapter concludes with a look at some tips and tricks for optimizing your movies.

What Types of Content Can Macromedia Flash MX Publish?

In addition to the .swf file, Macromedia Flash MX is able to publish several different file formats. Here's a short table to describe some of the publishing options in Macromedia Flash MX.

Macromedia Flash MX Publishing Choices	
Web Delivery	If you plan to publish Web content, you will need to create minimal HTML to embed the Macromedia Flash MX movie, as well as to determine how the movie will appear. You'll learn how to generate this HTML code in the exercises provided in this chapter.
CD-ROM Delivery	If you want to use Macromedia Flash MX on a CD-ROM, you can create a projector file. You'll learn to do this in the exercises provided in this chapter.
Email Attachment	If you want to create a Macromedia Flash MX movie as an email attachment, you would create a projector file. You'll learn to make a projector file in this chapter.
QuickTime	It's possible to generate a Flash track for QuickTime. This offers the opportunity to create Macromedia Flash MX controllers or buttons for QuickTime content.
Image File	If you want to create an image file, such as a JPEG, PNG, or GIF, from your project file, you can use the Publish settings to create an image. You will learn how to do this and what the limitations are in this chapter.

I. —————————Macromedia Flash MX and HTML

This exercise will walk you through the Publish settings interface to learn how to create the necessary HTML files for Web delivery of Macromedia Flash MX content. The following steps will show you how changes that you make in the Publish settings affect the way your movie is viewed in a Web browser.

1. Copy the **chap_16** folder, located on the **H•O•T CD-ROM**, to your hard drive. You need to have this folder on your hard drive in order to save files inside it.

2. Open the **publish.fla** file from the **publishTesting** folder inside the **chap_16** folder. Notice that this is the only file inside the **publishTesting** folder.

3. Choose **Control > Test Movie** to preview the movie. This is the finished version of the effects movie you created in Chapter 8. Notice the title **publish** at the top of the window.

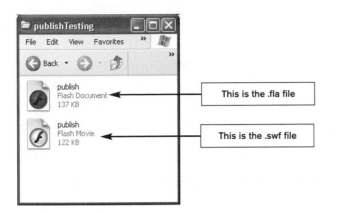

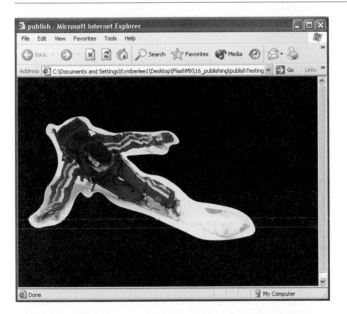

4. Leave Macromedia Flash MX for a moment and open the **chap_16** folder on your hard drive. Open the **publishTesting** folder. Inside you will now see two files: one .fla file and one .swf file. When you chose **Control > Test Movie**, Macromedia Flash MX created the .swf file in the folder as well.

5. Back in the project file, choose **File > Publish Preview > Default - (HTML)**, or use the shortcut key **Ctrl+F12** (Windows) or **Cmd+F12** (Mac). This will trigger the **Publish Preview** command, which launches the default browser on your machine and displays an HTML page with the .swf file embedded inside it.

When you use the Publish Preview command, the Publish settings determine how Macromedia Flash MX decides to publish the documents. You will work with the Publish settings in just a few steps.

> **WARNING | Publish Preview Versus Test Movie**
>
> The Publish Preview command, compared to using Control > Test Movie, gives you the most accurate indication of how your movie will look on the Internet. The preview you see when using Control > Test Movie will not always be exactly the same as the published movie will appear on a Web server. For example, sound in your movie may vary slightly, and complex animations may animate slightly slower using the Test Movie command. To be safe, use the Publish Preview or Publish command to view the movie before you upload it live to the Internet.

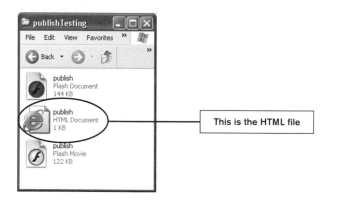

This is the HTML file

6. Open the **chap_16** folder on your hard drive. Browse again to the folder titled **publishTesting** and open it. Inside you will now see *three* files: the .fla file, the .swf file, and the HTML file. When you preview your movie in a browser by choosing File > Publish Preview > Default - (HTML), Macromedia Flash MX will create an HTML file in the same folder that you saved your .fla file in.

Notice that all three files have the same name. By default, Macromedia Flash MX names the additional files with the same name as the .fla file. You will change these names in the next few steps.

7. Back in the project file, choose **File > Publish Settings**. This will open the **Publish Settings** dialog box, which always opens to the Formats tab first.

The Formats tab is used to specify which file formats will be created when you publish the movie. The other tabs will appear or disappear according to which boxes you check.

Uncheck this box

8. Make sure there are checks in the boxes next to the Format Types **Flash** and **HTML**. Notice that all the **Filenames** are set to have the prefix **publish**. This is because the **Use default names** box is checked. Uncheck the **Use default names** box and type **movie.swf** inside the **Flash Filename** field. Then type **webPage.html** inside the **HTML Filename** field.

9. Click the **Publish** button to publish these two files with the names you just gave them. Macromedia Flash MX will create these new files and save them in the same folder as the original .fla file.

10. To make sure the new files have been published, open the **publishTesting** folder again. Inside you will now see *five* files: the three files that were already there, each with the **publish** name, and two new files named **webPage** and **movie**.

Each time you click the Publish button in the Publish settings dialog box (or you use File > Publish), Macromedia Flash MX writes and creates all of the files you have selected on the Formats tab in the Publish Settings dialog box (in this case, .swf and HTML). If you publish two or more times with the same settings, Macromedia Flash MX will overwrite the existing files each time.

11. In the **Publish Settings** dialog box, click on the **Flash** tab, which is next to the **Formats** tab. For **Load Order**, select **Top down**. This will load each layer in the movie from the top layer first and continue downward. Selecting this option is a good habit to get into since, as you learned in Chapter 11, "*ActionScripting Basics*," you should always place your actions on the top layer. When you select Top down, your ActionScripting layer will always load first in the Macromedia Flash Player.

Don't click OK or Publish just yet; you will change another setting in the next step.

12. Place a check in the box next to **Generate size report**. Click the **Publish** button.

13. Open the **publishTesting** folder. Notice the new file **movie Report**.

Why is it named movie Report? When you generate a size report, Flash creates a detailed report about the current .swf file. In this case, you renamed the .swf file movie, so the size report is named movie Report.

movie Report - Notepad

File Edit Format View Help

Movie Report

FrameFrame #	Frame Bytes	Total Bytes	Page
1	118	118	Scene 1
2	156	274	2
3	219	493	3
4	264	757	4
5	325	1082	5
6	124823	125905	6
7	13	125918	7
8	13	125931	8
9	13	125944	9
10	13	125957	10
11	13	125970	11
12	13	125983	12
13	13	125996	13
14	13	126009	14
15	13	126022	15
16	13	126035	16
17	13	126048	17
18	13	126061	18
19	13	126074	19
20	87	126161	20
21	17	126178	21
22	13	126191	22
23	13	126204	23
24	13	126217	24

movie Report - Notepad

File Edit Format View Help

44	2	126373	44
45	2	126375	45

Page	Shape Bytes	Text Bytes
Scene 1	1005	0
Embedded Objects	61	0

Page	Symbol Bytes	Text Bytes
origImage	0	0
boarder	330	0

Bitmap	Compressed	Compression	
boarderCloseup	124473	886788	Imported JPEG

14. Double-click on the **movie Report** file to open it. This is the size report file. Whenever you select **Generate size report**, Macromedia Flash MX will create a special text file that gives a breakdown of the file size contributions of all of the symbols, fonts, and other elements in the movie. This is a handy tool to use when you want to know, frame by frame, how big the movie is and how many different elements are present in the movie. When you are done reviewing the file, you can close it.

15. Back in the **Publish Settings** dialog box, under the **Flash** tab, place a check mark in the box next to **Protect from import**. Checking this box prevents someone from importing your .swf movie file into Flash and converting it back to a project file.

Be aware that checking Protect from import is not 100 percent secure. You can still import a protected movie into a Macromedia Director movie, and hackers can also use a utility called SWIFFER to break into any Macromedia Flash MX movie. To be safe, don't put highly sensitive information into Macromedia Flash MX movies, but do check the Protect from import box to safeguard against at least the average person opening the .swf file.

16. Click on the **HTML** tab. Notice that the **Dimensions** setting default is **Match Movie**. The Dimensions setting determines the dimensions at which the Macromedia Flash MX movie will be set in the HTML tags. This value can be in pixels or can be a percentage of window size. As you will see in the next step, the Match Movie option will not allow the .swf file to scale.

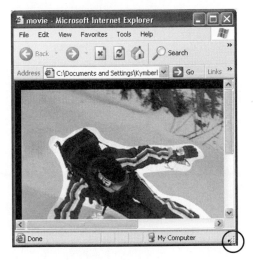

17. In the **chap_16** folder on your hard drive, open the **publishTesting** folder. Double-click on the **webPage** file to open it. Resize the browser window by clicking and dragging the bottom right corner of the window. Notice that the .swf file doesn't scale with the browser window and that, as you make the window smaller, the image becomes cut off. You will change the scalability restrictions by changing the Dimensions setting next.

18. In the **Publish Settings** dialog box, under the **HTML** tab, choose **Dimensions: Percent**. Click **Publish**. This will replace the previous version of the **webPage.html** page.

It is important that you remember to click the Publish button if you wish to preview the new settings you have created. Macromedia Flash MX will update the HTML document with the new setting applied to it only if you click the Publish button or choose File > Publish.

19. To see the difference this setting makes, open the file **webPage** file again. Try resizing the browser window by clicking and dragging the bottom right corner of the window. Notice that the .swf file scales this time! This is because the Percent setting allows the movie to fill the browser window 100 percent by 100 percent, so that no matter how you resize it, the movie will scale to fit the entire browser window and will not be cut off.

> **NOTE | Important Uploading Advice!**
>
> Macromedia Flash MX publishes the HTML file with the assumption that the .swf file will be located in the same folder as the HTML file, so when you upload the HTML file to a Web server, make sure you put both files in the same directory.

This exercise has taken you through many of the common Publish settings on the Flash and HTML tabs. For a more in-depth look at what each of the settings on these tabs can do, refer to the tables at the end of this chapter. Also, in Chapter 18, "Integration," you will learn how to control the .swf file inside an HTML document using Dreamweaver.

---

20. Save and close this file.

---

2. ——————————Creating Projectors

Have you ever received an email attachment that had the extension .exe or .hqx and found when you opened it that it was a Macromedia Flash movie that played right in its own window, without a browser? If you have, you may be more familiar with projector files than you think. Projector files are often sent via email because they are stand-alone files that can play with or without the Macromedia Flash MX Player on most computers! Projector files can also be distributed via floppy disks or CD-ROMs or shown from your hard drive without a browser (as a great PowerPoint substitute!). This exercise will teach you how to create a projector file using the Publish Settings dialog box.

1. Open the **projector.fla** file from the **chap_16** folder. This is the project file you used in the sound synchronizing exercise in Chapter 13. You'll take the file one step further by turning it into a stand-alone projector file in the steps that follow.

2. Choose **Control > Test Movie** to preview the movie. When you do this, Macromedia Flash MX will create the .swf file and save it in the same folder as the .fla file, as you learned in the last exercise.

3. Close the **Preview Window** and, back in the project file, choose **File > Publish Settings**. This will open the **Publish Settings** dialog box.

4. Uncheck the boxes next to the Format Types **Flash** and **HTML**, because you will be working with projector files in this exercise. Check the boxes next to **Windows Projector** and **Macintosh Projector**.

5. Uncheck the box next to **Use default names** and enter the name **wProjector.exe** in the **Windows Projector Filename** field and **mProjector** in the **Macintosh Projector Filename** field. This will give each of your projector files its own unique name. Click **Publish** when you are finished.

When you click Publish, Macromedia Flash MX automatically saves the projector files to the same folder as your .fla file.

6. Click OK **to close the** Publish Settings **dialog box.** Open the **chap_16** folder on your hard drive. Inside you will see five files and one folder: the **publishTesting** folder from Exercise 1, the original project file, **projector**, the .swf file that was created when you chose Control > Test Movie in step 2 of this exercise, the **exportingImages.fla** that you will use for Exercise 4, and two new projector files named **mProjector** and **wProjector**.

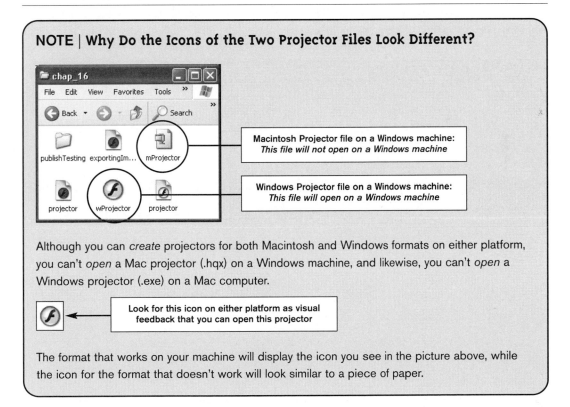

NOTE | Why Do the Icons of the Two Projector Files Look Different?

Macintosh Projector file on a Windows machine:
This file will not open on a Windows machine

Windows Projector file on a Windows machine:
This file will open on a Windows machine

Although you can *create* projectors for both Macintosh and Windows formats on either platform, you can't *open* a Mac projector (.hqx) on a Windows machine, and likewise, you can't *open* a Windows projector (.exe) on a Mac computer.

Look for this icon on either platform as visual feedback that you can open this projector

The format that works on your machine will display the icon you see in the picture above, while the icon for the format that doesn't work will look similar to a piece of paper.

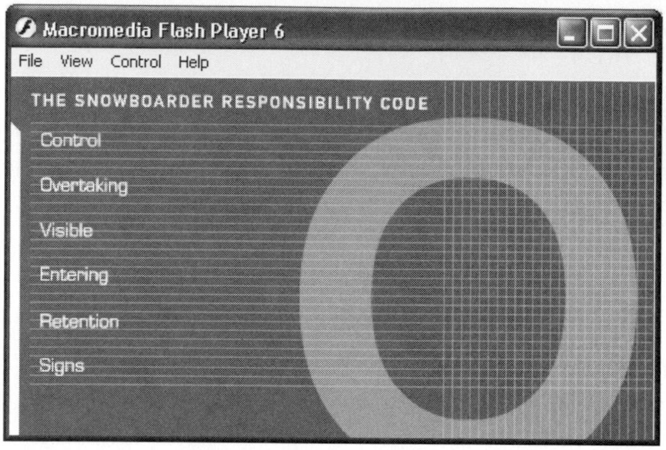

7. If you're using Windows, double-click on the file named **wProjector** to open it. If you're on a Mac, double-click on the file named **mProjector** to open it. You have just created your first projector file. Notice that the sound and animation play. This is because the projector file takes the entire movie, sound and all, and displays it in its own player.

NOTE | Missing Tabs in the Projector Publish Settings?

When you select the projector file types from the Formats tab in the Publish Settings dialog box, no additional tabs become available for you to alter the settings. However, you can control the way your projectors behave by using ActionScript and FSCommands. You will do this in the next exercise.

---

8. Click **OK** to close the **Publish Settings** dialog box. Save this file and keep it open for the next exercise.

---

3. ———————————Modifying Projectors with FSCommands

In the last exercise, you learned how to create a projector file. This exercise will show you how to modify the original project file by adding ActionScript to control the stand-alone player. The following steps will teach you how to use **FSCommands** to force the movie to take up the full screen of the computer and to disable the menu so that users cannot right-click or Ctrl+click on the movie and see a list of menu items.

1. You should have the same file open from the last exercise, **projector.fla**. Save this file under a new name, **fsProjector.fla**.

2. Click the **Insert Layer** button to add a new layer to the movie. Rename the new layer **actions**. Make sure this layer is on top of all the other layers.

3. Click on the first keyframe of the **actions** layer, and press **F9** to open the **Actions** panel. You will add the ActionScript to control the stand-alone player in this keyframe next.

NOTE | FSCommands as Frame Actions

It is usually most effective to add the FSCommands that control the window behavior to one of the first keyframes in the movie. This enables your commands to take effect immediately, as soon as the player opens.

What Are FSCommands?

FSCommands are actions that invoke JavaScript functions from Macromedia Flash MX. They include a command that is similar to an instruction, and an argument that checks to see if the command should be allowed (true) or not (false). A chart at the end of this exercise describes the FSCommands for the stand-alone player.

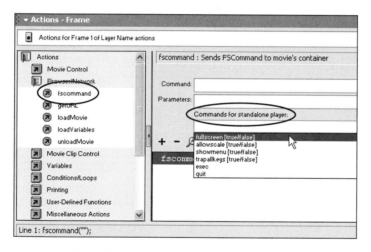

4. In the **Actions Toolbox**, choose **Actions > Browser/Network** and double-click on **fscommand** to add it to the **Script** pane. In the **Commands for standalone player** drop-down menu, select **fullscreen [true/false]**. This will make the projector launch and completely fill the user's screen.

Notice that this command automatically populates the Command and Parameters fields. The fullscreen command makes the player take up the whole screen and prevents screen resizing when the parameter is set to true.

5. Choose **File > Publish Settings**. In the **Publish Settings** dialog box, rename the projector files **fsWprojector.exe** and **fsMprojector.hqx**. This will allow Macromedia Flash MX to publish two new files without replacing the old projector files you made in the last exercise. When you are finished, click **Publish** to publish the projectors with the FSCommands added.

6. Open the **chap_16** folder on your hard drive. Inside you will see all the files you have created this far. If you are using Windows, double-click on the file named **fsWProjector**. If you are on a Mac, double-click on the file named **fsMProjector** to open it. Now the projector will launch full screen! To exit the full-screen mode, simply press **Esc** on the keyboard.

7. In the project file, make sure that **Frame 1** is still selected in the **actions** layer. In the **Actions** panel, double-click on the **fscommand** action again to add it to the **Script** pane. This will add another FSCommand to the projector file.

8. In the **Script** pane, in the drop-down menu for the **Commands for standalone player**, select the **showmenu [true/false]** option. This will populate the Command and Parameters fields. Change the **Parameters** field text to **false**. When the Parameters field is set to false, this command prevents the user from being able to right-click (Windows) or Ctrl+click (Mac) to access the full list of menu items.

While a projector is playing, the user can either right-click (Windows) or Ctrl+click (Mac) to view a list of menu items. If the projector is set to full screen, you may not want to allow your users to zoom in or out or manipulate the way the movie is presented to them. By disabling the menu (setting show-menu to false), you can limit the control that users have.

9. Choose **File > Publish**. This will publish the changes you made (adding the new FSCommand) to the file formats that you specified in the Publish Settings dialog box.

10. Open the **chap_16** folder on your hard drive. If you are using Windows, double-click on the file named **fsWprojector**. If you are using a Macintosh, double-click on the projector file named **fsMprojector**. Try to right-click (Windows) or Ctrl+click (Mac) to access the drop-down menu and see the full list of menu items. You should not be able to do it! You should see only the About Macromedia Flash Player 6 and Settings menu items. This is because you set the argument to false in the Parameters field, thereby preventing the user from seeing the full menu and using any of the options within it.

11. When you are finished testing the projector, save and close this file.

FSCommands for the Stand-Alone Player Defined		
Command	**Arguments**	**Function**
fullscreen	true/false	Sets the movie to fill the full screen when set to true, and returns the movie to a normal window when set to false. Setting the movie to full screen without also setting *allowscale* to false can result in the movie changing scale in some cases.
allowscale	true/false	Enables or disables the user's ability to scale the movie. If the argument is set to false, the movie will always be presented at the original size and can never be scaled. It also prevents the scaling that occurs when the movie is set to full screen. It is important to note that this option refers to the Macromedia Flash movie itself and not the stand-alone player window, since the user can still scale the player window bigger or smaller by clicking and dragging on an edge of it. However, the movie will remain at the original size if *allowscale* is set to false. Note also that if *showmenu* is not set to false, the user can still scale the movie by right-clicking (Windows) or Ctrl+clicking (Mac) to access the drop-down Options menu, which includes Zoom In and Zoom Out options.
showmenu	true/false	When set to true, enables a user to right-click or Ctrl+click on the projector and have access to the full set of context menu items. When this command is set to false, it disables the user's ability to access any of the menu items except for the About Flash Player item.
trapallkeys	true/false	When set to true, enables the movie to capture keystrokes that the user enters on the keyboard.
exec	path to application	Allows you to launch another application file on the local system. For this to work properly, you must know the correct path and name of the application. You must type the correct path and name of the application in the Parameters field. If you are calling a file in the same directory, all you need is the file name.
quit	none	Closes the projector.

To Publish or to Export?

In Macromedia Flash MX, in addition to the publishing features that you have learned in the last three exercises, you can also use the Export features, which will allow you to export content that can be edited in other programs such as an Adobe Illustrator document or a bitmap image. Many of the Export settings are very similar to the Publish settings, but the workflow involved in exporting an image is different from that of publishing an image, for example. In the following exercise, you will learn how to export a PNG image from a Macromedia Flash MX file. A chart follows with the file formats you can export from Macromedia Flash MX.

Export File Types Supported by Macromedia Flash MX			
File Format	**Extension**	**Windows**	**Mac**
Adobe Illustrator 8.0 or earlier	.ai	x	x
Animated GIF and GIF Image	.gif	x	x
Bitmap	.bmp	x	
AutoCAD DXF Image or DXF Sequence	.dxf	x	x
Enhanced Windows Metafile	.emf	x	
EPS (6.0 and earlier)	.eps	x	x
Flash Movie	.swf	x	x
FutureSplash Player	.spl	x	x
JPEG Image and JPEG Sequence	.jpg	x	x
PICT sequence	.pct	x	
PNG Image and PNG Sequence	.png	x	x
Macromedia Freehand	fh7, .ft7, fh8, .ft8, .fh9, .ft9, .fh10	x	x
QuickTime Video	.mov	x	
WAV Audio	.wav	x	
Windows AVI	.avi	x	
Windows Metafile	.wmf	x	

4. ——————Exporting Image Files

In the last three exercises, you worked with the Publish settings in Macromedia Flash MX, and you learned how to publish different types of files. This exercise will show you another option for producing different file types from your project file: the Export options. If you know that you want to export only an image from your project file so that you can work with it in another application, using the Export settings can be a great solution. You will learn how to do this in the steps that follow.

1. Open the **exportingImages.fla** file from the **chap_16** folder. This is a project file similar to the one you made in Chapter 10, "*Movie Clips.*"

2. Choose **Control > Test Movie** to preview the movie. Notice the animating logo. This is a Movie Clip symbol instance that you will work with next. When you are finished, close the **Preview Window**.

Suppose that you love the logo you made inside Macromedia Flash MX, but you want to have it as an image file all by itself, so that you can use it on a business card. In the following steps you will learn how to export only the logo in the picture above from the project file as a PNG image.

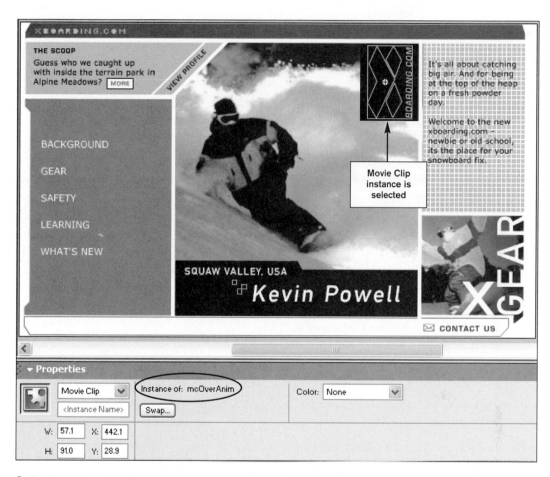

THE SCOOP
Guess who we caught up with inside the terrain park in Alpine Meadows? [MORE]

BACKGROUND

GEAR

SAFETY

LEARNING

WHAT'S NEW

VIEW PROFILE

XBOARDING.COM

It's all about catching big air. And for being at the top of the heap on a fresh powder day.

Welcome to the new xboarding.com – newbie or old school, its the place for your snowboard fix.

Movie Clip instance is selected

SQUAW VALLEY, USA
"Kevin Powell

X GEAR

✉ CONTACT US

▼ Properties

Movie Clip
<Instance Name>
Swap...

Instance of: mcOverAnim

Color: None

W: 57.1   X: 442.1
H: 91.0   Y: 28.9

3. Back in the project file, select the logo on the **Stage** and notice the setting in the **Property Inspector**—this is an instance of the Movie Clip named **mcOverAnim**.

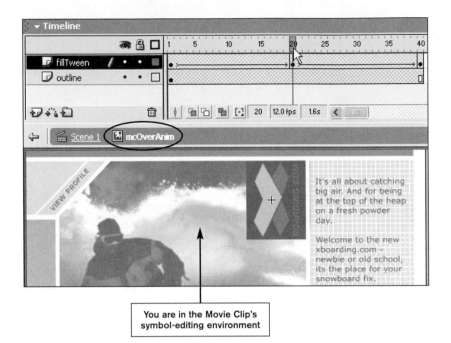

You are in the Movie Clip's
symbol-editing environment

4. Double-click on the Movie Clip instance to open the Movie Clip's **Timeline**. Scrub the **Playhead** to find out where in the tween animation the logo is in full color.

You want to export the logo in full color, not the logo outline, so you need to find the frame that has the full-color logo. This happens to be Frame 20.

*At this point, you might be wondering, Don't I need to select the image or the frame? When you choose Export Image, you have several ways to decide what is being exported. Macromedia Flash MX will either export the **frame that the Playhead is over** (and all layers under that frame), export a **selected frame** (and all layers under and over that frame), or export a **selected image** (including the frame the image is on and all layers under and over that frame). Therefore, based on what is selected or where the Playhead is, Macromedia Flash MX will export the appropriate artwork.*

5. Position the **Playhead** over **Frame 20** and choose **File > Export Image**. In the **Export Image** dialog box that pops up, name the file **logo** and choose **PNG** from the **Save as type** drop-down list. Make sure you save the image in the **chap_16** folder. Click **Save**.

6. When you click the **Save** button, you will be presented with another dialog box specific to the file type you've chosen to export: a PNG file. In this window, you can leave the settings at their defaults and click **OK**.

*The chart that follows details the settings available to you. **Note:** If you were saving this image for use in a page layout program, you might want to increase the resolution to 150 to 300 dpi so it would print at a higher quality than the screen resolution.*

PNG Export Settings	
Option	**Description**
Dimensions	Allows you to set the size of the exported PNG image by entering the width and height into the corresponding fields.
Resolution	Allows you to specify the resolution in dots per inch. Clicking on the **Match Screen** button will generate a PNG image that uses the screen resolution and maintains the aspect ratio of the original image in the project file.
Include	Lets you export either the minimum image area or the full document size.
Colors	Sets the number of colors (bits per pixel) that will be used in the exported file. As the bit depth increases, the file size increases as well. **8-bit:** Creates a 256-color image. **24-bit:** Creates an image using thousands of colors. **24-bit with Alpha:** Creates an image with thousands of colors and allows transparency.
Filter Options	Allows you to choose a filtering method that produces an image at the best quality and smallest file size.
Options	**Interlaced:** Causes the image to appear in stages as it is downloaded. **Smooth:** Causes the PNG image to become antialiased, which can increase file size. **Dither solid colors:** Matches colors that are not part of the 256-color palette as closely as possible by mixing similar colors.

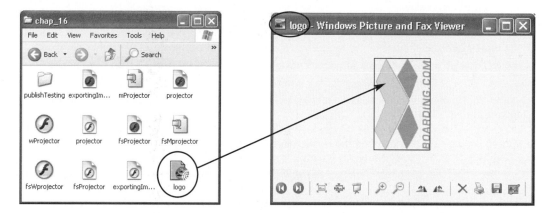

7. Open the **chap_16** folder on your hard drive. Inside you will see all the files you have created so far. Notice the **logo** file. Double-click on the **logo** file to open it in your default image viewing program. You will see the logo all by itself, without any other images from the project file. Neat!

8. When you are finished, save and close this file.

TIP | Export Versus Publish for Image Files

In this exercise you learned to export an image using the export feature in Macromedia Flash MX. You can also publish an image using the Publish settings, although the workflow is a bit more involved and there are considerable limitations. If you want to use the Publish settings to publish a PNG file, for example, you need to enter a frame label of #Static on the keyframe you want to publish. (This will publish the keyframe and all the layers above and below it on that same frame.) If you do not enter the frame label of #Static, Macromedia Flash will export the first frame (with all the layers) of the movie as a PNG file. Beyond a more labor-intensive workflow, a major drawback to using the Publish settings to output a PNG file from your project file is that the Publish settings don't recognize the #Static label inside a Movie Clip, Button, or Graphic symbol, so you are limited to frames on the Main Timeline. The export feature, on the other hand, will recognize the location of the Playhead no matter where it is, so you have a more streamlined workflow and more flexibility.

More About the Publish Settings

The first three exercises in this chapter taught you firsthand how to use some of the Publish settings. I'm sure you noticed many settings that weren't covered in the exercises. This section covers how to export other kinds of media from Macromedia Flash MX using the Publish settings. I will begin with the settings on the Flash tab and then move on to HTML, GIF, JPEG, PNG, and QuickTime, ending with a description of the settings for projector files.

The Publish settings are all located in the Publish Settings dialog box, displayed by choosing **File >** **Publish Settings**. You can change these settings at any point while developing or editing your project file (.fla). The Publish Settings dialog box is divided into a number of tabs.

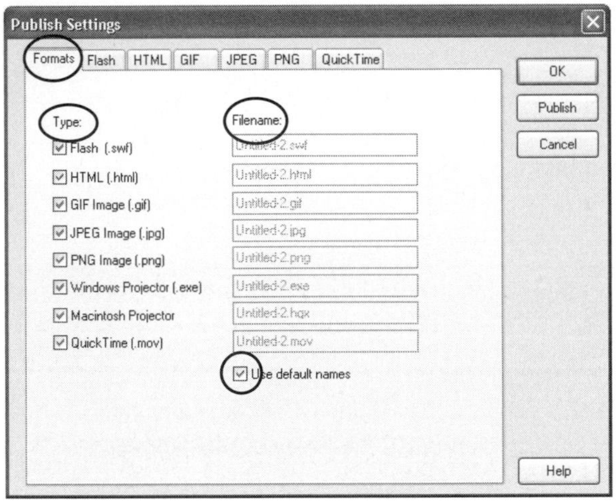

Formats Tab

The first tab is the Formats tab. It allows you to select the file formats that Macromedia Flash MX will publish. As each format is selected, additional tabs will appear to the right of the Formats tab, with the exception of the Windows Projector and Macintosh Projector types. Each tab holds settings specific to the selected format that can be modified. I will cover each of the format types in detail below. The Formats tab also allows you to modify the filename of each selected format that Macromedia Flash MX will publish.

Filename

As you saw in Exercise 1, if the **Use default names** box is checked, all file formats you choose to create will have the same name as the original project file. If the **Use default names** box is unchecked, you can create a unique name for each of the file formats you select.

Type

In the Type section under the Formats tab, you can select the type of files you wish to publish. I will cover each of the types in the pages that follow.

Flash Settings

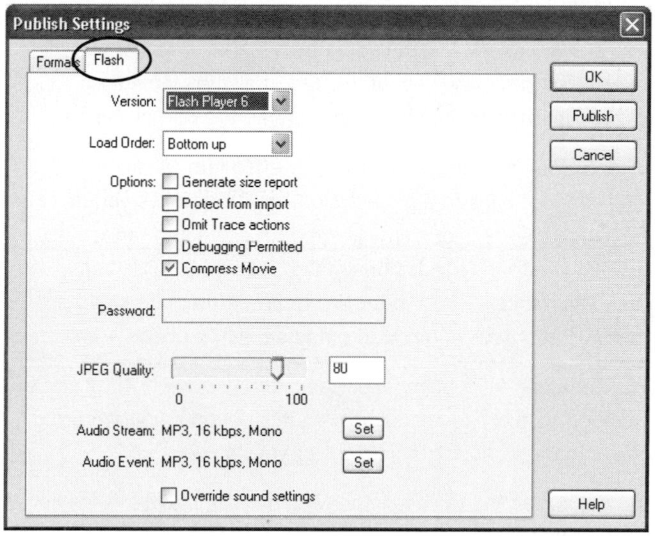

The Flash tab contains all of the settings that will be used for the .swf file, which is the file you have been viewing when you choose Control > Test Movie. The .swf file is embedded in the HTML document so that the movie can be seen on the Web. A detailed description of each option under the Flash tab appears below.

Flash Publish Settings	
Version	Allows you to export earlier formats of Macromedia Flash .swf files. The real value of this feature is that it provides you the means to import work you did in Macromedia Flash MX into earlier versions of Macromedia Flash, such as Macromedia Flash 5.
Load Order	Sets whether the layers will be loaded from the top down or the bottom up. For example, **Bottom up** means that the lowest layer will be shown first, the second lowest next, etc. The reverse is true of **Top down.** This load setting takes place only when you have multiple elements loading in different layers in the same frame slot, and on a fast connection you may never see this happen. However, as you learned in Chapter 11, "*ActionScripting Basics*," you should always place your actions on the top layer. For this reason, you should select **Top down** so that your ActionScripting layer will load first. The frames (not layers) will always load in numeric order.

continues on next page

Flash Publish Settings *continued*	
Generate size report	Checking this box will cause Macromedia Flash MX to create a text file that contains detailed information about the size of all the elements in your movie. It will be published to the same directory as the rest of the files.
Protect from import	Prevents anyone from importing your .swf movie file into Macromedia Flash and converting it back to a project file (.fla). This allows you to protect your work. However, you can still import a protected movie into a Macromedia Director movie. Additionally, the SWIFFER utility can break into any Macromedia Flash movie, so to be on the safe side, don't put sensitive information into Macromedia Flash movies.
Omit Trace actions	Blocks the Trace action from being exported with your movie. (The Trace action is a debugging tool.) You should select this option if you are using Trace actions and are producing a final cut of your movie.
Debugging Permitted	Activates the debugger and will allow the Macromedia Flash MX movie to be debugged remotely.
Compress Movie	Compresses the Macromedia Flash MX movie to reduce file size and download time. This option is selected by default and works best when a movie has a lot of text or ActionScripting. This option is available only for Macromedia Flash MX.
Password	Allows you to set a password that others have to enter before they debug your movie. This can prevent unauthorized users from debugging a movie.
JPEG Quality	Allows you to set the default image quality Export setting for all of the bitmap graphics in your movie. To retain greater control over your image fidelity and file size, I recommend that you bypass this setting and use the individual settings for each file in the Library instead.
Audio Stream	Allows you to set separate audio compression types and settings for all sounds in the movie that have a Stream Sync type and that have a compression type of Default.
Audio Event	Allows you to separately set the audio compression type and settings for all sounds in the movie that have a Start or Event Sync type and whose compression type is set to Default.
Override sound settings	Checking this box allows you to force all sounds in the movie to use the settings here, instead of using their own compression settings.

HTML Settings

The HTML tab allows you to set values that determine how the HTML file is created for your movie. The HTML file is needed as a container to embed the .swf file if you plan to publish to the Web. By changing the settings under the HTML tab, you can change the appearance of your .swf file when viewed from a browser. The chart that follows describes the available options.

HTML Publish Settings	
Template	Allows you to choose from a list of premade HTML templates. Each of these templates was built to provide different types of support for the movie. If you don't choose a template, the default template will be used.
Dimensions	Allows you to set the dimensions that the Macromedia Flash movie will be set to in the HTML tags. This value can be in pixels or it can be a percentage of window size. A setting of **Match Movie** will not allow the .swf file to scale in the browser. A percentage setting will allow the .swf content to scale if the user resizes the browser window.

continues on next page

HTML Publish Settings *continued*	
Playback	Allows you to define how the movie will act in the browser. You can check **Paused at Start** to force the movie to start in a stopped position, without using a Stop action in the first keyframe. You can deselect the **Loop** check box to make the movie play only once. If you deselect the **Display Menu** option, the Control menu will be disabled in the browser window. The **Device Font** option applies to a Macromedia Flash movie playing on a Windows Macromedia Flash Player. If this option is selected, it allows the movie to use the local antialiased system font on the user's system instead of the font(s) embedded in the movie.
Quality	Sets whether the movie will be played back with emphasis on graphics quality or playback speed. **High** emphasizes graphics quality over speed, whereas **Low** emphasizes playback speed over appearance.
Window Mode	Determines how the movie interacts in a DHTML environment. This setting has an effect only on browsers that are using absolute positioning and layering.
HTML Alignment	Sets the horizontal alignment of the Macromedia Flash movie within the HTML page in a browser window.
Scale	Determines how the Macromedia Flash movie resizes within the movie window on the HTML page.
Flash Alignment	Determines how the movie is aligned within the Macromedia Flash movie window. This determines how the movie will look if it is zoomed or cropped.
Show Warning Messages	Toggles whether or not the browser will display error messages that occur within the Object or Embed tags.

GIF Settings

The GIF file format can be used to produce animated graphics and static graphics. For example, if you create an icon in Macromedia Flash MX that you want to save to use in other applications, you can select the GIF file type under the Formats tab. By default, Flash will output the first frame of the movie as a GIF unless you specify a particular keyframe by entering the frame label #Static on the keyframe you select. Use caution, because Macromedia Flash MX will publish all the frames in the current movie as an animated GIF unless you designate a range of frames by entering the frame labels #First and #Last in the corresponding keyframes. The GIF settings are explained in detail in the chart that follows.

GIF Publish Settings	
Dimensions	Allows you to set the size of the GIF by entering the width and height into the corresponding fields. Checking the **Match Movie** box will generate a GIF that has the same dimensions that were set in the Movie Properties dialog box in the project file.
Playback	Determines whether the GIF will be static or animated. If the **Static** radio button is selected, the first keyframe of the movie will be used as the GIF image. If you would like a different keyframe to be used as the GIF image, you can add the label #Static to the selected keyframe, and Macromedia Flash MX will export the labeled keyframe instead. If the **Animated** radio button is selected, Macromedia Flash MX will export the whole project file as an animated GIF. If you want to export only a selection of frames, add these labels to the first and last keyframes: #First and #Last. If **Loop Continuously** is selected, the GIF will repeat the animation over and over. If **Repeat** is selected, you can manually enter the number of times you want the animated GIF to loop before it stops.

continues on next page

GIF Publish Settings *continued*	
Options	**Optimize Colors:** Removes unused colors to decrease file size. **Interlace:** Causes the image to appear in stages as it is downloaded. **Smooth:** Causes the GIF to become antialiased, which can increase file size. **Dither Solids:** Matches colors that are not part of the 256-color palette as closely as possible by mixing similar colors. **Remove Gradients:** Changes all gradients to solid colors, thereby reducing file size.
Transparent	**Opaque:** Causes the background of the image to appear solid. **Transparent:** Causes the background of the image to appear invisible. **Alpha:** Controls the background and all shapes that have an alpha setting applied to them. Allows you to set the threshold so that all colors above the specified amount will be solid and all colors that have an alpha setting below the specified amount will be transparent.
Dither	**None:** Matches any color that is not within the 256-color palette with the closest color from within the 256 colors, rather than using dithering. **Ordered:** Matches any color that is not within the 256-color palette, using dithering from a pattern of colors. **Diffusion:** Matches any color that is not within the 256-color palette, using dithering from a random pattern of colors. This creates the closest match of colors but has the greatest increase in file size of these three options.
Palette Type	**Web 216:** Creates a GIF file using the 216 Web-safe colors. **Adaptive:** Creates a GIF file using only the Web-safe colors that were actually used within the GIF. **Web Snap Adaptive:** Creates a GIF file that substitutes Web-safe colors for any colors that are not Web safe but are a close match. **Custom:** Allows you to use a custom palette for the GIF file. When you select this option, the **Palette** option becomes active as well (see below).
Max Colors	Determines the maximum number of colors created within the palette when either the **Adaptive** or **Web Snap Adaptive** option is selected. The smaller the number, the smaller the file size, but this can degrade the image colors.
Palette	Allows you to select your own custom color palette from your hard drive.

JPEG Settings

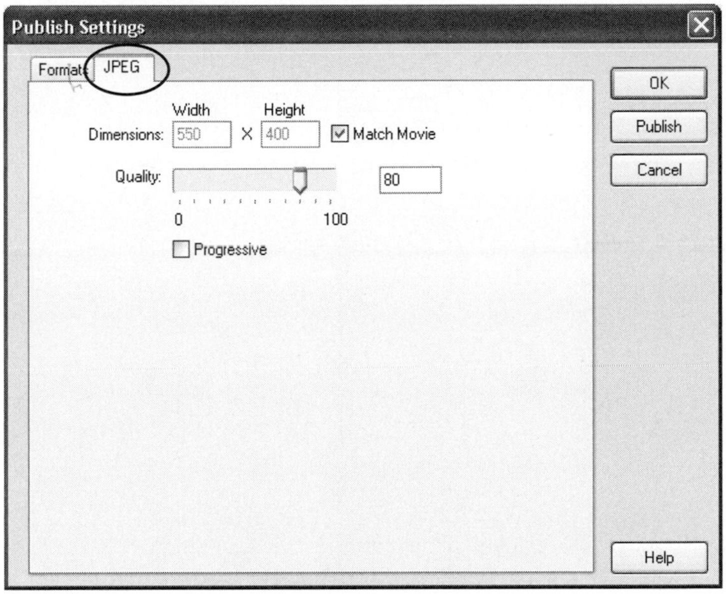

The JPEG file format can be used for images that have more detail than GIF images generally do, such as photographs. Although JPEG images cannot be animated, they can have an unlimited number of colors, rather than having to fall within a specific color palette. By default, Flash will output the first frame of the movie as a JPEG unless you specify a particular keyframe by entering the frame label #Static on the keyframe you select. The chart below describes the available options for publishing a JPEG image.

JPEG Publish Settings	
Dimensions	Allows you to set the size of the JPEG by entering the width and height into the corresponding fields. If the **Match Movie** box is checked, the JPEG will have the same dimensions as the project file's Movie Properties settings.
Quality	Sets the amount of compression, from 0 (lowest quality and smallest file size) to 100 (highest quality and largest file size).
Progressive	Allows the image to appear in stages as it is downloaded.

PNG Settings

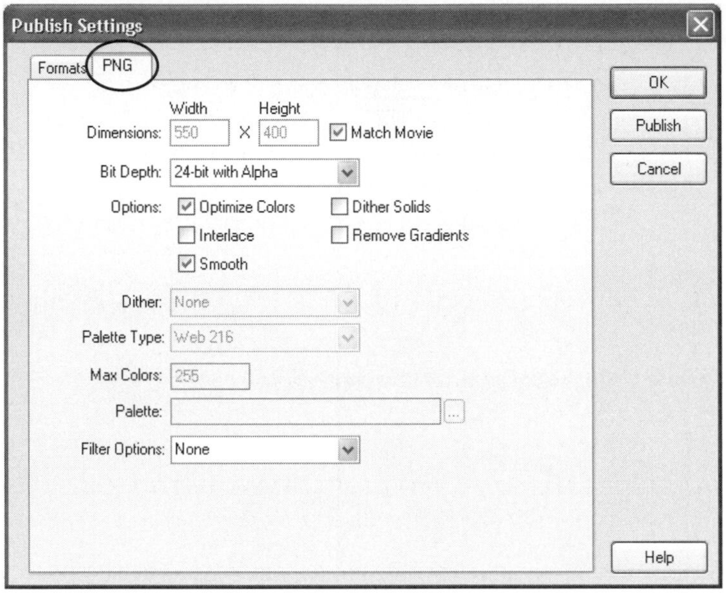

The PNG file format can be used to produce static graphics. Similar to the GIF format, the PNG format supports transparency. By default, Flash will output the first frame of the movie as a PNG unless you specify a particular keyframe by entering the frame label #Static on the keyframe you select. The PNG settings, which are similar to the GIF settings, are explained in detail in the chart below.

PNG Publish Settings	
Dimensions	Allows you to set the size of the PNG image by entering the width and height into the corresponding fields. Checking the **Match Movie** box will generate a PNG that has the same dimensions as those set in the Movie Properties dialog box in the project file.
Bit Depth	Sets the number of colors (bits per pixel) that will be used in the published file. As the bit depth increases, the file size increases as well. **8-bit:** Creates a 256-color image. **24-bit:** Creates an image using thousands of colors. **24-bit with Alpha:** Creates an image with thousands of colors and allows transparency. (The higher the bit depth, the larger the file.)

continues on next page

PNG Publish Settings *continued*	
Options	**Optimize Colors:** Removes unused colors to decrease file size. **Interlace:** Causes the image to appear in stages as it is downloaded. *Smooth:* Causes the PNG to become antialiased, which can increase file size. **Dither Solids:** Matches colors that are not part of the 256-color palette as closely as possible by mixing similar colors. **Remove Gradients:** Changes all gradients to solid colors, thereby reducing file size.
Dither	**None:** Matches any color that is not within the 256-color palette with the closest color from within the 256 colors, rather than using dithering. **Ordered:** Matches any color that is not within the 256-color palette, using dithering from a regular pattern of colors. **Diffusion:** Matches any color that is not within the 256-color palette by dithering from a random pattern of colors, creating the closest match of colors, but with the greatest increase in file size of these three options.
Palette Type	**Web 216:** Creates a PNG file using the 216 Web-safe colors. **Adaptive:** Creates a PNG file using only the colors within the 256 colors that were actually used within the PNG. **Web Snap Adaptive:** Creates a PNG file that substitutes Web-safe colors for any colors that are not Web safe but are a close match. **Custom:** Allows you to use a custom palette for the PNG file. When you select this option, the Palette option becomes active as well (see below).
Max Colors	Determines the maximum number of colors created within the palette when either the **Adaptive** or **Web Snap Adaptive** option is selected.
Palette	Allows you to select your own custom color palette (in the ACT format) from your hard drive.
Filter Options	Allows you to choose a filtering method that produces an image at the best quality and smallest file size.

QuickTime Settings

The QuickTime settings allow you publish the Macromedia Flash MX project file as a QuickTime 4 movie (.mov). The layers of the Macromedia Flash MX file will be converted to what is called the "Flash track" within the QuickTime movie. Chapter 18, "*Video*," will cover working with QuickTime in a step-by-step exercise. The chart that follows explains the QuickTime tab options in detail.

QuickTime Publish Settings	
Dimensions	Allows you to set the size of the QuickTime movie by entering the width and height into the corresponding fields. Checking the **Match Movie** box will generate a QuickTime movie that has the same dimensions as those set in the Movie Properties dialog box in the project file.
Alpha	Controls the transparency (alpha) of the Flash track in the QuickTime movie. **Auto:** Makes the Flash track opaque if it is the only track in the QuickTime movie or if it is located on the bottom of the other tracks. Makes the Flash track transparent if it is located on the top of other tracks. **Alpha Transparent:** Makes the Flash track transparent. Other tracks below the Flash track will show through the Flash track. **Copy:** Makes the Flash track opaque. Tracks below the Flash track will be masked.
Layer	Determines where the Flash track will reside relative to other tracks inside the QuickTime movie. **Top:** Positions the Flash track on top of all other tracks. **Bottom:** Positions the Flash track below all the other tracks. **Auto:** Positions the Flash track in front of the other tracks if Macromedia Flash MX content is placed in front of QuickTime content in the Macromedia Flash MX movie. Positions the Flash track behind the other tracks if Macromedia Flash MX content is placed in back of QuickTime content in the Macromedia Flash MX movie.
Streaming Sound	Allows you to convert all streaming audio in the Macromedia Flash MX project file into a QuickTime soundtrack.
Controller	Specifies the type of QuickTime controller that will be used to play the QuickTime movie.
Playback	**Loop:** The movie starts over at the beginning once the end is reached when this box is selected. **Paused at start:** The movie will start paused if this box is checked. When the user clicks a button, the movie will play. **Play every frame:** All sound is disabled and each frame plays without skipping when this box is checked.
File	**Flatten (Make self-contained):** Combines Macromedia Flash MX content and video content in one QuickTime movie. The Macromedia Flash MX file and video file will be referenced externally if the box is not selected.

Settings for Projector Files

Macromedia Flash MX can also be used to produce stand-alone applications for Windows or Mac machines.

Although there are no additional settings to choose from in the Publish Settings dialog box, you can select **Windows Projector** and **Macintosh Projector** in the Type options under the Formats tab. These projectors are self-contained files that can run on any computer, regardless of whether the user has the Macromedia Flash MX Player installed or not. You learned about projector files in depth in Exercise 3, earlier in this chapter.

Top Tips for Optimizing Movies

All movies in Macromedia Flash MX are not created equal. You can, however, use a few tricks and follow some simple guidelines to reduce the file size and increase the playback performance of your movie. The list below provides helpful tips to generate the best performance in your Macromedia Flash MX files.

Use symbols. Any time you use artwork multiple times in your project file, turn the artwork into a symbol. This will allow the artwork to be downloaded only once and used over and over without having any significant impact on file size.

Use solid lines wherever possible. Try to avoid using the dashed, dotted, or jagged line styles. Each dot, dash, or squiggle in these lines will be tracked as an independent object when the file is published. The jagged line style is the worst of the three. Lines using the jagged style contribute more than 100 times more bytes to the file size of your movie than do plain lines.

Use alpha sparingly. The more alpha, or transparency, that you have in the movie, the slower the playback performance will be. Using alpha will not increase file size, but it can have a dramatic impact on playback performance. If you do use alpha, try not to have too many transparent elements stacked on top of one another.

Use gradients sparingly. Although their impact is not as serious as alpha, gradients can also slow down playback performance.

Use the Optimize command on your vector artwork. By selecting an object and using the **Modify > Optimize** command, you can reduce the file size of your movie.

Use vector graphics rather than bitmaps wherever possible. Vector graphics are usually significantly smaller than bitmaps, which can keep the file size down.

Be aware of complex objects in animation. The more complex your object is, the slower the playback performance will be.

Use device fonts where appropriate. When you use device fonts, Macromedia Flash MX will not embed the outlines for your movie's fonts, as it otherwise does by default. Instead, Macromedia Flash MX will display the font on the user's machine that is closest to the specified font, saving file size.

Be cautious of looping streaming sound. When a sound's Sync option is set to Stream, it will play the sound at the same rate the animation is played. If you loop the streaming sound, Macromedia Flash MX will multiply the file size by the number of times you loop the sound. This is because when the Sync is set to Stream and you specify a number of loops, Macromedia Flash MX actually adds frames to the Timeline—so be careful of adding looping to streaming sound.

Turn layers into Guide layers. To prevent unwanted content from being exported, convert unwanted layers into Guide layers. For example, if you have artwork that you are using only for inspiration on a particular layer and you don't want to delete it but don't want that layer to end up in the movie, turn the layer containing the content into a Guide layer. Guide layers are not exported with the final movie, and this may save file size also.

Use the individual compression settings to compress imported bitmap graphics and sound files. By compressing each file individually, you can control the file size and image/sound quality, and often you can drastically reduce the image/sound file size from the original while keeping the image/sound quality relatively high.

Use the Load Movie command to keep file sizes small and to display content only on demand. With this command, rather than having one huge movie, you can create several smaller .swf files and load them into the main movie when the user requests the content by clicking on a button, for example.

Use the Generate Size Report feature to look at the breakdown of the .swf file, frame by frame. This report helps you identify places where you may be able to reduce the file size by compressing an image further, for example, or lets you spot a frame that is significantly larger than other frames.

Be aware of platform performance. Macromedia Flash MX plays slightly faster (frames per second) on a Windows machine than it does on a Macintosh. Ideally, before you distribute Macromedia Flash MX files or upload them to a live Web site, test the files on both a Mac and a Windows-based machine to make sure the movie performs to your expectations on both platforms.

You have completed another chapter and should be ready to distribute your Macromedia Flash MX movies all over the world! Before you do, you may want to hang on and finish the last two chapters—"Putting It All Together" and "Integration"—because they contain some valuable information.

17.

Putting It All Together

The Big Picture	Examining the Scenes and Layers
Managing Layers	Organizing the Library
Using the Movie Explorer	Building a Preloader	The Bandwidth Profiler
Printing from the Project File and the Macromedia Flash Player
Exporting the Scenes	Creating Draggable Movies

chap_17

Macromedia Flash MX
H•O•T CD-ROM

You may not realize it, but after working through the exercises in the previous chapters, you have actually created all the parts that make up a full, working Web site. This chapter will take you through the completed xboarding.com Web site and will point out many elements in the site that you've created within the exercises of this book. You will then have a chance to rebuild sections of the site to enhance it even further, such as adding a Preloader and creating draggable movies. Additionally, you will be introduced to several features within Macromedia Flash MX that allow you to maximize your production efficiency, including the Movie Explorer. Finally, you'll learn about the program's print capabilities.

I. ————————The Big Picture

This exercise introduces you to the completed xboarding.com Web site, which includes many of the exercise files you have created in previous chapters in this book. As you look through the site, you'll see references to previous chapters in which you covered the associated technique. You might find that you know more than you think you do!

1. Copy the **chap_17** folder, located on the **H•O•T CD-ROM**, to your hard drive. You need to have this folder on your hard drive in order to save files inside it.

2. Open the **xboardingSiteFinal.fla** file from the **siteFinal** folder inside the **chap_17** folder. This fully functional project file was created ahead of time for you, using many of the techniques that you learned in this book. You will learn how this was done in the following steps.

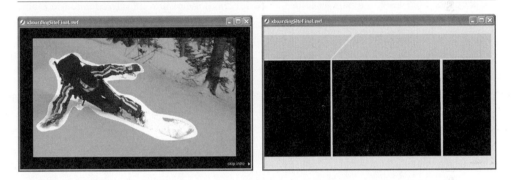

3. Choose **Control > Test Movie** to preview the movie. Notice the animation of the outline being drawn and the snowboarder fading up. You created this animation in Chapter 8, "*Bitmaps.*" Notice the next animation of the shapes turning into the interface. You created a piece similar to this in Chapter 5, "*Shape Tweening.*"

NOTE | Missing Fonts

When you choose Control > Test Movie, you may see a dialog box that says, "One or more of the fonts used by this movie are unavailable. Substitute fonts will be used for display and export. They will not be saved to the Macromedia authoring document." This simply means that your computer does not have some of the fonts that were used to create the artwork in this file. Go ahead and choose Use Default so that your computer will pick a default font to replace the unrecognizable fonts in the movie.

When creating your own projects, you can avoid this missing font issue altogether by working with your designer to select fonts that are common across multiple platforms, such as Arial, Verdana, or Helvetica. If you choose fonts that are likely to be included on all platforms, you will not see the "Missing Font" warning message. Also, please note that the end user will not encounter this problem, since the font outlines are embedded in the movie to be viewed with the Macromedia Flash Player. The only time this error message will occur is when you try to view a project file containing a font that is not installed on your computer.

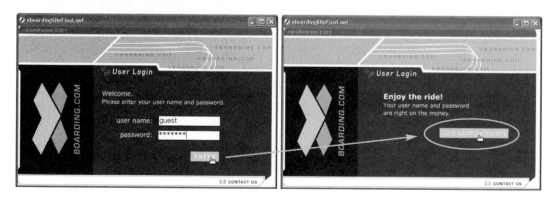

4. On the **User Login** screen, enter the user name **guest**, and for the password enter **gotsnow** in lowercase letters. On the next screen, click the **Click to Enter the Site** button, circled above, to enter the Web site. (You built a similar user name and password file in Chapter 11, "*ActionScripting Basics*.")

5. Notice the snowflake slowly falling down the screen. Does it look familiar? It is the same Motion Guide you created in Chapter 7, "*Motion Tweening*." Notice the logo animating near the top of the screen. You created this in Chapter 10, "*Movie Clips*." Click on the **Sound Off** and **Sound On** buttons to stop and start the sound. You created similar buttons to control sound in Chapter 13, "*Sound*."

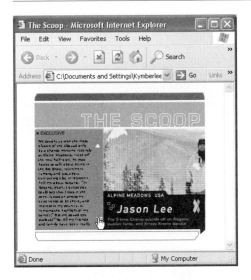

6. In the upper left corner of the interface, click the **More** button. This opens a browser window with the **thescoop.html** file embedded inside it. You created this file in Chapter 11, "*ActionScripting Basics*." Close the browser window when you are finished previewing the file.

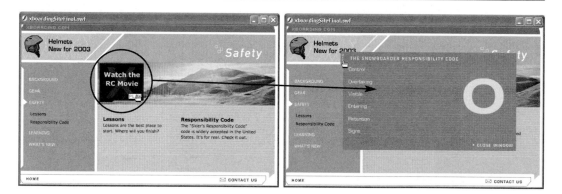

7. Back in the **Preview Window**, click on the **XGear** button in the lower right corner of the interface. This will load an order form into a level in the Macromedia Flash Player. This form is similar to the file you created in Chapter 14, "*Components and Forms*." Go ahead and test the components and click on the **Drag** button to drag the form around the window. When you are finished, click the **Close Window** button in the lower right corner of the form to unload the form from the Macromedia Flash Player. You will learn how to make the form draggable and make the Close Window button work in a later exercise in this chapter.

8. Click on the **Safety** button in the navigation menu. You'll see the same drop-down menu you built in Chapter 11, "*ActionScripting Basics*." On the **Safety** page of the Web site, click **Play** on the **Watch the RC Movie** button. This will load the Responsibility Code movie you made in Chapter 13, "*Sound*," into a level above the Main Timeline. Click the **Drag** button to drag the movie around the screen, and click the **Close Window** button to unload the movie from the Macromedia Flash Player.

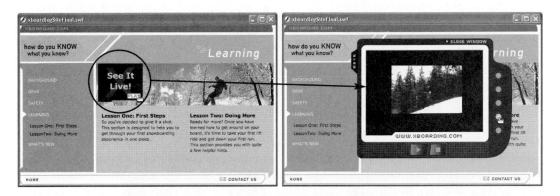

9. Click on the **Learning** button in the navigation menu. On the **Learning** page of the Web site, click **Play** on the **See It Live** button. This will load a movie similar to the one you made in Chapter 15, "*Video*," into a level above the Main Timeline. Click the **Drag** button to drag the movie around the screen, click the buttons inside the movie to see the different snowboarders, and click the **Close Window** button to unload the movie from the Macromedia Flash Player.

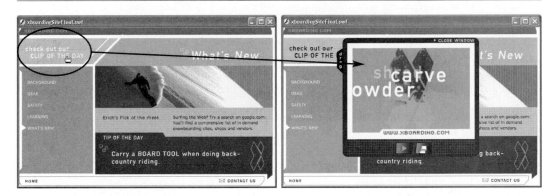

10. Click on the **What's New** button in the navigation menu. On the **What's New** page of the Web site, click the **Check Out Our Clip of the Day** button. This will load a movie that has features similar to the file you made in Chapter 15, "*Video*," into a level above the Main Timeline. Click the **Drag** button to drag the movie around the screen, click the **Start** and **Stop** buttons to play and stop the movie, and click the **Close Window** button to unload the movie from the Macromedia Flash Player.

Go ahead and explore this Web site to see how many of the pieces you recognize from your lessons thus far in the book. In later exercises of this chapter, you'll re-create parts of this project file to learn how to add some of the sections that are new, such as the draggable movie and Close Window button. When you are finished, keep the Preview Window open—you have one more area to look at next.

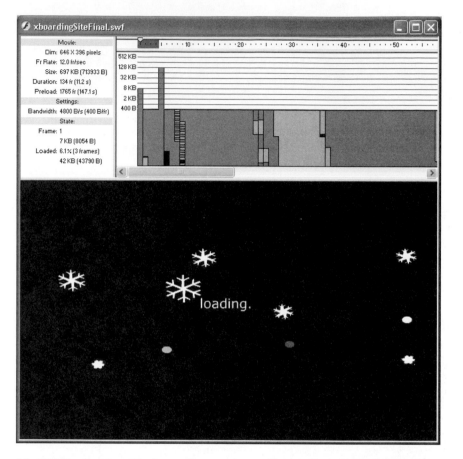

11. With the **Preview Window** still open, choose **View > Bandwidth Profiler**. Next choose **View > Show Streaming**. This will allow you to see the Preloader for the xboarding.com site.

A Preloader is a short animation that plays while ActionScripting checks to see how many frames from the main movie have downloaded to the user's computer. This technique is often used as a "loading" screen while a large Flash movie downloads to your end user's computer. You will build this Preloader in Exercise 6 in this chapter. The Bandwidth Profiler is a feature in the Test Movie environment. It allows you to see how the movie streams based on different connection speeds.

---

12. When you are finished, close the **Preview Window**, but keep the project file open for the next exercise.

After investigating the complete movie in the previous exercise, it is now time to take a closer look at the .fla file to see how the Web site was put together. The next several exercises will show you how the xboarding.com site was created, will highlight certain workflow techniques, and will introduce you to a few tools, including the Movie Explorer.

2. ————————Examining the Scenes

Scenes can be used to organize sections of content within the project file. You can use scenes to break up large projects into smaller, more manageable pieces. By default, Macromedia Flash MX will play all the scenes continuously in order unless you use ActionScript to tell it to do otherwise. If no ActionScripting is present in the Main Timeline to stop the movie, the Playhead will continue on to the next scene and will play the frames in each scene, one after another, until the end is reached or a **stop** action is encountered. You'll see when the **stop** action was added in this exercise. This exercise will also point out how scenes were used in the xboardingSiteFinal project file.

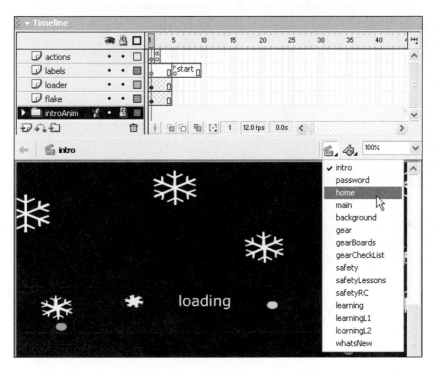

1. Inside the **xboardingSiteFinal** project file, click on the **Edit Scene** button in the **Information Bar** to reveal a menu listing the scenes within this project. Select the **home** scene to open that scene's Timeline.

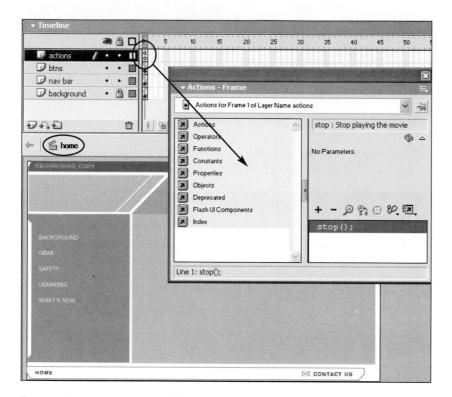

2. In the **home** scene, select **Frame 1** in the **actions** layer and open the **Actions** panel (**F9**). Notice that there is a **stop** action in the Script pane. This action will prevent Macromedia Flash MX from playing one scene right after another, since as soon as the Playhead hits the **stop** action in Frame 1 of the scene, it will stop.

3. Using the **Edit Scenes** button, select the **gear** scene to open that scene's Timeline.

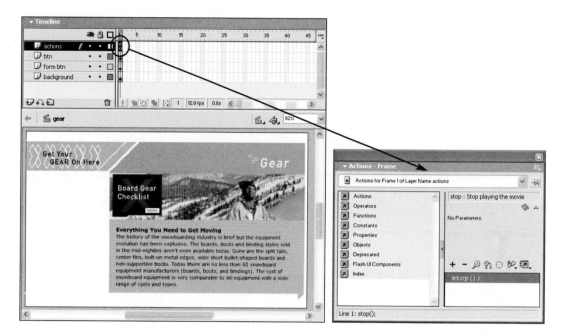

4. Click **Frame 1** of the **actions** layer to see another **stop** action. The purpose of this action is to cause Macromedia Flash MX to stop as soon as the Playhead reaches this frame and wait until the user interacts with the buttons before it continues.

5. Go ahead and use the **Edit Scenes** button to investigate each of the different scenes inside the **xboardingSiteFinal** project file.

The artwork in these scenes may look familiar to you. You used the .swf file for each of these scenes when you worked through the Loading movies exercise in Chapter 11, "ActionScripting Basics." What you never saw in Chapter 11 was the .fla file that created them. Did you suspect that there was a different .fla file for each of the .swf files? Although the xboarding Web site could have been created that way, it would have been a hassle to open each of the 15 different .fla files to change something. Instead, I used a different scene for each different "page" of the xboarding Web site, exported each scene individually using the Test Scene command, and then used the load movie ActionScripting, just as you did in Chapter 11, to load the correct page on demand when the user clicks a button. You will have a chance to export each of the scenes to re-create this same workflow in Exercise 9 of this chapter.

6. When you are finished, leave the file open for the next exercise.

Layer Management

Layers in Flash are similar to transparent sheets stacked one on top of another. Layers help you organize the content of the frames in the project file. For example, in Chapter 11, "*ActionScripting Basics*," you learned to get in the habit of adding an action layer on top of all other layers so that frame actions can always be found in the same place. In Chapter 13, "*Sound*," you learned to add a sound layer to the Timeline to keep the sounds consistently on the same layer and separate from others. Layers also play an important role in animation in Macromedia Flash MX. For instance, you learned in Chapter 5 "*Shape Tweening*," that if you want to tween multiple elements, each element that is tweened must be on its own separate layer. By default, all movies in Macromedia Flash MX have at least one layer, although you can add as many layers as you want to your movie.

Adding and Removing Layers

You can add a new layer by choosing **Insert > Layer** or by clicking on the **Insert Layer** button in the bottom left corner of the Timeline. You can click on the **Add Motion Guide** button to add a Guide layer. You can click on the **Insert Layer Folder** button to add a Layer Folder. You can remove a layer by clicking on the **Delete Layer** button (the Trashcan icon).

Types of Layers

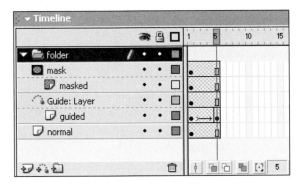

Throughout this book, you have worked with several kinds of layers in addition to a standard layer. There are three special types of layers: Guide layers, Mask layers, and Layer Folders.

Guide Layers

Guide layers come in two flavors: Motion Guide layers (Guide layers) and Guided layers. The difference between the two is that Motion Guide layers serve as a path for an object to follow and Guided layers contain the objects that follow the path.

Motion Guide layers are special layer types that are not exported when the movie is published or tested, and therefore they do not add to the size of the .swf file. These layers are visible only in the development environment. Use caution: While artwork on a Guide layer is not exported, actions on the layer *are* exported.

Mask Layers

Mask layers come in two flavors also: Mask layers and Masked layers. A Mask layer is a special layer that defines what is visible on the layer (or layers) below it. The layers that are attached or indented under the Mask layer are called Masked layers. Only layers that are beneath the shapes in the Mask layer will be visible.

Layer Folders

A Layer Folder is a special kind of layer that can hold other layers inside it. It is important to note that you cannot have artwork in a Layer Folder—the Layer Folder's sole purpose is to hold multiple layers so that you can keep your Timeline compact and organized.

In the next exercise, you will see an example of both a Motion Guide layer and a Layer Folder in the **xboardingSiteFinal.fla** project file.

3. _____Examining the Layers

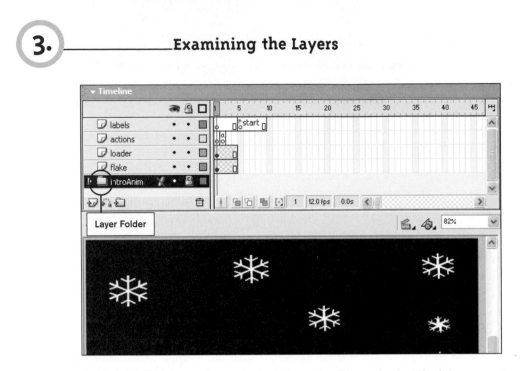

1. Click the **Edit Scene** button in the **Information Bar** and select the **intro** scene to open that scene's Timeline. Notice the **Layer Folder** in the Timeline.

Note: The layers above the Layer Folder (labels, actions, loader, and flake) make up the Preloader. You will re-create the Preloader in Exercise 6 of this chapter. The section preceding Exercise 6 describes how to create Layer Folders and discusses how they can benefit your workflow.

2. Click on the arrow to the left of the **Layer Folder** to expand all the layers inside the **Layer Folder**. **Tip:** You may have to resize the Timeline in order to view all of the layers. These layers make up the introductory animation that you saw when you previewed the movie in Exercise 1 of this chapter.

Tip: You can choose View > Magnification > Show All to resize the Stage so you can see everything.

3. Click on the **Edit Scene** button in the **Information Bar** and select the **main** scene to open that scene's Timeline.

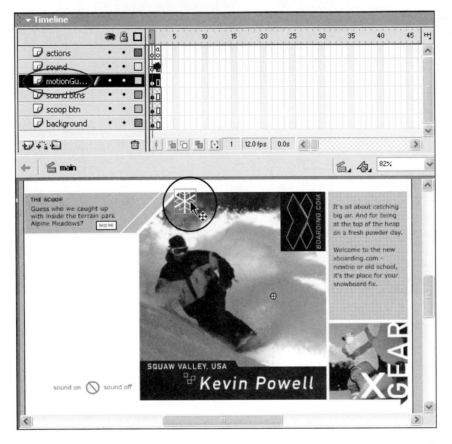

4. Click on the **snowflake** to select it. Notice that the **motionGuide** layer is highlighted in the **Timeline**. This snowflake travels down the Motion Guide that you created in the Chapter 7, "*Motion Tweening*."

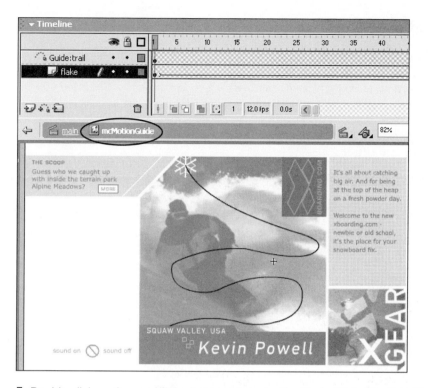

5. Double-click on the **snowflake** instance to enter the Movie Clip's Timeline. Once inside you will see the Guide layer, **Guide:trail** (which contains the path the snowflake will follow) and the Guided layer, **flake** (which contains the snowflake tween). This is similar to the file you create in Chapter 7, "*Motion Tweening*."

6. When you are finished, leave this file open for the next exercise.

Library Organization

Through your production work on Macromedia Flash MX projects, you will frequently use the Library for a variety of purposes, including opening files, dragging sounds or Movie Clips out to add them to the Timeline, renaming elements, or finding elements within a project, to name a few. Since you will often use the Library, it is important to keep it organized and consistent in its naming schemes.

| Organized Library | Unorganized Library |

These two examples show an organized Library on the left and an unorganized Library on the right. Would you rather search for a Movie Clip symbol in the Library on the left, which has consistently named elements, or in the Library on the right, which is disorganized and uses many different naming schemes, as well as inconsistently placed items in the folders?

In addition to helping improve your efficiency, organizing your Library can also help other individuals who may be working on the project with you. Here are several basic "Library etiquette" guidelines to keep in mind:

• Be consistent in your naming conventions. There is no "right way" to name the items within your project file, but once you decide on a structure to follow, stick to it. Since the Library sorts elements alphabetically, I recommend using prefixes at the beginning of the item name, such as btnHome or mcMenu. Again, there is no perfect way to name your elements. Instead, consistency is what matters.

• Choose brief, descriptive names, such as mcEffects, rather than meaningless letters, such as ef. This way, when you look for the Movie Clip at a later point, you can find it a lot easier, knowing that you have given it an accurate, descriptive name.

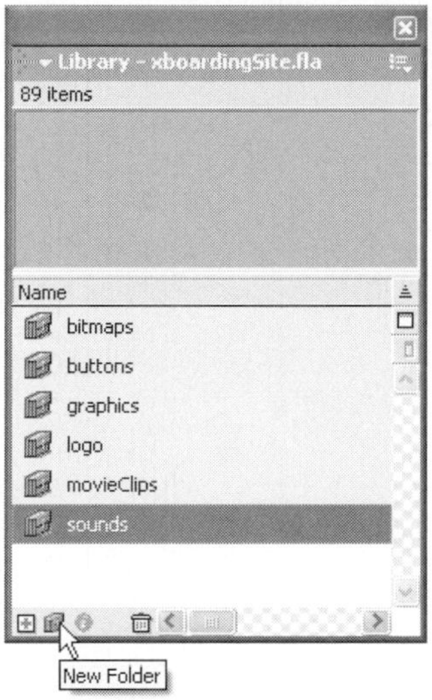

• Use folders to organize the Library elements, and stay consistent with the folder names. You can create a folder by clicking the New Folder button, shown in the picture above. Short, descriptive names will help you navigate through the Library faster, and you will know what to expect inside each folder before you open it.

4. ————————————Investigating the Library

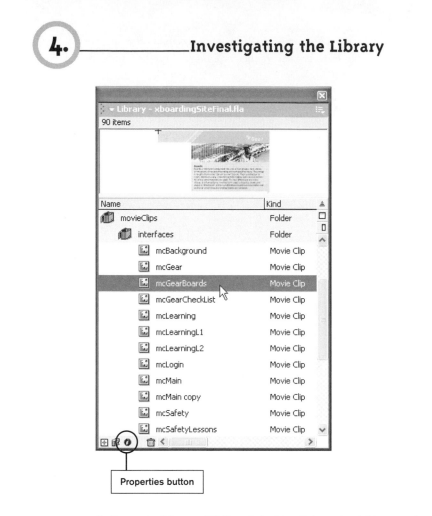

Properties button

1. Open the **Library** (**F11**) and double-click on the folders to view the elements inside them. Notice that all of the elements are named consistently and are located in the corresponding folders. Double-click on any Library item that intrigues you to open the symbol's Timeline, or select an item and click the Properties button to open the Properties dialog box to learn more about the element.

2. Continue to click around, expand and collapse the folders, and examine other elements inside the Library.

3. Click on the **Options** menu in the upper right corner of the Library window to view the drop-down list. Choose **Collapse All Folders**. This will collapse all the folders inside the Library.

4. Notice that there is one file named **bitmapBCloseUp** that is not inside a folder. Click once on the **bitmaps** folder to expand it and reveal the files inside. Try to drag the **bitmapBCloseUp** file that is outside the bitmaps folder into the **bitmaps** folder.

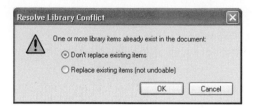

5. You will be presented with the **Resolve Library Conflict** dialog box. Choose **Don't replace existing items**, and click **OK**.

> **NOTE** | **What Is Library Conflict Resolution?**
>
> New to Macromedia Flash MX, the **Library Conflict Resolution** feature will detect when you try to put two items with the same name into the same Library folder. If you choose to replace the existing item, it will be replaced with the new one. If you choose not to replace the existing item, the new item will be given a slightly different name, keeping the original name and adding the word "copy" at the end.

6. After you click OK, notice that Macromedia Flash MX automatically added the word "copy" after the bitmap name. The conflict resolution feature is a great safeguard against accidentally writing over files!

7. When you are finished, save this file and leave it open for the next exercise.

5. —————————Using the Movie Explorer

The **Movie Explorer** is a handy tool that provides you with a visual representation of every aspect of the project file, organized into a hierarchical structure. You can use the Movie Explorer to view and locate just about every type of element within the project, including Graphic symbols, Button symbols, Movie Clip symbols, text, ActionScripts, frames, and scenes. This exercise will introduce you to the basic features of the Movie Explorer while looking at the **xboardingSiteFinal.fla** project file.

1. Choose **Window > Movie Explorer** to open the Movie Explorer.

TIP | Why Use the Movie Explorer?

The Movie Explorer can be used for many different purposes. It acts as a detective that displays a map that is customized to show what you want to see. For example, the Movie Explorer can be used to search and display all the text within a movie that uses the Verdana font. It can also be used to list all the Graphic symbols or even all the sounds within a scene. Additionally, it can locate a particular element when you know its name but not its location. The following steps take you through some of these examples.

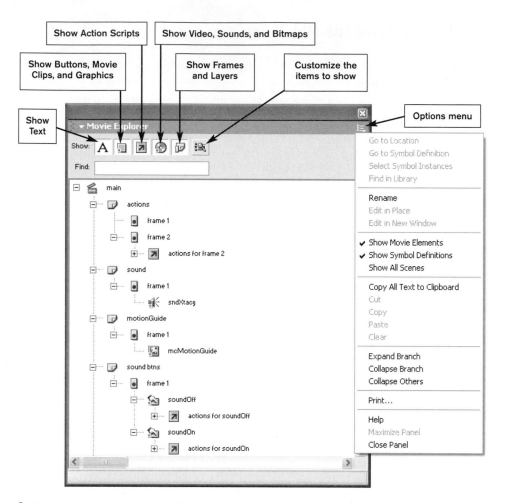

2. Click on the buttons next to **Show** to select the elements to be displayed. Once you have selected the categories you want to see, you can expand and collapse the folders within the display list window to reveal or hide the contents inside.

The Movie Explorer also allows you to search for an item by name, including font names, symbols, ActionScript, and frame numbers. You'll search for a specific item next.

3. From the **Options** menu, choose **Show All Scenes** to reveal the categories for all of the scenes.

4. In the **Find** text box, type the item name **btnClipOfDay** to search for this element within the project file. When Macromedia Flash MX finds the item, it will display it in the window. **Tip:** Make sure that the Show Buttons, Movie Clips, and Graphics filter button is depressed.

WARNING | Finding Files in the Movie Explorer

When you use the Find feature in the Movie Explorer, Macromedia Flash MX will search all the categories that are currently selected, not all the categories in the project file.

If, for example, you are searching for a button, make sure you have the second button (Show Buttons, Movie Clips, and Graphics) selected. Otherwise, the Movie Explorer will not find the item you are searching for. When you open the Movie Explorer for the first time, by default, the first three buttons (including the Show Buttons, Movie Clips, and Graphics category) are selected for you.

The Movie Explorer will also reveal ActionScript applied to frames and objects within the project file. You will see this next.

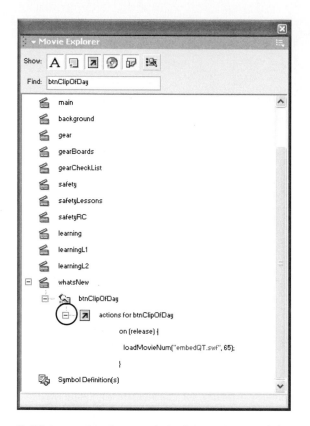

5. If it is not already expanded, click on the **plus** (+) sign next to the **actions for btnClipOfDay** text to reveal more elements related to that object. In this case, the Movie Explorer will reveal the actual ActionScript that is attached to the button instance. Using the Movie Explorer is a great way to learn how projects were built, since you can drill down to the actual ActionScripting on any object in the movie.

TIP | Viewing the Full Path

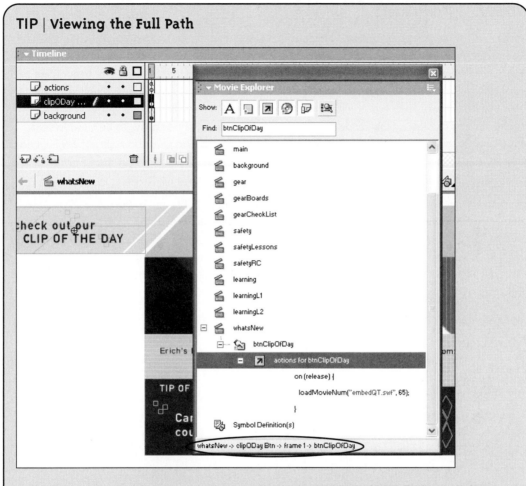

You can view the full path to the object selected at the bottom of the Movie Explorer window. Also, if the layer is not locked in the project file, Macromedia Flash MX will select the element on the Stage when you select it in the Movie Explorer.

6. When you are finished investigating the Movie Explorer, close the **xboardingSiteFinal** project file. You will be re-creating the Preloader in the xboarding.com Web site in the next exercise.

What Is a Preloader?

Macromedia Flash MX is a streaming format, which means that the movie can begin playing before it is completely downloaded. In many cases, this is good because the user doesn't have to wait until the whole movie finishes loading in order to see the beginning of the movie. On the other hand, there are times when you may not want the movie to be seen until all the frames have been downloaded–to assure smooth playback or synchronization with sound and the animation, for example. Additionally, there is no way of knowing the bandwidth available to the person who is going to be viewing your movie–dial-up, broadband, T1, or T3. Therefore, you may want to give users on a slower connection some type of visual feedback that the movie is being downloaded while they wait. One method of achieving both proper playback and giving visual feedback is to use a **Preloader**.

A Preloader can exist in the very first frames of the movie, in the first scene of the movie, or even at different points within the movie. It uses ActionScript that detects whether the .swf file has finished downloading or not. Once the whole movie (or an amount you specify) has downloaded onto the user's machine, the movie will play. You can put different artwork or animation into your movie to be displayed while the Preloader is doing its detection work. The animation or artwork can keep users interested while they wait for the movie to download.

The following exercise will teach you how to create a simple Preloader.

6. ——————————Building a Preloader

As you build more complex projects in Macromedia Flash MX, you may find that the users will see the movie differently depending on their connection speed. Rather than allowing users to view a choppy animation or to click on a button that doesn't work yet because the movie is not completely downloaded, you can add a Preloader to the movie that permits the movie to play once all the necessary frames have downloaded. This exercise will teach you how to create a basic Preloader so that you can control what your users see.

1. Open the **xboardingSite.fla** file from inside the **siteInProgress** folder in the **chap_17** folder. This file was created to get you started.

The siteInProgress folder contains all the files you need to recreate the xboarding.com Web site. Some files are already complete, while others have been partially created to get you started. You will complete these in the next few exercises.

2. In the project file, click the **Edit Scenes** button in the **Information Bar** to access the drop-down list. Choose **intro** to open the intro scene's Timeline. You will create the Preloader in this scene.

The order of the scenes listed in the Edit Scenes drop-down list is the order in which they will play in the movie unless you tell the Timeline otherwise. When you have a Preloader in the movie that will control the number of frames downloaded for the entire movie, the Preloader needs to occur in the first scene.

3. In the **Property Inspector**, choose **black** for the **Background** color.

Although the Stage looks black at first glance, it is actually white with a black Graphic symbol over the top of it. Changing the Background color in the Property Inspector will temporarily change the background color of the movie to black so that you can see the artwork in the new few steps.

In the next steps, you will be previewing Movie Clips in the Library that have white artwork and text. When the movie also has a white background, you cannot see the animation. Changing the background color of the movie temporarily will allow you to preview the animations.

4. Open the **Library** (**F11**). Inside the **movieClips** folder, click on the Movie Clip named **mcLoading** to select it. In the **Library Preview Window**, click the **Play** button to preview the Movie Clip. This will serve as the part of the looping animation that will play over and over until all the frames you specify are loaded.

5. Inside the **movieClips** folder, click on the Movie Clip named **mcFlakes** to select it. In the **Library Preview Window**, click the **Play** button to preview the Movie Clip. Notice the falling snowflakes. This will serve as the background of the looping animation that will play until all the frames you specify are loaded.

6. Click the **Insert Layer** button to add a new layer to the **Timeline**, and name it **flake**.

NOTE | Whoa! Where Did All Those Frames Come From?

When you insert a new layer in the Timeline, Macromedia Flash automatically adds frames up to the current last frame in the Timeline. In this case, there are frames up to 100 inside the introAnim folder, so Macromedia Flash adds frames up to 100 each time you insert a new layer. Since you don't need all those extra frames, you can highlight Frames 2 through 100 and right-click (Windows) or Ctrl+click (Mac) to access the drop-down menu and choose **Remove Frames**. This will delete all the extra frames from 2 to 100.

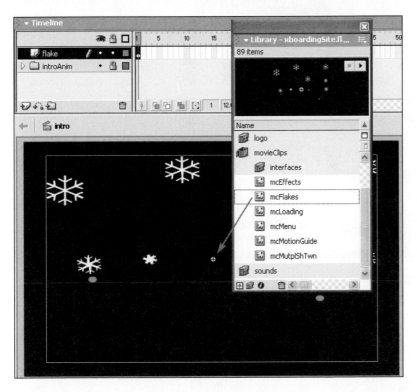

7. From the **Library**, drag an instance of the **mcFlakes** Movie Clip onto the center of the **Stage**.
Tip: You can use the **Align** panel (**Window > Align**) to center the **mcFlakes** Movie Clip instance on the **Stage**. You can also use the **Free Transform** tool to stretch the **mcFlakes** Movie Clip instance so that it covers more of the Stage, as in the picture above. When you are finished, lock the **flake** layer.

8. Click the **Insert Layer** button to add a new layer to the **Timeline**, and name it **loader**. Make sure the **loader** layer appears above the **flake** layer.

9. Highlight **Frames 2 through 100** on the **loader** layer and right-click (Windows) or Ctrl+click (Mac) to access the drop-down menu. Choose **Remove Frames**. This will delete all the extra frames from 2 to 100.

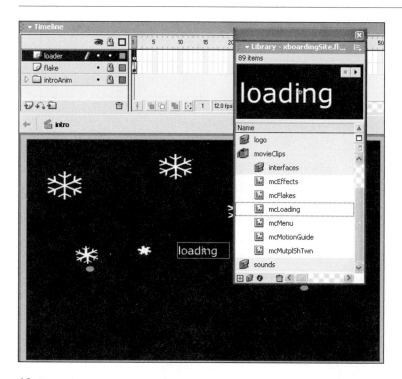

10. From the **Library**, drag an instance of the **mcLoading** Movie Clip onto the center of the **Stage**. **Tip:** You can use the **Align** panel to center the **mcloading** Movie Clip instance on the **Stage**. When you are finished, lock the **loader** layer.

11. Click and drag down on **Frame 4** of the **loader** and **flake** layers to select Frame 4 on both layers. Press **F5** to add frames up to Frame 4 on both layers.

12. Click away from the **Stage** to deselect everything, and in the **Property Inspector**, choose **white** for the **Background** color. This will change the background color of the movie back to white.

13. Click the **Insert Layer** button to add a new layer to the **Timeline**. Move it above the **loader** layer and rename it **labels**. Highlight **Frames 2 through 100** on the **labels** layer and right-click (Windows) or Ctrl+click (Mac) to access the drop-down menu. Choose **Remove Frames**. This will delete all the extra frames from 2 to 100.

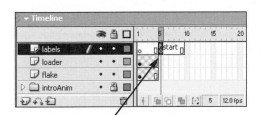

14. Select **Frame 5** and press **F7** to add a blank keyframe to the frame. In the **Property Inspector**, type **start** for the **Frame** Label. Press **F5** with **Frame 9** selected to add frames so that you can see the **start** label.

Why did you have to put the start label on Frame 5? The reason for this is that the intro animation begins at Frame 5, and in the next few steps you will be adding ActionScripting for the Preloader that will check to see whether all the frames are loaded in the movie. If they are, the Playhead will be sent to the start frame and the intro animation (which begins at Frame 5) can play.

15. Click the **Insert Layer** button to add another new layer to the **Timeline**. Make sure it is above all the other layers in the Timeline, and rename it **actions**. Press **F7** to add a second blank keyframe to the **actions** layer. Highlight **Frames 3 through 100** on the **actions** layer and right-click (Windows) or Ctrl+click (Mac) to access the drop-down menu. Choose **Remove Frames**. This will delete all the extra frames from 3 to 100.

16. Select **Frame 2** in the **actions** layer and open the **Actions** panel. In the **Actions Toolbox**, select **Actions > Conditions/Loops** and double-click on the **if** action to add it to the **Script** pane.

*The **if** action allows you to set up a condition that tests whether or not something is true.*

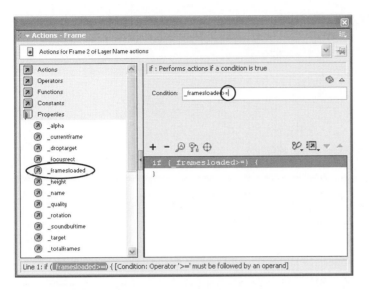

17. In the **Actions Toolbox**, choose **Properties** and double-click on the **_framesloaded** property to add it to both the **Parameters** pane and the **Script** pane. Click inside the **Condition** field in the **Parameters** pane and, after the **_framesloaded** property, type **>=**. This tells Macromedia Flash MX that if the frames that are loaded in the movie are greater than (>) or equal to (=) something, then something else will happen. You will be adding those "somethings" next.

18. In the **Actions Toolbox**, double-click on the **_totalframes** property to add it to both the **Condition** field and the **Script** pane.

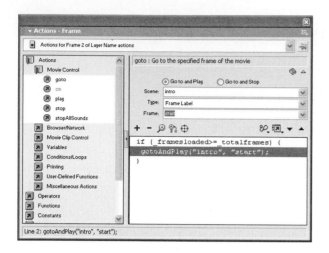

19. In the **Actions Toolbox**, choose **Actions > Movie Control** and double-click on **goto** to add it to the **Script** pane. In the **Parameters** pane, for **Scene** choose **intro**, for **Type** choose **Frame Label**, and for **Frame** choose **Start**. This ActionScript tells Macromedia Flash MX to check to see whether the frames that have been loaded in the movie are greater than or equal to the total frames in the movie. If they are, it should go ahead and play the intro scene, beginning at the start label.

You have just added ActionScript to have Macromedia Flash MX determine whether all the frames in the movie have been downloaded to the user's system. But what if the frames have not downloaded yet? You need to add one more condition to the ActionScript, which will cause this command to loop. You will do this next.

20. In the **Actions Toolbox**, select **Actions > Conditions/Loops** and double-click on the **else** action to add it to the **Script** pane.

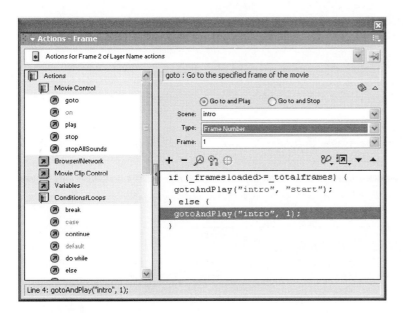

21. In the **Actions Toolbox**, select **Actions > Movie Control** and double-click on the **goto** action to add it to the **Script** pane. In the **Parameters** pane, for **Scene** choose **intro**, for **Type** choose **Frame Number**, and for **Frame** choose **1**.

This ActionScript tells Macromedia Flash MX that if the frames loaded are not greater than or equal to the total number of frames, it should go back to Frame 1. This creates a loop that checks repeatedly to see whether all the frames are loaded. If they are not, the Playhead will go back to Frame 1, but if they are, the Playhead will go to the start label and play the intro animation.

```
if (_framesloaded>=_totalframes) {
    gotoAndPlay("intro", "start");
} else {
    gotoAndPlay("intro", 1);
}
```

When you are finished, your ActionScripting should look like the script above.

22. Choose **Control > Test Scene** to preview the movie. Make sure you select Test Scene and not Test Movie, since you need to test only the intro scene in this exercise. You may not see the Preloader!

Why? Because all the frames may load so fast that you can't even see the Preloader in action. The next step will show you how use the Bandwidth Profiler to simulate the way the movie will appear on the Internet, so that you can view the Preloader hard at work.

Note: *When you choose Control > Test Scene, you may see a dialog box that says, "One or more of the fonts used by this movie are unavailable. Substitute fonts will be used for display and export. They will not be saved to the Macromedia authoring document." This simply means that your computer does not have some of the fonts that were used to create the artwork in this file. Go ahead and choose Use Default so that your computer will pick a default font to replace the unrecognizable fonts in the movie.*

NOTE | What Is the Bandwidth Profiler?

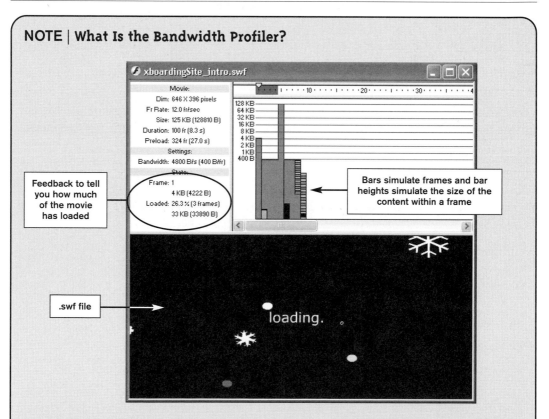

The **Bandwidth Profiler** is a feature in the Test Movie environment. It allows you to see how the movie streams based on different connection speeds. You can use the Bandwidth Profiler to simulate how a user would view your movie using a 28.8 modem or a 56k modem, for example. You can also use the Bandwidth Profiler to view the Preloader before the movie plays.

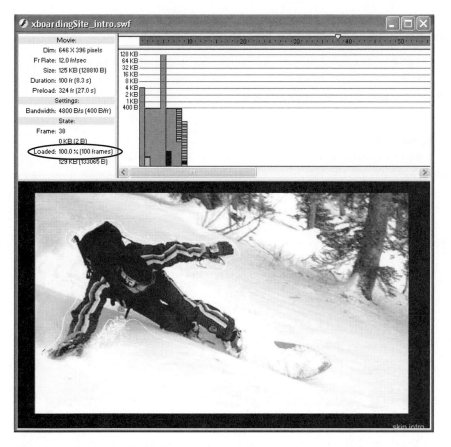

23. With the **Preview Window** open, choose **View > Bandwidth Profiler**, and then select **Debug >
56K (4.7 Kb/s)** to set the test to a bandwidth connection similar to a 56k modem connection. Choose
View > Show Streaming to see your Preloader work!

*This allows you to see the movie as it will appear when streamed on a live 56k connection. Notice
that the loading animation loops until all the frames are loaded (you will see Loaded: 100% in the
State section of the Bandwidth Profiler), and then the intro animation begins.*

24. When you are finished previewing the Preloader, choose **View > Bandwidth Profiler** to deselect it so that the Preview Window will show only the movie and not the Bandwidth Profiler.

Note: What if you don't want all the frames in the movie to load before the intro animation begins? For example, what if you want only 50 frames to load before the animation will play? If this is the case, then your ActionScripting on Frame 2 would instead look like this:

```
if (_framesloaded>=50) {
    gotoAndPlay("intro", "start");
} else {
    gotoAndPlay("intro", 1);
}
```

25. Nice work; you have made your first Preloader! Save this file and keep it open for the next exercise.

7. ——————————Printing from the Project File

One capability of Macromedia Flash MX that many users are not aware of is the ability to print from inside the project file (the .fla file). You can use this feature to show a client the page layouts for a Web site or even your progress on a project. In the project file, you can choose to print all frames in the movie or just the first frame of each scene. This exercise will show you how to set up the parameters and print a section of the movie from inside the project file. Then, the following exercise will show you how to allow your users to print from the Macromedia Flash Player.

1. The **xboardingSite.fla** project file should still be open. Select **File > Page Setup** (Windows) or **File > Print Margins** (Mac) to open the corresponding dialog box.

The Windows and Macintosh dialog boxes differ slightly, although the Layout options (circled above) are the same.

2. From the **Frames** option in the **Layout** section of the **Page Setup** dialog box, choose **First Frame Only** to print the first frame in each scene.

Tip: The other option, All Frames, will print all the frames in the movie.

3. From the **Layout** drop-down menu, choose **Storyboard – Boxes**. This will determine how the frames will appear on the printed page.

4. After you are finished setting up the options, click **OK**.

Layout Settings

The Layout settings allow you to select from five layout options. These options are described in the table below.

Printing Layout Options	
Option	**Description**
Actual Size	Prints the frame at full size.
Fit On One Page	Increases or decreases the size of each frame so that it fills the print area of the page.
Storyboard – Boxes	Prints multiple thumbnails on one page and creates a rectangle around each thumbnail.
Storyboard – Grid	Prints multiple thumbnails inside a grid on each page.
Storyboard – Blank	Prints multiple thumbnails on one page and prints only the artwork inside each thumbnail.

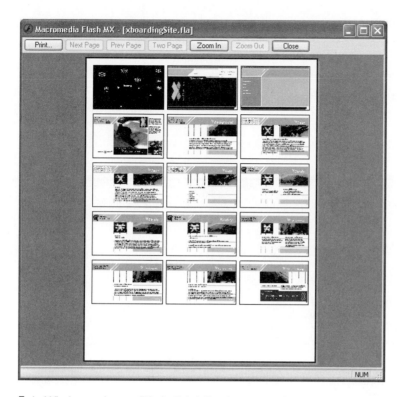

5. In Windows, choose **File > Print Preview** to preview how the printed page will look based on the settings you selected in the steps above. On a Mac, choose **File > Print** and then click the **Preview** button. This generates a PDF of the preview page.

6. Choose **Print** from the **Print Preview** window to print the first frames of each scene from the project file.

This is a great way to quickly show a client the page layouts for a Web site or even your progress on a project without having to show your client the entire project file.

NOTE | Printing Platforms Supported by the Macromedia Flash Player

In Macromedia Flash 5, Mac users experienced problems printing to PostScript printers. These issues have been resolved with the release of Macromedia Flash MX. Using the Macromedia Flash Player 6, you can now print to PostScript and non-PostScript printers. This includes most common printers, such as black-and-white and color, laser and inkjet, and PostScript and PCL printers. You can view a list of all the printing platforms supported by the Macromedia Flash Player at **http://www.macromedia.com/software/flash/open/webprinting/faq.html**.

7. You have just printed your first document from inside Macromedia Flash MX! Save the file and leave it open for the next exercise.

NOTE | Printing Macromedia Flash MX Content from a Browser

When an end user is viewing a Web site created using Macromedia Flash MX, different results occur when the user attempts to print the Web site, depending on the method used:

- If the user clicks the Print button in the browser window, the page of the Web site that he or she is currently viewing will be printed. Since you cannot control the user's browser, there is no way to completely control or disable printing inside the user's browser using Macromedia Flash MX.

- If the user right-clicks (Windows) or Ctrl+clicks (Mac) and chooses the Print option in the drop-down contextual menu, every frame in the movie will print. However, you can change this by labeling certain keyframes as printable in the project file and thus restricting users to print only the frames you specify. You will learn to do this in the next exercise.

- If the user clicks a Print button that you created inside the Macromedia Flash movie, all the frames to which you have added a #p in the Timeline will print. (You will learn how to add this in the next exercise.)

Tip: You can also disable printing entirely in the Macromedia Flash Player by adding the label !#p to a keyframe. This will make the entire movie nonprintable from the drop-down contextual menu in the Macromedia Flash Player.

---

8. ———————Printing from the Macromedia Flash Player

In addition to printing files from within the project file, you can allow users viewing the movie in the Macromedia Flash Player to print Macromedia Flash content. You would add this feature if you wanted to allow visitors to your Web site to be able to print certain pages within your site. By default, all the frames in the Timeline will print unless you either specify certain frames as printable by a user viewing the movie or disable printing altogether. This exercise will show you how to control printing by adding a special label to the chosen printable frames. It will also teach you how to add ActionScripting to a button and set up the printing parameters for your users.

1. In the project file, click on the **Edit Scenes** button in the **Information Bar** to access the drop-down list. Choose **learningL1** to open the learningL1 scene's Timeline.

If you see the "missing font" message, go ahead and choose Use Default so that your computer will pick a default font to replace the unrecognizable fonts in the movie.

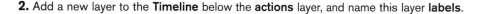

2. Add a new layer to the **Timeline** below the **actions** layer, and name this layer **labels**.

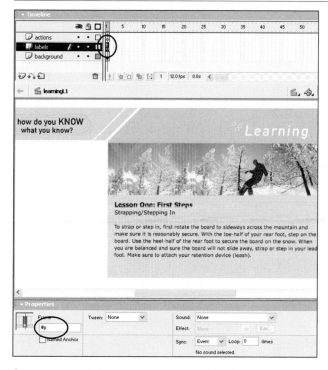

3. With the first frame selected in the **labels** layer, open the **Property Inspector (Window > Properties)**. Type **#p** in the **Frame Label** field of the **Property Inspector** to define that keyframe as printable.

NOTE | Printing from the Contextual Menu

You can permit your users to access the Print command from the drop-down contextual menu. The contextual menu will appear in the Macromedia Flash Player when a Windows user right-clicks or a Mac user Ctrl+clicks on the movie.

By default, the Print option in the contextual menu will print every frame in the movie. However, you can change this by labeling certain keyframes as printable in the project file (as you did in step 3 by adding the #p label to the keyframe) and thus restricting the users to printing only the frames you specify.

Further, you can also disable printing entirely in the Macromedia Flash Player by adding the label !#p to a keyframe. This will make the entire movie nonprintable from the Macromedia Flash Player. It is important to note that although you disable printing from the Macromedia Flash Player, the user can still choose the Print command from the browser. Since you cannot control the user's browser commands, there is no way to disable printing inside the user's browser using Macromedia Flash MX.

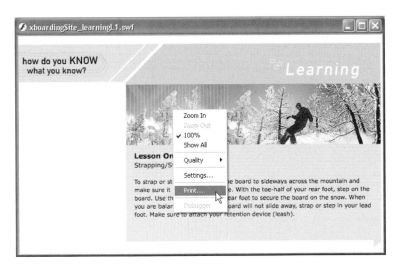

4. Choose **Control > Test Scene**. **Note:** Make sure you choose Test Scene and not Test Movie, since you need to preview only the scene at this point. Right-click (Windows) or Ctrl+click (Mac) on the movie to access the drop-down contextual menu. Choose **Print** to print the frame you labeled in step 3.

Note: After you have defined a keyframe as printable, when a user accesses the drop-down menu and chooses Print, Macromedia Flash MX will print only the frames labeled as #p. When you add the #p label to a frame, you must attach the label to a keyframe, not a frame.

In addition to allowing access to the drop-down menu, you can allow the user to print frames within the movie by attaching ActionScript to a button that will print the frames you specify. To do this, you must first create the printable frame labels, as you did in the steps above, and then you can create the button, which you will do in the steps that follow.

5. Lock the three existing layers in the **Timeline** and click the **Insert Layer** button to add another new layer to the Timeline. Move the new layer below the **labels** layer and rename this layer **print btn**.

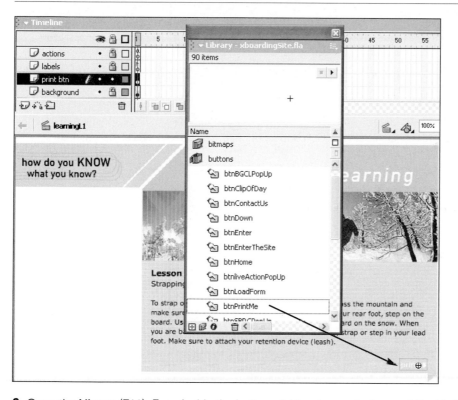

6. Open the **Library** (F11). From inside the **buttons** folder, drag an instance of the **btnPrintMe** button onto the lower right corner of the **Stage**, as in the picture above.

7. Make sure the **Print** button is selected, and open the **Actions** panel (**Window > Actions**).

8. In the **Actions Toolbox**, choose **Actions > Printing**, and double-click on the **print** action to add it to the **Script** pane. Since you are adding an action to a button, the **on** Event Handler will automatically be added to the Script pane as well.

9. In the **Parameters** pane, choose **Print: As bitmap**. This will print all the content in the frame as a bitmap, honoring any transparency and color effects in the frame.

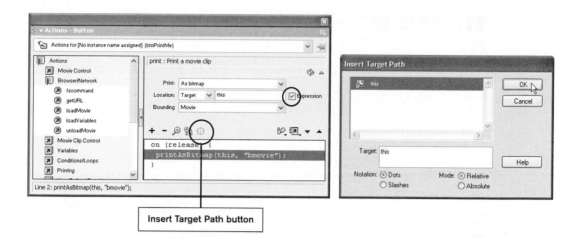

Insert Target Path button

10. For **Location**, select **Target** from the drop-down menu. Next to the **Target** field, highlight the **0** and click the **Insert Target Path** button. Click on **this** in the **Insert Target Path** dialog box, and click **OK**. In the **Parameters** pane, check the **Expression** box. These parameters will determine the location of the printable frame. When the ActionScript is attached to a button, **this** refers to the Timeline that contains the button. Because that Timeline is where you added the frame label #p, Frame 1 will be printable.

11. In the **Parameters** pane, leave **Bounding** (Windows) or **Bounds** (Mac) at the default setting of **Movie**, since this parameter is optional.

The chart at the end of this exercise details all the available **print** *action parameters.*

Note: *The print area is determined by the Stage size of the movie, by default. Any movies loaded into levels will use their own Stage size as the print area unless you specify otherwise. Also, if any object is located off of the Stage, it will be cut off and will not print.*

12. Choose **Control > Test Scene** and test the **Print** button by clicking on it in the **Preview Window**. Your printer will display a **Print** dialog box. Click **Print** and your printer will print the frame you labeled with the #p.

Tip: You can use the `print` action to print frames in either the Main Timeline or the Timeline of any Movie Clip or movie that is loaded into a level. **Note:** *For a Movie Clip to be printable, it must be on the Stage or work area, and it must have an instance name.*

13. When you are finished, save this file and keep it open for the next exercise.

Print Action Parameters

Option	Setting	Description
Print	As Vectors	Prints frames that do not use transparency (alpha) or color effects.
	As Bitmap	Prints frames that contain bitmap images, transparency, or color effects.
Location	Level	Specifies the level in the Macromedia Flash Player to print. By default, all of the frames in the level will print unless you specify otherwise. You can assign a #p frame label to print only specific frames in the level, rather than all the frames.
	Target	Identifies the instance name of the Movie Clip or Timeline to print. By default, all of the frames in the movie are printed. However, you can designate frames for printing by attaching a #p frame label to specific frames.
Bounding	Movie	Sets the print area for all printable frames in the movie to the bounding box of a specific frame in a movie. You can assign a #b label to the frame whose bounding box you want to use as the print area.
	Frame	Sets the print area of each printable frame to the bounding box of that frame. This can change the print area for each frame and scales the objects to fit the print area.
	Max	Merges all of the bounding boxes of all the printable frames and assigns the resulting bounding box as the print area.

9. ————————Exporting the Scenes

Now that you have created the Preloader and identified the printable frames, you need to export the .swf file for each scene so that the site will work correctly. This exercise will show you how to do this by testing each scene in order to export its .swf file. You will then rename the scenes to shorten their existing names so that they can be loaded into the Main Timeline on demand.

1. Click on the **Edit Scenes** button in the **Information Bar** to access the drop-down list. Choose **home** to open the home scene's Timeline.

2. On the **Stage**, double-click on the **menu** Movie Clip to open the Timeline for the Movie Clip. Notice that it looks familiar. This is the same drop-down menu you created in Chapter 11, "*ActionScripting Basics*." Click on **Frame 5** of the **actions** layer and press **F9** to open the **Actions** panel. The ActionScripting should also look familiar: it is the same ActionScripting that you programmed in Chapter 11. This particular ActionScript stops the Playhead when it reaches the frame that the ActionScripting resides in (Frame 5), and it loads a movie named **background.swf** into Level 50.

In the following steps, you are going to create the background.swf file by exporting the background scene from this project file and renaming it to match this ActionScripting. You will also create all the other interface .swf files that are loaded into levels.

3. Click on the **Edit Scenes** button in the **Information Bar** to access the drop-down list. Choose **intro** to open the **intro** scene's Timeline. Choose **Control > Test Scene**. As soon as you see the **Preview Window**, you can close it, since you do not need to spend time previewing the scene—instead the goal here is to export the .swf file for the scene.

NOTE | Why Am I Choosing Control > Test Scene?

As you learned in Chapter 16, "*Publishing and Exporting*," each time you choose Control > Test Movie, the .swf file of the entire movie is created inside the same folder that the project file (.fla) is saved in. Choosing Control > Test Scene also creates a .swf file, although instead of containing the whole movie, the .swf file will contain only the contents of the scene.

4. Leave the project file open and open the **siteInProgress** folder inside the **chap_17** folder. Notice the **xboardingSite_intro.swf** file. This is the file that was just created when you chose Control > Test Scene. When you choose the Control > Test Scene command, Macromedia Flash MX automatically names the exported file, using the name of the .fla file (xboardingSite) followed by an underscore and the name of the scene. Notice also the file named **xboardingSite_learningL1.swf**. This is the file that was created in the last exercise when you chose the Control > Test Scene command to test the printing functionality. When you are finished, close the **siteInProgress** folder.

---

5. Back in the project file, click the **Edit Scenes** button in the **Information Bar** to access the drop-down list. Choose **password** to open the password scene's Timeline. Choose **Control > Test Scene**. As soon as you see the **Preview Window**, you can close it, since the goal here is to export the .swf file for the password scene.

---

6. Repeat step 5 to export a .swf file for each of the remaining scenes: home, main, background, gear, gearBoards, gearCheckList, safety, safetyLessons, safetyRC, learning, learningL1, learningL2, and whatsNew.

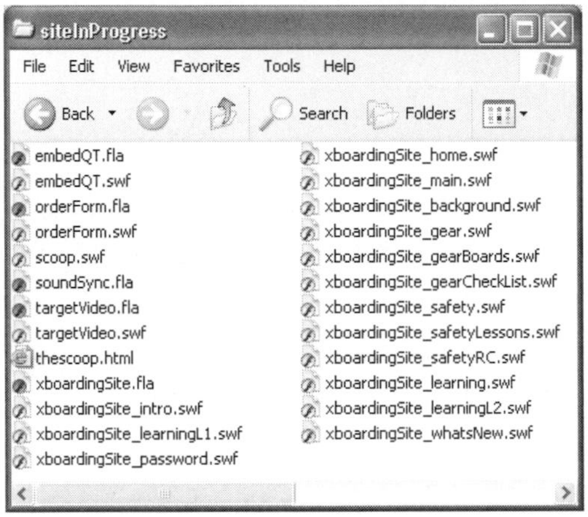

7. Open the **siteInProgress** folder again. You should now see 15 .swf files—one from each scene in the project file, as in the picture above.

The last task to complete in order for the site to function properly is to rename the .swf files you just exported so that they match the ActionScripting in the drop-down menu that you originally created in Chapter 11.

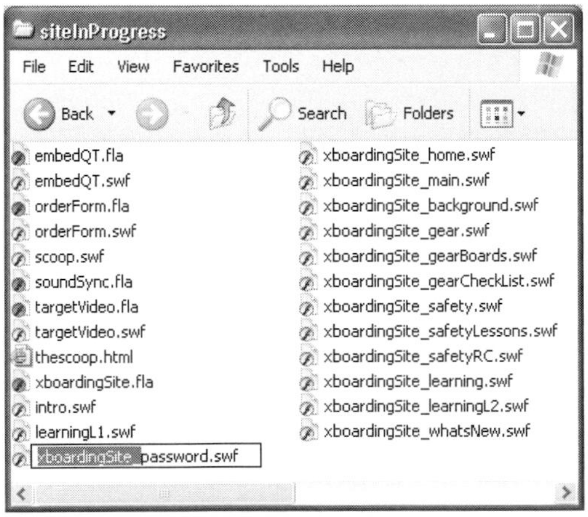

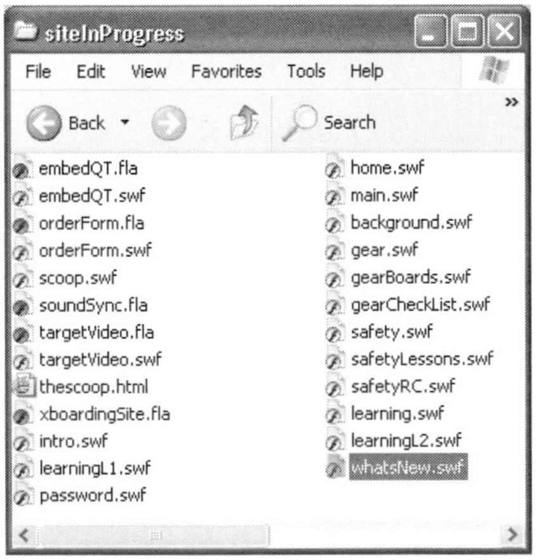

8. Inside the **siteInProgress** folder, rename each .swf file, deleting the xboardingSite name and the underscore so that it contains only the name of the scene. When you are finished, the 15 .swf files should be named just like those in the picture above.

9. Back in the project file, choose **Control > Test Movie** (yes, Test Movie and not Test Scene this time) to preview the Web site. In the **Preview Window**, choose **View > Bandwidth Profiler** to hide the Bandwidth Profiler. Enter the user name **guest** and the password **gotsnow** and click to enter the site. Test all the menu buttons to make sure they work!

Tip: *If you click on one of the menu buttons and nothing happens, chances are that you have some-how named the .swf file incorrectly. If this is the case, go back to the siteInProgress folder and check the name of the .swf file in question to make sure that it matches the picture above.*

10. When you are finished, save this file and keep it open for the last exercise.

Note: *Even though you can change the name of the .swf file by using the Publish settings, doing so changes the name of the .swf file for the whole movie, not just the scene. For example, if you choose the Control > Test Scene command after you have changed the name of the .swf file in the Publish settings to xSite, Macromedia Flash MX will use the new name of the movie (xSite) followed by an underscore and the name of the scene.*

10. Creating Draggable Movies

When you load movies into levels, you can add functionality so that they not only will load but can also be dragged around the interface by the user. This exercise will teach you how to do that. As well, this exercise will teach you how to add the ActionScripting to allow the user to close the window when he or she is finished with it.

1. Click on the **Edit Scenes** button in the **Information Bar** to access the drop-down list. Choose **safety** to open the safety scene's Timeline.

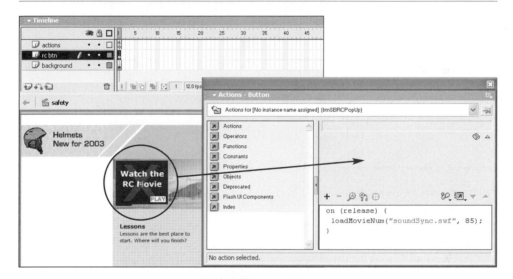

2. On the **Stage**, click on the **Watch the RC Movie** button to select it. Press **F9** to open the **Actions** panel. This ActionScripting will tell Macromedia Flash MX that when a user clicks on the selected button, it should load the movie named **soundSync.swf** into Level 85.

3. Save and close the **xboardingSite.fla** file. You will not be needing it anymore.

In order to make the soundSync.swf file draggable, you need to modify the soundSync.fla file. You will do this next.

4. Open the **soundSync.fla** file from the **siteInProgress** folder. This file has been created to get you started. It is similar to the one you created in Chapter 13.

5. Choose **Control > Test Movie** to preview the file. Notice that if you try to drag the movie, you can't. This is because no button or ActionScripting has been added to make the movie draggable. You will add the button and the ActionScripting in the following steps. Close the **Preview Window**.

6. Back in the project file, click the **Insert Layer** button to add a new layer to the Timeline. Rename the new layer **btn invisible**. Make sure the **btn invisible** layer is just below the **labels** layer.

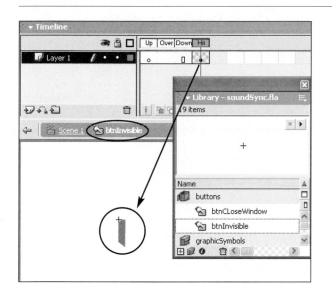

7. Open the **Library** (**F11**) and click on the **buttons** folder to expand it. Double-click on the **btnInvisible** symbol to open the Button symbol's Timeline. Notice that this button has only a Hit frame; therefore, it will serve as an invisible button in the movie.

8. In the **Information Bar**, click on **Scene 1** to return to the **Main Timeline**.

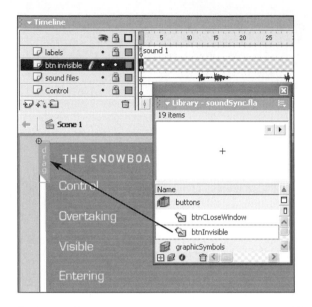

9. Back in **Scene 1**, drag an instance of the **btnInvisible** symbol onto the **Stage**. Position it so that it is on top of the tab on the upper left side of the Stage, as in the picture above. You will add the ActionScripting to make the button draggable next.

10. Press **F9** to open the **Actions** panel. In the **Actions Toolbox**, choose **Actions > Miscellaneous Actions** and double-click on **comment**. This will add two slashes (//) to the Script pane. In the **Comment** field in the **Parameters** pane, type the text **Add the ActionScripting to start the drag here**.

You have just created your first ActionScripting comment. In the Actions panel, comments can be used to describe scripts or add notes inside the Script pane.

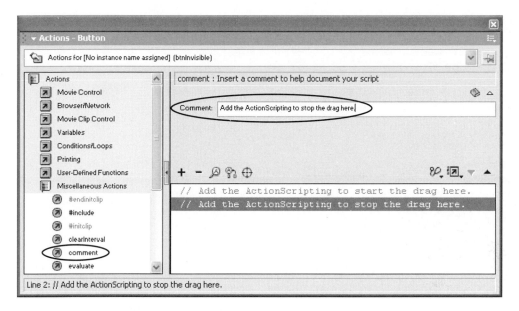

11. In the **Actions Toolbox**, choose **Actions > Miscellaneous Actions** and double-click on **comment** again. In the **Comment** field in the **Parameters** pane, type the text **Add the ActionScripting to stop the drag here**.

Note: Comments are not exported with the .swf file, so they can be any length without affecting the size of the exported file. Also, comments do not need to follow rules for ActionScript syntax or keywords.

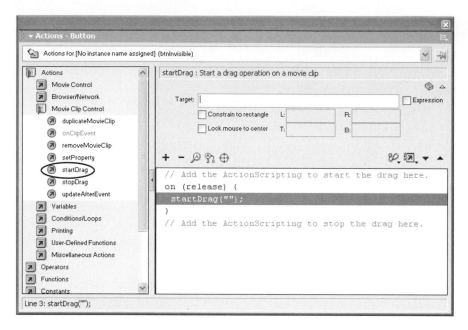

12. Select the top comment and, in the **Actions Toolbox**, choose **Actions > Movie Clip Control** and double-click on the **startDrag** action to add it to the **Script** pane. This will place the ActionScripting below the comment. Since you are adding the ActionScripting to a button, the **on** Event Handler will automatically be added.

Tip: If you don't see the **on (release) {** *line added to the Script pane when you double-click on the startDrag action, you may be placing your action on a frame, rather than on the button. Make sure that you have the button selected and that the top of the Actions panel reads Actions – Button so that you know you are applying the ActionScripting to the button.*

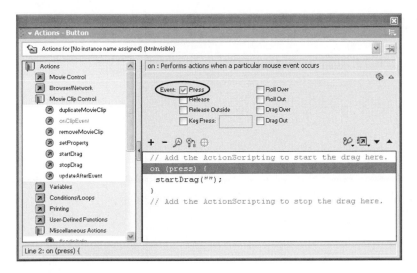

13. In the **Script** pane, select the **on (release) {** line. In the **Parameters** pane, click the **Event: Release** check box to deselect it, and then select the **Press** check box. This will tell Macromedia Flash MX to start the drag when the user presses the button, not when the user releases the button. When you are finished, your Script pane should look like the picture above.

14. In the **Script** pane, select the **startDrag("")**; line and in the **Parameters** pane, type the word **this** in the **Target** field. Make sure the **Expression** box is selected. This ActionScripting will make the whole movie draggable when the user clicks on the Hit state of the button. Since the **on** Event Handler is attached to a button, the **this** parameter refers to the Timeline that contains the button.

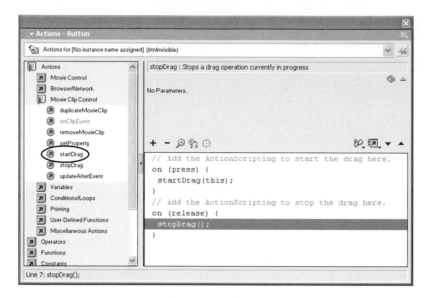

15. Select the second comment in the **Script** pane and, in the **Actions Toolbox**, choose **Actions >
Movie Clip Control** and double-click on the **stopDrag** action to add it to the **Script** pane. This will
place the ActionScripting below the comment, and the **on** Event Handler will automatically be added.
This ActionScripting will stop the movie from being draggable when the user lets go of the mouse.

16. Choose **Control > Test Movie** to preview the draggable button. Go ahead and click on the **Drag**
button to drag the movie around the screen. When you are finished, close the **Preview Window**.

You will add the Close Window button next.

17. Back in the project file, click the **Insert Layer** button to add a new layer to the **Timeline**. Rename the new layer **close btn**, and move it above the **btn visible** layer.

18. From the **Library**, drag an instance of the **btnCloseWIndow** symbol onto the lower right corner of the **Stage**, as in the picture above.

19. With the **Close Window** button selected on the **Stage**, open the **Actions** panel.

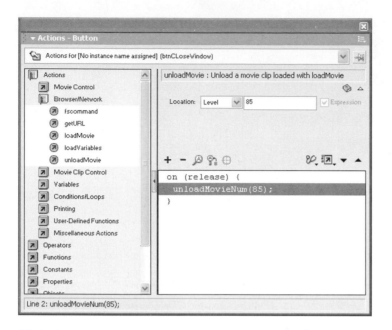

20. In the **Actions Toolbox**, choose **Actions > Browser/Network** and double-click on the **unloadMovie** action to add it to the **Script** pane. In the **Parameters** pane, enter **85** in the field next to **Level**. Remember from step 2 of this exercise that the xboarding Web site used ActionScripting to load the **soundSync.swf** file into Level 85. Therefore, the ActionScripting you just added in this step will unload the movie from Level 85.

21. Choose **Control > Test Movie**. The Close Window button will not work yet, since you are viewing the **soundSync.swf** file, but you still need to test the movie in order to export the .swf file. Close the **Preview Window**.

22. Save and close the **soundSync** file. From the **siteInProgress** folder, double-click on the **xboardingSite.swf** file to preview the site movie again.

23. Enter the same user name and password you have been using in this chapter and, once you are inside the site, click on the **Safety** button in the menu.

24. Click on the **Watch the RC Movie** button and drag the Snowboarder Responsibility Code movie around the screen!

25. Click on the **Close Window** button to unload the movie!

26. When you are finished, close the **Preview Window**.

You have conquered another chapter! You should now have a more solid understanding of how the different pieces within this book come together to make a whole. Now there is only one more important chapter left: Chapter 18, "Integration."

I8.

Integration

| Fireworks Editable Content |
| Fireworks Flattened Content | FreeHand Content |
| Dreamweaver and Macromedia Flash MX |
| Illustrator Content | Accessible Content |

chap_18

Macromedia Flash MX
H•O•T CD-ROM

Although many designers work exclusively in Macromedia Flash MX, the program doesn't have to be an island unto itself. There are many opportunities to combine it with other tools. The following hands-on exercises show how to use Fireworks, FreeHand, and Illustrator content with Macromedia Flash MX. It also shows you how to incorporate Macromedia Flash MX content into a Dreamweaver Web site. Keep in mind that in order to try these exercises, you must have these programs installed on your system. The **H•O•T CD-ROM** contains trial versions of Fireworks MX and Dreamweaver MX. If you don't own the other software, save the exercises for another time. You never know when you'll be adding new programs to your system, or working for someone else who has them.

Importing Vector Files

When you want to import vector files that were created in another program into Macromedia Flash MX, you can choose from many file types that the program supports. A chart follows listing the supported file types.

Vector File Types Supported by Macromedia Flash MX			
File Type	**Extension**	**Windows**	**Mac**
Adobe Illustrator 8.0 or earlier	eps, .ai	x	x
AutoCAD DXF	.dxf	x	x
Enhanced Windows Metafile	.emf	x	
Macromedia FreeHand	fh7, .ft7, fh8, .ft8, .fh9, .ft9, .fh10	x	x
FutureSplash Player	.spl	x	x
Macromedia Flash movie	.swf	x	x
Windows Metafile	.wmf	x	
PNG	.png	x	x

For a list of the bitmap file types supported by Macromedia Flash MX, see Chapter 8, "*Bitmaps.*"

I. ―――――――Bringing Fireworks Editable Content into Flash

As you continue to develop your skills, you may find from time to time that you want to use content that was created outside of Macromedia Flash MX. While there are many applications to choose from for creating artwork (such as Photoshop or PaintShop Pro), the advantage to using Macromedia Fireworks is that colors and text can remain as editable objects when you import the Fireworks MX file into Macromedia Flash MX. The following exercise will take you through some basic techniques for importing and working with Fireworks PNG files with editable objects and text.

Note: You must have Fireworks MX installed in order to complete this exercise. A trial version of Fireworks MX is located inside the **software** folder on the **H•O•T CD-ROM**.

1. Copy the **chap_18** folder, located on the **H•O•T CD-ROM**, to your hard drive. You need to have this folder on your hard drive in order to save files inside it.

2. Open the **fireworksFlash.fla** file inside the **chap_18** folder.

3. Choose **File > Import**. Select the **gearSale.png** file in the **chap_18** folder and click **Open**.

4. Macromedia Flash MX will automatically detect that you are trying to import a Fireworks PNG file. The **Fireworks PNG Import Settings** dialog box will open.

5. Choose the following settings in the **Fireworks PNG Import Settings** dialog box: **File Structure: Import into new layer in current scene**, **Objects: Keep all paths editable**, and **Text: Keep all text editable**. Click **OK**. This will import the PNG image in a new layer and allow all the text and paths to be editable. See the chart that follows for a description of each of the options in this dialog box.

Note: Importing a PNG file with editable paths and editable text allows all the vector information to remain as vector information and allows text to be editable. However, you will lose bitmap effects, such as bevels and glows.

Fireworks PNG Import Settings		
Option	**Settings**	**Description**
File Structure	Import as movie clip and retain layers	Allows you to import the PNG file as a Movie Clip with the layers and frames intact.
	Import into new layer in current scene	Allows you to import the PNG file into a single new layer at the top of the stacking order. When you use this setting, the Fireworks layers are compressed into one single layer. The Fireworks frames are contained within the new layer.
Objects	Rasterize if necessary to maintain appearance	Maintains the appearance to preserve Fireworks fills, strokes, and effects.
	Keep all paths editable	Keeps all objects as editable vector paths, but fills, strokes, and effects may be lost on import.
Text	Rasterize if necessary to maintain appearance	Maintains the appearance to preserve Fireworks fills, strokes, and effects applied to text.
	Keep all text editable	Keeps all text editable, but fills, strokes, and effects may be lost on import.
Import as a single flattened bitmap		Turns the PNG file into a single flattened image.

6. After you click OK, notice that Macromedia Flash MX places the Fireworks PNG file on its own layer and even names it for you. This is because you chose the **File Structure: Import into new layer in current scene** option in the Fireworks PNG Import Settings dialog box.

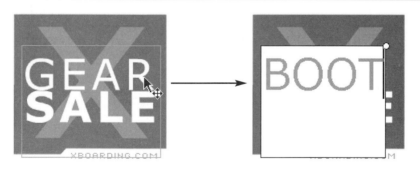

7. Using the **Arrow** tool on the **Stage**, double-click on the **GEAR** text. This will allow you to edit the text. Type the word **BOOT**. See how easy it is to make changes? Select your **Arrow** tool again and reposition the **BOOT** text so it is centered above the **SALE** text.

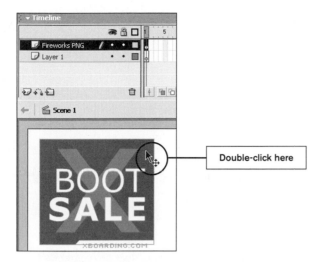

Double-click here

8. Double-click on a corner of the background artwork to enter the **group** for that object.

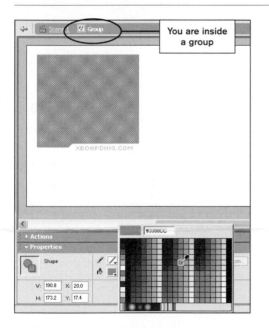

You are inside
a group

9. Using the **Property Inspector**, change the fill by selecting a new color from the **Fill Color** pop-up window.

When you double-click on the background of the artwork in the Main Timeline, the group for the object will open and the background will be automatically selected. If you click somewhere else to deselect it, just remember to make sure the shape is selected before you choose a new color.

10. When you are finished, click on **Scene 1** in the **Information Bar** to return to the **Main Timeline**. Preview your changes.

---

11. Save this file and keep it open for the next exercise.

You just learned how to import a Fireworks PNG file as a new layer using editable paths and editable text, which allows you to modify object attributes such as the type and object color. In the next exercise, you will learn how to import the same Fireworks document as a flattened bitmap. However, with that method, you lose the ability to edit the object as a vector because it is imported as a bitmap graphic.

---

2. ———————Bringing Fireworks Flattened Content into Flash

There will be times when you find you just can't create the artwork that you want in Macromedia Flash MX, such as artwork that contains bevels or glows. In addition to importing editable Fireworks MX content, as you did in the last exercise, you can also import a rasterized or flattened image, which is necessary if you want to preserve any bevels and/or glows contained in the original Fireworks artwork. Additionally, you can modify the flattened image in Fireworks MX without ever leaving Macromedia Flash MX! In this exercise, you will learn how to do just this.

1. You should still have the **fireworksFlash.fla** file open from the last exercise.

2. In the **Main Timeline**, lock the **Fireworks PNG** layer and select **Frame 1** of **Layer 1**.

3. Choose **File > Import** to open the **Import File** dialog box. In the **chap_18** folder, select the same **gearSale.png** file that you imported in the last exercise. Click **Open**.

4. Macromedia Flash MX will automatically detect that you are trying to import a Fireworks PNG file, and the **Fireworks PNG Import Settings** dialog box will appear again. This time, check the **Import as a single flattened bitmap** check box. Click **OK**. This will import the PNG image into Layer 1 as a bitmap graphic.

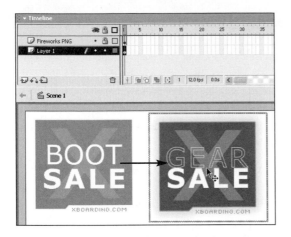

5. Click and drag the new Movie Clip symbol to the right of the **Stage** so you can see it better. **Tip:** By default, Macromedia Flash MX automatically places imported artwork in the top left corner of the Stage. Since Layer 1 is below the Fireworks PNG layer, it will appear behind it in the stacking order.

6. With the new artwork you just imported still selected, notice that the **Property Inspector** calls it a **Bitmap**. This is visual feedback that the artwork has been imported as a bitmap. Notice also the glow around the artwork. You imported the same file in Exercise 1, but there was no glow. Why? When you import a Fireworks PNG file using editable paths and editable text, some fills, strokes, and effects may be lost. However, when you import a Fireworks PNG file as a flattened bitmap, you lose the ability to edit the text and paths, but glows and bevels are preserved.

You will learn how to edit the bitmap using Macromedia Fireworks MX next.

7. Press **F11** to open the **Library** and highlight the **gearSale** bitmap in the Library.

8. From the **Options** menu in the upper right corner of your **Library** window, choose **Edit with Fireworks**. This automatically will open **gearSale.png** in the Fireworks MX program.

9. In Fireworks MX, select the **SALE** text and, in the **Property Inspector**, select **red** for the text color to change the color of the **SALE** text to red. When you are finished, click the **Done** button in the upper left corner of the document window, circled above. This will close Fireworks MX and return you to Macromedia Flash MX.

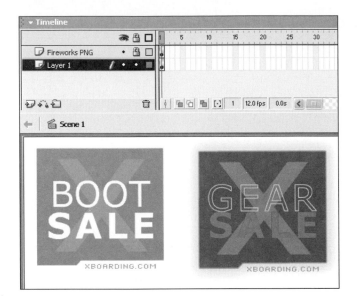

10. Back in Macromedia Flash MX, notice that your file has been instantly updated!

11. Save and close the file; you won't need it for future exercises.

TIP | **Learning More About Macromedia Fireworks**

If you are interested in learning more about Fireworks, here are a couple of learning resources
and support sites:

http://www.macromedia.com/support/fireworks/

http://www.macromedia.com/support/fireworks/programs/fw_to_flash/

---

3. ─────────Importing FreeHand Content as Keyframes

With the release of Macromedia Flash MX, Macromedia has strengthened the compatibility between Macromedia Flash and FreeHand. Macromedia Flash MX allows you to import FreeHand 7, 8, 9, or 10 files and turn them into a Macromedia Flash MX Web site in a few easy steps. The next exercise will show you how.

1. In Macromedia Flash MX, open the **fhKeyFrames.fla file** from the **chap_18** folder.

2. Choose **File > Import**. Inside the **chap_18** folder, select the **mockUp.FH10** file. Click **Open**.

Tip: If you import a FreeHand 10 file that contains symbols into Macromedia Flash MX, it will automatically add those symbols to the Library.

NOTE | Pages in FreeHand

When working in FreeHand, it's best to set up your document as Pages, as opposed to Layers (though Pages can contain Layers!). If you set up your file using Pages, you will have the maximum flexibility when importing the file into Macromedia Flash MX. A file created as Pages can be imported into Macromedia Flash MX as scenes or keyframes, whereas a file created in Layers can be imported only as keyframes.

To access the Pages feature of Macromedia FreeHand 10, click on the **Document panel** tab. Using the **Options** arrow in the upper right corner of the tab, select **Add Pages**.

This will open the **Add Pages** dialog box.

3. Macromedia Flash MX will automatically detect that you are trying to import a FreeHand file and will open the **FreeHand Import** dialog box. In the **Mapping** section of the dialog box, choose **Pages: Key Frames** and **Layers: Flatten**. In the **Options** section, deselect **Include Invisible Layers** and **Include Background Layer**, and click **OK**.

NOTE | The FreeHand Import Dialog Box

The FreeHand Import dialog box appears whenever you import FreeHand files into Macromedia Flash MX. The settings allow you to control specific aspects of your file. See the chart below for an explanation of its features.

FreeHand Import Settings		
Option Group	**Setting**	**Description**
Mapping	Pages	Controls how the Macromedia FreeHand document pages are imported into Macromedia Flash MX. If you select *Scenes*, each page will be transformed into a scene in Macromedia Flash MX. If you select **Key Frames**, each page in your FreeHand file will be transformed into a keyframe. You can choose the method that you prefer.
	Layers	Controls how individual layers are imported into Macromedia Flash MX from your FreeHand file. Selecting **Layers** allows the layers in your FreeHand file to remain as layers when imported into Macromedia Flash MX. Selecting **Key Frames** allows Macromedia Flash MX to convert the layers into keyframes. Selecting **Flatten** will convert multiple layers in FreeHand into one layer in Macromedia Flash MX.
Pages		Allows you to either import all pages from your FreeHand file or specify a range of pages to import into Macromedia Flash MX.
Options	Include Invisible Layers	If this box is checked, Macromedia Flash MX will include all hidden layers from your FreeHand document.
	Include Background Layer	If this box is checked, the background layer in your FreeHand file will be included during import.
	Maintain Text Blocks	If this box is checked, Macromedia Flash MX will preserve the text blocks in your FreeHand file so that they will remain editable in Macromedia Flash MX.

4. On the **Timeline**, click on **Frames 1**, **2**, **3**, and **4** (or scrub the **Playhead**) to see the content that Macromedia Flash MX imported as separate keyframes. Can you imagine how easy it would be to mock up a Web site inside FreeHand and simply import it into Macromedia Flash MX? This is truly powerful integration!

5. When you import FreeHand pages as keyframes, all your objects will still be editable, even if you select the Layers: Flatten option in the dialog box (they will just all be on one layer). Click in **Frame 1**. Double-click on the green background on the right side of the artwork. This opens the group for this object. Notice that it is editable!

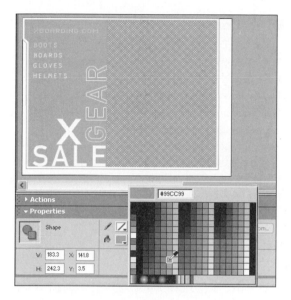

6. With the green shape still selected, choose a different **Fill Color** in the **Property Inspector**.

7. In the **Information Bar**, click on **Scene 1** to return to the **Main Timeline**. Preview your changes.

8. Choose **File > Save** and then close this file.

4. ——————Importing FreeHand Content as Scenes

In Chapter 11, "*ActionScripting Basics*," you learned to work with scenes. In this exercise, you'll get a chance to bring FreeHand content in as scenes instead of as keyframes. There is an ongoing debate within the Macromedia Flash MX developer community as to whether it is better project management to use scenes or keyframes to organize sections of a Macromedia Flash MX project. As you become more and more proficient in Macromedia Flash MX development, you will ultimately choose the style that works best for you. In the meantime, since there is not one "correct" way to import content from FreeHand into Macromedia Flash MX, I want to show you both methods.

1. In Macromedia Flash MX, open the **fhScenes.fla** file from the **chap_18** folder.

2. Choose **File > Import**. Inside the **chap_18** folder, select the same FreeHand file you imported in the last exercise (**mockUp.FH10**). Click **Open**.

3. In the **FreeHand Import** dialog box that comes up, choose to have all the pages brought in as scenes by clicking on the **Pages: Scenes** button in the **Mapping** section. Click **OK**.

4. Click on the **Edit Scenes** icon in the **Information Bar** to reveal that Macromedia Flash MX has imported the content from the FreeHand file as four separate scenes! Now click on a different scene to see the content within that scene. It's really easy to import a FreeHand file into Macromedia Flash MX and transform each page into a separate scene.

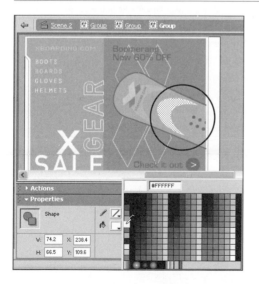

5. Choose **Scene 2** using the **Edit Scenes** icon and double-click on the lower boomerang on the snowboard. Keep double-clicking until you see a dotted selection mesh over the boomerang. This is an indication that you can change the color of the shape. Using the **Property Inspector**, choose **white** for the **Fill Color**.

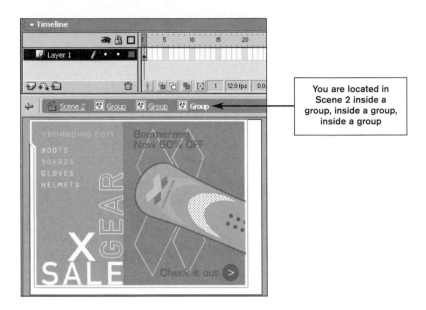

Note: Why all this double-clicking? Depending on how the FreeHand file was originally created, Macromedia Flash MX will automatically group certain objects when you import the file into Macromedia Flash MX. Grouping objects will not change the design, so just keep in mind that although you may need to click a few times, you will be able to edit any object you want, eventually! Also note that this file contains fonts that were created as outlines (because it's likely that you don't own the fonts used). If you want to keep type editable between FreeHand and Macromedia Flash MX, don't convert your type to outlines in FreeHand. If you want to use Macromedia Flash MX to edit the text of a FreeHand file that was created without using type outlines, you will also need to have the font installed on the computer on which you plan to edit the content.

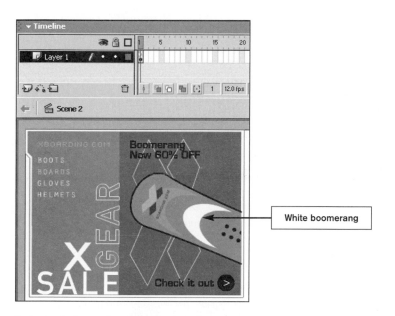

White boomerang

6. In the **Information Bar**, click on **Scene 2** to return to the **Main Timeline**. Preview your changes.

Just as with importing FreeHand pages as keyframes, when you import FreeHand pages as scenes, your shapes will still be editable inside Macromedia Flash MX.

7. Save and close this file.

TIP | **Learning More About FreeHand**

If you are interested in learning more about FreeHand, here are a couple of learning resources and support sites:

http://www.macromedia.com/support/freehand/

http://www.freehandsource.com/

5. ——————————Dreamweaver and Macromedia Flash MX

Many designers create .swf files using Macromedia Flash MX and then use Macromedia Dreamweaver MX to integrate the .swf file with the required HTML documents. Dreamweaver MX is also a great tool for managing large numbers of Web site files, and it also provides a way to FTP the files to a Web server. This next exercise shows how to combine HTML and Macromedia Flash MX using Dreamweaver. Why not just use the publishing features of Macromedia Flash MX for your HTML? That's fine for simple pages with only Macromedia Flash content, but Dreamweaver offers more control if you plan to integrate Macromedia Flash MX with a lot of different HTML pages, as you would want to do in a complicated Web site. After you import the .swf file into Dreamweaver, you can alter many attributes of your Macromedia Flash MX file, such as size and positioning. You can even insert Macromedia Flash MX content inside frames, tables, or layers within a Dreamweaver HTML document. Fortunately, the process is quite simple, and the following exercise will show you how.

Note: You must have Dreamweaver MX installed in order to complete this exercise. A trial version of Dreamweaver MX is included inside the **software** folder on the **H•O•T CD-ROM.**

1. Open the **homePage.fla** file from the **chap_18** folder.

2. Test the movie (**Control > Test Movie**) to produce the .swf file you will need in later steps in this exercise. Notice the logo animating.

3. Close the file when you are finished previewing it.

4. Open Dreamweaver MX, choose **File > Open**, and select the **index.htm** file from the **chap_18** folder.

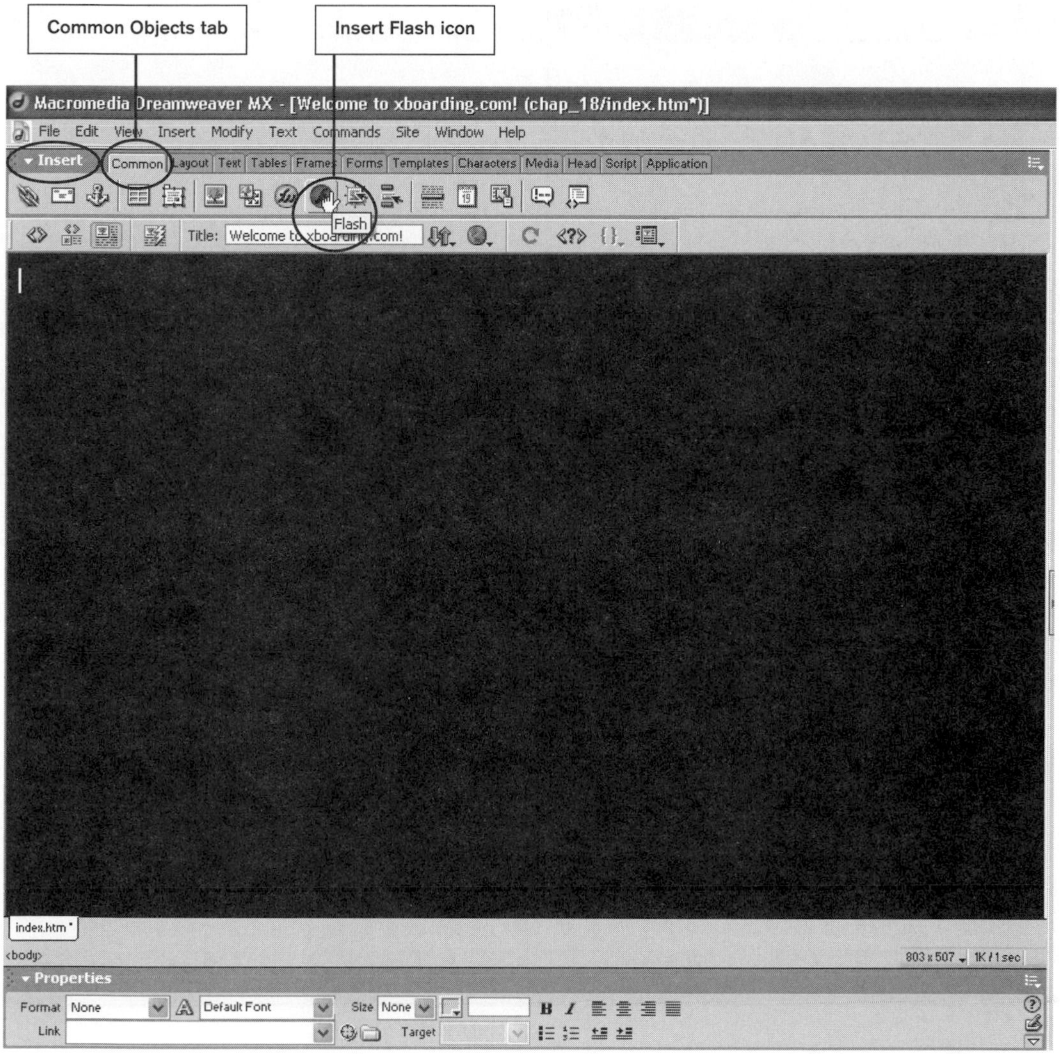

Common Objects tab

Insert Flash icon

5. You will see a document that simply has a black background. In the **Insert Bar**, on the **Common Objects** tab, click on the **Insert Flash** icon (shown above). This will insert a .swf file into the HTML document.

Tip: You can also insert a .swf file into your document using several other methods: In the Insert Bar, select the Media tab and then click on the Insert Flash icon, or simply drag the Insert Flash icon to the document window. Additionally, you can choose Insert > Media > Flash.

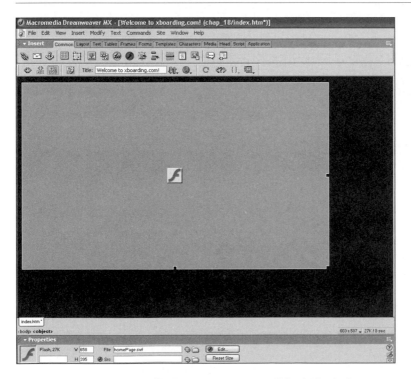

6. In the **chap_18** folder, select the **homePage.swf** file and click **OK**. Make sure you choose the .swf file and not the .fla file!

This is what the Macromedia Flash MX content will look like in Dreamweaver.

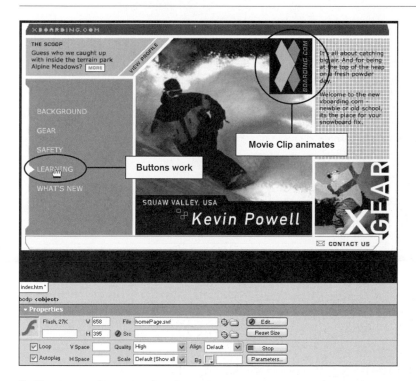

7. In the **Property Inspector**, click the small arrow in the lower right corner to expand the Property Inspector. Notice the green **Play** button. Click the **Play** button to preview the Macromedia Flash MX file right on the screen inside Dreamweaver.

8. Check the rollover functionality of the buttons to make sure they turn white when you roll your mouse over them. Notice that the logo is animating also.

Using the Play button, you can have Dreamweaver MX preview Graphic, Button, and Movie Clip symbols inside your Macromedia Flash MX movie.

9. As you preview the file, notice that the green Play arrow in the **Property Inspector** changes to a red Stop square. Once you've previewed the file, click the **Stop** button to return to your work environment.

10. In the **Property Inspector**, make sure the .swf file is selected, and click the **Edit** button. This immediately opens Macromedia Flash MX and allows you to make changes to the source file, which will immediately be updated in the .swf file in Dreamweaver MX.

Tip: You can also right-click (Windows) or Ctrl+click (Mac) to access a drop-down menu and then select Edit with Flash to open the file inside Macromedia Flash MX.

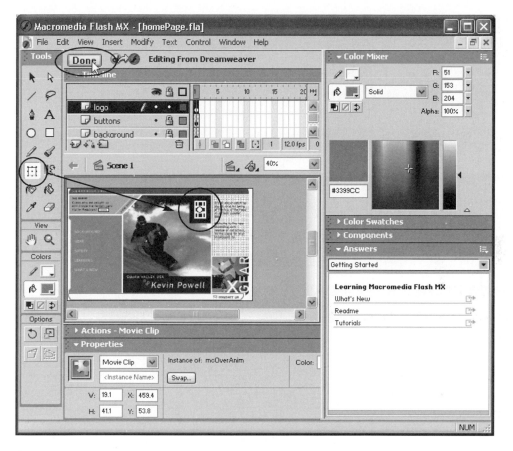

11. Once inside the Macromedia Flash MX source file, select the **Free Transform** tool and scale the logo down to a tiny size. When you are finished, click the **Done** button, circled in the picture above.

Once you click the Done button, you will be returned to Macromedia Dreamweaver MX.

18. Integration | Macromedia Flash MX **H•O•T**

12. Back in Dreamweaver MX, click the **Play** button in the **Property Inspector**. Notice that Dreamweaver has automatically updated the .swf file inside the document to reflect the change you made to the logo. Cool!

Note: Using the Property Inspector in Dreamweaver MX is an easy way to edit the .fla file, assign attribute tags, change the background color, change how the content will be aligned or how the movie will scale, and plenty of other useful properties. Dreamweaver MX offers a lot of control over how the content is displayed.

13. When you are finished, save and close the file.

| 754 |

6. ——————Illustrator and Macromedia Flash MX

Many digital artists are familiar with Adobe Illustrator and prefer to use its drawing capabilities over other vector tools. The good news is that an excellent .swf export feature was added to the release of Illustrator 9 and 10. This exercise will walk you through the process of exporting content from Illustrator and importing it into Macromedia Flash MX. You will need Illustrator 9 or 10 to follow this exercise.

1. Open Illustrator 9.0 or 10.0. In Illustrator, open the file **store-items.ai** from the **chap_18** folder.

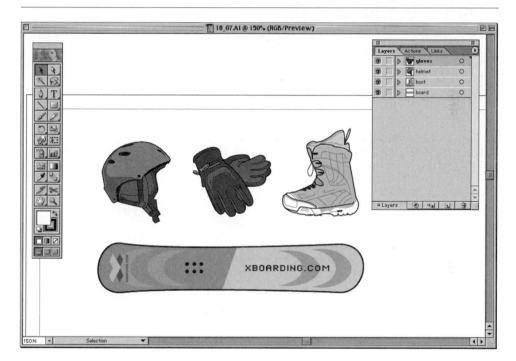

This file contains multiple layers, as well as shapes that would be difficult to create in Macromedia Flash MX. Note that transparency is supported in Illustrator 9 and 10, but it will not be honored by Macromedia Flash MX. Therefore, it's best to leave your objects fully opaque inside Illustrator and add transparency after you bring them into Macromedia Flash MX. You would have to convert them to symbols in Macromedia Flash MX before you could lower their transparency there.

2. Choose **File > Export**. From the **Format** menu, choose **Macromedia Flash (SWF)**. You will be prompted to save the file with the .swf extension. Save it somewhere that makes sense (remember where!) and click **Export**. The **Macromedia Flash (SWF) Format Options** dialog box will appear.

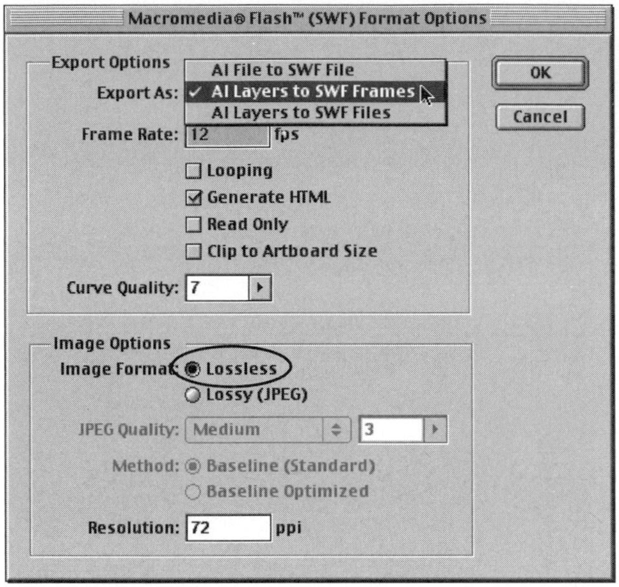

3. For **Export As**, choose **AI Layers to SWF Frames** and click **OK**. It's important that you select **Image Format: Lossless** if you want to preserve the vectors from Illustrator (which in this case, you do!). Save your file in Illustrator and quit the program. **Note:** The chart at the end of this exercise describes all the options in the dialog box in detail.

This setting will take the content of each layer and save it to a separate frame in Macromedia Flash MX. I like this technique, because it separates all my artwork into separate frames so I can easily convert them to symbols. You can also make other appropriate settings in this dialog box, many of which are geared to creating a finished .swf movie (such as frame rate, looping, and generating HTML). For the purposes of this exercise, I am interested only in getting this artwork out of Illustrator and into Macromedia Flash MX, so I can ignore the other settings.

4. Open Macromedia Flash MX, and choose **File > New**. Choose **File > Import**, and locate the **store-items.swf** file that you just saved. Click **Open** to import the file. After a few moments to process the artwork, four frames will appear inside the Macromedia Flash MX Timeline.

5. Create three new layers, and move or copy each frame to its own layer.

You have now brought all the artwork from the Illustrator file successfully into Macromedia Flash MX and isolated each Illustrator layer on its own layer and frame in the Timeline. From here, you can do just about anything!

6. Save and close this file.

Illustrator's Macromedia Flash (SWF) Format Options Explained

Export Options	Setting	Description
Export As	AI File to SWF File	Groups all the objects into a single .swf file.
	AI Layers to SWF Frames	Creates an animation based on layer information. Each layer will import into Macromedia Flash MX as a separate frame.
	AI Layers to SWF Files	Exports each layer as a separate .swf file.
Frame Rate		You enter a frame rate here. This is useful if you want to match your Macromedia Flash MX frame rate to the Illustrator frame rate.
Read Only		Creates a protected .swf movie that cannot be imported into Macromedia Flash MX.
Clip to Artboard Size		Trims the canvas size to fit the artwork.
Curve Quality		Offers settings from 1 to 10, with 1 representing the lowest quality.

Image Options	Setting	Description
Image Format	Lossless	Lossless is best for images that have solid colors and when you want to preserve vector information from the file.
	Lossy (JPEG)	Lossy is best for images that have gradations.
Resolution		Use the default setting of 72 dpi. Even if you change this setting, Macromedia Flash MX will only recognize 72 dpi.

7. ——————Creating Accessible Content

An increasing number of Web sites require **accessible** content. This means that the content must be usable by people who have disabilities. In Macromedia Flash MX, you can make the content in your movie accessible to visually impaired individuals who have access to screen reader software. Screen reader software uses audio to describe what is seen on the screen. In order for the screen reader to be able to read your content properly, you must set up the content in a certain way. This exercise will teach you how to make content in your Macromedia Flash MX project file accessible.

System Requirements: The Macromedia Flash 6 Player uses MSAA (Microsoft Active Accessibility) technology, which is technology that communicates with screen readers. This technology is available only on Windows operating systems. It is also important to note that the Windows Internet Explorer Plug-in (ActiveX) version of the Macromedia Flash 6 Player *does* support MSAA, although the Windows Netscape and Windows stand-alone players do not.

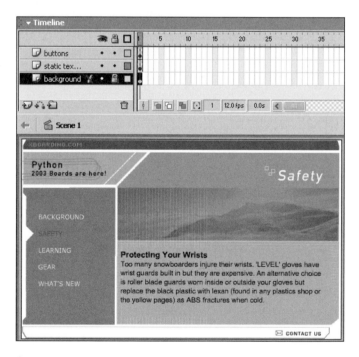

1. Open the **accessibleContent.fla** file from the **chap_18** folder. This file contains a background image, buttons, and text.

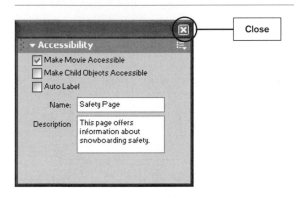

Edit Accessibility Settings button

2. In the **Property Inspector**, make sure nothing is selected in the project file and click the **Edit Accessibility Settings** button.

Close

3. In the **Accessibility** dialog box that opens, select the **Make Movie Accessible** box. In the **Name** field type **Safety Page**, and for **Description** type **This page offers information about snowboarding safety**. This will allow the whole movie (which resides on one frame in the Main Timeline) accessible to screen readers. The chart that follows describes the options in this dialog box.

4. When you are finished, close the Accessibility dialog box by clicking the **X** in the upper right corner.

Accessibility Dialog Box Options

Option	Description
Make Movie Accessible	Allows the movie to be readable by screen readers; this includes all text, Input Text fields, Buttons, and Movie Clips. If this option is deselected, it will hide the movie from screen readers.
Make Child Objects Accessible	Allows the accessible objects (text, Input Text fields, Buttons, and Movie Clips) located inside Movie Clips to be readable by screen readers. If this option is deselected, it prevents accessible objects within Movie Clips from being accessed by screen readers.
Auto Label	Uses text objects, such as Buttons or Input Text fields contained in the movie, as automatic labels for accessible content. If this option is deselected, screen readers will read text objects as text objects, not labels. (You will learn how to label individual items later in this exercise.)
Name	Allows you to enter a title (name) for the movie, since the screen reader will read the name of the movie even if there is no other accessible content in the movie. This option is available only if you select the Make Movie Accessible option.
Description	Allows you to enter a description of the movie that will be read by the screen reader software. This option is also available only if you select the Make Movie Accessible option.

NOTE | Accessible Objects

The Macromedia Flash 6 Player will include text, Input Text fields, Buttons, Movie Clips, and entire movies as accessible objects that can be read by screen readers. However, individual graphic objects are not included as accessible objects, since graphics can't be easily turned into spoken words. On the other hand, Movie Clips are included as accessible objects, as are the objects inside Movie Clips, as long as they are either text, Input Text fields, Buttons, or other Movie Clips.

5. Select the text field on the **Stage** and choose **Window > Accessibility** to open the **Accessibility** dialog box again. Once the window opens, notice the message in the dialog box. This message appears because the text field you have selected on the Stage is a Static Text field, and the contents of Static Text fields are automatically hidden to screen readers by default.

If you want more control over what the screen reader will read, you can convert the text field to a Dynamic Text field. You will do this next.

Tip: You can open the Accessibility dialog box by selecting an object or text on the Stage and choosing either Window > Accessibility or clicking the Accessibility button in the Property Inspector, or you can select nothing and either choose Window > Accessibility or click the Accessibility button in the Property Inspector.

6. In the **Property Inspector**, change the **Text Type** to **Dynamic Text** and type **wrist protection** for the **Instance Name**. In the **Accessibility** dialog box, type **In order to protect your wrists, it is important to wear wrist guards**. This will give the text field a descriptive name (wrist protection) that will be read first by the screen readers, and the description that you just typed in the Accessibility dialog box will be read after the name.

It is very important that each accessible object in your movie have a name. The screen readers will identify an object by reading the object's name first and then the description of the object. Rather than allowing Macromedia Flash MX to name objects generically (by selecting the Auto Label option in step 3), it is better to take control over the names of your objects and name them yourself. By default, the Macromedia Flash Player automatically provides the names for Static and Dynamic Text objects because the names of these text objects are the actual text. Although you don't have to provide the names for Static and Dynamic Text objects, it will make more sense to the screen reader user if you do.

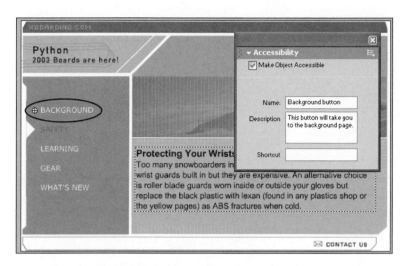

7. Select the **Background** button on the **Stage** and, with the **Accessibility** dialog box still open, type **Name: Background button** and for the **Description** type **This button will take you to the background page**. Again, rather than leaving it up to Macromedia Flash MX to name your button (it may name it something like "button 17"), it is much better to name your buttons individually. When you are finished, close the **Accessibility** dialog box.

8. Even if you test your movie, unfortunately, it is not possible to test your movie's accessibility content using Macromedia Flash MX's test movie features. If you have access to a screen reader, however, you can test the movie's accessibility by playing it in a screen reader. Additionally, demonstration versions of screen reader software are available, so you can download one and test your movie that way.

TIP | Learning More About Accessibility

If you are interested in learning more about Macromedia Flash MX and accessibility, here are a few resources:

http://www.macromedia.com/macromedia/accessibility/features/flash/overview/

http://www.macromedia.com/macromedia/accessibility/gettingstarted/validate.html

http://www.macromedia.com/macromedia/accessibility/features/flash/faq/

---

9. Save and close this file. You are finished with the book!

Congratulations! You did it! I really hope this book helped you learn Macromedia Flash MX quickly, and that you are now armed and ready to create your own animated and interactive projects. I wish you the best of luck with all of your future Flashing!

A.

Troubleshooting FAQ and Technical Support

| Troubleshooting | Frequently Asked Questions |
| Technical Support |

H•O•T

Macromedia Flash MX

Troubleshooting

If you run into any problems while following the exercises in this book, you might find the answer in this troubleshooting guide. This section will be maintained and updated at this book's companion Web site: **http://www.lynda.com/products/books/flmxhot**.

If you don't find what you're looking for here or at the Web site, please send an email to: **flmxhot@lynda.com**.

If you have a question related to Macromedia Flash MX but unrelated to a specific step in an exercise in this book, visit the Macromedia Flash site at **http://www.macromedia.com/support/flash/**, or you can contact them by email at **http://www.macromedia.com/support/email/complimentary/main.cgi**.

Frequently Asked Questions

Q: On the Macintosh, why can't I see any .fla files when I choose File > Open?

A: If the .fla file was created on a PC, you might experience a problem seeing those files when you choose File > Open from within Macromedia Flash MX on a Macintosh. You can correct this by changing the **Show: All Formats** option to **All Files**.

Q: On the Macintosh, when I try to double-click on the .fla file to open it, it will not open. Why?

A: If the .fla file was created on a PC, you might not be able to double-click on it to open the file. If this is the case, open Macromedia Flash MX and choose **File > Open** to open the .fla file. If you don't see the .fla file listed when you choose File > Open, see the previous question. Once you save the .fla file (originally created on a PC) on your Mac, you will be able to double click on the .fla to open it.

Q: My Toolbox has disappeared. What should I do?

A: If your Toolbox has vanished, you can easily make it reappear again. Choose **Window > Tools** to show/hide the Toolbox. Chapter 2, "*Interface*," explains the Toolbox in detail.

Q: All of my panels have disappeared. What should I do?

A: If you lose your panels, you can press the **Tab** key on the keyboard to show them and even hide them again. If you don't like their arrangement, you can restore them to their default positions by choosing **Window > Panel Sets > Default Layout**. This will cause all of the panels to reappear in their default positions on the screen. This command is especially helpful when someone else has undocked and changed the combination of your panels. Chapter 2, "*Interface*," describes each of the panels in detail.

Q: I undocked one of the panels but I can't redock it again. Why?

A: To redock a panel, make sure that you drag it over the location where you want dock it. A black outline will appear, symbolizing the area that panel will be docked in when you release the mouse. Chapter 2, "*Interface*," explains docking and undocking in detail.

Q: Why does Macromedia Flash MX create extra files when I press Ctrl+F12 (Windows) or Cmd+F12 (Mac)?

A: Pressing Ctrl+F12 or Cmd+F12 is a shortcut for the Publish Preview command. This means that Macromedia Flash MX will publish the .swf file and an HTML file when you press this key. These files will be created in the same directory as the .fla file. If you want to preview your movie without publishing any other files, choose **Control > Test Movie** or **File > Publish Preview > Flash**, and only the .swf file will be created. Chapter 16, "*Publishing and Exporting*," explains the publish features in detail.

Q: I tried to create my own shape tween but it won't work, and the Timeline has a broken line. What does this mean?

A: You cannot create a shape tween using symbols, groups, or text blocks (text that hasn't been broken apart). A solid line with an arrow indicates that the tween is working properly. This is a good tween. A dashed line in the Timeline indicates there is a problem with the tween. This is a bad tween. Make sure you are using only objects that work with shape tweens. In Chapter 5, "*Shape Tweening*," you will find a detailed list of the objects you can use to create shape tweens.

Q: Why do all of the objects on my Stage appear faded?

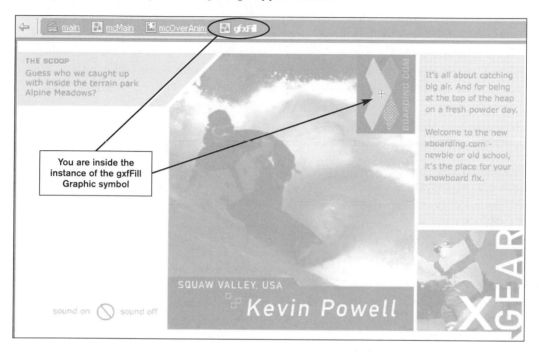

You are inside the instance of the gxfFill Graphic symbol

A: This occurs when you double-click on an instance or right-click on one and choose Edit in Place. This is a quick way to make changes to a symbol without having to access the Library; however, it can be confusing if that's not what you intended to do. Click on **Scene 1** in the Information Bar to exit this editing mode and return to the Main Timeline. In the picture above, Scene 1 was renamed **main** so you would click on the word main in the Information Bar.

Q: I tried to create my own motion tween, but it won't work. And the Timeline has a broken line. What does this mean?

A: You cannot create a motion tween using shapes or broken-apart text. A solid line with an arrow indicates that the tween is working properly. This is a good tween. A dashed line in the Timeline indicates that there is a problem with the tween. This is a bad tween. Make sure you are using only objects that work with motion tweens. In Chapter 7, "*Motion Tweening,*" you will find a detailed list of the objects you can use to create motion tweens.

Q: I tried to motion tween multiple objects, but it's not working. What could be wrong?

A: Motion tweening multiple objects requires that each different object exist on a separate layer. If you have all the objects on a single layer, the tween will not behave as expected. You can use the **Modify > Distribute to Layers** command to quickly distribute each object to its own layer. Also, make sure you are trying to tween objects that are capable of being motion tweened. Objects such as shapes and broken-apart text cannot be motion tweened.

Q: Why won't my Movie Clips play when I click the Play button on the Controller?

A: You can't preview your Movie Clips on the Stage within the Macromedia Flash MX authoring environment. Movie Clips can be previewed only in the Library or by selecting **Control > Test Movie** to preview the Movie Clip in the Flash Player.

Q: I made an Input Text field, but when I test it using Control > Test Movie and I type inside it, nothing happens. Why?

A: Most likely, you are having this problem because when you created the text box, the Text Color was set to the same color as the background of the movie. Try changing the text color and testing the movie again. Also make sure that you do have **Input Text** set for the **Text Type**.

Q: I see many actions in the Actions Toolbox that I want to learn the meaning of. How can I quickly do this?

A: In the **Actions Toolbox**, click on an action that you want to learn about. On the right side of the **Actions panel**, above the Parameters pane, click on the **Reference** button. This will open the Reference panel with a complete description of the action you selected in the Toolbox.

Technical Support

Macromedia Technical Support

http://www.macromedia.com/support/flash/ or
http://www.macromedia.com/support/email/complimentary/main.cgi.

If you're having problems with Macromedia Flash MX, please visit the first link above to access the Macromedia Flash Support Center. To contact Macromedia Technical Support, use the email form at the second link listed above. They can help you with typical problems, such as the trial version has expired on your computer or your computer crashes when you try to launch the application. Please note that lynda.com cannot help troubleshoot technical problems with Macromedia Flash MX.

Peachpit Press

customer_service@peachpit.com

If your book has a defective CD-ROM, please contact the customer service department at the above email address. We do not have extra CDs at lynda.com, so they must be requested directly from the publisher.

lynda.com

We have created a companion Web site for this book, which can be found at

http://www.lynda.com/products/books/

Any errors in the book will be posted to this Web site, and it's always a good idea to check there for up-to-date information. We encourage and welcome your comments and error reports to **flmxhot@lynda.com**. Kymberlee will receive these emails. Please allow a 72-hour turnaround and longer on weekends or holidays.

B.

Macromedia Flash MX Resources

| Online Forums | Web Sites |
| CD-ROMs | Movie Library | Books |

H•O•T
_____
Macromedia Flash MX

There are many great resources for Macromedia Flash MX users. You have ample choices among a variety of newsgroups, conferences, and third-party Web sites that can really help you get the most out of Macromedia Flash MX. This appendix lists some of the best resources for developing your Macromedia Flash MX skills.

Macromedia Flash MX Application Development Center

http://www.macromedia.com/desdev/mx/flash/

Macromedia has created a section of its Web site called the Macromedia Flash MX Application Development Center. This is a one-stop shop for everything Flash. For example, you can read tutorials and articles on Macromedia Flash MX, download sample applications, access links to other Macromedia Flash MX resources, and even read the White Papers written on topics related to Macromedia Flash MX. This is the perfect link to use if you want to learn more about components or even video in Macromedia Flash MX.

Macromedia Online Forums

http://webforums.macromedia.com/flash/

Macromedia has set up several Web-based online forums for Macromedia Flash. This is a great place to ask questions and get help from thousands of Macromedia Flash MX users. These online forums are used by beginning to advanced Macromedia Flash MX users, so you should have no problem finding the type of help you need, regardless of your experience with the program. A list follows describing several of Macromedia's online forums.

Flash General Discussion
Online forum for general issues related to using Macromedia Flash.

Flash Handhelds
Online forum for technical issues related to creating Macromedia Flash content for handheld devices, such as the PocketPC.

Flash Site Design
Online forum for design feedback on your Macromedia Flash MX animations. This forum is dedicated to the discussion of Macromedia Flash design and animation principles and practices. Other issues not specific to the Macromedia Flash tools yet important to Macromedia Flash designers can also be discussed here.

Flash Remoting
Online forum that discusses issues involved with Flash Remoting. Flash Remoting supplies the infrastructure that allows users to connect to remote services exposed by application server developers and Web services. Examples of these are message boards, shopping carts, and even up-to-the-minute stock quote graphs.

Flash Exchange Extensions
Online forum for issues relating to Macromedia Flash MX extensions, including how to use them and how to troubleshoot any problems with them. (See also the "Macromedia Exchange for Flash" section next.)

Macromedia Exchange for Flash

http://www.macromedia.com/exchange/flash/

Macromedia has set up another section of its Web site called the Macromedia Flash Exchange. There you'll find hundreds of free extensions written by third-party users and developers that can help you build new features into your Web site. These features are not part of the Macromedia Flash MX product, but they can be downloaded when you need them. Many of these extensions have features that normally would require an advanced level of ActionScripting. For example, some of these behaviors can give you the ability to password-protect areas of your site and to create pop-up menus, scroll bars, complex text effects, etc.

The Macromedia site is not just for developers but for any Macromedia Flash MX user who wants to take Macromedia Flash MX to the next level. If you are a developer, this is a great place to learn how to write your own behaviors to share with the rest of the Macromedia Flash community.

You can also visit **http://webforums.macromedia.com/flash/** and click on the Flash Exchange Extensions link to access the online forum for Flash Extensions.

Macromedia TechNotes

http://www.macromedia.com/support/flash/technotes.html

Macromedia has another section of its Web site listing all the issues that have been reported and answered by Macromedia Flash staff. This can be a valuable learning resource as well.

Third-Party Web Sites

http://www.flashkit.com/

http://www.ultrashock.com/

http://virtual-fx.net/

http://www.actionscripts.org/

http://www.flzone.net/

http://flashmove.com/

http://flazoom.com/

http://www.were-here.com/

http://www.popedeflash.com/

http://www.macromedia.com/support/flash/ts/documents/flash_websites.htm

Flashforward

Flashforward is an international educational Macromedia Flash conference created by Lynda Weinman of lynda.com and Stewart McBride of United Digital Artists, and sponsored by Macromedia. Additionally, Kymberlee has recently accepted the position of Conference Coordinator for the Flashforward conferences. It's a great conference to attend once you know Macromedia Flash MX and want to take your skills to a new level. The best Macromedia Flash developers and designers in the world present their technical and artistic work in an educational setting. You can learn more about Flashforward and its offerings by visiting `http://www.flashforward2003.com`.

CD-ROMs from Lynda.com

`http://www.lynda.com/products/videos/index.html`

Learning Flash MX
Learning Flash MX ActionScripting

Online Training Movie Library from Lynda.com

`http://movielibrary.lynda.com/html/index.asp`

Lynda.com now offers a subscription service that allows you to see over 1,600 movies on a variety of subjects, including Macromedia Flash MX.

Books for Further Learning about Macromedia Flash MX

Flash MX Bible
by Robert Reinhardt and Snow Dowd
John Wiley & Sons, 2002
ISBN: 0764536567
`http://www.flashmxbible.com`

Macromedia Flash MX ActionScript Bible
by Robert Reinhardt and Joey Lott
John Wiley & Sons, 2002
ISBN: 0764536141
`http://www.actionscriptbible.com`

ActionScript: The Definitive Guide
by Colin Moock and Gary Grossman
O'Reilly & Associates, 2001
ISBN: 1565928520

Flash Web Design: The V5 Remix
by Hillman Curtis
New Riders Publishing, 2001
ISBN: 0735708967

MTIV: Process, Inspiration and Practice for the New Media Designer
by Hillman Curtis
New Riders Publishing, 2002
ISBN: 0735711658

Macromedia Flash MX Video
by Kristian Besley, Hoss Gifford, Todd Marks, and Brian Monnone
Friends of Ed, 2002
ISBN: 1903450853

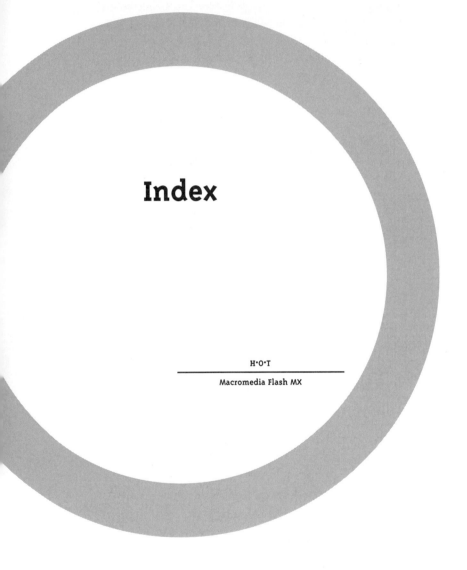

Index

H•O•T

Macromedia Flash MX

A

absolute addresses, 404
Accessibility dialog box, 761–763
  Auto Label box, 762
  defined, 33
  Description field, 761, 762,
    764, 765
  illustrated, 33
  Make Child Object Accessible
    box, 762
  Make Movie Accessible box,
    761, 762
  message in, 763
  Name field, 761, 762, 765
  opening, 761, 763
accessible content
  creating, 760–765
  defined, 760
  resources, 765
  testing, 765
accessibleContent.fla file, 760
accessible objects, 762
  defined, 762
  naming, 764
actions
  adding, 373, 378
  adding, to button instances,
    397, 583
  adding, to keyframe, 378
  application feedback, 377
  button, 388
  choosing, 373
  code display, 374
  comment, 720–721
  controlling Movie Clips with,
    385–393
  defined, 367
  description, 374
  dragging, 373
  else, 494, 696
  feedback, 378
  frame, 367
  fscommand, 636, 638
  getURL, 402–407
  goto, 379, 395–401, 416,
    426, 493, 494
  goToAndPlay, 522
  if, 492, 694
  information display, 441
  interactivity and, 380
  layer placement, 626

learning, 770
list of, 373
loadMovie, 434
loadVariables, 468, 472
nextFrame, 399
object, 367
on, 492
parameters, entering, 368
play, 369, 376, 583, 612
print, 708–711
renaming, 418
startDrag, 722–723
stop, 369, 373, 377, 419,
  425, 426
stopAllSounds, 519
stopDrag, 724
unloadMovie, 452, 726
ActionScript
  arguments, 394
  braces {}, 375
  button application, 389
  code, working with, 366
  Coding Standards, 485
  defined, 13, 366
  dot syntax, 394
  for draggable movies,
    720–726
  functions, 559
  importance, 366
  overview, 366
  parentheses (), 375, 394
  placement, 367
  for Preloader, 693–700
  semicolon ;, 375, 394
  syntax errors, 388
Actions panel, 366
  accessing, 371, 387, 396
  Add (+) button, 367, 373, 387,
    390
  Condition field, 492, 696
  default location, 372
  defined, 32, 367–368
  Delete (-) button, 367
  Expert mode, 367, 368
  feedback, 388
  Frame field, 416, 427, 493,
    494
  Go to and Play radio button,
    522
  Go to and Stop radio button,
    401, 416, 427, 493,
    494

gripper, 372
illustrated, 32, 367
Insert a Target Path button,
  391
Jump menu, 374, 378
Key Press box, 382
Location field, 438, 443, 446,
  452
Movie Clip Control category,
  722
Normal mode, 367
Object field, 389, 391
options, 367
Options menu, 373
Parameters pane, 403, 404,
  406, 416, 427, 443
Pin button, 368
redocking, 372
Reference button, 441, 770
Scene field, 417
Script pane, 367, 368, 373,
  374, 375
Toolbox, 396
Type field, 398, 399, 401,
  416, 427, 493
undocking, 372
URL field, 403, 406, 438,
  443, 473, 474
Variables option, 405, 406,
  438, 443, 446
Window field, 404, 406
Actions Toolbox
  Actions category, 373
  Browser/Network category,
    403, 405, 437, 442,
    472
  Conditions/Loops category,
    492, 494, 694, 696
  Miscellaneous category, 720
  Movie Control category, 373,
    396, 398, 416, 419
  Printing category, 708
Add Pages dialog box
  (FreeHand), 739
addresses
  absolute, 404
  Load Movie and, 438
  relative, 404
ADPCM compression model,
  502, 505
Advanced Effect dialog box, 203
.ai files, 729

size, 424
targeting, 590–592
video targeting, controlling, 586–596
visibility in Timeline, 425
frame rate
animation length and, 124
defined, 122
lower, 123
maximum, 125
playback, 125
playback time calculation, 124
previewing, 122
recommended, 125
setting, in Property Inspector, 102, 133
Timeline readout, 99
understanding, 122–123
variance, 125
frames
adding, 148, 174, 288, 290, 579
adding, to background layer, 224, 233
adding actions to, 371
adding loadMovie action to, 437
beginning animation, 218
block of, repositioning, 332
copying, 134–135, 417, 426
current, Timeline readout, 99
cutting, 341
defined, 107
deleting, 131–132
downloading, checking, 696
dragging, 332
expanding, 609
ghosted representations, 236
in Hit state, 311
inserting, 126–130, 217
light gray, 128, 134
loading after intro animation, 700
matching number of to video, 609
moving, 332, 758
multiple, editing, 231–237
pasting, 342, 417, 426
printing, 706, 707, 710
printing, at full size, 702
range of, 128
range of, selecting, 131

removing, 107, 343, 589, 691, 692, 693
rendering time, 125
reversing, 135
selected, removing, 132
selecting, 226, 233, 241
selecting, before inserting keyframes, 115
selecting, in Graphic Symbol Timeline, 213, 215
selecting all, 134, 340, 341
sound, 535
total number, in playback time calculation, 124
viewing, 525
frames.fla file, 126, 136
frames.html file, 141
frames.swf file, 139
FreeHand, 739–747
editable type and, 746
imported content, viewing, 742
importing content as keyframes, 739–743
importing content as scenes, 744–747
object grouping and, 746
Pages in, 739
resources, 747
FreeHand Import dialog box, 740–741
accessing, 740
illustrated, 740
Mapping section, 740, 741, 744
Options section, 740, 741
Pages option, 740, 741, 744
Free Transform tool, 7, 117–121, 163–164, 205–207, 606
bounding box, 229, 555
click+drag, 121, 163, 164
defined, 40, 117
flipping with, 252
functions, 121
illustrated, 40
over bounding box, 121
in resizing components, 555
rotating with, 119, 251, 252
scaling with, 251, 252
selecting, 117, 163, 206, 229

Shift+drag, 206, 229, 230
skewing with, 205, 252
fscommand action
adding, 636, 638
Command field, 637, 638
Commands for standalone player, 638
double-clicking, 636, 638
Parameters field, 637, 638
See also actions
FSCommands
adding, 636, 638
allowscale, 640
defined, 636
exec, 640
as frame actions, 636
fullscreen, 640
modifying projectors with, 635–639
publishing projectors with, 637
quit, 640
showmenu, 640
trapallkeys, 640
FScrollBar Skins folder, 561
fullscreen FSCommand, 640
functions, 559

G

Gear button, 421, 427, 429, 430, 450, 453
gearExtra button, 451
gearSale.png file, 730, 735
getURL action, 402–407
addresses, 404
defined, 402
double-clicking, 405
as email link, 405
link creation, 403–405
link preview, 405
selecting, 403
URL field, 403, 406
Variables option, 405, 406
Window parameter options, 404, 406
See also actions
getURL.fla file, 402
.gif files, 257
GIF settings, 653–654
Global Skins folder, 561

resources, 500
selecting, 500, 501
settings, modifying, 514–516
on Stage, 508
Start, 509, 515
starting, 522, 665
start point, 513
Stop, 515
stopping, 665
Stream, 509, 515
synchronizing, to narration
cues, 529–535
testing, 503, 504, 508, 509,
512, 535
in Timeline, 508
uses, 496
visual feedback, 508
soundSyncFinal.fla file, 524
soundSync.fla file, 524, 529, 718
soundSync.mov, 535
soundz.fla file, 326
spatial compression, 572
Speech compression, 524
format, 502
global, 528
selecting, 527, 528
setting, 527–528
See also sound compression
.spl files, 729
squares, drawing, 58
Stage
aligning instances on, 354
animation preview on, 108,
113, 127
button preview on, 302–303
centering bitmaps on, 289
clearing, 46
clicking on blank area, 332
content, deselecting, 602
defined, 16
dragging bitmaps onto, 266
dragging ComboBox
component onto,
541–542
dragging instances onto, 216,
224, 325, 329, 339
dragging ListBox component
onto, 543
dragging Movie Clip instances
onto, 344, 363,
691, 692
dragging PushButton
component onto,
547

dragging RadioButton
component onto,
543
dragging ScrollBar component
onto, 546
dragging sounds to, 508
faded objects on, 769
as instance storage location,
190
placing instances on, 316
play button, 582
resizing, 675
ruler units, 104
selecting all on, 46
stop button, 583
video clips on, 600
viewing content as outlines,
319
width, changing, 345, 352
work area, 16, 250
Start button, 667
startDrag action, 722–723
adding, 722
double-clicking, 722
Expression check box, 723
Target field, 723
See also actions
Start sounds, 509
defined, 511, 515
Event sounds vs., 511
previewing, 511
setting, 511
starting, 522
See also sound(s)
Static Text
characteristics, 455
choosing, 457
object names for, 764
working with, 462–464
See also text; text blocks
staticText.fla file, 462
Status Bar, 17
defined, 18
Edit Multiple Frames button,
235, 266, 268
illustrated, 18
stop action, 369, 373, 669
adding, 373, 396, 419, 425,
426, 521
adding, to buttons, 584, 613
application, 375
for controlling Movie Clip, 387
description, 374

double-clicking, 374, 419,
425, 426, 521
executing, 521
selecting, 387–388
testing, 375, 392
See also actions
stopAllSounds action
adding, 519
double-clicking, 519
execution, 519
stopping sound with, 522
See also actions
stopAndPlayFinal.fla file, 369, 370
stopAndPlayMC.fla file, 385
Stop button, 369, 370, 375, 378,
379, 667
stopDrag action, 724
store-items.ai file, 755, 757
streaming
color effects and, 608
defined, 5
playback, 608
sound, exporting, 616
Stream sounds, 509
benefits, 510
defined, 515
looping and, 531
Main Timeline and, 509
setting, 510, 530
testing, 530
See also sound(s)
strokeAnim.fla file, 282, 286
strokes
adding, to shape, 54, 194
attaching, to fills, 41
color, 50, 53, 69, 70
cutting, 283
defined, 41
deleting, 197
double-clicking, 197
drawing over, with Eraser tool,
284, 285
modifying, 64–70, 194
pasting, 283
removing, from shape, 55
selecting, 197
style, 49, 69
width, 49, 51, 70
strokes.fla file, 47
Stroke Style dialog box, 50
stroking bitmaps, 282–285
Submit button, 559

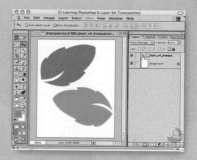